MW01639844

GÜNTER BEER · PATRIK JAROS

ENCYCLOPEDIA OF COOKING

GÜNTER BEER · PATRIK JAROS

ENCYCLOPEDIA OF COOKING

LOVE FOOD is an imprint of Parragon Books Ltd

LOVE FOOD and the accompanying heart device is a registered trademark of Parragon Books Ltd in Australia, the UK, and the EU.

This is a Parragon Publishing book
This edition published in 2010

Parragon Publishing
Queen Street House
4 Queen Street
Bath BA1 1HE, UK

ISBN: 978-1-4054-9577-6

Printed in China

Original German edition
Photography: Günter Beer I www.beerfoto.com
Written by: Günter Beer, Gerhard von Richthofen, Patrik Jaros, Jörg Zipprick
Photography assistants: Sigurd Buchberger, Aranxa Alvarez
Kitchen assistants: Magnus Thelen, Johannes von Bemberg
Design by Estudio Merino I www.estudiomerino.com
Produced by Buenavista Studio S.L. I www.buenavistastudio.com

English-language edition produced by Cambridge Publishing Management Ltd
Translators: Elisabeth Moser, Rónat O'Neill, Cathryn Siegal-Bergman

Concept: Patrik Jaros & Günter Beer

The visual media is on file at the OHIM as a registered design of Buenavista Studio s.l. under the number 000252796-001.

Notes for the reader:

This book uses imperial, metric, and US cup measurements. Follow the same units of measurement throughout; do not mix imperial and metric. All spoon measurements are level: teaspoons are assumed to be 5 ml, and tablespoons are assumed to be 15 ml. Unless otherwise stated, milk is assumed to be whole, eggs and individual vegetables such as potatoes are medium, and pepper is freshly ground black pepper.

The times given are an approximate guide only. Preparation times differ according to the techniques used by different people and the cooking times may also vary from those given as a result of the type of oven used. Optional ingredients, variations or serving suggestions have not been included in the calculations.

Recipes using raw or very lightly cooked eggs should be avoided by infants, the elderly, pregnant women, convalescents, and anyone with a chronic condition. Pregnant and breastfeeding women are advised to avoid eating peanuts and peanut products. Sufferers from nut allergies should be aware that some of the ready-prepared ingredients used in the recipes in this book may contain nuts. Always check the packaging before use.

Photo credits: All photographs taken by Günter Beer, Barcelona

Except: p. 303, Gettyimages–3rd row middle; p. 423, Davies + Starr–2nd row middle, Eising–3rd row left and middle, Foodcollection–3rd row right.

Contents

6 How to Use This Cookbook
8 Consumer Guide

26 Salt, Butter, Oil, Vinegar
48 Cold Sauces
64 Salads & Appetizers
100 Egg Dishes
130 Sauces & Stocks
160 Soups
182 Pasta
230 Rice
266 Grains & Legumes
300 Potatoes
340 Vegetables
402 Plant Proteins
420 Freshwater Fish
440 Saltwater Fish
476 Crustaceans & Shellfish
514 Poultry
544 Beef & Veal
598 Pork
622 Lamb & Wild Game
648 Fruit & Desserts
700 Cakes & Bread
732 Cheese
744 Wine

760 Glossary
762 Index

How to Use This Cookbook

The list of ingredients with their images at the top left side of the page is like a flip book that can be used as an index. Without having to read the book, you can quickly flip through and find recipes according to the ingredients you want to use.

↓

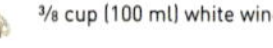

⅜ cup (100 ml) white wine
5 eggs
1 pinch of salt
1½ cups (350 g) butter
½ lemon
1 tbsp tarragon vinegar
1 pinch of cayenne pepper

This sauce is too runny either because the butter was too hot when it was added, or it was added too quickly.

Hollandaise Sauce

1. Bring 1¼ inches (3 cm) water to a boil in a pot (to form the bottom of a double boiler). Pour the white wine in a bowl with a rounded bottom. Separate the eggs, putting the yolks in the bowl, and the egg whites in a container for later use. Place the bowl over the double boiler, ensuring the bottom does not touch the water, add salt, and mix with a whisk.

2. Beat the egg yolks vigorously until they are thick and white.

3. Melt the butter in a small pot until it is warm, not hot, then slowly ladle it into the foamy egg yolks. Keep whisking so the butter blends with the yolks and creates a thick, creamy sauce. The preparation is exactly like for mayonnaise, except this sauce is warm. Finally, add salt, lemon juice, tarragon vinegar, and cayenne pepper to taste.

Makes about 4 cups (1 liter).

The yolk was beaten too vigorously over the boiling water. The egg has now curdled and it won't be possible to smooth it by adding more butter.

Kitchen doctor: The sauce is runny here too. Add 1 tbsp of hot water and try stirring it again with small movements in one spot, then stir in more and more of the rest of the sauce.

■ To whip up a really good Hollandaise sauce, 5 eggs yolks are best. Never use fewer than 3 egg yolks, otherwise the sauce will not reach the correct volume. Place the finished sauce over a pot of hot water, not letting it touch the stove, and cover with parchment paper. This allows the sauce to stay warm for up to an hour. This sauce goes best with steamed asparagus, poached fish, or eggs.

25

152 | Sauces & Stocks

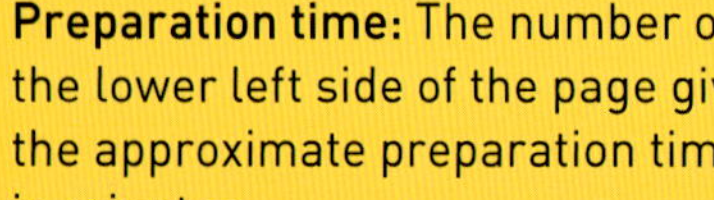

Preparation time: The number on the lower left side of the page gives the approximate preparation time in minutes.

Tips: Substitutions and variations for the recipe, useful suggestions, or possible menu combinations.

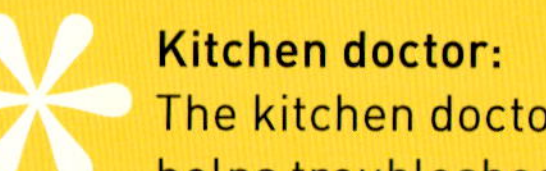

Kitchen doctor: The kitchen doctor helps troubleshoot if something goes wrong.

Level of difficulty: The stars indicate the level of difficulty. One star is for easy, two stars are for intermediate, and **three** stars are for advanced.

The recipes will generally serve four people using the amounts given, unless otherwise specified.

A teaspoon equals 5 ml; a tablespoon equals 15 ml. If milk is called for and nothing else is specified, use whole milk. The amounts specified for potatoes, vegetables, and eggs refer to medium sizes. Pepper always means freshly ground pepper.

You've been here before—you want to make something delicious. You look for the perfect recipe, one that delivers the goods. You shop for the ingredients and get going in the kitchen. And soon the problems begin, perhaps while cutting a classic ingredient, such as the onion. It looked so easy: dice the onion—but how do you do that?

This is exactly where this book comes in. Words and pictures clearly explain the essential steps of preparing basic ingredients. How do I peel tomatoes correctly? How do I seed a bell pepper? When do I slice artichokes, and when do I leave them whole? It will soon be clear that "cut into small pieces" does not always mean the same thing: mushrooms are cut differently for sauces and omelets than they are for stews. And that goes for all vegetables, too.

Problems also arise while carrying out a recipe. Who hasn't cooked rice that got sticky while boiling, although it was supposed to be light and fluffy? It may have been because partially polished brown rice is not cooked in the same way as basmati rice, for example. The same goes for potatoes. Why do mashed potatoes get gluey and heavy? This book finally explains how to make light, creamy mashed potatoes. You will find basic recipe foundations that clearly explain how to make pasta, gnocchi, bread, dumplings, pizza, and flaky pastries successfully. Basic recipes for stocks and sauces, required for many dishes, are also included.

This book offers numerous recipes with clear step-by-step photography—recipes that have been expanded to include additional ingredients, as well as preparation techniques and methods.

So you need no longer worry your onion will get soggy with tears as you cut it, or have the oh-so-promising dish literally leave a bitter taste in your mouth. You will not just *plan* to cook something delicious, you *will* cook something delicious!

Consumer Guide

Contents

10 General Consumer Guide
12 Staples
14 Basic Ingredients and Equipment
18 The Food Pyramid
20 Cooking for Yourself Is the First Step to Better Eating
22 Picnic Menu Suggestions
24 Party Time

General Consumer Guide

Good kitchens need good ingredients. Even an amateur can create a special menu with a Blue Foot chicken or a freshly caught sea bass—a simple recipe is all that's needed for the greatest enjoyment if the food's quality is decent. It's true that a little precision is required, especially with cooking times. If mediocre ingredients are all that's available, even an outstanding cook won't be able to make them taste good.

Despite the abundance of ingredients, it is getting more and more difficult to pick out really good food from the range available. When is the last time you ate a tomato, for example, that didn't taste like water with food coloring in it? Most people judge food purely in terms of how it looks. Meat and fish counters have the right lighting, and vegetables look spotless, as though torn from a picture book—no one talks about flavor anymore.

In every chapter in this book, we will take a closer look at the most important ingredients. However, there are some ground rules for shopping:

Even experts find it hard to tell if a fish has been properly scaled, gutted, and filleted without examining it further. The meat in a fillet should be firm and (other than "red" fish, such as salmon) have a nice white shimmer without looking dull. In the end, you can taste the difference.

Whole fish should always have glossy, clear eyes, with meat that is firm to the touch and, depending on the species, the gills should have a reddish shimmer. Fillets should always be purchased fresh and, if possible, eaten within two hours or, at best, on the same day. Otherwise the fish oxidizes and loses its flavor.

Cheap meat is often pale, flabby, and watery. It shrivels up in the pan. Visible signs of quality are not easy to discern because the lighting at the meat counter can be deceptive. Do not generally spurn meat for having rims of fat, because fat is an important flavor carrier.

You cannot recognize definitive quality based on the regional origin or breed, either. There is both superior and inferior Angus beef, yet they are sold under the same name.

No one can really determine the quality of packaged broiler-fryer chicken either. The skin should not be spotty, and visible damage should ring an alarm bell. Unlike with other meats, chicken labels can give reliable indications of quality. A free-range chicken always tastes much better than a caged one. And a Blue Foot chicken with certification of its origins is even better.

Looking at vegetables alone does not tell you which ones have the best flavor. *Note:* Dehydration is the vegetable's natural enemy. Spots on skins and cracked stalks are, therefore, signs of poor quality. Choose smaller or medium-size vegetables over larger ones, which often contain a lot of water that will end up in the pan.

Fruit is almost always nice to look at these days—all shiny, glossy, and crisp-looking in its display. Organic foods are better: Organic apples may be either lightly wrinkled or completely worm-eaten, but they simply have more flavor. And that is the bottom line.

Staples

Many cookbook readers make the same mistake: They look for a particularly attractive recipe, and the first thing they do is buy each and every ingredient on the list. Then, after complaining all the way home about how much it cost, they decide that cooking at home may be too expensive.

The truth is cooking for yourself is not expensive. But you should avoid shopping for each individual recipe.

To have a sensible kitchen you can work in, you need a primary "foundation" of nonperishable ingredients. Fill your kitchen cabinets with, for example:

1. Rice (basmati and jasmine (Thai))
2. Flour
3. Spaghetti and tagliatelle
4. Lentils, bulgur, other dried legumes
5. Unsweetened cocoa powder
6. Dark chocolate with a high cocoa content (above 70 percent)
7. Slivered almonds
8. Raisins
9. Dried fruit, e.g. apricots
10. Dried mushrooms, e.g. porcini
11. Tomato paste
12. Sugar
13. Salt
14. Pepper, black and white, whole corns
15. Peanut oil
16. Olive oil
17. Balsamic vinegar
18. Cinnamon sticks
19. Nutmeg
20. Thyme
21. Rosemary
22. Sesame seeds
23. Bay leaves
24. Peas (dried or frozen)
25. Canned fish (e.g. tuna)
26. Alcohol, such as cognac, port, rum, or Cointreau

Groceries that need to be stored in a refrigerator spoil faster. To start cooking, you need:

27. Butter
28. Cream
29. Plain yogurt
30. Milk
31. Eggs
32. Fresh lemon

■ **Warning: Nothing lasts forever. Always check the expiration date on the item before using.**

1

2

3

4

5

6

7

8

9
10
11
12
13
14
15
16
17
18
19
20
21
22
23
24
25
26
27
28
29
30
31
32

Basic Ingredients and Equipment

Aluminum foil (1): To cover cooked foods. It protects food surfaces from overbrowning.

Baking powder (2): This helps dough and batter rise and stay fluffy while baking.

Bamboo mat (3): To roll sushi or other rolls.

Cotton kitchen towel (4): To dry potatoes and uncut vegetables.

Round nonstick skillet (5): To make crépes and for frying potatoes, vegetables, meat, poultry, and fish.

Colander (6): For rinsing and draining lettuce, vegetables, fruit, or cooked foods.

Steamer pot (7): Relatively flat pot with a cover for steaming vegetables and fish.

Meat fork (8): For removing roasts and poultry from pots, or for turning meat over in a pot.

Ricer (9): Used to press through potatoes, vegetables, or chunky vegetable sauces.

Stock (10): Always a good base for soups, stews, sauces, and risottos.

Active dry yeast (11): Important ingredient in bread, pastries, and dough. Only mix into lukewarm liquids.

Gelatin (12): To bind creams, desserts, savory, and sweet mousses. Soak in cold water first, then let it dissolve in a hot liquid.

Paring knife (13): Curved slightly from the front end downward, this knife is used for peeling, or for cutting and cleaning vegetables and fruit.

Vegetable bouquet I. (14): Comprised of root vegetables and herbs for fish soups and sauces.

Vegetable bouquet II. (15): Comprised of root vegetables, except carrots, with lemon peel and herbs for fish soups and sauces.

Gratin dish (16): For dishes topped with cheese, such as vegetable casseroles, stuffed vegetables, or lasagna.

Grill pan (17): Cast iron grill pan for grilling meats, fish, vegetables, or side dishes. The pan has to be brushed with oil first, then heated well, otherwise the food will stick to it.

Large grater (18): For grating vegetables and fruit.

Large salad bowl (19): For making and mixing salads, for making fillings, or for keeping cooked ingredients.

Fish-bone tongs (20): Important for getting the smaller bones out of fish fillets so you can make a fish dish clear of any bones.

Terrine mold (21): Able to hold 7⅔ cups (1.8 liters) for pâtés, meat loaf, aspic, vegetables, and fish loaf.

Stainless steel skillet (22): Pan for frying all foods and for heating up sauces.

Loaf pan (23): For baking bread and cake—first grease with butter and sprinkle with a little flour so that the contents slide out of the pan better after baking.

Ceramic casserole dish (24): For baking fish in the oven and for making casseroles and some desserts.

Ceramic roasting dish (25): For roasting poultry, fish, or vegetables in the oven.

Plastic wrap (26): For keeping cooked food or prepared, marinated meats or fish in the refrigerator. This prevents them from taking on the taste and odor of other foods, and vice versa.

Small stainless-steel roasting pan (27): For roasting smaller dishes in the oven.

Small ladle (28): For removing foam from soups or stocks.

1

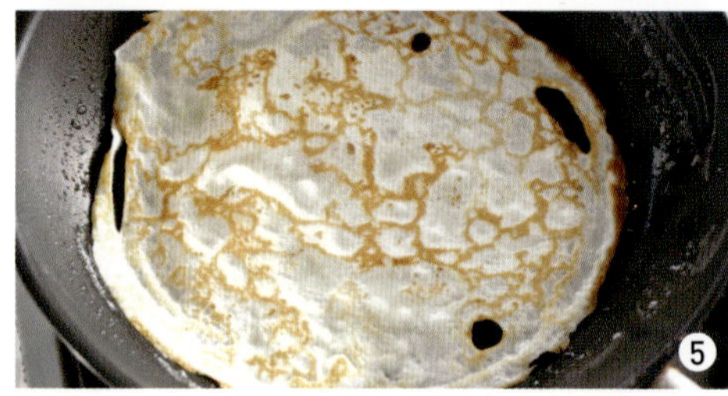
5

9

13

17

21

25

2
3
4
6
7
8
10
11
12
14
15
16
18
19
20
22
23
24
26
27
28

Small whisk (29): For stirring salad dressings, warm sauces, cake mixes, and soups.

Rubber spatula (30): For spreading fillings or stuffings, or scraping sauces out of pots or bowls.

Garlic press (31): To press peeled garlic for marinades or salad dressings.

Springform pan (32): Normally nonstick and 11 inches (28 cm) in diameter. For cakes and tortes.

Melon baller (33): With its sharp edges, the melon baller is also good for scraping out pumpkins, cucumbers, or zucchini.

Kitchen brush (34): For brushing off and cleaning shellfish.

Kitchen twine I. (35): For trussing bacon, herbs, roasts, or even two different kinds of meat together, so that they hold their shape while cooking.

Kitchen twine II. (36): For securing one ingredient to another one, such as a lemon slice to a piece of artichoke, or bacon to meat or poultry.

Blender (37): For mixing sauces, soups, milkshakes, smoothies, or vegetable purees.

Paper towels (38): For blotting fried foods to soak up the extra oil or fat.

Kitchen shears (39): For cutting shellfish shells to be used in sauces, or poultry bones used in stocks and sauces.

Measuring cup (40): For measuring solids, liquids, and creams.

Nutmeg grater (41): For grating whole nutmeg. Important for clear soups and mashed potatoes.

Oval nonstick pan (42): For frying fish or shellfish.

Parchment paper (43): For covering delicate foods in the oven, so they don't come in direct contact with the heat.

Parsley bouquet (44): Tie up any leftover parsley stems into a bouquet with kitchen twine and cook it in sauces, soups, or stews—it adds a nice, fresh flavor.

Plastic cutting board (45): A board on which to cut foods. Always use a separate board for cutting raw meat to avoid cross-contamination.

Round cutters (46): You can buy sets in different sizes. For cutting dough, and making potato or carrot scales for fish.

Round, heatproof mixing bowl (47): For whipping Hollandaise or egg yolks over a double boiler.

Skimmer (48): For removing cooked foods from soups or stocks.

Soda siphon (49): For foaming cream or cream-like liquids while adding it to gelatins.

Soufflé dish (50): Round ceramic dishes varying in diameter for sweet and savory soufflés.

Piping bags and decorating tips (51): For decorative egg fillings or decorating small buns, cakes, and tortes.

Steel saucepan (52): For cooking and heating up sauces, soups, or stews.

Pastry or cookie cutter (53): For working with cookie, pastry and puff pastry doughs.

Truffle slicer (54): For slicing truffles over dishes, of course, but also for shaving Parmesan cheese over dishes or pasta.

Wok (55): Large pan with high, sloping sides used for stir-frying.

Toothpicks (56): For sealing poultry cavities closed and for securing ham or bacon to small cuts of meat.

29

33

37

41

45

49

53

30
31
32
34
35
36
38
39
40
42
43
44
46
47
48
50
51
52
54
55
56

The Food Pyramid

The food pyramid is designed to help you make healthy food choices.

It shows the proportions of servings of the different foods we should consume.

The bottom section shows foods that should be consumed frequently; for example, starchy foods such as pasta, bread, or rice.

The foods at the top, such as fats and sugar, should be eaten in smaller portions.

However, the pyramid has been disputed for years. There are alternatives, for example, that use a glycemic index measure. Some scientists believe red meat, cheese, and white bread should be closer to the top of the pyramid.

The food pyramid can be a guide to healthy eating, but it should not be taken as gospel. Most food models fall short because they assume the human body works like a machine. A diesel engine always needs diesel fuel, whether it's driven with a light foot or a leaden one. Our bodies, however, are not machines. Our food requirements depend on how we live our lives—on whether we lead active or sedentary lifestyles. Do we exercise during free time, or sit in front of the TV?

Genetic factors also play a role. It's a fact that some people can eat whatever they like and still stay thin their whole lives. Others can eat just the same amount and yet they get fat. Everyone metabolizes food differently.

Regular exercise,
a minimum of
2–3 times a week
(20–30 minutes)
Alcohol in moderation

Animal fats, sweets, salt

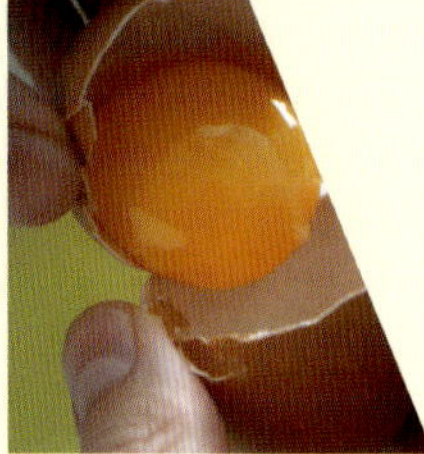

Meat 2–3 times a week **Eggs** 2–3 per week

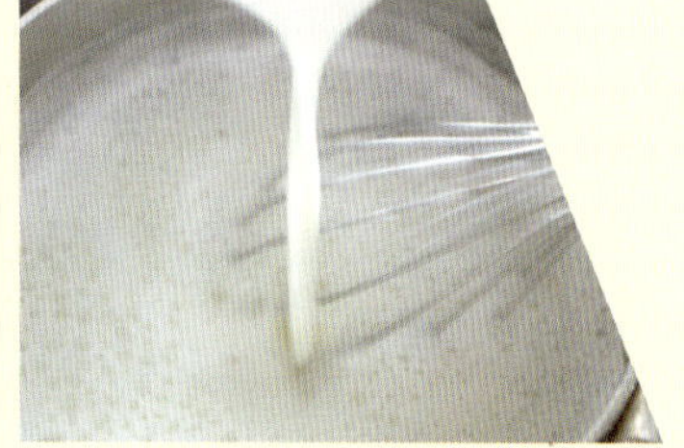

Fish 1–2 portions per week **Milk & dairy products** min. 2 portions per day

Vegetables min. 2–3 portions per day **Fruit** min. 2–3 portions per day

Grains several portions per day, e.g. bread, potatoes, pasta, legumes

Drink min. 8 glasses of water a day

Cooking for Yourself is the First Step to Better Eating

When you cook, you know what is going into the pots and pans. You can decide between fatty and lean meats, you can choose between cooking with butter or olive oil. And you can spare your body all the additives hiding in junk foods: for example, substances that preserve junk foods, make them look nicer, or just give them flavor. The last group, flavor enhancers, are especially controversial.

Energy Density

Even though Calories have asserted themselves in the public eye, many experts in food-energy density see a better option for healthy eating. Energy density is the energy content in food in relation to weight (Calorie/oz /30 g). That sounds abstract, but it has concrete implications. Foods with less energy density are more filling with lower Calorie intakes.

Food Energy Density Cal/oz (30 g)

Food	Cal/oz (30 g)
Wheat rye bread	63
Whole-grain roll	66
Croissant	129
Cheesecake	111
Cookies	147
Gingerbread	120
Cow's milk, 1.5% fat	12
Cow's milk, 3.5% fat	12
Fruit yogurt, added sugar, 1.5 % fat	24
Fruit yogurt, added sugar, 3.5 % fat	27
Sour cream	36
Whipped cream	93
Jam	81
Honey	99
Hazelnut spread	156
Low-fat butter/margarine	111
Light margarine	240
Butter	240
Ham, cooked (lean)	39
Leberkaese	90
Salami	111
Bratwurst	93
Tuna fish (no oil)	33
Pickled herring	63
Emmental/Gruyère cheese, fat content 45%	120
Apple, grapefruit, honeydew melon, cherries, kiwi, mandarins, nectarines, plums	15
Gummi bears	102
Granola bars	33–126
Whole chocolate milk	162
Beef, lean	30
Veal, lean	30
Pork cutlet	33
Pork cutlet, breaded (cooked)	96
Chicken breast	30
Trout	30
Breaded fish (cooked)	96
Potatoes	21
White rice, cooked	30
Fried potatoes	39
Pasta, cooked	42
French fries	63
Eggs	45
Beans, broccoli, cress, pumpkin, carrots, leeks, savoy cabbage, onion	9
Fruit sorbet	24–36
Ice cream, scoop	30–117

The ideal average is about 45 Cal/oz (30 g). Eating cheesecakes and pizza is perfectly allowed on occasion, but using the energy density table cleverly ensures you'll be able to put together palatable meals on your own. So it might be better to limit bread consumption at breakfast and by all means eat a little more cooked ham instead. Potatoes have a lower energy density than rice or pasta, and avoiding pasta means you can dish up a little more meat. And don't forget, the energy density table guarantees less hunger, after all it directly relates to the satiety effect of each food.

- Under 45 Cal/oz (30 g)
- 45–75 Cal/oz (30 g)
- Above 75 Cal/oz (30 g)

Excerpted from the energy density table from the Else Kröner Fresenius Center at the Technical University of Munich, Germany.

Calories

Calories are a measure of energy: 1 Calorie is the amount of energy needed to heat 2 lb 4 oz (1 kg) water by 1.8°F (1°C). The term Calorie comes directly from the era of steam engines. To make one work, it was important to know how wood or coal could be used to heat water, and so create energy. The human body, however, does not burn food like a steam engine—and it does not work as consistently either. Despite all the tables in women's and fitness magazines, human energy conversion depends heavily on your individual constitution. The brain is considered the largest energy user. By weight, it equals about 2 percent of total body mass, but monopolizes about 20 percent of the body's own converted energy.

Caloric content of each item for every 3½ oz (100 g) unless otherwise specified:

Hare	105
Venison	94
Veal	94
Calf's liver	115
Rabbit	121
Lamb	178
Venison saddle	94
Beef tenderloin	115
Ground beef	212
Beef, fatty	281
Beef, lean	164
Round steak	162
Pork tenderloin	171
Pork knuckle	189
Pork, fatty	311
Pork, lean	143
Pork cutlet	105
Roast chicken	99
Chicken leg	80
Chicken breast	75
Duck	192
Goose	227
Turkey	122
Wiener sausage	257
Frankfurter sausage	249
Ham, cooked	264
Sole	59
Tuna fish	239
Turbot	42
Hamburger, ¼ lb (105 g)	273
Cheeseburger, ¼ lb (120 g)	324
Fish burger, 5½ oz (150 g)	380
French fries, 4 oz (120 g)	420
Curry sausage with ketchup, 5½ oz (150 g)	516
Frikadeller, 5½ oz (150 g)	280
Sausage, 5½ oz (150 g)	460
Mayonnaise (80% fat)	765
Whole chocolate milk	569
Semisweet chocolate	521
Potatoes with skins	70
Potatoes, without skins	86
Potato chips	598
Mushrooms	12
Carrots	29
Eggplants	21
Tomatoes	16
Butter	776
Margarine	748
Apricots	49
Apricots, dry	308
Bananas	70
Olive oil	930
White wine	69
Red wine	67
Beer	43
Apple turnover, approx. 3 oz (80 g)	220
Jelly donut, approx. 2 oz (60 g)	310
Croissant, approx. 2 oz (60 g)	280

Picnic Menu Suggestions

Generally speaking, recipes do not usually follow the rules of mathematics. You will not often find a recipe serving four that allows you to neatly divide all the ingredients and cooking times in half to serve two people. And, likewise, you can't just double all the ingredients in a recipe for four to serve eight people. For example, the cooking time for a piece of meat for eight people is not double the cooking time for a piece of meat for four—there is a formula for calculating cooking times based on weight after an initial fixed cooking period. The same goes for fish, too. But there are exceptions. You can, in fact, multiply the ingredients needed for a cold salad. In most cases, multiplying the ingredient quantities will work for soups as well. However, you should be especially careful with cakes and homemade breads. This is definitely where doing the math has its limits.

You can have a picnic with a variety of smaller dishes. Simply make several different recipes for four people and serve them as finger foods. The only important thing is to calculate the total amount of food you'll need. Most adults eat a main dish equal to about 10–17 oz (300–500 g), including side dishes. People take in closer to 1 lb (500 g) at a restaurant, where there are multiple courses served over several hours. For 8 people, you have to figure on filling about a 6–9-lb (2.4–4-kg) picnic basket, depending on the occasion and cost. But you should include plenty of fruit or vegetable salads.

1. **Herb Butter and Tomato Basil Butter** (see p. 36)

2. **Tomato Pesto with Black Olives, and Genovese Pesto** (see p. 60)—For a cold salad, or as a bread spread.

3. **Fresh Chicken Liver Pâté** (see p. 80)–Cut into slices and serve on brioche or toast and pair with a sweet wine.

4. **Waldorf Salad** (see p. 84)

5. **Potato and Cucumber Salad with Bacon Strips** (see p. 86)—Always a success with cold Veal Patties (see p. 590), cold chicken, or cold cuts.

6. **Pasta Salad with Tuna and Boiled Egg** (see p. 94)

7. **Spanish Tortilla** (see p. 117)—Cut into pieces and serve in ciabatta buns, with aioli and green olives on the side.

8. **Nigiri Sushi** (see p. 242)—Also a delicious picnic snack with other sauces and wasabi filling.

9. **Quiche Lorraine with Leeks** (see p. 394)—Bake and bring to the picnic in the dish—it will avoid damage that way.

10. **Cornish Hens Roasted with Lemon and Garlic** (see p. 540)—Roast the day before and serve it cold. Don't forget napkins.

11. **Exotic Fruit Salad** (see p. 657)—Fresh and easy to eat.

12. **Chocolate Brownies** (see p. 710)—These stay moist, are easy to bake, and make everyone happy (as chocolate is known to do!).

1
2
3
4
5
6
7
8
9
10
11
12

Party Time

Good preparation is everything. After all, you want to spend the evening with your guests and not in the kitchen. The same goes here that if you have a recipe conceived for four people, you can't easily convert it for eight or sixteen people using multiplication. It's easier to stick with the recipes as they are in the book and prepare a nice buffet for your guests with several delicious little dishes. It's difficult with warm dishes; it definitely can be a lot of work to get everything on the table at the right temperature if you have a lot of guests. But there is one exception that is appropriate for parties—and that's grilling.

Simply cooking meat or fish over an open fire—it doesn't get much more natural and authentic than that. For the meat to turn out well, you should pay attention to a few easy tips.

— The grill should not be too hot. Otherwise, it won't take long for the outside to burn and for the meat to become tough. So it's better to reduce the heat by spreading the coals apart, to place the grill a little higher over the flame, and let the food cook for a few more minutes. You can test the heat by holding your hand about 5 inches (12 cm) over the grill; if you have to move after only one or two seconds, the grill is too hot. About five seconds means it's a medium heat.

— Grilled meat should sit for a few minutes on a plate, covered with foil. Doing this keeps the juices from running out of the meat with the first cut.

— Marinades or spice mixtures taste even better when they're homemade. Packaged grilling spices often contain flavor enhancers, such as monosodium glutamate.

Beef and pork are great without a marinade as long as there is fat marbled through the meat. Chicken breasts can simply be brushed with a mixture of the juice of 1 lemon, ½ bunch chopped parsley, 3 tbsp olive oil, and one pressed garlic clove. Let them rest for two hours before putting them on the grill.

Fish, such as salmon, herring, porgy, or mackerel, also taste good on the grill. Shrimp and shellfish should be grilled in the shell. Grilling time is only two or three minutes.

1. **Tartar Sauce** (see p. 52), **Cocktail Sauce** (see p. 53), and **Aioli** (see p. 53), for dipping bread and vegetables.

2. **BBQ Sauce** (see p. 56) for steaks and grilled pork chops.

3. **Ham Aspic with Radishes** (see p. 74)

4. **Tomato Mousse with Pesto** (see p. 76)

5. **Lobster Cocktail with Mushrooms** (see p. 82)—Fill glasses and set on the table.

6. **Potato and Cucumber Salad with Bacon Strips** (see p. 86)—Always a hit with cold Veal Patties, chicken, or cold cuts.

7. **Italian frittata** (see p. 116)—Prepare this in the morning and serve it lukewarm.

8. **Deviled Eggs** (see p. 118)—A classic must-have for any "retro" party! These decorative eggs also work well as a garnish for salads.

9. **Fried Quail Egg Canapés with Beef Tartare** (see p. 120)—The beef tartare is prepared ahead of time, and the quail eggs are fried only at the last minute, so you can serve the canapés with beer right at the beginning of the party.

10. **Gazpacho** (see p. 162)—Prepare the day before and let the flavors meld overnight. Then serve it in large bowls.

11. **Penne Bolognese** (see p. 202)—Precook and just bake in the oven later to finish. Pasta is a real winner at parties and, with the exception of spaghetti, can be eaten while standing.

12. **Indian Chickpea Curry with Cinnamon, Yogurt, and Mint** (see p. 290)—Easily prepared, it tastes nice and spicy, and it's also vegetarian.

13. **Stuffed Eggplants with Goat Cheese Filling and Oregano** (see p. 366)—Bake ahead of time, warm it up quickly when your first guests arrive, and bring it to the table hot.

14. **Mussels in Herb Marinade** (see p. 506)–Can also be made the day before.

15. **Chicken Legs in BBQ Sauce** (see p. 522)—Easy to prepare in large batches and marinate the day before. The chicken pieces can also be baked slowly at 275°F (140°C). The low temperature extends the cooking time, allowing the chicken legs to stay in the oven longer without browning.

16. **Chili con Carne** (see p. 554)—Especially popular at later hours, or warmed up with a sunny-side up egg the next day—your guests will thank you for it!

17. **Bavarian Cream** (see p. 658)—Easily multiplied. Either portion it into individual glass bowls, or fill a large bowl and serve with various fruit sauces (see p. 695).

18. **Panna Cotta with Coffee** (see p. 674)—So easy, you can hardly go wrong, and it's also a favorite dessert at every party.

1
2
3
4
5
6
7
8
9
10
11
12
13
14
15
16
17
18

Salt, Butter, Oil, Vinegar

Contents

28 Salts
30 Butter
30 Whipped Butter
32 Butter From Around the World
34 Melted Butter
34 Beurre Noisette
34 Clarified Butter
36 Tomato Basil Butter
36 Herb Butter
38 Oils
40 Oil Lexicon
42 Infused and Speciality Oils
44 Vinegar
46 Truffle Vinegar
46 Chili Pepper Vinegar
46 Garlic Cilantro Vinegar
46 Vanilla Cardamom Vinegar
46 Lemon Rosemary Vinegar

1. Hibiscus flower salt
2. Portuguese sea salt
3. Himalayan salt
4. Fleur de sel
5. Rock salt
6. Iodized salt
7. Coarse Atlantic sea salt
8. Maldon sea salt
9. Smoked salt
10. Mallorcan sea salt

Salts

Not all salts are the same. The most important kinds are table salt, with or without iodine supplements. Then you have sea salt and coarse salt. Sea salt comes from the salt mines in Guerande (Brittany, France), Aigues-Mortes (Languedoc-Roussillon, France), the Camargue, the French Atlantic coast, Maldon (Essex, England). The size and shape of the crystals and their flavor can vary slightly. The light gray "Fleur de Sel" (salt flower) from Guerande, which is harvested by hand from June to September, apparently forms only if the wind blows from the East. People say that the "salt rose" from the "Salins du Midi" has a mild peppery note, while the coarse salt from the Atlantic coast, on the other hand, has slightly sour notes. Salt should always be stored dry. Metal boxes are not good for storing salt, because salt crystals contain chlorine.

Coarse salt is often used for soups and vegetable dishes. Smaller salt granules season fish, meat, and sauces. Meat should be salted as it begins to cook, because the salt releases the flavors drawing the natural juices to the surface. Likewise, salt fish inside and out before cooking. Then place it immediately in the pan or on the grill.

Salt should be used sparingly, but it does bring out the flavor in dishes.

Some reference books count monosodium glutamate as a culinary salt. But it's really a flavor enhancer, and it can cause nausea. If you cook with good ingredients, you won't need such flavor enhancers.

An increasing number of "high-end salts" have appeared in the last few years—red-wine-infused salts are included among them, as are Hawaiian salts available in green, red, and black; Himalayan salt; and Korean bamboo salt. They can add color accents to certain dishes and are a unique gift idea. But if you use only a little salt, you'll barely notice a difference in taste. These are not kitchen must-haves. Generations of cooks have created first-class dishes without using "such luxuries."

English Maldon salt is good-quality variety that tastes great on a boiled egg or on roasted meat.

Coarse white sea salt from Mallorca and lavender-colored Hibiscus salt, also from Mallorca. Hibiscus flowers mixed with the salt lend it a fruity flavor.

1
2
10
3
9
8
4
7
6
5

1. Danish butter
2. Irish butter
3. French butter, low salt
4. Belgian butter

Butter

Butter is made from the fat, or cream, that comes from milk. It's rarely made in a traditional butter churn anymore. Most of the time the cream is put in a centrifuge, where the fat separates from the rest of the liquid. Roughly 2½–4 gallons (10–15 liters) of milk goes into just over 2¼ cups (500 g) of butter. In principle, butter can be made from the milk of all animals. Yak butter is served with tea in Tibet.

All types of butter differ in salt and moisture content. But other factors affect the quality, too. For example, a cow's diet affects the taste of her milk.

Butter browns and burns easily when heated because of its high water content. This is why some people start with a little oil in the pan, then add the butter to it.

Soft, slightly warm butter can be mixed easily with other ingredients. These include shallots, parsley, garlic, and horseradish. Anyone can whip up herb butter. You can also add almonds, sardines, or mustard.

Beurre noisette (literally, "hazelnut butter") is a term for lightly browned butter. The name refers to the color and taste, not the ingredients. There are no nuts in beurre noisette, but rather caramelized milk sugars. It is traditionally served with fish.

Butter turns rancid quickly and should only be kept up to three weeks in the refrigerator.

Low-fat butter contains 50 percent less fat than usual. Emulsifiers, food dyes, stabilizers, and preservatives are added to make it look like real butter.

The traditional way of making butter is very different. Only a few companies still follow it today—it takes about three days to produce butter this way. These small producers allow the customer to specify the salt and moisture content, as well as the shape. The milk spins in a horizontal metal drum for 90 minutes. It turns into flakes in a kind of white mash. When cooled with ice water, the flakes come together. The butter then sits for three days. Afterward the butter is kneaded on a wooden surface.

The butter has to sit for at least two hours while the salt sets in. Salt content in traditional butter varies according to what the customer wants, but usually lies between 1.8 and 7 percent.

Traditionally made butter will keep for three weeks, but it begins to lose its natural flavor after seven days.

Whipped Butter

Bring **1⅛ cups (250 g) butter** to room temperature and beat with a whisk for as long as it takes to increase the volume by a third, and for the butter to take on a creamy consistency. This butter can be worked into mixtures or used in baking recipes.

To serve butter on the dining table, cut thin slices of a little less than ¼ inch (5 mm) and then cut the slices in half. Then put the slices in a bowl with ice and water. The butter won't melt and you can take one piece at a time.

Store opened butter in a well-sealed container. Uncovered butter can take on various odors from other foods in the refrigerator.

It's best to keep the butter container on a separate shelf in the refrigerator door. It's not too cold there, and the butter will be easier to spread or work with.

Butter From Around the World

1. Buffalo milk butter—for melting over pasta and for roasting Italian meat dishes, on bread or baked goods, or for binding pasta sauces.

2. Cultured butter from Italy—for bread, or for binding pasta sauces.

3. French butter, half salted—works well for roasting meats, for binding sauces, and for spreading on fresh baguettes.

4. French sweet cream butter—works well in butter or cream sauces, French cakes, and fine pastries.

5. German farmer's butter—for baking and cooking.

4
3
5
2
1

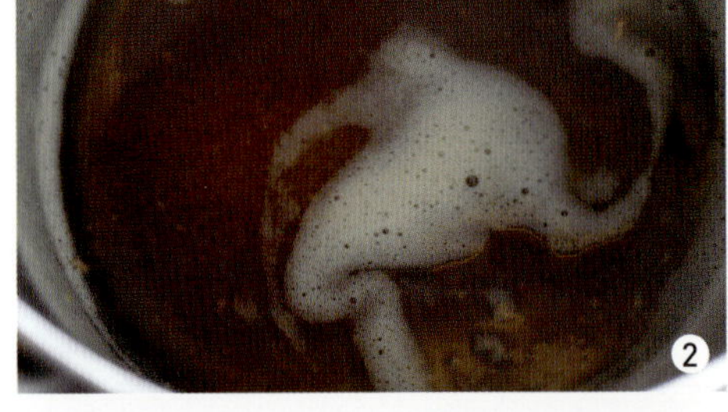

Melted Butter

Put **1⅛ cups (250 g) butter** in a small pot and melt over medium heat, then pour over boiled potatoes or steamed white asparagus.

Beurre Noisette

1. Melt **1⅛ cups (250 g) butter** in a small pot over medium heat, until the liquid takes on a light brown color.

2. As soon as it reaches the desired color, remove the pot from the heat, because the butter will continue to brown in the pot. For best results, immediately place the pot on a wet kitchen towel. This cools the pot somewhat so the butter doesn't brown too much and burn.

Clarified Butter

Run **1⅛ cups (250 ml) beurre noisette** through a conical strainer lined with cheesecloth to separate the browned solids from the butterfat.

Clarified butter is used for roasting or baking. It's known as *ghee* in Indian cooking. Clarified butter can be heated to high temperatures without burning because it does not contain whey.

 ½ cup (125 g) butter

 3 tsp tomato paste

 1 bunch fresh basil

 ½ garlic clove

 1 pinch of salt
1 pinch of black pepper

Tomato Basil Butter

1. Whip the butter until it forms peaks.

2. Add the tomato paste. Cut the basil into thin ribbons, finely chop the garlic, and then add both to the tomato and butter. Add the salt and pepper, then stir.

3. Fill small bowls, cover, and store in the refrigerator.

Serve with grilled or roasted meat or fish. Another option is to spread it on oven-toasted bread and serve as an appetizer with a rosé wine.

 ½ cup (125 g) butter

 1 bunch fresh chives
1 bunch fresh parsley

 ½ garlic clove

 3 shallots

 1 tsp hot mustard

 1 pinch of salt

 1 pinch of nutmeg, freshly grated

 ½ tsp Worcestershire sauce

Herb Butter

1. Whip the butter until it forms peaks.

2. Rinse the chives and chop into small rings. Pick the parsley leaves from the stems, rinse, and chop finely. Peel the garlic and chop finely. Peel and finely dice the shallots. Add the herbs, mustard, salt, nutmeg, and the Worcestershire sauce to the butter.

3. Mix everything well with a whisk. Fill small bowls, cover, and store in the refrigerator.

Serve this butter with grilled steaks or with reheated potato dishes.

Oils

There's oil for cooking, for frying, and for seasoning, but an oil that does everything—that doesn't exist.

You need at least two oils in your kitchen, and usually they are olive and sunflower or peanut oils.

A relatively neutral-tasting oil, such as peanut, is ideal for frying. It starts to smoke when it reaches 425°F (220°C), and then it can catch fire. A deep fryer with a temperature display can prevent that from happening.

Even with something simple such as French fries, throwing them in hot oil is not enough. They have to be fried first at 300°F (150°C), drained, then left to sit. Next, bake them at 375°F (190°C) briefly, until golden brown, and then drain on paper towels.

Oil Lexicon

On the label

Extra virgin olive oil, olio extra virgine, or huile vierge extra: oil from the first pressing. It contains a portion of free oleic acids, less than 0.8 percent.

Virgin olive oil: "second class" oil, with less than 2 percent free oleic acids.

Olive oil: the "third class." These oils can be extracted and refined using chemical solvents. A blend of virgin and refined olive oils is suitable for cooking and frying in most cases.

Olive pomace oil: Oil that has been chemically extracted from olive pomace (the residue of pressed olives).

100 percent pure oil: The contents of the bottle were obtained from a single oil; blending is prohibited.

Cold press: A gentle press done at 63°F (17°C), often carried out using hydraulic presses.

The designations "first pressing" and "cold pressed" are outdated. Virgin olive oil is always cold pressed; the second pressing, which once served to increase the yield, is not common anymore. In addition, the acidity levels say very little about the taste of the oil itself.

The label should show the year the oil was pressed, the name of the mill, and the name of the "cultivation area." This is how inferior oil blends from different countries can be avoided. Different labels, such as Appellation d'Origine Contrôlée (AOC), Appellation d'Origine Protégée (AOP), or Identification Géographique Protégée (IGP), speak to the care taken in production.

Olive oil should be stored upright and in a cool (50–60°F/10–16°C), dark place. Do not put oils in the refrigerator, because they will turn cloudy.

1. Hazelnut oil
2. Walnut oil
3. Grapeseed oil
4. Pumpkin Seed oil
5. Argan oil
6. Sunflower Seed oil

Infused and Specialty Oils

Almond oil pairs well with mussels, pistachio oil tastes good with lobster or rock lobster, and hazelnut oil can make fish more refined or refresh the taste of cold chicken or turkey.

Aside from the simple all-purpose oils for the deep fryer or pan, there is also a wide variety of specialty oils—oils that have their own flavor and can spice other dishes or refine them. Styrian pumpkin seed oil, which is sometimes enjoyed straight on a boiled tri-tip in Austria, for example. Hazelnut and almond oil from the Perigord region of France taste outstanding on salads. A strong sesame seed oil lends a simple vegetable salad an exotic flavor. These oils are only as good as the mills that pressed them though. Purists do not buy oils at a store, but have them shipped from remote farms, where the fruits are milled between two large stone blocks according to centuries-old tradition.

For example, nutty argan oil comes from the fruit of the argan tree, which grows only in southwest Morocco, not far from the Atlantic. Moroccan women consider it a beauty secret. They use the rare liquid as a natural moisturizer for hair and skin, as a body gel, and as a strengthener for nails. The outer flesh becomes animal feed, and the extremely hard kernel beneath is crushed with two stones. A nut is stored inside. Once gathered, these nuts are toasted in an oven, their shells a useful source of "fuel." Then the Berber women mill the toasted nuts by hand—a process that takes hours.

Gourmet shops carry, among other things, diverse infused oils for pepping up salads or fresh seafood—sometimes with just a little caraway added, sometimes enriched with sophisticated spice blends. Oils like this can be made easily at home. Just put a little basil or lemon in a bottle of neutral oil and wait. After a week, a new scent comes storming through the bottle. Wait about six weeks and it's ready to serve. Try it first with just half a vanilla bean (cut it open and scrape out the beans with the tip of a knife) in a small bottle of peanut oil—it works wonders with a simple tomato salad.

Infused oils, such as a chili-garlic oil, can easily be made at home.

1
2
3
4
5
6

1. White balsamic
2. Balsamic
3. Apple vinegar
4. Raspberry vinegar
5. Sherry vinegar
6. Brown rice vinegar
7. White wine vinegar
8. Red wine vinegar
9. Tarragon vinegar

Vinegar

Alcohol is turned into vinegar by a bacteria called *Mycoderma aceti*. The acid content of vinegar is about 4–12 percent. The best vinegars are made from wine or apple cider. But, in principle, almost any alcohol can be made into vinegar. Sherry, cider, champagne, rioja, white wine, red wine, malt, or even rice and palm wine vinegars—all provide variety in the kitchen. Of course, another familiar type is the conventional distilled white vinegar used for pickling.

Aside from these vinegars, there are several infused varieties available on the market—made with garlic, shallots, tarragon, rosemary, nutmeg, cherry, or raspberry. You can make these infused vinegars at home. Bring 2¼ cups (500 ml) wine vinegar to a boil, pour it over the herbs, shallots, or fruit (approx. 2¼ oz/60 g), and store in a well-sealed bottle for two weeks, stirring occasionally. Alternatively, you can slowly heat herbs, such as thyme, in a pot with the vinegar and let them steep for 30 minutes before putting the mixture in a bottle. Vinegar is nearly non-perishable at room temperature, but homemade vinegar is probably better when stored in the refrigerator.

Balsamic vinegar (aceto balsamico)
Italian balsamic vinegar is used as a spice. It's obtained from the filtered, heated must of the Trebbiano grape and has to mature. As the years go by, it's moved into smaller and smaller barrels that can be made of oak, chestnut, cherry, ash, or other woods. This is how it survives cold winters and hot summers. It can take 12, 25, or even 50 years before the syrupy, dark brown liquid makes it into a glass bottle. After 20 years of proper storage, only about 3¼ quarts (3 liters) of balsamic remain from the original 74 quarts (70 liters) of must. A good name alone does not mean quality though. Depending on its age, balsamic is not cheap. Special deals are often a lot younger than genuine balsamic vinegar, and they are often pepped up with artificial flavors. On the other hand, balsamic labeled "traditional" has spent at least 12 years in a barrel, and older balsamics proudly carry "extra vecchio" on the label.

Not all balsamic vinegars taste the same. Taste it on a spoon or knife tip first before using it as a seasoning. Balsamic is low maintenance. As long as you seal the bottle well, storage won't be a problem. Only strong odor carriers, such as onions, can affect the flavor.

1
2
3
4
8
9
5
7
6

1. Truffle Vinegar

Slice about **1¾ oz (50 g) black truffles**, then cut the slices into strips, and put them in a container with **6 blackberries**. Pour **3 tbsp (50 ml) red port wine** and **1⅛ cups (250 ml) sherry vinegar** over them, seal the container, and place it in the refrigerator for about one week. Use this vinegar for strong vinaigrettes, to season mayonnaise, or for deglazing kidneys or sweetbreads.

2. Chili Pepper Vinegar

Put **1⅛ cups (250 ml) white wine vinegar**, **10 dried red chiles**, **1 tbsp black peppercorns**, and **1 tsp coriander seed** in a bottle and seal. Let stand for about one week. Use on summer salads with tomatoes and cheese, for poaching eggs, or for seasoning sauce reductions. The spiced vinegar lends the dish a strong, piquant note.

3. Garlic Cilantro Vinegar

Pour **½ cup (125 ml) white wine vinegar** and **½ cup (125 ml) rice wine vinegar** into a bottle. Add **5 pressed garlic cloves**, **½ bunch fresh cilantro**, **2 slices galangal** to the vinegar. Seal and place in the refrigerator for a few days. Use for salad dressings, to accompany fish and shellfish with fruit, or when making Asian dips.

4. Vanilla Cardamom Vinegar

Pour **½ cup (125 ml) white wine**, **⅜ cup (100 ml) red wine vinegar**, and **1 tbsp balsamic vinegar** into a bottle. Cut **2 vanilla beans** in half, and scrape out the insides. Along with the vanilla scrapings, add **3 star anise seeds** and **5 black cardamom pods** to the vinegar. Seal and shake well once so the vanilla can be better distributed. Use on winter salads with red cabbage and oranges, or in stewed quince with venison.

5. Lemon Rosemary Vinegar

Pour **1⅛ cups (250 ml) white wine vinegar** into a container. Crush together **3 bay leaves**, **1 sprig fresh rosemary** (removing the leaves from the stem), half **a lemon** (cut in slices), and **10 white peppercorns**. Add everything to the vinegar and place in the refrigerator for a few days. Use in salad dressings or for seasoning mayonnaises.

■ **Because these vinegars don't get cooked, they won't keep as long as cooked ones, but they'll be far more flavorful.**

1
2
3
4
5

Cold Sauces

Contents

50 Mayonnaise
52 Tartar Sauce
52 Remoulade
52 Rouille Sauce
53 Cocktail Sauce
53 Dill Mustard Sauce
53 Aioli
54 Preparing Herbs
55 Yogurt Sauce with Herbs
55 Green Chervil Cress Sauce
55 Lingonberry Horseradish Sauce
56 BBQ Sauce
58 French Dressing
59 Thousand Island Dressing
59 Caesar Dressing
60 Tomato Pesto with Black Olives
60 Genovese Pesto
62 Classic Vinaigrette
63 Herb-Mustard Vinaigrette
63 Tomato Vinaigrette
63 Soy Vinaigrette with Cilantro

6 eggs

1 tsp hot mustard

1½ tsp salt

3½ cups (800 ml) sunflower oil

½ lemon

1 large pinch cayenne pepper

Mayonnaise

Important: All ingredients must be used at the same temperature; that means oil and eggs should either both come out the refrigerator, or both be at room temperature.

1. Separate the eggs. Put the egg yolks in a bowl and place the egg whites in the refrigerator for later use.

2. Add the mustard and the salt to the egg yolks and beat.

3. Add half of the oil a little at a time and whisk briskly.

4. Then, add the lemon juice and a pinch cayenne pepper. Quickly beat in the rest of the oil.

Makes 4 cups (1 liter).

■ **Lay a damp towel under the bowl so it doesn't slide while you stir the oil. If the mayonnaise breaks, you can save it by carefully stirring at the side of the bowl. The runny part will get mixed in a little at a time and the mayonnaise will bind again.**

2
3
4

Tartar Sauce

Boil **2 eggs** for 10 minutes. Shock the eggs under cold water and peel them. Peel **1 shallot**, cut it in half, and dice it finely. Rinse **1 bunch fresh chives**, removing any damaged parts, and snip into small rings. Grate the hard-boiled eggs on the finest grater. Mix the ingredients with **7 oz (200 g) mayonnaise**. Next, add **1 tsp hot mustard**, the juice of half **a lemon**, and **½ tbsp Worcestershire sauce**. Finish it with **1 pinch salt** and **pepper** to taste.

Makes about 14 oz (400 g).

■ To make the sauce a little lighter, add 1 tbsp sour cream. **Serve with sliced, cold roast beef, beef aspic, or warm or cold fish dishes.**

Remoulade

Peel **3 shallots**, cut them in half, and dice finely. Cut **3 small pickles** into thin slices, then into strips, then dice finely. Rinse **½ bunch fresh parsley** and **½ bunch fresh chervil**, removing any damaged leaves, and chop finely. Chop **3 anchovies** and **1 tbsp capers** finely. Stir all ingredients into **7 oz (200 g) mayonnaise**. Add **1 tsp hot mustard** and **½ tsp Worcestershire sauce**, stir, and add **1 pinch salt** and **pepper** to taste.

To make the sauce a little lighter, add **1 tbsp sour cream**.

Makes about 14 oz (400 g).

■ **Serve with warm meat, cold roast beef, baked vegetables, or egg dishes.**

Rouille Sauce

Peel **3 garlic cloves** and cut them into slices. Peel **1 small, starchy cooked potato** and dice finely. Add everything to a small pot with **1 tbsp extra virgin olive oil** and sweat lightly. Add **6 saffron threads**, **½ tsp paprika**, and **½ tsp salt**. Pour in **⅞ cup (200 ml) water** and simmer slowly for 10 minutes. Crush the potato pieces with a fork and stir into the liquid. Let cool until the mixture is lukewarm. Then mix with **7 oz (200 g) mayonnaise**.

Makes about 14 oz (400 g).

■ **Rouille sauce is an important part of bouillabaisse, but it also tastes good with cold poached fish or shellfish, or simply with a fresh baguette and a glass of wine.**

Cocktail Sauce

Add **3 tbsp ketchup**, **2 tsp grated horseradish**, **3 tbsp cognac**, and the juice of **half an orange** to **1 cup (200 g) mayonnaise**. Blend with a whisk until smooth. Add **1 pinch salt**, **1 pinch cayenne pepper**, and **3 drops Worcestershire sauce** to taste.

Makes about 14 oz (400 g).

■ **Great as a dressing on shellfish salads or as a dip with cold or baked vegetables. Tastes really good with fondue.**

Dill Mustard Sauce

Rinse **1 bunch fresh dill**, remove the stems, and chop finely. Combine with **2 tbsp coarse mustard**, **2 tbsp hot mustard**, **5 tbsp honey**, and **7 oz (200 g) mayonnaise**. Finish it with **1 pinch salt** and **1 pinch pepper** to taste.

Makes about 14 oz (400 g).

■ **Goes best with marinated fish, such as salmon, halibut, or trout—but it can also be served with fresh steamed shrimp or crayfish.**

Aioli

Peel **3 garlic cloves**, slice them, then grind them together with **½ tsp salt** in a mortar and add to **7 oz (200 g) mayonnaise**. Squeeze **half a lemon** and mix the juice with the mayonnaise. For best results, let the sauce sit for 30 minutes before serving.

Makes about 9 oz (250 g).

■ **Serve with cooked fish, cold fried fish, or shellfish. Also great as a dip with raw vegetable sticks. For a Spanish-themed evening, it makes an essential appetizer spread on white bread and served with ice-cold Chablis.**

Preparing Herbs

1. Rinse the chives, removing any damaged pieces, and chop them into fine rings.

2. Rinse the basil, pick the leaves from the stems, removing any damaged pieces, and cut into thin ribbons.

3. Rinse the tarragon, pick the leaves from the stems, removing any damaged pieces, and cut into thin ribbons.

4. Rinse the chervil, pick the leaves from the stems, removing any damaged pieces, and chop finely.

5. Rinse the parsley, pick the leaves from the stems, removing any damaged pieces, and chop finely. Hold the herbs together to chop them finer.

6. A food processor works faster, but it can make herbs bitter. The best thing is to cut gently through the herbs with the rocking motion of a sharp knife.

Yogurt Sauce with Herbs

Rinse **1 bunch fresh chervil**, **½ bunch fresh basil**, **1 bunch fresh parsley**, **1 bunch fresh chives**, and **½ bunch fresh tarragon**, and chop them finely. Peel **2 shallots**, cut them in half, and dice them finely. Put **1 cup (250 g) yogurt** and **7oz (200 g) crème fraîche or sour cream** in a bowl, then add the chopped herbs and the garlic. Add **1 tsp sugar**, **1½ tsp salt**, **1 pinch of black pepper**, and **4 tbsp extra virgin olive oil**, and mix well.

Makes about 1 lb 5 oz (600 g).

■ **Serve this sauce as a dip for raw vegetables, cooked meat or fish, cold roast beef, or roasted chicken or turkey—or simply with fresh white bread.**

Green Chervil Cress Sauce

Rinse **1 bunch fresh chervil** and **1 bunch fresh watercress**, and pick the leaves from the stems, removing any damaged pieces. Boil the herbs in salted water for 1 minute and shock them immediately in a bowl of cold water. Combine **7 oz (200 g) mayonnaise**, **1 tbsp extra virgin olive oil**, **3½ oz (100 g) crème fraîche or sour cream**, **1 tsp salt**, and **1 pinch cayenne pepper**. Squeeze **½ lemon** over a sieve to keep the seeds out of the bowl. Mix everything well with a whisk. Put the herbs and **3 tbsp water** in a food processor, and process until it is an evenly fine mass. Then mix it with the sauce.

Makes about 2¼ cups (500 g).

■ **Serve with shellfish, such as shrimp or lobster, cold steamed salmon, warm veal, or cold chicken.**

Lingonberry Horseradish Sauce

Using a whisk, stir about **¾ cup (200 g) plain yogurt** with **1 pinch salt**, **1 pinch white pepper**, and the juice from **½ lemon** until smooth. Add **1 tbsp lingonberry jam** and about **5½ oz (150 g) grated horseradish**, then mix together. Finish by mixing in about **3½ oz (100 g) whipped cream**.

Makes about 1 lb (500 g).

■ **This lingonberry horseradish sauce goes very well with warm beef, cold roast venison, and cold poultry, such as turkey.**

 2¼ cups (500 ml) ketchup

 1 garlic clove

 5 tbsp sugar

 1 orange

 1 lemon

 3 tbsp soy sauce

 2 tbsp peach jam

 3 tbsp (50 ml) cognac

 2 tbsp maple syrup

 1 tsp Tabasco sauce

 2 tbsp hot mustard

 1 tsp Worcestershire sauce

 1 tbsp sweet paprika

 1 tbsp curry powder

 1 tbsp ground ginger

 1 sprig fresh rosemary

 1 tbsp dried thyme

BBQ Sauce

1. Put the ketchup in a bowl. Peel the garlic cloves, chop them finely, and add them to the bowl with the sugar, the juices of the orange and the lemon, and the soy sauce. Briefly stir everything with a whisk.

2. Then add the peach jam, cognac, maple syrup, Tabasco, hot mustard, Worcestershire sauce, paprika, curry powder, and ground ginger, and stir again.

3. Pick the rosemary leaves from the stem, chop and add them to the sauce along with the thyme, and mix.

Serve as a marinade for spareribs, use with pork chops, steaks, or grilled chicken wings.

Makes 4 cups (1 liter).

■ BBQ sauce will keep up to three months in the refrigerator if it is well sealed. Keep heat low when grilling, broiling, or roasting with BBQ sauce to avoid burning the sugars in the sauce.

2

3

 2 eggs

 4 tsp hot mustard

 2 tsp salt

 1 pinch of white pepper

 ⅔ cup (150 ml) white wine vinegar

 1 pinch of freshly grated nutmeg

 2⅔ cups (600 ml) sunflower oil

 ⅜ cup (100 ml) water

French Dressing

1. Separate the eggs, putting the yolks in a bowl. Place the egg whites in the refrigerator for later use. Add the mustard to the egg yolks.

2. Add the salt, pepper, white wine vinegar, and nutmeg.

3. Mix everything with a handheld blender and add the oil a little at a time. Then add the water and stir. Season with white pepper and salt to taste.

Makes 4 cups (1 liter).

■ **This classic salad dressing goes with most leafy salads. It serves as a foundation for other dressings, such as Thousand Island and Caesar.**

Thousand Island Dressing

Rinse ½ **green bell pepper** and ½ **red bell pepper**, cut them in half, seed, and dice finely. Peel **2 shallots**, cut them in half, and dice finely. Then mix everything with **2¼ cups (500 ml) French dressing**. Now add **2 tbsp ketchup**, **1 tbsp sugar**, and **1 pinch cayenne pepper** and stir everything well together. The diced peppers look like tiny islands in the sea—that's why it's called "thousand island" dressing.

Makes about 3⅓ cups (800 ml).

■ **As a simple variation, you can add a variety of pickles instead of bell peppers and shallots. Chop the pickles in a food processor and add them to the dressing.**

Caesar Dressing

Grate **2¾ oz (80 g) Parmesan cheese**, and finely chop **1 tsp capers** (without the brine). Finely chop **5 anchovies** and crush them with the back of the knife. Combine **1⅛ cups (250 ml) French dressing**, about **7 oz (200 g) sour cream**, the capers, the anchovies and the Parmesan cheese, and mix. Season with a **pinch of black pepper** to taste.

Makes about 2⅓ cups (550 ml).

■ **Mix in romaine lettuce and finish with a sprinkle of crisp bacon strips and Parmesan shavings on top. This one is a salad classic.**

 3½ oz (100 g) Parmesan cheese

 7 oz (200 g) sun-dried tomatoes in oil

 1 tsp salt
1 pinch of black pepper

 4½ oz (125 g) skinned almonds

 1⅛ cups (250 ml) extra virgin olive oil

 1¾ oz (50 g) pitted black olives

1

2

3

Tomato Pesto with Black Olives

1. Grate the Parmesan cheese. Put the sun-dried tomatoes, salt and pepper, the almonds, and half the oil in a food processor and mix, then combine with the Parmesan cheese.

2. Now pour in the rest of the oil and process for 3 minutes, until the pesto has a pastelike consistency.

3. Finish by adding the black olives. Process for just 30 seconds to retain some olive pieces.

Makes about 1 lb 10 oz (750 g).

■ **Serve the tomato pesto with broiled or grilled fish or pasta dishes.**

 3½ oz (100 g) Parmesan cheese

 3 bunches fresh basil

 3 garlic cloves

 4½ oz (125 g) pine nuts

 1 tsp salt
1 pinch of black pepper

 1 pinch of freshly grated nutmeg

 ⅞ cup (200 ml) extra virgin olive oil

1

2

3

4

Genovese Pesto

1. Grate the Parmesan cheese. Rinse the basil and remove any damaged leaves. Peel the garlic and cut into thin strips. Put these ingredients in a food processor.

2. Add the pine nuts; season with salt, black pepper, and nutmeg.

3. Pour in half the oil and mix everything in the food processor.

4. Finally, add the remaining oil and process another 1 or 2 minutes, until the pesto has a pastelike consistency.

Makes about 1 lb 7 oz (650 g).

■ **Serve this classic basil pesto on pasta or broiled vegetables, or use it to marinate olives.**

1 garlic clove

1½ tsp hot mustard

1 pinch of white pepper

1 tsp salt

1 tbsp sugar

4 tbsp white wine vinegar

½ cup (125 ml) extra virgin olive oil

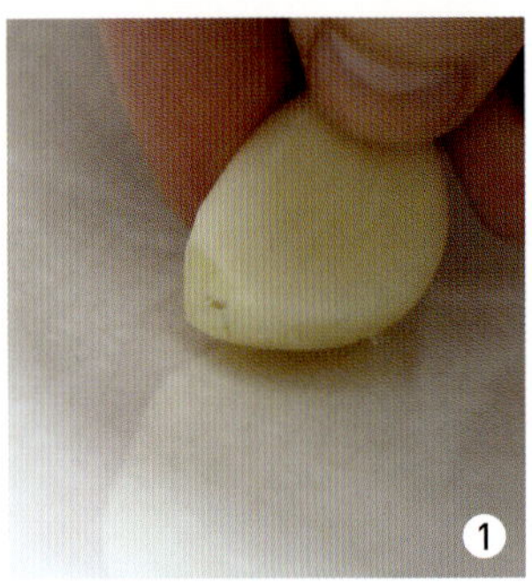

Classic Vinaigrette

1. Rub the inside of a bowl with the garlic clove to infuse the vinaigrette with flavor.

2. Add the mustard, pepper, salt, and sugar to the bowl. Then pour in the white wine vinegar and stir until the salt and sugar have dissolved.

3. Next, pour in the olive oil. Beat well with a whisk until the vinaigrette becomes creamy. This is how to make a basic vinaigrette, a simple yet very tasty salad dressing.

Makes about ¾ cup (180 ml).

Herb-Mustard Vinaigrette

Rinse ½ **bunch parsley**, **1 bunch chives**, ½ **bunch basil**, and ¼ **bunch tarragon**, removing any damaged pieces, and chop finely. Peel **2 shallots**, cut them in half, and dice them finely. Mix all of the ingredients with ⅔ **cup (140 ml) classic vinaigrette** and **1 tsp mustard**.

Makes about 1⅛ cups (250 ml).

■ **This herb-mustard vinaigrette works as a marinade for roasted vegetables such as artichokes, steamed asparagus, or beans, or as a dressing on tomatoes, endive, or a mixed salad.**

Tomato Vinaigrette

Skin **2 tomatoes** (see p. 347), remove the seeds, and dice them finely. Peel **1 shallot** and ½ **garlic clove** and dice them finely. Rinse ½ **bunch basil**, removing any damaged pieces, and cut into thin ribbons. Pour **4 tbsp balsamic vinegar** into a bowl. Add **1 pinch of salt**, **1 pinch of black pepper**, and **1 tbsp sugar** to the vinegar and beat with a whisk until the sugar and salt have dissolved. Now stir in ½ **cup (125 ml) oil** a little at a time. Add the tomatoes, garlic, shallots, and basil and mix everything together.

Makes about 1⅛ cups (250 ml).

■ **This vinaigrette tastes very good on roasted fish, calamari, or steamed mussels. Fried mushrooms with tomato vinaigrette are a delicious side dish with anything broiled or grilled.**

Soy Vinaigrette with Cilantro

Rinse ½ **bunch fresh cilantro**, removing any damaged pieces, and chop finely. Peel and finely grate **1 thumb-size piece of ginger**. Combine the ginger, **4 tbsp brown rice vinegar**, **1 tbsp soy sauce**, **1 tbsp sesame seeds**, and **1 pinch of crushed pepper**. Pour in **1 tbsp sesame oil** and **5 tbsp peanut oil** and mix. Stir in cilantro.

Makes about 1⅛ cups (250 ml).

■ **Serve mixed with cold Asian noodles, or as a dip with small pieces of raw vegetables, such as carrots, fennel, celery stalks, or Chinese cabbage.**

Salads & Appetizers

Contents

66 Lettuce & Herbs
68 Iceberg Lettuce
69 Green Batavia (Loose Leaf) Lettuce
70 Preparing Ginger
70 Preparing Horseradish
72 Green and White Asparagus Salad with Poached Egg
74 Ham Aspic
76 Tomato Mousse with Pesto
78 Beef Mango Salad with Cherry Tomatoes and Mint
80 Fresh Chicken Liver Pâté
82 Lobster Cocktail with Mushrooms
84 Waldorf Salad
86 Potato and Cucumber Salad with Bacon Strips
88 Mixed Bean Salad with Parsley
90 Seaweed Salad with Spinach Leaves and Sesame Dressing
92 Rice Salad with Curry Mayonnaise and Fruit
94 Pasta Salad with Tuna and Boiled Egg
96 Homemade Yam Chips
98 Beef Carpaccio with Parmesan Cheese and Lemon Juice

Lettuce & Herbs

Lettuce should be eaten as soon as possible, otherwise it can wither and rot. Wrapped in a moist towel, it will keep two to four days in the crisper, depending on how fresh it is.

Fresh herbs can be stored in a half-full glass of cool water. Herbs will also keep for up to five days in a plastic bag in the crisper. Dried herbs do not like light or heat.

Lollo rosso

Lollo biondo

Romaine

Frisée

Green oak leaf lettuce

Yellow dandelion leaves

Oak leaf lettuce

Iceberg lettuce

Buttercrunch

Belgian endive

Radicchio

Red endive

Arugula

Hijiki seaweed

Dulse seaweed

Bean sprouts

Watercress

Purslane

Chives

New Zealand spinach

Parsley

Iceberg Lettuce

1. Iceberg lettuce should have a crisp heart, and the stalk should not be too dried out.

2. Cut off the stalk.

3. Cut out any brown spots on the ribs in the centers of the outer leaves.

4. Rinse the whole iceberg head under running water. Then let it drain well.

5. Now cut the lettuce into pieces and toss with salad dressing, or wrap in plastic and store it in the refrigerator.

6. The washing water helps keep the lettuce fresh for a good week in the refrigerator.

6

Green Batavia (Loose Leaf) Lettuce

1. The lettuce should have a firm heart and the stalk should not be too dried out.

2. Cut off about ¾ inch (2 cm) of the stalk and likewise cut off any wilted tips of lettuce.

3. Place the lettuce in a large colander and separate the leaves under running water to remove any dirt.

4. Rinse the leaves well under running water, removing any rotten pieces at the same time. Let the leaves drip dry or shake them dry. Then toss with salad dressing or place in a bowl, cover with plastic wrap, and store in the refrigerator for later use.

Preparing Ginger

1. Ginger stays fresh longer if you store it in a plastic bag in the refrigerator, keeping it moist with a few drops of water.

2. Peel with a small paring knife.

3. Grate it with a small grater.

Preparing Horseradish

1. Peel the horseradish.

2. Grate the amount needed with a grater.

3. Rub the remaining portion with lemon so the horseradish stays white while stored.

4. Then wrap it in plastic to keep it fresh.

1. Ginger
2. Horseradish

14 oz (400 g) white asparagus

14 oz (400 g) green asparagus

2 shallots

2 sprigs fresh mint

½ bunch fresh chives

½ bunch fresh parsley

½ bunch fresh chervil

2 tbsp sugar

2 tbsp salt

½ lemon

⅔ cup (150 ml) vinaigrette (see p. 62)

4 eggs

2 tbsp water

2 tbsp cream

1½ tbsp mayonnaise

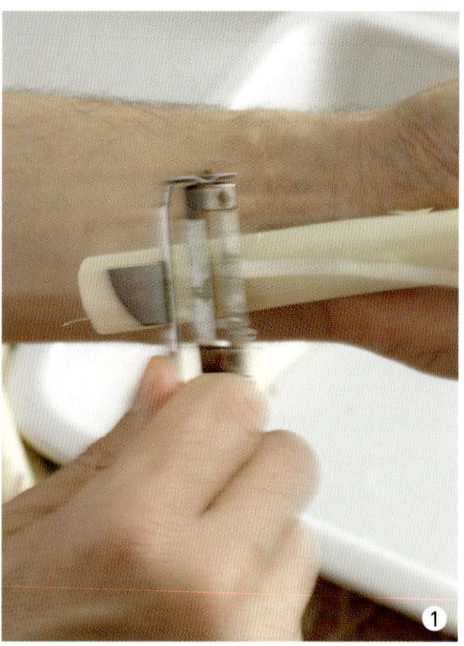

Green and White Asparagus Salad with Poached Egg

1. Peel the white and green asparagus. Peel both shallots, cut them in half, and dice them finely. Rinse the mint, removing any damaged pieces, pick the leaves from the stems, and cut them into thin ribbons. Rinse the chives, removing any damaged pieces, and chop into small rings. Likewise, rinse the parsley and chervil, removing any damaged pieces, pick the leaves from the stems, and cut them into ribbons.

2. In a pan, combine the white asparagus, the sugar, half the water, half the salt, and the lemon juice, and cook for about 8 minutes. In another pan, combine the green asparagus, the rest of the water and the salt, and cook about 5 minutes. Remove the asparagus and briefly shock in cold water. The asparagus must remain warm to absorb the marinade. Arrange the asparagus in a baking dish. Sprinkle the shallots and herbs over the asparagus stalks.

3. Pour the vinaigrette over the asparagus. Meanwhile, poach the eggs in vinegar water (see p. 110).

4. Mix the asparagus carefully with the marinade and leave it to marinate for about 10 minutes. Then divide the asparagus onto plates and drizzle with the herb vinaigrette from the marinade. Lay one poached egg on top of the asparagus and garnish with a little of the cooking water and cream mixed with mayonnaise.

■ **This salad tastes great with steamed crayfish, poached quail eggs, sautéed mushrooms (for example morels), roasted veal medallions, or veal tri-tip.**

3

4

 1 tbsp salt

 12 oz (350 g) leeks

 5½ oz (150 g) celery

 5 oz (140 g) celeriac

 2¾ oz (80 g) parsnip

 10½ oz (300 g) carrots

 3 ham hocks

 9 oz (250 g) onions

 1 head of garlic

 3 sprigs fresh thyme

 3 bay leaves

 10 cloves

 10 juniper berries

 1 pinch nutmeg, grated

 1 tsp white peppercorns

 1 tsp black peppercorns

3 sheets gelatin

2¼ cups (500 ml) beef broth

 ½ bunch fresh parsley

+ 2½ hours cooking time
+ 6 hours cooling time

Ham Aspic

1. Bring a large pot with 21 cups (5 liters) water to a boil and add the salt. Clean and peel all the vegetables except the onion and garlic. Reserve half of the carrots and of the leeks. Now put the ham hocks in the boiling water and add the unpeeled onions, remaining leeks and carrots, celery, unpeeled head of garlic, thyme, bay leaves, cloves, juniper berries, nutmeg, and white and black peppercorns. Let it simmer 2¼ to 2½ hours, depending on the size of the ham hocks, adding more water when needed. Soak the gelatin in cold water.

2. Bring a pot of water with salt to a boil and cook the reserved carrots and leeks, the parsnips, and the celeriac until very soft to make a broth. Pay attention to the different cooking times for the vegetables—the celeriac needs the longest time, followed by the carrots, the parsnip, and the leeks. Dissolve the gelatin in the beef broth, adding salt to taste, if necessary. Place the broth in the freezer, cooling it to room temperature. Cut the vegetables in wide strips.

3. Cut the ham hocks into pieces and remove any undesirable parts, such as fat and remaining skin. Using your hands, pull the meat apart into pieces about ¾–1¼ inches (2–3 cm). Pour a little broth into a terrine mold so the plastic wrap doesn't stick to the bottom. Then line the mold with plastic wrap, pressing down in the corners so that it sits flat and doesn't crease. Layer the vegetables, meat, and the parsley, filling the dish with broth in between layers.

■ Crisp fried potatoes and remoulade work well as side dishes with the aspic. The aspic shown here is served with radish slices and some classic vinaigrette, marinated with chives.

4. Continue to alternate the meat and vegetables in layers, adding pressure each time so no air pockets are left, otherwise the aspic will fall apart when cut.

5. When the dish is completely filled in, finish by pouring in the remaining broth and pressing down the aspic with a flat hand.

6. Take the overlapping wrap from the sides, cover the aspic, and seal it in.

7. Take a board the same size as the aspic and lay in on top, weighing it down to apply pressure. Place the aspic in the refrigerator for at least 6 hours (for best results, leave in overnight), so the gelatin can set until firm.

8. Remove the aspic from the dish and carefully unwrap. With a sharp knife, cut about ¾-inch (2-cm) thick slices, plate, and serve.

 1 lb 5 oz (600 g) tomatoes

 2 garlic cloves

 3 shallots

 2¼ oz (60 g) celery

 1 sprig fresh rosemary

 2 sprigs fresh thyme

 3 tbsp water

 2 tbsp sugar

 3 tbsp tarragon vinegar

 4 tbsp extra virgin olive oil

 2½ tsp salt

 1 pinch of black pepper

 2¼ cups (500 ml) tomato juice

 4 sheets of gelatin

 1 lb 2 oz (500 g) whipping cream

 4 tbsp pesto

Tomato Mousse with Pesto

1. Skin the tomatoes (see p. 347), cut them in eighths, remove the cores, and cut into about ½-inch (1-cm) pieces. Peel the garlic and cut it into thin slices. Peel the shallots and cut into rings. Dice the celery finely. Likewise, chop the rosemary and thyme finely.

2. Put the water in a pot and dissolve 1 tbsp sugar in it. Heat until the sugar has a golden color. Then add the tarragon vinegar.

3. Now add the olive oil, shallots, garlic, and herbs and sweat for 1 minute over medium heat. Add the celery and let it sweat for 5 minutes.

4. Now add the tomatoes, salt, and pepper to the pot. Pour in the tomato juice and simmer for 8–10 minutes over medium heat. Last, puree it with an immersion blender and cool to room temperature. This makes 3⅓ cups (750 ml) of the tomato liquid.

5. Soak the gelatin for about 10 minutes in cold water. Put the soaked gelatin into a pot and let it melt.

6. In the meantime, whip the cream until stiff and place in the refrigerator to chill. Pour the tomato liquid into a bowl, stir in the melted gelatin, and season once more with tarragon vinegar, salt, and pepper to taste.

+ 3 hours cooling time

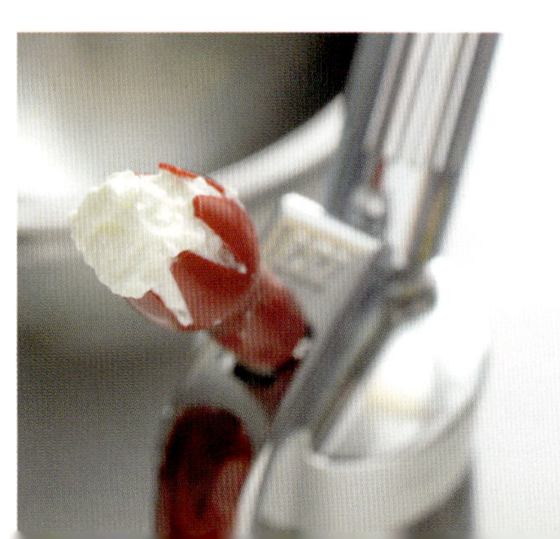

■ You can save time by putting 2¼ cups (500 ml) cream in a soda siphon, whipping the cream using two capsules.

7. Now add half the whipped cream and, using a whisk, fold it into the tomato liquid.

8. Fold in the remaining cream carefully with a rubber spatula, then stir with a whisk to get rid of any lumps in the cream. Next, put some of the pesto in glasses, fill them with the tomato mousse, cover with plastic wrap and let stand for 3 hours in the refrigerator to cool. Top with some pesto and serve with white bread.

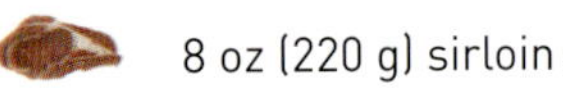

8 oz (220 g) sirloin steak

5 tbsp Thai fish sauce

7 oz (200 g) cherry tomatoes

3½ oz (100 g) onion

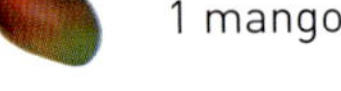

1 mango

2 tsp sugar

1½ limes

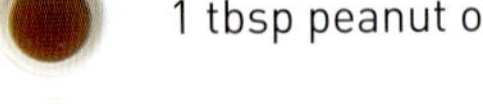

1 tbsp peanut oil

1 tsp roasted sesame oil

5 sprigs fresh mint

1 small head of lettuce

Beef Mango Salad with Cherry Tomatoes and Mint

1. Cut the steak into strips and marinate it in 2 tbsp Thai fish sauce. Cut the cherry tomatoes into quarters. Peel the onion, cut in half, and dice finely.

2. Wash the mango and peel it, removing it from the pit, then cut the mango into strips.

3. Put the onion, tomatoes, mango, and sugar in a medium-size bowl and squeeze the lime juice over it.

4. Put both the peanut and sesame oils in a pan and set over a high heat. Sear the meat for 1 minute, turning frequently.

5. Rinse the mint, removing any damaged pieces, and pick the leaves from the stems. Remove the tips from the leaves and set them aside as a garnish, cutting the remaining leaves into ribbons. Add the meat and the mint to the bowl. Add the remaining 3 tbsp of Thai fish sauce and mix. Decorate with some lettuce leaves and the mint tips, and serve.

■ **Chopped, roasted peanuts or spelt berries would lend this dish a special note.**

2
3
4
5

 1 lb 9 oz (700 g) chicken livers

 1⅛ cups (250 ml) red port wine

 1⅛ cups (250 ml) cognac

 2⅔ cups (600 g) butter

 9 oz (250 g) thin bacon slices

 3 eggs

 1½ tsp salt
½ tsp black pepper

 1 pinch of freshly grated nutmeg

 4 juniper berries

 1 sprig fresh thyme

Fresh Chicken Liver Pâté

1. Clean the livers and, with a small kitchen knife, remove the skin, veins, and any blood.

2. In a pot, boil the port and cognac down to a fifth of the original volume and cool to room temperature. Use the butter to prepare a beurre noisette (see p. 34) and cool to room temperature.

3. In the meantime, line a terrine with the bacon slices so they overlap and hang over the edges of the dish.

4. Put the chicken livers, eggs, salt, pepper, and the reduced spirits into a blender.

5. Grate in the fresh nutmeg, pour in the beurre noisette, and blend everything until it all looks like a smooth chocolate milkshake.

6. With a ladle, put the blended ingredients in the bacon-lined dish.

7. Fold the overhanging bacon over the filled dish.

8. Lay the juniper berries and the thyme over the bacon. Cover with aluminum foil and cook for 90 minutes at 210°F (100°C). Remove and let cool overnight in the refrigerator for best results. Then carefully remove it from the dish. With a long knife soaked in hot water, cut ¾-inch (2-cm) slices and lay them on plates. Serve with bread or brioche. Garnish with pickles and/or orange chutney.

+ 6 hours cooling time

■ **Alternatively, you can use ingredients such as pickled green peppercorns, sautéed mushrooms or morels, black truffle pieces, or apple slices sautéed in sugar and butter. The ingredients should be lukewarm.**

5
6
7
8

 2 lobsters, cooked

 1 Belgian endive

 7 oz (200 g) mushrooms

 3 tbsp (50 ml) white wine

 ½ lemon

 4½ oz (120 g) cocktail sauce (see p. 53)

Lobster Cocktail with Mushrooms

1. Remove the lobster meat from the shell and cut it in half. Using the tip of a knife, pull out the vein (see p. 482). Keep one claw per person as a garnish. Cut the lobster into ¼-inch (5-mm) pieces. Set aside four nice Belgian endive leaves, cutting the rest into thin ribbons.

2. Clean the mushrooms and cut them into quarters. Bring the white wine to a boil in a pot and add the mushrooms. Squeeze the lemon juice into the pot over a sieve so the seeds don't fall in the pot. Let everything steam lightly for about a minute.

3. Drain the mushrooms in a sieve and let them cool. Keep the liquid for possible later use in a fish sauce or hollandaise sauce.

4. Mix the mushrooms in a bowl with the lobster meat and cocktail sauce. Stick a few Belgian endive ribbons and one leaf in a champagne glass. Then fill with the lobster cocktail and decorate with the claws.

■ **You can make this cocktail with crab meat or shrimp and garnish with different herbs.**

2
3
4

 9 oz (250 g) celeriac

 1 lemon

 12 walnuts, shelled

 3 apples

 ½ tsp salt

 1 tsp sugar

 1 pinch of black pepper

 3½ oz (100 g) crème fraîche (or sour cream)

 3½ oz (100 g) mayonnaise

Waldorf Salad

1. Peel the celeriac and rub it with lemon to keep it from browning. Chop the walnuts and set them aside.

2. Peel the apples, removing the tops and bottoms. Remove the core from the fruit.

3. Grate the apple pieces and celeriac using a fine grater.

4. Put the apple and celeriac strips in a bowl. Squeeze half a lemon over a sieve into the bowl. Add salt and pepper to taste.

5. Add the crème fraîche (or sour cream) and the mayonnaise, mixing everything together well. Finish by serving in a glass and garnishing with walnuts.

■ **You can cut the celeriac into thin, even slices using an automatic slicer. Celeriac strips can also be blanched for a more refined flavor. Walnuts are easier to peel if you boil them briefly in equal parts milk and water.**

2
3
4
5

3 lb 5 oz (1.5 kg) potatoes

1 lb (450 g) cucumber

3½ oz (100 g) bacon

2 onions

⅞ cup (200 ml) sunflower oil

3 tbsp hot mustard

1⅛ cups (250 ml) chicken broth

⅔ cup (140 ml) cider vinegar

1½ tsp salt

1 large pinch of black pepper

Potato and Cucumber Salad with Bacon Strips

1. Boil and cool the potatoes, peel, and while they are still warm, cut them into slices about ¼ inch (5 mm) thick.

2. Peel the cucumbers and cut them into thin slices.

3. Next, cut the bacon into strips. Peel and dice the onions.

4. Add sunflower oil to a pot and fry the bacon until crisp. Then add the onions and sweat them. Add the mustard as well and stir. Pour the chicken broth and vinegar into the pot and season with salt and pepper to taste. Let everything marinate for 3 minutes.

5. Pour the hot dressing over the potatoes and stir carefully. Season again with salt and pepper to taste. Serve while still warm.

■ If you cook the potatoes with caraway, they'll have a spicier flavor. The salad tastes even more substantial served with mayonnaise and is a wonderful side dish with roast beef, baked fish, or ham aspic, or with a variety of sausages.

2
3
4
5

 7 oz (200 g) pinto beans

 7 oz (200 g) white beans

 7 oz (200 g) fava beans

 10½ oz (300 g) green beans

 1 tsp salt

 3 scallions

 1 pinch of black pepper

 4 tbsp cider vinegar

 5 tbsp sunflower oil

 1 tbsp chopped parsley

Mixed Bean Salad with Parsley

1. Boil the beans (see p. 282), drain them well, measure out, and put them in a bowl.

2. Cut the green beans into diagonal strips and cook in salted water until firm to the bite. Pour them into a sieve and shock under cold running water.

3. Add the lukewarm green beans to the other beans.

4. Cut the scallions in half and cut into thin slices. Add them to the beans.

5. Season with salt and black pepper. Pour the cider vinegar and sunflower oil over the beans and mix well. Let stand for 10 minutes for everything to marinate. Next, rinse the parsley, pick the leaves from the stems, and chop finely, then mix it in.

This dish goes well with broiled or grilled fish or veal patties.

■ **You can tell if the beans are old if they break apart when soaking (left)—fresh beans stay whole (right).**

2
3
4
5

 2 packages dried seaweed

 6 tbsp soy sauce

 2 tbsp roasted sesame seeds

 2 tbsp roasted sesame seed oil

 10½ oz (300 g) spinach leaves

Seaweed Salad with Spinach Leaves and Sesame Dressing

1. Soak the seaweed in lukewarm water according to the package instructions—about 30 minutes.

2. Drain the soaked seaweed in a colander.

3. For the dressing, mix the soy sauce with the roasted sesame seeds and the roasted sesame seed oil.

4. Rinse the spinach leaves, shake them thoroughly dry, and add them to the dressing bowl.

5. Next, add the drained seaweed on top of the spinach and mix together.

Put in a bowl and serve.

■ **The following ingredients can be mixed into the seaweed salad to give it more color and substance: julienned carrots or radishes, small fried tofu squares, small pieces of raw tuna or salmon. These ingredients make this salad a wholesome dish.**

2
3
4
5

 14 oz (400 g) cooked long-grain rice

 7 oz (200 g) cooked, diced ham

 7 oz (200 g) canned fruit cocktail

 3 tbsp mayonnaise

 1 tbsp curry powder

 1 pinch of salt
1 pinch of black pepper

 Juice of 1 lemon

Rice Salad with Curry Mayonnaise and Fruit

1. Put the rice and diced ham in a bowl.

2. Strain the fruit cocktail and cut up the large pieces, if necessary.

3. Add the fruit pieces and mayonnaise to the rice.

4. Sprinkle with curry powder; add salt, pepper, and lemon juice to taste.

5. Mix everything together and let sit for about 30 minutes.

Serve in bowls or cocktail glasses and garnish them with a lettuce leaf and lemon slice.

■ **You can use fresh fruit salad (see p. 656) instead of canned fruit.**

4

5

2 eggs

14 oz (400 g) penne pasta

2 scallions

5½ oz (150 g) canned tuna, drained

1 pinch of salt
1 pinch of black pepper

2 tbsp mayonnaise

2 tbsp plain yogurt

1 tbsp honey mustard

Pasta Salad with Tuna and Boiled Egg

1. Boil the eggs well (see p. 102). Cook the penne, drain, and let cool under cold running water (see p. 189). Peel the eggs and chop coarsely. Trim the scallions and snip into small rings.

2. Put the cold cooked pasta in a bowl. Add the eggs, scallions, and tuna.

3. Add the salt, pepper, mayonnaise, and yogurt to the salad.

4. Add the honey mustard last and mix everything well.

Serve in bowls or plates and garnish with herbs.

■ **You can make this salad with other types of pasta as well, such as farfalle, rigatoni, or short-cut spaghetti.**

2
3
4

2 yams

8 cups (2 liters) vegetable oil for frying

1 pinch of salt

1 pinch of sugar

1

2

3

4

Homemade Yam Chips

1. Using a knife, cut away the skin from the yams.

2. Cut the yams into thin slices.

3. Lay the slices in cold water for 15 minutes to draw the starches out.

4. Then rinse well under running water.

5. Dry the slices well in a kitchen towel.

6. Heat the oil in a tall pot to 340°F (170°C) and fry the yam slices until crisp.

7. Using a skimmer, take the chips out of the oil when they are fried to a golden brown.

8. Spread them over paper towels to dry.

Sprinkle with salt or sugar to taste, and serve in paper towel-lined bowls.

■ **Serve a light herb sauce or a piquant tomato salsa with the homemade yam chips.**

5
6
7
8

 ½ cup (125 ml) extra virgin olive oil

 1 pinch of sea salt

 1 pinch of black pepper

 5 basil leaves

 14 oz (400 g) beef tenderloin

 Juice of 1 lemon

 1 piece of Parmesan cheese

Beef Carpaccio with Parmesan Cheese and Lemon Juice

1. Brush four plates each with 1 tbsp olive oil, and sprinkle with salt, pepper, and some thin ribbons of basil.

2. Using a long, sharp knife, cut the beef into very thin slices.

3. Lay the beef slices next to each other on the preseasoned plates and drizzle with 1 tbsp olive oil. Add salt and pepper to taste.

4. Sprinkle ribbons of basil and drizzle some lemon juice over the beef.

5. Grate the Parmesan cheese with a vegetable peeler over the dishes and serve with fresh bread.

■ **Instead of beef, you can also use freshly cut raw salmon, tuna, mussels, or fresh veal tenderloin or saddle of veal.**

2
3
4
5

Egg Dishes

Contents

102 Boiled Egg
102 Duck, Chicken, and Quail Eggs
103 Thousand-Year Egg
103 Pickled Eggs
104 Scrambled Eggs
105 Scrambled Eggs with Herbs
105 Scrambled Eggs with Tomato
105 Scrambled Eggs with Mushrooms
105 Scrambled Eggs with Cheese
106 French Creamy Scrambled Eggs with Truffles
108 Fried Eggs
109 Strammer Max
109 Spicy Fried Eggs
110 Poached Egg
111 Deep-Fried Egg
111 Eggs Florentine
112 Classic French Omelet
112 French Omelet with Creamed Mushrooms
114 Cheese Soufflé
116 Italian Frittata
117 Spanish Tortilla
118 Deviled Eggs
120 Fried Quail Egg Canapés with Beef Tartare
122 Boiled Egg In Mustard Sauce with Parsley Potatoes
124 Crêpe Batter
126 Apple Crêpes with Crisp Bacon and Maple Syrup
128 Mirabelle Crêpes

Boiled Egg

1. Five-Minute Egg: The egg yolk is still quite runny.

2. Seven-Minute Egg: The breakfast egg. The yolk is still soft.

3. Ten-Minute Egg: The egg white and yolk are equally firm.

4. Overcooked egg: Has a green ring around the yolk—this happens when eggs are boiled for longer than 15 minutes, then not cooled in cold water.

5. A fresh egg: The egg white is very tight and compact.

6. An egg that is not very fresh: The egg white is no longer compactly framed around the egg yolk. Instead, it separates and runs all over the plate.

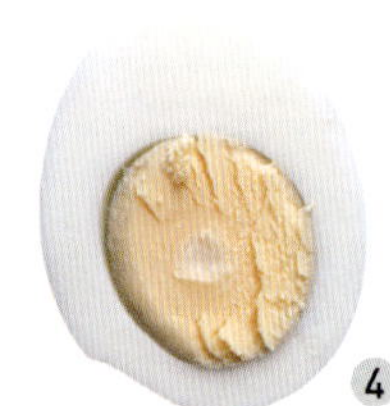

Duck, Chicken, and Quail Eggs

1. A comparison of duck, chicken, and quail egg sizes.

2. Duck, chicken, and quail eggs cracked open.

3. To open a quail egg, use the tip of a knife to scratch the eggshell carefully to avoid breaking the egg yolk.

4. Then cut a hole and let the egg run into a bowl. The thickness of the shell makes it hard to simply crack it open.

Thousand-Year Egg

It is also called a century egg, but of course it's not that old. For this Chinese specialty, raw, fresh duck eggs are covered in a mixture of limestone, ashes from various woods, tea, and salt. After three months, the eggs are washed. Because the shell is so porous, the lime mixture reacts with the egg inside. The egg becomes a yellowish green, gelatinous mass with a strong odor reminiscent of cheese. In China, it is served for breakfast and in other dishes.

Pickled Eggs

Bring **4½ cups (1 liter) water** to a boil with **4 tbsp salt**, **1 tsp white peppercorns**, **1 dried chile**, **3 cloves garlic** and **1 tsp mustard seeds**. Put **10 eggs** in the boiling water and cook them for 5 minutes. Remove them from the stove and pour the eggs and the liquids into a mason jar.

The eggs will keep in the jar in cool storage for more than a month. Serve with vinegar and bread.

 2 eggs

 1 tbsp cream

 1 pinch of salt
1 pinch of black pepper

 2 tsp (10 g) butter

Scrambled Eggs

1. Beat the eggs with a fork in a deep dish. Use a quick circular motion.

2. Add the cream, season with salt and pepper to taste, and mix.

3. Put the butter in a pan and let it foam up over medium heat. Pour the eggs into the pan. Let the eggs become firm while you stir. They should be creamy, slightly shiny, and moist.

Scrambled Eggs with Herbs

In a deep dish, beat together **2 eggs**, **2 tbsp chopped herbs**, **1 tbsp cream**, and **a pinch each of salt** and **pepper**. As with scrambled eggs (see p. 104), cook with **2 tsp (10 g) butter** in a pan. Good herbs for this dish are chives, basil, and cilantro.

Scrambled Eggs with Tomato

In a deep dish, beat together **2 eggs** with **1 tbsp cream** and **a pinch each of salt** and **pepper**. Wash **a tomato**, skin it, remove the core (see p. 346) and cut into small dice. Cut **5 basil leaves** into ribbons and, along with the tomato, mix them into the eggs. Heat **2 tsp (10 g) butter** in a small pan, and pour in the egg mixture, letting it coagulate as you stir it. This tastes very good on toasted **white bread**, garnished with a few pieces of **mozzarella**.

Scrambled Eggs with Mushrooms

Trim **1 oz (30 g) mushrooms** (see p. 360) and cut into slices. Heat **2 tsp (10 g) butter** in a small pan, add the mushrooms, and sweat them, then season with **a pinch each of salt** and **pepper**. Beat together **2 eggs** with **1 tbsp cream**, and add to the mushrooms, allowing them to coagulate as you stir them (see p. 106).

■ **You can use button mushrooms, oyster mushrooms, chanterelles, porcinis, or shiitakes in this dish. Truffles go well with eggs too.**

Scrambled Eggs with Cheese

In a deep dish, beat together **2 eggs**, **1½ oz (40 g) grated cheese**, **1 tbsp cream**, and **a pinch each of salt** and **pepper**. As with scrambled eggs (see p. 104), put **2 tsp (10 g) butter** in a pan and add the egg mixture. Let the eggs set and the cheese melt.

■ **You can use Gruyère, aged Gouda, Appenzeller, or Swiss cheeses. For a milder choice, pick up some fresh goat cheese, feta cheese, or brie.**

4 eggs

2 tbsp crème fraîche (or sour cream)

¼ oz (10 g) pickled black truffles from a jar

4 tsp (20 g) butter

1 pinch of salt
1 pinch of black pepper

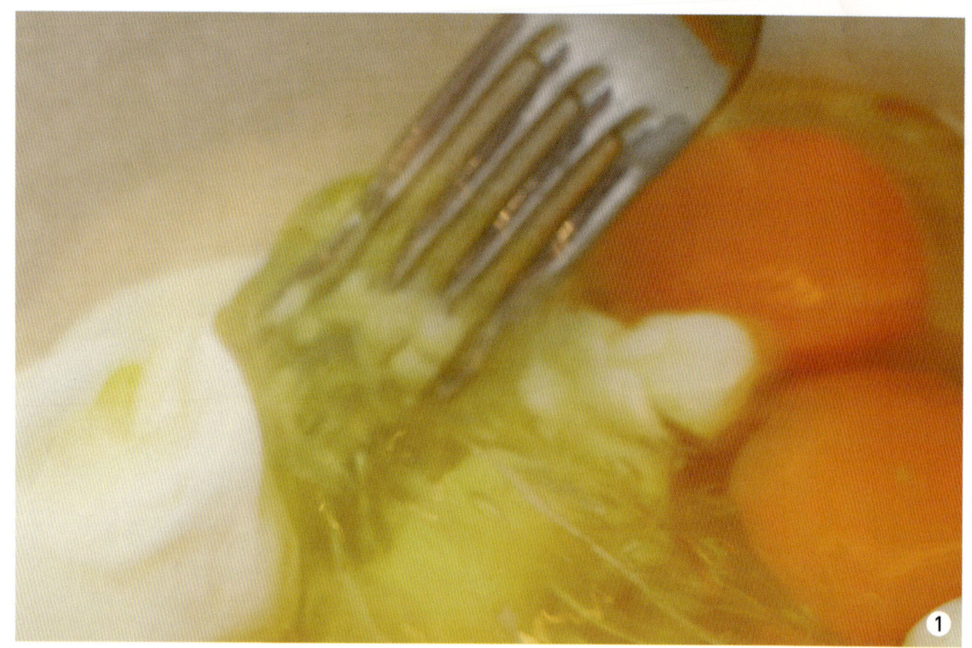

French Creamy Scrambled Eggs with Truffles

1. Beat the eggs in a bowl and stir in the crème fraîche, or sour cream.

2. Cut the truffles into thin slices. You can also use fresh or frozen truffles for this dish.

3. Add the truffle slices to the eggs, mix, cover, and let stand for 1 hour in the refrigerator to infuse the eggs with truffle flavor.

4. Put the butter in a pan over medium heat and let it foam. Season the beaten eggs with salt and pepper and put them in the pan. Slowly stir the scrambled eggs continuously so they coagulate evenly.

5. Truffle-scrambled eggs are finished when they are consistently creamy and light. Put them on a plate and serve with white toast.

■ If you prefer to make this dish with white truffles, make the scrambled eggs first, then grate the white truffles over them with a truffle slicer. White truffles should not be cooked, otherwise they lose flavor.

2
3
4
5

2 tsp (10 ml) vegetable oil

2 eggs

1 pinch of salt
1 pinch of pepper

2 tsp (10 g) butter

Fried Eggs

1. Put the vegetable oil in a nonstick pan and bring it to medium heat. Crack the eggs into a cup and slide them into the pan.

2. Add salt to the egg white only, avoiding the yolk—salt leaves white spots on the yolk. Pepper the whole egg. Take the butter and move it along the sides of the pan with a fork, so the eggs maintain a more delicate flavor.

3. Then take the eggs out of the pan with a spatula and put them on a plate.

■ Cracking the eggs into a cup keeps shells from ending up in the pan and makes it less likely the yolks will break. The longer an egg is fried, the harder it is to digest!

10

Strammer Max

Spread **2 tsp (10 g) butter** on **1 slice of multigrain toasted bread** and lay **2 slices of cooked ham** on top. Add **2 fried eggs** (see p. 108) to the toast using a spatula. Sprinkle it with parsley leaves or watercress and serve. You can also make Strammer Max with prosciutto.

■ **For a fuller flavor, grate a little garlic over the toast first.**

Spicy Fried Eggs

Break **2 eggs** into a cup and slide them into a hot pan. Put **salt** on only the egg white, avoiding the yolk. **Pepper** the whole egg. Slice **2 hot green chili peppers**, cut **1 tbsp scallion rings**, and cut **1 tbsp dried bell peppers** into strips, then add them over the eggs. Lift the eggs onto a plate with a spatula and finish by sprinkling with a **pinch of hot paprika**.

■ **Serve with a fresh roll or a bagel. Spicy chili beans also go well with this dish, as does crispy fried bacon.**

8 cups (2 liters) water

3 tbsp (50 ml) white wine vinegar

1 egg

Poached Egg

1. Heat the water in a deep pot, then add the vinegar. The water should not boil. Crack the egg into a glass bowl and then carefully slide it into the vinegar water. Continue to turn the egg gently with a spoon, enclosing the yolk in the egg white. A medium-size egg poaches in about 3–5 minutes, but the required cooking time also depends on personal taste.

2. Carefully lift the egg out of the pot with a skimmer and let it drain on a plate. If necessary, remove any overhanging strands of egg white with a knife. Then serve it on a salad, with toast, or just with butter and fresh herbs.

■ **Eggs should be taken out of the refrigerator shortly before using them, so they stay firm during cooking. The vinegar helps the egg coagulate. Never salt the boiling water because that would have the opposite effect.**

Deep-Fried Egg

Fill a pan with **1 cup (250 ml)** vegetable oil. Heat over medium. Crack **1 egg** into a bowl and carefully slide it into the oil. Turn the egg over in the pan and fry both sides, each for about 1 minute. Remove the egg from the pan with a skimmer and place on a **slice of white toast**. Season with **a pinch of salt** and **pepper**.

■ **Caution: When you put the egg into the oil, some oil can splash. Put the egg on white toast, to soak up the excess grease. Serve the egg on toast, with a piquant tomato sauce, or on scaloppini.**

Eggs Florentine

Poach **2 eggs** as described on the preceding page. Put **2 tsp (10 g) butter** in a pan and let it foam. Add **5½ oz (150 g) cleaned** and **rinsed spinach leaves**. Season with **a pinch each of salt**, **pepper**, and **freshly grated nutmeg**. Let the spinach wilt in the pan. Toss it for about 1 minute. Divide the spinach between **2 slices of white toast**. Place a poached egg on top and pour **5 tbsp of Hollandaise sauce** (see p. 152) over each one.

3 eggs

1 pinch of salt
1 pinch of black pepper

1 pinch of freshly grated nutmeg

1 tbsp cream

2 tsp (10 g) butter

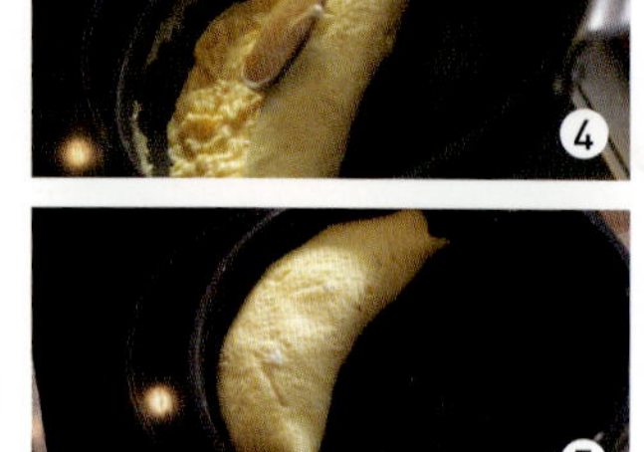

Classic French Omelet

1. Beat the eggs in a bowl and season with salt, pepper, and freshly grated nutmeg to taste. Add the cream and beat the eggs with a fork.

2. Heat butter in a nonstick pan at least 8 inches (20 cm) in diameter, letting it foam. Add the eggs to the pan, stirring continuously with a wooden spoon.

3. Reduce the heat and stop stirring the eggs so that they can set underneath. Tilt the pan slightly.

4. Roll the omelet into a half moon using the wooden spoon.

5. Spread a little butter over the finished omelet and slide it onto a plate.

Spread a little more butter over the top to make it glisten. The omelet should look smooth and moist on the outside and be creamy on the inside.

French Omelet with Creamed Mushrooms

Finely dice ½ **shallot**. Let **2 tsp (10 g) butter** foam in a pan and sweat the shallot until translucent. Cut about **2¾ oz (80 g) mushrooms** into slices and add them to the shallots. Cook for about 2 minutes, until the liquids have evaporated. Add **salt** and **pepper**, and drizzle with **10 drops of lemon juice**. This keeps the mushroom white. Add **⅜ cup (100 ml) cream** and let it simmer another 2 minutes, until the sauce thickens. Prepare an omelet (see above) and cut it lengthwise. Fill the omelet with the creamed mushrooms and pour sauce over it. Garnish with **parsley leaves** and serve with **white toast**.

■ **Fillings made with asparagus, crayfish, shrimp, tomatoes, and ground beef also pair with omelets.**

¼ cup (50 g) butter

⅓ cup (50 g) breadcrumbs

8 eggs

1 pinch of salt
1 pinch of black pepper

1 tsp cornstarch

1 pinch of freshly grated nutmeg

8 oz (250 g) Swiss cheese

Cheese Soufflé

1. Preheat the oven to 375°F (190°C/Gas Mark 5). Grease soufflé cups, about 3 inches (8 cm) in diameter, with butter and line with breadcrumbs.

2. Separate the eggs. Add salt to the egg whites. Beat the egg whites with a whisk until stiff, and fold in the cornstarch. Add the egg yolks, pepper, and a pinch of freshly grated nutmeg.

3. Cut the rind of the Swiss cheese away and coarsely grate the remaining cheese. Set aside 7 oz (200 g) grated cheese, add the remaining grated cheese to the eggs, and carefully fold it into the eggs with a rubber spatula. Don't stir too much, otherwise the egg mixture will collapse and the soufflé will not rise properly.

4. Using a ladle, distribute the egg mixture into the soufflé cups until they are three-quarters full.

5. Sprinkle the reserved cheese over the soufflés. Line a porcelain casserole dish with parchment paper and fill it with ¾ inch (2 cm) hot water. Place the soufflé cups inside.

Put the cups in the oven. Bake 20 to 25 minutes. Remove the soufflés immediately, either serving in the dish or on a plate. You can serve them with a light tomato butter sauce or a mushroom cream sauce.

■ **It is important to grease the soufflé cups all the way to the top. Otherwise, the soufflé could stick. Make sure the eggs are cold so they whip to the proper volume.**

2
3
4
5

5 eggs

1 pinch of salt

1 pinch of ground fennel seeds

7 oz (200 g) zucchini

1 garlic clove

1 sprig fresh rosemary

5 tbsp extra virgin olive oil

4 tbsp aioli (see p. 53)

1 pinch of black pepper

1

2

3

Italian Frittata

1. Preheat oven to 350°F (180°C). Crack the eggs into a bowl. Season with salt and ground fennel seeds to taste. Then beat with a fork.

2. Cut the zucchini in half lengthwise, then cut into thin slices. Peel the garlic and cut it into thin slices. Chop the rosemary leaves coarsely. Heat the olive oil in a nonstick pan. Add the garlic and cook until golden. Add the zucchini and rosemary to the pan and brown them for about 5 minutes. Add the eggs to the pan, covering the zucchini slices. Heat the pan for about 30 seconds on the stove.

3. Then put it in the preheated oven and bake for 8–10 minutes. The frittata is finished when it has risen nicely and the surface is golden yellow. Then slide it out of the pan onto a cutting board, let it cool, and cut it into ¾-inch (2 cm) thick slices. Serve on a plate with aioli (see p. 53) and garnish with coarse pepper.

■ **Instead of using ground fennel seeds, you can use them chopped. Serve the frittata pieces on toothpicks for a light appetizer. Pesto or balsamic vinegar work nicely as a dip for this dish.**

2 garlic cloves 

14 oz (400 g) potatoes 

4 tbsp extra virgin olive oil 

1 pinch of salt
1 pinch of black pepper 

4½ oz (130 g) onion

3 eggs

Spanish Tortilla

1. Crush the garlic cloves. Peel the potatoes and cut them into thin slices. Heat 2 tbsp olive oil in a nonstick pan and add the garlic and potatoes. Add salt and pepper to taste. Cook the potatoes slowly over medium heat for about 15 minutes, without letting them brown.

2. Cut the onion in half and cut into thin slices. After 5 minutes, add the onion slices to the potatoes in the pan. Crack the eggs into a bowl and add salt and pepper to taste. Beat them with a fork, then add the cooked potatoes from the pan and mix.

3. Next, heat another 2 tbsp olive oil in an 8-inch (30-cm) diameter nonstick pan. Add the egg-potato mix to the pan and fry it over a low heat for 6–8 minutes. Then flip the tortilla out onto a plate and, with the fried side on top, slide it back into the pan. Fry for another 5–7 minutes. Slide the finished tortilla onto a plate and serve.

■ **Aioli (see p. 53) goes really well with this dish, as do olives. The tortilla tastes best lukewarm.**

6 eggs

½ cup (80 g) butter

1 pinch of salt

1 pinch of cayenne pepper

1 tbsp medium-hot mustard

1 lemon

10 drops Worcestershire sauce

Deviled Eggs

1. Boil the eggs for 10 minutes. Then shock them under cold water to cool. Peel and cut them lengthwise. Carefully remove the egg yolk with a small spoon.

2. Beat room-temperature butter in a bowl with salt and cayenne pepper until peaks form. Add the mustard and whisk.

3. Season with the juice of half a lemon and Worcestershire sauce to taste. Add the egg yolks and stir until smooth.

4. Press the egg yolk mix through a fine sieve and then put it in a piping bag fitted with a star tip. Rinse the hard-boiled egg whites under warm running water. Place on a plate with paper towels to drain.

5. Pipe the egg yolk filling into the egg whites. Decorate them with cherry tomatoes, chiles, capers, anchovies, or small parsley leaves.

■ Russian-style eggs: Cook 4½ oz (120 g) potatoes, 2¾ oz (80 g) parsnips, and 2¾ oz (80 g) carrots whole, let them cool, and then cut in ¼-inch (5-mm) dice. Place the diced vegetables and potatoes in a bowl. Toss them with 2 tbsp mayonnaise, 1 tsp medium-hot mustard, 1 tbsp white wine vinegar, salt, and pepper. Arrange on plates and lay the filled eggs on top.

2
3
4
5

 7 oz (200 g) lean ground beef

 1 shallot

 2 anchovies

 1 pinch of salt
1 pinch of black pepper

 1 tsp hot mustard

 1 tbsp ketchup

 ½ tsp hot paprika

 1 egg, separated

 a few drops of Worcestershire sauce

 2 tbsp pickle or caper juice

 8 quail eggs

 2 tbsp vegetable oil

 4 slices of multigrain bread, toasted

 Parsley

Fried Quail Egg Canapés with Beef Tartare

1. Place the ground beef in a bowl. Peel and finely dice the shallot. Finely chop the anchovies. Add both ingredients to the beef and, using a tablespoon, delicately toss the mix with pepper, salt, mustard, ketchup, paprika, egg yolk from the separated egg, Worcestershire sauce, and pickle or caper juice.

2. Carefully scratch the surface of each quail egg open with a small knife (see p. 102) and put it in a glass bowl.

3. Heat the vegetable oil in a nonstick pan over medium heat. Place each egg in the pan using a tablespoon, and ensure that the edges don't run together while frying. Season with black pepper.

4. Quail eggs are done when the egg white coagulates but the egg yolk glistens and is still runny. Generously spread the toasted multigrain bread with the beef tartar. Cut the bread slices in half and place a quail egg on each half. Garnish with parsley leaves and serve.

40

■ **This dish should be served with a cold beer as an aperitif. "Lean" beef refers to the low fat content of the meat.**

2
3
4

2¼ cups (500 ml) Béchamel sauce (see p. 156)

1 tbsp crème fraîche (or sour cream)

⅞ cup (200 ml) heavy cream

2 tbsp medium-hot mustard
1 tsp hot mutard

8 eggs

1 lb 5 oz (600 g) boiled potatoes

½ bunch fresh parsley

2 tsp (10 g) butter

Boiled Egg in Mustard Sauce with Parsley Potatoes

1. Slowly bring the Béchamel sauce (see p. 156) to medium heat, stirring constantly. Add the crème fraîche and cream to the Béchamel sauce.

2. Stir in both mustards using a whisk. As soon as the mustard is added, stop cooking the sauce. In the meantime, mix the boiled potatoes with butter and the finely chopped parsley leaves.

3. Immerse the peeled hard-boiled eggs in the sauce. Arrange the parsley potatoes on a plate. Place two eggs on each plate with the mustard sauce and garnish with parsley leaves.

■ **Alternatively, this dish can be served with a cold green sauce (see p. 55). In that case, the eggs should be freshly boiled, cut in half, and placed over the sauce.**

2

3

 2 cups (240 g) flour

 2¼ cups (500 ml) milk

 3 tbsp sugar

 3 eggs

 ⅔ cup (150 g) butter

 2 tbsp oil

Crêpe Batter

1. Place the flour in a mixing bowl. Add half the milk and the sugar.

2. Using a whisk, mix the batter until smooth.

3. Pour in the remaining milk and beat in the eggs. The batter should have the consistency of heavy cream.

4. Heat the butter in a small pot until it is golden brown and has a nutty aroma.

5. Using the whisk, stir in the browned butter a little at a time.

6. Put enough oil in a pan to coat the bottom. Heat over medium heat. Using a ladle, add the crêpe batter and let it spread by tilting the pan in circles.

7. Once the crêpe is set and light golden, loosen the batter with a spatula and flip the crêpe, or grasp one edge of the crêpe with your fingertips and gently turn over.

8. Cook the crêpe briefly after turning. Flip the crêpes onto a plate and let them cool.

■ **Spread crêpes with jam or roll them up and sprinkle with confectioners' sugar. A combination of fruit and cottage cheese filling with vanilla sauce is also delicious. Or, fill with a savory mixture, such as chicken or shrimp in cream sauce.**

5
6
7
8

 2 ripe apples (Golden Delicious)

 12 slices bacon

 1 tbsp vegetable oil

 1¾ cups (400 ml) crêpe batter (see p. 124)

 4 tbsp sugar

 ⅜ cups (100 ml) maple syrup

Apple Crêpes with Crisp Bacon and Maple Syrup

1. Peel the apples, cut them in half, and remove the cores. Fry the bacon in a nonstick pan until slightly crisp.

2. Heat the vegetable oil in a pan. Pour in a quarter of the crêpe batter.

3. Distribute the batter evenly by tilting the pan.

4. Cut the apple in thin slices and add a quarter of the slices into the wet crêpe batter in the pan.

5. Sprinkle the crêpe with about 1 tbsp sugar and flip. Cook for another 2 minutes on the apple side and let it caramelize until golden brown. Repeat the process with the three remaining crêpes.

Arrange on plates, ladle with maple syrup, and top with crispy bacon.

■ **Instead of apples, thin banana slices can also be cooked into the pancakes. Top with a drizzle of maple syrup.**

2
3
4
5

3 medium mirabelle plums

1 tbsp butter

2 tbsp brown sugar

4 crêpes (see p. 124)

Mirabelle Crêpes

1. Using a knife, cut the plums in half and remove the pits. Slice.

2. Let the butter foam in a pan. Add the brown sugar and melt.

3. Place the plums in the pan.

4. Cook the plum slices over a low heat until the sugar has completely dissolved and the slices begin to fall apart easily—about 5 minutes. Fold the pancakes into triangles and warm them up for 2 minutes in a 400°F (200°C/Gas Mark 6) preheated oven.

Put two pancakes on each plate and distribute the plum slices over them.

■ **Slather crêpes with chocolate-hazelnut spread (such as Nutella). Fold into triangles or roll into logs, dust with confectioners' sugar and serve.**

2
3

4

Sauces & Stocks

Contents

132 Vegetable Stock
134 Chicken Stock
136 Fish Stock
137 White Wine Sauce
137 Chive Sauce
137 Whipped Butter Sauce
138 Gravy/Jus
140 Thick Poultry Cream Sauce
141 Thick Tarragon Cream Sauce
141 Coarse Mustard Sauce
142 Shellfish Stock
143 Shellfish Cream Sauce
144 Simple Tomato Sauce
146 Green Curry Sauce
146 Red Curry Sauce
146 Yellow Curry Sauce
148 Green Peppercorn Cream Sauce
150 Paprika Cream Sauce
151 Balsamic Vinegar Sauce
152 Hollandaise Sauce
154 Béarnaise Sauce
155 Choron Sauce
155 Foyot Sauce
156 Béchamel Sauce
158 Simple Bolognese Sauce

 ½ fennel bulb

 1 leek

 3 carrots

 2 celery stalks

 1 tomato

 2 onions

 1 head of garlic

 1 sprig fresh rosemary

 1 bay leaf

 1 pinch of white pepper

 ½ tsp fennel seeds

Vegetable Stock

1. Remove any brown spots from the fennel and cut into large dice.

2. Trim the remaining vegetables as well, peel them, and cut them into large dice. Cut the head of garlic in half horizontally.

3. Pour 2⅔ quarts (2.5 liters) cold water into a pot and place all the vegetables in the pot.

4. Now add the seasonings and slowly bring to a boil.

5. Let the vegetable stock simmer for about 20 minutes. Then strain it through a sieve and let cool.

Place in the refrigerator until further use. The stock will keep for up to 7 days.

Makes about 2⅓ quarts (2.2 liters).

■ **The stock is good for stretching out or thinning substantial soups or sauces, for light soups, and for steaming vegetables.**

2
3
4
5

 1 chicken, about 2 lb 4 oz (1 kg)

 3 carrots

 5 shallots

 1 onion

 1 leek

 2 celery stalks

 4¼ quarts (4 liters) water

 1 head of garlic

 1 sprig fresh rosemary

 2 sprigs fresh thyme

 2 bay leaves

 1 tsp white peppercorns

 5 cloves

 3 sprigs fresh parsley

1

Chicken Stock

1. Cut the chicken into large portions, separating the legs and cutting the backbone from the breast. Cut the head of garlic in half horizontally and peel the other vegetables, and then cut them into large pieces.

2. Put the water on the stove and add the chicken and salt. Slowly bring it to a boil. Add the vegetables, garlic, herbs, and seasonings.

3. Cook the stock for about 45 minutes and remove the foam that builds up with a—foam makes the stock cloudy.

4. Just before the stock finishes cooking, add the parsley and turn off the heat.

5. Remove the chicken legs and breasts and set aside for later use.

Pass the broth through a fine-mesh strainer and let it cool.

Makes about 2⅔ quarts (2.5 liters).

■ **The stock is good for stretching out or thinning substantial soups or sauces, for light soups, and for steaming vegetables.**

Kitchen doctor: Carefully skim the foam from the chicken broth again and again, otherwise the foam cooks down into the broth and makes it cloudy.

2
3
4
5

 2 lb 4 oz (1 kg) fish carcasses

 1 onion

 3 shallots

 ½ fennel bulb

 3 celery stalks

 1 head of garlic

 3 tbsp vegetable oil

 10 white peppercorns

 ½ tsp fennel seeds

 4 tsp (20 g) sea salt

 2 bay leaves

 1⅛ cups (250 ml) white wine

 3 tbsp (50 ml) dry vermouth

 6¼ quarts (1.5 liters) water

 2 lemon slices

 1 sprig fresh basil

 1 sprig fresh thyme

Fish Stock

1. Soak the fish carcasses for 30 minutes to completely wash out the blood—to keep the stock from getting cloudy. Peel all the vegetables and cut them into medium-size pieces (see pp. 348–55). Then sweat the vegetables in the oil without browning. Add the spices, sea salt, and bay leaves.

2. Add the soaked and well-drained fish carcasses and sweat briefly. Add the white wine and dry vermouth. Then pour in the cold water and slowly bring it to a simmer.

3. Using a small ladle, remove any foam floating on top—this protein can make the stock cloudy. Let it simmer gently for 15 minutes. About 5 minutes before it's finished, add the lemon slices, basil leaves, and the sprig of thyme. Strain the stock before using.

Makes about 2⅔ quarts (2.5 liters).

■ **White fish carcasses lend the best flavor to stocks. Use sole, turbot, flounder, wolf fish, or anglerfish. Use this fish stock as a base for cream sauces and for fish soups.**

White Wine Sauce

Cut **1 small white mushroom** and **2 shallots** into thin slices. Let **⅛ cup (30 g) butter** foam in a pot over medium heat. Add the shallots and mushrooms, letting them sweat. Pour in **1⅛ cups (250 ml) white wine** and **⅜ cup (100 ml) dry vermouth**. Let it boil down almost completely. This concentrates the flavor and evaporates the alcohol. Add **2¼ cups (500 ml) fish stock** and cook until it has a souplike consistency, concentrating the flavor a second time. Pour in **1⅓ cups (300 ml) cream** and **7 oz (200 g) crème fraîche (or sour cream)**, and bring it to a boil just once. Remove it from the heat and season with a few drops of **lemon juice**, **1 pinch of salt**, and **1 pinch of cayenne pepper** to taste. Pass the sauce through a fine sieve, pushing the remnants through well, and then puree using an immersion blender. Round it off with **2 tbsp whipped cream**.

Makes about 2½ cups (600 ml).

■ **White wine sauce goes well with steamed or lightly fried fish fillets.**

Chive Sauce

Rinse **2 bunches chives**, removing any damaged parts, and snip into small rings. Make **1¾ cups (400 ml) butter sauce** and add to it the chives along with **1 tbsp whipped cream**. Stir and serve.

Makes 2 cups (450 ml).

■ **This sauce goes well with fried or steamed fish fillets, such as sole, walleye, or tilapia, or with lobster.**

Whipped Butter Sauce

Dice **2 shallots** finely. Cut **⅞ cup (200 g) butter** into large dice and chill immediately. Heat an additional **4 tsp (20 g) butter** in a steel saucepan over medium heat until it foams, then add the shallots and sweat them. Then pour in **⅜ cup (100 ml) white port wine** and **⅞ cup (200 ml) white wine** and let it cook down to a fifth of the volume. Add **1¾ cups (400 ml) fish stock** and cook it down to about half the volume. Add **1 tbsp cream** to emulsify the sauce with the butter. Add the cold butter cubes. Mix with an immersion blender. The sauce should not be allowed to cook down any longer. Season with **salt** and **cayenne pepper** according to taste.

Makes about 1¾ cups (400 ml).

■ **The butter should be particularly cold, or the sauce won't bind. This is a classic with fish, or shellfish—full bodied, but very delicate. Goes with fried or poached white fish, but also with salmon and pasta dishes containing large shrimp and mussels.**

 6 lb 8 oz (3 kg) beef bones

 4 tbsp vegetable oil

 9 oz (250 g) carrots

 14 oz (400 g) onions

 4½ oz (120 g) celeriac

 4½ oz (120 g) celery stalks, with leaves

 2 heads of garlic

 10 cloves

 1 tsp white peppercorns

 1 tsp allspice

 2 sprigs fresh thyme

 2 sprigs fresh rosemary

 5 bay leaves

 2 tsp salt

 2 tbsp tomato paste

 2 tbsp flour

 1⅛ cups (250 ml) red wine

+3 hours cooking time

Gravy/Jus

1. Chop the bones into walnut-size pieces. It's best to leave this work to the butcher. Then put them in a wide pot with the vegetable oil and fry all sides for about 30 minutes, until golden brown. Keep stirring, continuously scraping the residue from the bottom of the pot, otherwise it could burn, making the gravy bitter.

2. Peel the carrots, onions, and celeriac, then wash the celery. Set aside the green leaves from the celery. Cut the vegetables into ¾-inch (2-cm) dice and add them to the pot. Fry them for another 20 minutes, stirring continuously.

3. Cut the heads of garlic in half horizontally and press all the spices into them with the flat side of the knife. This intensifies the flavor. Rinse the herbs and cut through the stems twice. Add the garlic, spices, herbs, and bay leaves to the sauce. Sprinkle with salt.

4. Push the bones and vegetables to the side and add the tomato paste to the middle. Toast the paste for 30 seconds to mellow its acidity.

5. Sprinkle with the flour and cook another 10 minutes. The flour binds the sauce.

6. Add the celery leaves, pour in half of the red wine, and cook it down completely. Pour in the remaining half of the wine and let it boil down again to make a robust sauce.

7. Now pour in 3¼ quarts (3 liters) cold water, or just enough to cover the bones.

■ Jus, the mother of all sauces, is necessary for nearly every beef sauce and above all, for seared beef cuts that don't produce enough juice while searing. Gravy turns out well when enough meat is on the bones used to make it. Veal bones achieve a more refined flavor. The bones should come from the back or neck. Don't use a long bone—that works better for soups. Gravy may be frozen in small containers.

The amount will depend on the width of the pot. If you have veal stock available, use it instead of water.

8. Now let the sauce simmer slowly for at least 2 hours, though 3 hours would be better. Keep pouring in cold water so the bones stay covered.

Meanwhile remove any foam with a skimmer; otherwise it cooks into the sauce, making it cloudy. Finish by putting the sauce though a coarse sieve. Press the bones and vegetables lightly. Then pass the sauce though a fine sieve. Then bring the sauce back to a boil, removing the foam, and season with salt and pepper to taste. This jus is an important base for other sauces.

Makes about $2\frac{2}{3}$ quarts (2.5 liters).

 1 shallot

 2¼ oz (60 g) mushrooms

 ⅛ cup (30 g) butter

 10 white peppercorns

 2 cloves

 ⅞ cup (200 ml) white wine

 2¼ cups (500 ml) chicken stock

 1⅓ cups (300 ml) cream

 5½ oz (150 g) crème fraîche (or sour cream)

 1 pinch of salt

 1 pinch of cayenne pepper

 2 eggs

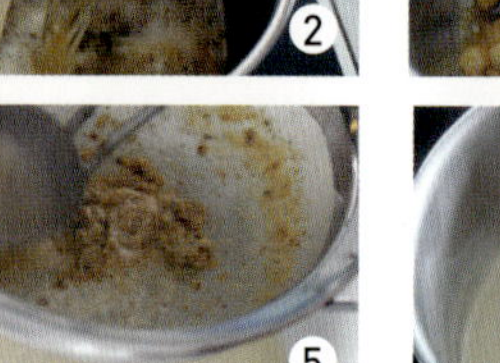

Thick Poultry Cream Sauce

1. Peel the shallot and dice it finely. Clean and slice the mushrooms. Heat the butter in a steel saucepan until it foams. Add the shallots and mushroom slices and sweat. Crush the peppercorns and cloves with the flat side of a knife and add them to the pot.

2. Pour in the white wine and let it boil down almost completely. Then pour in the chicken stock.

3. Let the chicken stock boil down almost completely, until it is syrupy.

4. Then pour in about ⅞ cup (200 ml) cream and the crème fraîche (or sour cream). Bring to a boil and season with salt and cayenne pepper to taste.

5. Mix with a handheld blender and pass it through a sieve. Use a ladle to push the remnants through. Return to a steel saucepan.

6. Separate the eggs, adding the yolks to the remaining cream and stirring with a whisk. Now add this egg yolk and cream combination (called a "liaison") to the hot sauce so that it binds and thickens. The sauce should not cook any further; otherwise the egg yolk will curdle.

Makes about 2 cups (500 ml).

■ **This sauce goes with lightly fried chicken, fried turbot or flounder, and also with steamed artichokes, cooked asparagus, steamed Belgian endive, or buttercrunch lettuce.**

Thick Tarragon Cream Sauce

Rinse **½ bunch fresh tarragon**, pick the leaves from the stems, and chop finely. Finish by adding the tarragon and **2 tbsp whipped cream** to **2¼ cups (500 ml) thick poultry cream sauce** and serve.

Makes about 2½ cups (550 ml).

■ **This sauce tastes great on all types of poultry, whether stewed or roasted, and also with rabbit fillets or veal medallions. If using with veal, you could substitute the chicken stock with a light veal stock. It goes best with roasted or stewed veal cutlets, young hen breasts, or other white meat from poultry.**

Coarse Mustard Sauce

Using a whisk, stir together **2 tbsp hot mustard** and **1 tbsp coarse mustard** with **2¼ cups (500 ml) thick poultry cream sauce**. Then add **2 tbsp whipped cream** and a **pinch of cayenne pepper** to taste, and stir.

Makes about 2½ cups (600 ml).

■ **Serve this sauce with stewed rabbit, cooked young hen, cooked calf's head, pork medallions, fillet of sole, or salmon and cucumber. The important thing is not to heat the mustard too high, otherwise it gets bitter quickly and the sauce tastes flat. It goes with veal medallions, with strong-flavored poultry, such as corn-fed young hen or guinea fowl, or with sweetbreads or calf's brain.**

 2 lb 4 oz (1 kg) shellfish shells

 3 tbsp (40 ml) olive oil

 ⅓ cup (80 g) butter

 1 head of garlic

 1 sprig fresh thyme

 1 sprig fresh rosemary

 2 bay leaves

 5½ oz (150 g) carrots

 10½ oz (300 g) onions

 3 shallots

 3½ oz (100 g) celery stalks

 3½ oz (100 g) fennel

 2 tsp tomato paste

 4 tsp (20 ml) cognac

 2 tbsp (30 ml) red port wine

 ⅞ cup (200 ml) white wine

 6⅔ cups (1.5 liters) water or vegetable stock

 10 white peppercorns

 2 cloves

 1 sprig fresh basil

Shellfish Stock

1. Cut the shellfish shells into small pieces or crush them with the back of a heavy knife. Heat them with oil and butter gently in a wide pot, stirring constantly. Cut the head of garlic in half, and coarsely chop the thyme, rosemary, and bay leaves.

2. Cut the vegetables in ½-inch (1-cm) dice and add them to the pot, along with the herbs and seasonings. Sauté everything until the vegetables become soft and collapse. Push the shells to the side and add the tomato paste, sautéing it lightly. This takes away the acidity. Next, mix it in with the shells and sauté it a little longer.

3. Finish by pouring in the cognac and port. Let the alcohol cook off and then add the white wine. Stir it as it cooks down. Pour in the water or, if available, vegetable stock. Add the peppercorns and cloves. Let it simmer gently for about 30 minutes. Ten minutes before it is finished, add the basil sprig and let it simmer down. Meanwhile, remove the foam that builds up on the surface. Next, pass it through a sieve twice and store it for later use. This stock can be stored in the refrigerator for up to a week, or frozen for up to two months.

Makes about 5⅓ cups (1.2 liters).

■ Shrimp shells produce a nice, strong stock. You can cut them with kitchen shears—they roast more evenly in smaller pieces. Use as a base for cream sauces or soups as well, or for pasta sauces with shellfish, or shrimp risotto. It's also good for bouillabaisse or paella.

Ingredients for shellfish stock, plus:

2¼ cups (500 ml) cream 

5 basil leaves 

10 tarragon leaves 

1 pinch of salt

1 pinch of cayenne pepper 

Shellfish Cream Sauce

1. Use the same ingredients and preparation as with the shellfish stock. As soon as the stock is cooked down so the shells are immersed only halfway, pour in the cream, add the basil and tarragon leaves, and simmer for 1 minute.

2. Using a handheld blender, carefully mix the sauce on the lowest speed. This will make the flavor more intense, and it mixes in the now orange-colored cream, which is responsible for the main flavor.

3. Pour everything through a small sieve and use a ladle to push it through well. Since so much sauce is contained in the shells, this ensures every possible drop is used. Bring the sauce to a boil again, season with salt and a little cayenne pepper to taste, and serve with steamed fish dishes or shellfish.

Makes about 4 cups (1 liter).

■ **When adding water to make the stock, add ¼ cup (50 g) short-grain rice. It helps the sauce combine nicely.**

120 ***

 2 red onions

 2 garlic cloves

 6 tbsp olive oil

 A few basil leaves

 1 pinch of salt
1 pinch of black pepper

 1 pinch of sugar

 1 lb 12 oz (800 g) canned peeled tomatoes

 1 tbsp tomato paste

Simple Tomato Sauce

1. Heat the finely diced onion and the chopped garlic in the olive oil. Add a few chopped basil leaves, and sweat them with the garlic and onion.

2. Season with salt, pepper, and a pinch of sugar.

3. Cook everything until the onions are translucent.

4. Drain the tomatoes in a colander. Dice the tomatoes, being sure to catch any juices and add them to the juice from the can.

5. Pour the tomato juice along with the tomato paste over the onions and garlic in the pan, and let it boil for about 20 minutes.

6. The tomato juice should boil down to about half of the original volume.

7. Now add the diced tomatoes and simmer for 5 minutes.

8. Season with salt, black pepper, and sugar to taste and mix in a few large, cut pieces of basil.

9. Fill mason jars with the warm tomato sauce, seal, and let cool. Store in the refrigerator.

Makes about 3⅓ cups (800 ml).

■ **The sauce will keep for 1 to 2 weeks in the refrigerator. This sauce is essential in cooking, whether served on any kind of pasta or as a base for the various tomato sauces, such as puttanesca, amatriciana, tomato mushroom sauce, or aurora sauce. It also tastes great with cream over vegetables au gratin, or with eggplant, zucchini, fennel, and Swiss chard, as well as with fried Mediterranean fish or calamari.**

4
5
6
7
8
9

1. Green Curry Sauce

Heat **2 tbsp peanut oil** in a pot. Add **1 tbsp green curry paste** and **1 tbsp brown sugar** and sauté lightly. Pour in **2 tbsp oyster sauce**, **1 tbsp soy sauce**, and a small portion of **2²/₃ cups (600 ml) coconut milk** and let it boil down. Add the remaining coconut milk and let it simmer gently for about 5 minutes. Finally, add leaves picked from **½ a bunch of cilantro** to the sauce. Mix with a handheld blender and serve.

Makes about 2½ cups (600 ml).

■ **Green curry tastes great as a vegetable curry and with beef dishes.**

2. Red Curry Sauce

Heat **2 tbsp peanut oil** in a pot. Add **1 tbsp green curry paste** and **1 tbsp brown sugar** and sauté lightly. Pour in **2 tbsp oyster sauce**, **1 tbsp soy sauce**, and a small portion of **2²/₃ cups (600 ml) coconut milk** and let it boil down. Add the remaining coconut milk and let it simmer gently for about 5 minutes. To make the curry sauce more aromatic, add extremely thin lemongrass slices shortly before serving.

Makes about 2½ cups (600 ml).

■ **Red curry sauce can be served with duck or beef, as well as with tofu.**

3. Yellow Curry Sauce

Heat **2 tbsp peanut oil** in a pot. Add **1 tbsp green curry paste** and **1 tbsp brown sugar** and sauté lightly. Pour in **2 tbsp oyster sauce**, **1 tbsp soy sauce**, and a small portion of **2²/₃ cups (600 ml) coconut milk** and let it boil down. Add the remaining coconut milk and let it simmer gently for about 5 minutes. To make the curry sauce more aromatic, add fresh Thai basil shortly before serving.

Makes about 2½ cups (600 ml).

■ **Yellow curry sauce goes best with chicken and vegetable or fruit curries.**

1
2
3

 2 shallots

 4 tsp (20 g) butter

 3 tbsp (50 ml) peppercorn brine

 3/8 cup (100 ml) cognac

 2¼ cups (500 ml) chicken stock

 1⅛ cups (250 ml) cream

 5½ oz (150 g) crème fraîche (or sour cream)

 2 tbsp green peppercorns in brine, drained

Green Peppercorn Cream Sauce

1. Peel the shallots and finely dice them. Heat the butter in a small pot over medium heat until it foams, add the shallots, and sweat them until they are translucent. Pour in the peppercorn brine and let the liquid cook down. Pour in the cognac and cook until the liquids are almost completely cooked down.

2. Pour in the chicken stock and cook down to a fifth of the volume. Then pour in the cream, add the crème fraîche (or sour cream), and bring it to a boil. Then remove it from the stove and mix using a handheld blender.

3. Pass the sauce though a fine sieve, and finally, add the green peppercorns to the sauce. If needed, add salt to taste.

Makes about 2 cups (500 ml).

■ **This base can also be used to make a mushroom cream sauce, in which case the peppercorns and brine should be left out. After sweating the shallots in butter, add 7 oz (200 g) cleaned, sliced mushrooms and sweat them. Then follow from step 2. Finally, pass the sauce through a sieve, blend, and add the mushroom slices again. Serve with omelets, pork medallions, or roasted chicken breast. But it tastes best with seared beef tenderloin, tenderloin tips, tournedos, or filet mignon.**

2

3

 1 lb 2 oz (500 g) red bell peppers

 3½ oz (100 g) onion

 2 garlic cloves

 4 tbsp extra virgin olive oil

 1 sprig fresh thyme

 2 bay leaves

 1 pinch of salt

 1 pinch of black pepper

 1 tbsp sugar

 ⅔ cup (150 ml) white wine

 3⅛ cups (700 ml) chicken stock

 7 oz (200 g) crème fraîche (or sour cream)

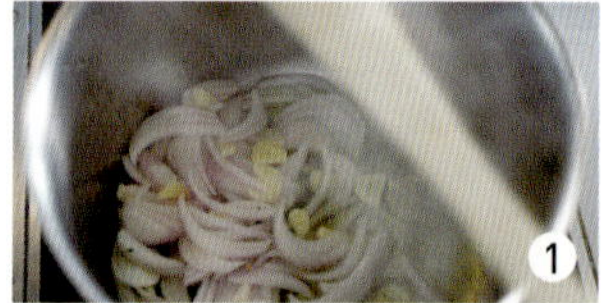

Paprika Cream Sauce

1. Clean the bell peppers and dice into large pieces. Peel the onion, cut it in half, and then into thin slices. Peel the garlic cloves and cut into thin slices. Warm up the olive oil in a pot, and slowly sweat the onion and garlic until translucent.

2. Add the thyme and bay leaves and sweat for about 1 minute. Then mix in the diced bell pepper, add salt, pepper, and sugar, and sweat another 2 to 3 minutes.

3. Pour in the white wine and the chicken stock and let it slowly simmer for about 15 minutes.

4. Add the crème fraîche (or sour cream) and let it come to a boil.

5. Take out the thyme sprig and bay leaves and mix the sauce with a handheld blender.

6. Then pass the sauce though a fine sieve. Using a ladle, push the pepper residue through the sieve well so the entire vegetable puree makes it into the sauce. This makes the sauce rich and thick.

Makes about 2½ cups (600 ml).

■ **This sauce goes well with roast rabbit, stewed or roast chicken, catfish or walleye fillets, or also with stuffed bell peppers.**

⅜ cup (100 ml) water

2 tbsp brown sugar

⅔ cup (150 ml) balsamic vinegar

3 shallots

4 garlic cloves

4 bay leaves

4 sprigs fresh thyme

1 sprig fresh rosemary

3 tbsp olive oil

1 pinch of salt
1 pinch of black pepper

2¼ cups (500 ml) chicken stock

1½ cups (350 ml) cream

5½ oz (150 g) crème fraîche (or sour cream)

2 tbsp whipped cream

Balsamic Vinegar Sauce

1. Put the water in a pot and dissolve the brown sugar in it, cooking until it is lightly caramelized and the water is boiled away. Pour in the balsamic vinegar and cook until it's syrupy.

2. Peel the shallots and cut them into thin slices. Crush the garlic cloves in their skins. Chop the bay leaves, thyme, and rosemary coarsely. Add the olive oil to the syrup first, then stir in the herbs, garlic cloves, and shallots.

3. Add salt and pepper and sweat for about 5 minutes.

4. Pour in the chicken stock and let it boil down to about a fifth of the volume for 15 minutes. Then add the cream and crème fraîche (or sour cream).

5. Bring the nearly finished sauce back to a boil. Then mix with a handheld blender.

6. Pass the sauce through a fine sieve. Using a skimmer, push the remnants through, and finally, stir in the whipped cream.

Makes about 2½ cups (600 ml).

■ **This sauce goes well with fried walleye, cod, or lentils, and with roasted young chicken or squab.**

 3/8 cup (100 ml) white wine

 5 eggs

 1 pinch of salt

 1½ cups (350 g) butter

 ½ lemon

 1 tbsp tarragon vinegar

 1 pinch of cayenne pepper

Hollandaise Sauce

1. Bring 1¼ inches (3 cm) water to a boil in a pot (to form the bottom of a double boiler). Pour the white wine in a bowl with a rounded bottom. Separate the eggs, putting the yolks in the bowl, and the egg whites in a container for later use. Place the bowl over the double boiler, ensuring the bottom does not touch the water, add salt, and mix with a whisk.

2. Beat the egg yolks vigorously until they are thick and white.

3. Melt the butter in a small pot until it is warm, not hot, then slowly ladle it into the foamy egg yolks. Keep whisking so the butter blends with the yolks and creates a thick, creamy sauce. The preparation is exactly like for mayonnaise, except this sauce is warm. Finally, add salt, lemon juice, tarragon vinegar, and cayenne pepper to taste.

Makes about 4 cups (1 liter).

■ To whip up a really good Hollandaise sauce, 5 eggs yolks are best. Never use fewer than 3 egg yolks, otherwise the sauce will not reach the correct volume. Place the finished sauce over a pot of hot water, not letting it touch the stove, and cover with parchment paper. This allows the sauce to stay warm for up to an hour. This sauce goes best with steamed asparagus, poached fish, or eggs.

This sauce is too runny either because the butter was too hot when it was added, or it was added too quickly.

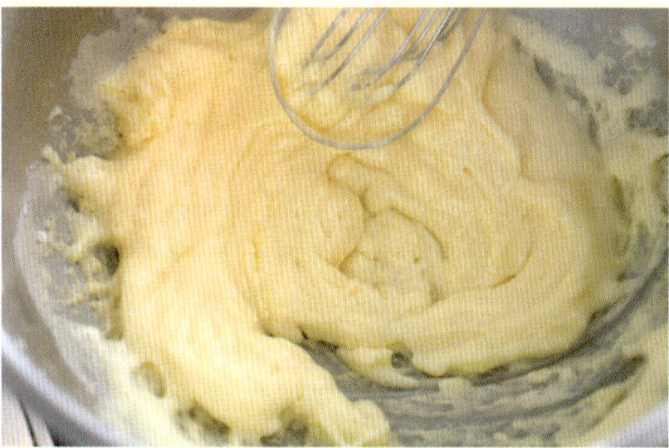

The yolk was beaten too vigorously over the boiling water. The egg has now curdled and it won't be possible to smooth it by adding more butter.

Kitchen doctor: The sauce is runny here too. Add 1 tbsp of hot water and try stirring it again with small movements in one spot, then stir in more and more of the rest of the sauce.

 7/8 cup (200 ml) white wine

 1 tbsp tarragon vinegar

 1 tsp white peppercorns

 1 cup (30 g) mushrooms

 1 shallot

 ½ bunch fresh tarragon

 5 eggs

 1½ cups (350 g) butter

 1 pinch of salt

 1 pinch of cayenne pepper

 ½ lemon

 ½ bunch fresh chervil

 ½ bunch fresh parsley

 ½ bunch fresh chives

Béarnaise Sauce

1. Put the white wine, tarragon vinegar, peppercorns, mushrooms, sliced shallot, and a tarragon sprig in a steel saucepan and boil it down to half the volume. Then pass it through a fine sieve into a bowl with a round bottom.

2. The rest of the recipe follows the same steps as with Hollandaise (p. 152), except the egg yolks are beaten with the vegetable stock instead of with white wine. Beat in the butter just as with the Hollandaise and season the sauce with salt and pepper to taste.

3. Rinse the rest of the tarragon and chervil, removing any damaged leaves, pick the leaves from the stems, chop them finely. Prepare the parsley and chives the same way. Cut the parsley into thin ribbons and the chives into small rings. Finally, stir the herbs into the sauce.

Serve with broiled, grilled, or roast beef, asparagus, boiled cauliflower, broccoli, or fried fish.

Makes about 4 cups (1 liter).

Choron Sauce

Make the **basic recipe** described for **Hollandaise sauce** (p. 152). Put **2 tbsp good tomato paste** in a bowl. You can tell if it's good tomato paste if it's red, not brownish. Stir **2 tbsp Hollandaise sauce** into the paste and then stir this mix into the Hollandaise bowl. This step is called blending and is necessary to prevent lumps

Makes about 4 cups (1 liter).

■ **This rich-flavored sauce goes well with steamed fish, with cooked vegetables, such as Swiss chard, spinach, or cauliflower, or with lightly fried chicken. Additionally, this sauce can be used in baked gratin dishes, or for a minestrone, which tastes particularly sophisticated with Choron sauce.**

Foyot Sauce

Make the **béarnaise sauce as described in the recipe** on the preceding page. Heat **3 tbsp roast beef gravy** in a small pot and, while continuously stirring, let it slowly run into the béarnaise sauce.

Makes about 4 cups (1 liter).

■ **Foyot sauce is sometimes erroneously confused with béarnaise sauce. Foyot sauce, however, contains beef gravy or beef extract, béarnaise sauce does not. Foyot sauce goes very well with large beef cuts, such as roasts and T-bone steaks, as well as with baked oysters.**

1 onion

1 bay leaf

2 cloves

¼ cup (60 g) butter

¼ cup (30 g) flour

3⅓ cups (750 ml) milk

1⅛ cups (250 ml) cream

1 pinch of salt

1 pinch of white pepper

1 pinch of freshly grated nutmeg

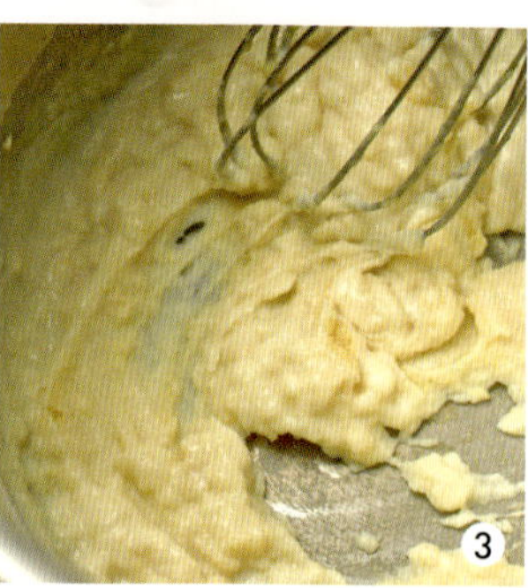

Béchamel Sauce

1. Peel the onion and tack the bay leaf to it using 2 cloves.

2. Melt the butter in the pot and sauté the flour in it lightly, making a roux.

3. Add a portion of the milk to the pot and stir it immediately so the roux dissolves.

4. Pour in the remaining cold milk and the cream and stir. Put the studded onion in the sauce.

5. Simmer gently for about 1 minute, stirring often. Season with salt, white pepper, and nutmeg to taste.

6. Then pass the sauce though a fine sieve.

Cover with plastic wrap to keep a skin from forming on the sauce. Use for lasagna or in other dishes and sauces.

Makes about 4 cups (1 liter).

■ **This is considered a base for other sauces—and it is certainly among the most important ingredients for a lasagna and for other baked gratin dishes.**

■ Thick Béchamel sauce: Stir in this sauce to bind soups or sauces until the desired consistency is reached. Cold, thick Béchamel sauce can also be used as a binding agent for vegetable or beef croquettes.

■ Creamy Béchamel sauce: This serves as the base for many white sauces, such as mustard sauce, for baking lasagna covered in cheese, or for horseradish sauce.

Kitchen doctor: This Béchamel sauce is too thin. You should make another attempt at making the butter and flour roux and pour in the sauce. Then simmer another 10 minutes.

Kitchen doctor: Pass the lumpy Béchamel sauce through a fine sieve again and then continue working.

Horseradish Sauce

Bring **2¼ cups (500 ml) Béchamel sauce** and **⅞ cup (200 ml) cream** to a boil and whisk until smooth. Next, remove it from the stove, add **1¾ oz (50 g) grated horseradish**, and stir. Season with **2 tbsp sugar**, **2 tbsp fruit vinegar**, **a pinch of salt**, and **a pinch of freshly ground white pepper** to taste, and serve.

Makes about 3⅓ cups (800 ml).

■ Horseradish sauce goes well with cooked beef, for example, tri-tip. It also tastes good with boiled calf's tongue, or calf's head, as well as with boiled potatoes or cauliflower.

Mustard Sauce

Bring **2¼ cups (500 ml) Béchamel sauce** and **⅞ cup (200 ml) cream** to a boil and whisk until smooth, then remove it from the stove and stir in **2 tbsp good medium-hot mustard**. Season with **a pinch of salt** and **a pinch of freshly ground white pepper** to taste, and serve.

Makes about 3⅓ cups (800 ml).

■ Serve this sauce with boiled eggs, boiled beef, or steamed saltwater fish. It goes well with poached shellfish, with braised onions, and with boiled beef, such as tri-tip.

3 tbsp olive oil

1 lb 5 oz (600 g) mixed ground meats

1 tsp salt
1 pinch of black pepper

1 onion

2 carrots

1 parsnip

1 garlic clove

2 tbsp tomato paste

1 lb 12 oz (800 g) canned peeled tomatoes

½ bunch fresh basil

Simple Bolognese Sauce

1. Heat the olive oil in a shallow pot and fry the meat in it.

2. Add salt and pepper to the meat, stir, and pay attention so that it doesn't burn and stick to the bottom.

3. Peel the onion, carrots, and parsnip. Grate the carrots and parsnip.

4. Add the grated vegetables, and the peeled and finely chopped onion, to the ground meat, and lightly sauté them.

5. When meat jus starts running, push the meat to the sides.

6. Put the tomato paste in the meat jus and sauté. This takes the acidity out of the tomato paste. Then stir the tomato paste in with the meat.

7. Add the canned tomatoes to the meat and split the tomato pieces with a wooden spoon.

8. Pour in 2¼ cups (500 ml) water and simmer gently for 45 minutes.

9. Finally, sprinkle with a chiffonade of basil.

Mix with cooked spaghetti, sprinkle with grated Parmesan cheese, and serve.

Makes about 8 cups (2 liters).

■ **Bolognese sauce is an important component for lasagna, but it tastes outstanding on other pasta dishes, too.**

5
6
7
8
9

Soups

Contents

162 Gazpacho
164 Tomato Soup with Basil Croutons
166 Italian Vegetable Soup
168 Chicken Soup with Butter Dumplings and Nutmeg
170 Potato Soup with Marjoram
172 Chervil Cream Soup
173 Cream of Asparagus Soup with Mint
173 Cream of Mushroom Soup
174 Squash Soup with Cheese Croutons
176 Lobster Bisque
178 Bouillabaisse Stock Base
180 Bouillabaisse

1 garlic clove

9 tbsp extra virgin olive oil

1 cucumber

2 red bell peppers

½ onion

3⅓ cups (750 ml) tomato juice

1 pinch of salt
1 pinch of black pepper

2 tbsp red wine vinegar

1

2

3

Gazpacho

1. To make garlic oil, peel the garlic cloves, crush them into 5 tbsp oil, and stir.

2. Rinse the cucumbers and peel them coarsely. Seed the peppers, rinse, and cut them in quarters. Peel the onions and cut all the vegetables into ½-inch (2 cm) dice.

3. Put the vegetables in a blender.

4. Pour in the tomato juice.

5. Season with salt and freshly ground black pepper, 2 tbsp red wine vinegar, and 4 tbsp olive oil.

6. Now puree for about 1 minute in the blender.

7. Pour into a bowl and place in the refrigerator for about 1 hour so the soup can chill thoroughly. Drizzle a little of the garlic oil over the soup shortly before serving. Place a tall container of ice in the soup bowl, so the soup stays cool longer on the table.

■ **During summer, use overripe, soft tomatoes instead of tomato juice.**

4
5
6
7

 ¼ cup (60 ml) olive oil

 2 tbsp sugar

 2½ oz (70 g) celery stalk

 5 oz (140 g) carrots

 5½ oz (150 g) onion

 2 garlic cloves

 4 cloves

 1 lemon

 1 tsp white peppercorns

 1 sprig fresh rosemary

 1 sprig fresh thyme

 1 bay leaf

 1 tbsp tomato paste

 2 lb 12 oz (1.2 kg) tomatoes

 1 tsp salt

 3⅓ cups (750 ml) chicken stock

Tomato Soup with Basil Croutons

1. Pour the olive oil into a large steel saucepan. Add the sugar and sauté it lightly, then add the finely diced vegetables (see p. 344) and sauté lightly for 5 minutes. Peel the garlic, cut it in half, and add to the vegetables, along with the cloves, 2 lemon peel strips (made using a vegetable peeler), crushed peppercorns, rosemary, thyme, and bay leaves. Sweat for another 5 minutes.

2. Add the tomato paste and sauté for 1 minute. Then add the washed and quartered tomatoes and season them with salt.

3. Pour in the chicken stock and bring it to a boil. Then reduce the heat to medium and let it simmer for 20 minutes.

4. Take out what is left of the sprigs of herbs and puree the soup for 1 minute using a handheld blender.

5. Using a ladle, pour the soup through a fine strainer and use the bottom of the ladle to push it through firmly until the remnants are almost dry. Put the soup in warmed bowls and serve with basil croutons.

■ **For the basil croutons, melt 4 tsp (20 g) butter in a nonstick pan, add 1¾ oz (50 g) cubed white bread and toast, stirring continuously, until golden brown. Add four basil leaves, cut into ribbons, lightly salt, and mix. Immediately put the croutons in a bowl and set aside to keep them from overbrowning.**

2
3
4
5

 3 small carrots, peeled

 1 small leek

 2 celery stalks

 ½ zucchini

 2 scallions

 8 cherry tomatoes

 1 garlic clove

 4 tbsp olive oil

 1 pinch of salt
1 pinch of black pepper

 ½ tsp fennel seeds

 6⅔ cups (1.5 liters) vegetable stock

 1 tbsp basil, chopped

 1 tsp fresh oregano, chopped

 2¾ oz (80 g) Parmesan cheese

Italian Vegetable Soup

1. Trim the carrots, leek, celery stalks, zucchini, and scallions, rinse, cut them into ¼-inch (5-mm) pieces. Cut the cherry tomatoes into quarters. Peel the garlic clove and mince it.

2. Heat the olive oil in a pot and slightly brown the garlic. Add the scallions and leek and sweat them lightly.

3. Now add the remaining vegetables, except the tomatoes, and sweat them without browning. Season with salt, pepper, and ground fennel seeds.

4. Add the tomatoes and pour in the vegetable stock. Let it simmer gently for about 10 minutes.

5. Finally, add the chopped basil and oregano leaves to the soup and serve immediately.

You can also add grated Parmesan cheese over the soup to taste.

■ **If the garlic clove is growing a green stem, remove it with a knife; it can taste bitter and sharp when cooked.**

2
3
4
5

 ½ cup (100 g) butter

 1 egg plus 1 egg yolk

 1 tsp parsley, chopped

 1 pinch of salt

 1 pinch of nutmeg, freshly grated

 ½ cup (60 g) all-purpose flour

 1 tbsp flour

 8 cups (2 liters) chicken stock

Chicken Soup with Butter Dumplings and Nutmeg

1. With the butter at room temperature, whip until it forms peaks. Next, add the egg and egg yolk, parsley, salt, and grated nutmeg. Beat until all the ingredients have blended.

2. Now, with a rubber spatula, work in the flour and let it sit for 10 minutes.

3. Use two teaspoons to form the dumpling.

4. Put the dumplings on a board sprinkled with flour and set the board in the refrigerator for 30 minutes.

5. Bring the chicken stock to a boil and add the dumplings. Maintain a gentle boil until the dumplings float. Then cover and let steep for 25 minutes.

Serve in soup cups or bowls and sprinkle with nutmeg.

- **Julienned root vegetables boiled in salted water, and chopped chicken can be added to this dish.**

2
3
4
5

 14 oz (400 g) potatoes

 3½ oz (100 g) leek

 1¾ oz (50 g) parsnip

 ½ garlic clove

 ⅛ cup (30 g) butter

 1 pinch of salt

 1 pinch of white pepper

 1 pinch of nutmeg, freshly grated

 4½ cups (1 liter) chicken stock

 ½ tsp marjoram, dried

 ⅞ cup (200 ml) cream

 5½ oz (150 g) crème fraîche (or sour cream)

 1 tbsp oil

 1 oz (30 g) bacon, cut into strips

 2 slices of white bread

Potato Soup with Marjoram

1. Peel the potatoes and cut them into ½-inch (1-cm) pieces. Put them in cold water until they're needed so they don't turn brown. Rinse and trim the leek, cut it in half lengthwise, and then cut into half rings (see p. 350). Rinse the parsnip, peel it, and cut it like the potatoes. Peel the garlic and cut into thin slices. Melt the butter in a pot until it foams, and sweat the garlic, leeks, and parsnip in it without letting them take on any color. Season with a pinch of salt and pepper.

2. Then add the potatoes, grate the nutmeg over the top, and sweat them. Don't let the vegetables brown or the soup will turn gray.

3. Pour in the chicken stock, add the marjoram, and bring to a boil. Then let it simmer gently over a low heat for about 20 minutes.

4. Now add the cream and crème fraîche (or sour cream) to the soup. Bring it back to a boil and puree using a handheld blender. Finally, heat the oil in a pan and fry the bacon until crisp. Cut the crusts off the slices of bread and cut into ½-inch (1-cm) pieces. Add the bread to the bacon and cook until golden. Serve the soup in deep bowls and sprinkle the bacon croutons on top.

■ **Cold potato leek soup: Pass 2¼ cups (500 ml) potato soup through a fine sieve. Then wash the leeks, cut them in rings, and sweat them in 1 tbsp olive oil. Add them to the soup. Let the soup cool and then serve over another bowl filled with ice. This popular French summer soup is called vichyssoise.**

3
4

2 onions

4 bunches fresh chervil

2 eggs

3 tbsp (40 g) butter

3⅔ cups (750 ml) chicken stock

1 pinch of salt

1 pinch of nutmeg, freshly grated

1¾ cups (400 ml) heavy cream

3½ oz (100 g) crème fraîche (or sour cream)

Chervil Cream Soup

1. Peel the onions, cut them in half, and dice them finely. Rinse the chervil and then pluck it, removing any damaged leaves. Set the leaves and stems aside. Boil the eggs for 6 minutes, shock them in cold water, and peel them. Melt the butter in a pot and sweat the onions until they look translucent. Now add the chervil stems and let them cook down briefly.

2. Pour in the chicken stock and season with salt and nutmeg. Bring to a boil, then lower the heat and let it simmer for about 10 minutes.

3. Add the cream and crème fraîche (or sour cream) and bring it briefly back to a boil.

4. Then pour the soup through a fine sieve and press it through with the bottom of a ladle.

5. Set aside a few chervil leaves as a garnish. Put the remaining leaves in a blender, pour in the soup, and mix it for 1 minute.

6. Season with a pinch of salt to taste. Serve the foamy soup topped with the remaining chervil leaves and 2 quarters of an egg.

■ **If you like it thicker, you can add 3½ oz (100 g) starchy potato to the recipe. Cut it into ½-inch (1-cm) pieces and add them before you add the chervil stems.**

Cream of Asparagus Soup with Mint

Peel the lower third of **12 oz (350 g) green asparagus** and rinse. Then cut off the tips at a length of about 1¼ inches (3 cm) and set them aside. Cut the asparagus stalks into pieces about ½-inch (1-cm) long. Peel **2¼ oz (60 g) starchy potato** and cut into ¼-inch (5-mm) cubes. Cut **1 shallot** in half lengthwise, then into thin slices. Melt **4 tsp butter** in a pot until it foams. Add the shallot and potatoes and briefly sweat them. Add the asparagus stalk pieces and likewise sweat them. Season with 1 pinch of salt, **1 pinch of freshly ground white pepper**, and **1 pinch of nutmeg**. Pour in **3⅓ cups (750 ml) chicken stock** and let it simmer for about 10 minutes. Boil the asparagus tips in salted water for 5 minutes and then shock them under cool water. Pour **⅞ cup (200 ml) cream** into the soup, bring to a boil briefly, and mix with a handheld blender. Add **2 tbsp whipped cream** to the soup and don't let it boil again. Cut the leaves from a **sprig of fresh mint** into thin ribbons and sprinkle them over the soup. Warm the asparagus tips in **2 tsp (10 g) butter** and drop them into the soup.

Cream of Mushroom Soup

Peel **1 shallot**, cut it in half, and dice finely. Peel **5½ oz (150 g) starchy potato** and cut into ¼-inch (5-mm) cubes. Clean **10½ oz (300 g) mushrooms** (see p. 360) and cut into slices. Peel **½ a garlic clove** and cut it in thin slices. Let **4 tsp (20 g) butter** foam up in a pot over medium heat. Add the shallots, garlic, and potatoes and sweat them. After about 1 minute, add the mushrooms and season with **1 pinch of salt**, **1 pinch of freshly ground black pepper**, and **1 pinch of freshly grated nutmeg**. Sprinkle with the juice of **½ a lemon** so the mushrooms don't darken too much while cooking. Pour in **3⅓ cups (750 ml) chicken stock** and let it simmer for about 10 minutes. Pour in **⅞ cup (200 ml) cream** and mix well with a handheld blender. Do not pass the soup through a sieve. Add **2 tbsp whipped cream** and remove from the heat. Divide the soup into warmed bowls and serve.

 3 lb 8 oz (1.6 kg) kabocha squash

 ½ bunch fresh dill

 ½ oz (15 g) fresh ginger

 1 garlic clove

 2¾ oz (80 g) carrot

 5½ oz (150 g) red bell pepper

 1 oz (30 g) celery stalk

 2¾ oz (80 g) onion

 3 tbsp (40 g) butter

 ½ tsp salt

 1 pinch of nutmeg, freshly grated

 3 cloves

 1 bay leaf

 1 tsp ketchup

 ½ tsp curry powder

 1½ tsp sweet paprika

 4½ cups (1 liter) chicken stock

 ⅞ cup (200 ml) cream

 3½ oz (100 g) crème fraîche (or sour cream)

Squash Soup with Cheese Croutons

1. Cut the top, from about 1¼ inches (3 cm) down, off the squash (best with kabocha or red kuri squash). Scrape out the seeds with a soup spoon. Rinse the dill and then pluck it, removing any damaged leaves.

2. Using a melon baller, scoop out the flesh from the squash and the top, without damaging the skin. Leave about a ½-inch (1-cm) thick wall. That yields about 8 oz (225 g) of flesh from the squash.

3. Peel the ginger and garlic and cut both into thin slices. Wash the vegetables and peel the carrot and onion. Cut the vegetables into ½-inch (1-cm) pieces. Melt the butter in a soup pot and sweat the garlic and onion together until they become translucent. Then add the other vegetables and the ginger and sweat them another 5 minutes.

4. Add the squash. Season with salt and nutmeg, and add the cloves and bay leaves. Sweat over medium heat for about 10 minutes, until the squash begins to fall apart.

5. Lightly sauté the ketchup, curry powder, and paprika in the middle of the pot for 1 minute, and then mix it in. This intensifies the flavor.

6. Pour in the chicken stock, bring it to a boil, and let it lightly simmer over medium heat for 15 minutes. Add the cream and crème fraîche and bring it briefly back to a boil.

■ Cheese croutons: Cut half a baguette in ¼-inch (5-mm) slices, sprinkle 2¼ oz (60 g) grated aged Gouda cheese over them, and bake them in the oven at 400°F (200°C/Gas Mark 6) for 5 minutes.

7. Then puree with an immersion blender for 1 minute and pour it through a fine sieve. Use the bottom of a ladle to press the remaining liquid out of the remnants.

Pour the soup into the hollowed-out squash, sprinkle with the finely chopped dill, and serve with the cheese croûtons (see Tip).

 3½ oz (100g) onion

 3 shallots

 2¾ oz (80 g) carrots

 2¾ oz (80 g) celery stalks

 3 garlic cloves

 10 black peppercorns

 2 lb 12 oz (1.2 kg) lobster, cooked

 3 tbsp olive oil

 ¼ cup (50 g) butter

 2 sprigs fresh thyme

 1 sprig fresh rosemary

 2 bay leaves

 4 peeled canned tomatoes

 ½ oz (15 g) short-grain rice

 3 tbsp (50 ml) dry vermouth
3 tbsp (50 ml) cognac

 ⅔ cup (150 ml) white wine

 4½ cups (1 liter) shellfish stock (see p. 142)

 1¾ cups (400 ml) cream

 2 basil leaves

 1 pinch of salt

 1 pinch of cayenne pepper

Lobster Bisque

1. Cut the onion, shallots, carrots, and celery into ¼-inch (5-mm) pieces. Crush the garlic in its skin. Crush the peppercorns with a knife. Crack open the lobster (see p. 482) and store the meat. Heat the olive oil in a wide pot, add the lobster carcasses (shells), and toast them for about 5 minutes. Then add the butter and toast the shells longer to extract their flavor.

2. Then add the vegetables, garlic, peppercorns, and the coarsely chopped herbs, and sweat until the vegetables are soft. Keep scraping any residue from the bottom of the pot to avoid letting it burn, which would make the soup bitter.

3. Add the peeled tomatoes, mash them, and sauté them. Add the rice, pour in the vermouth, cognac, and white wine, and let it boil another 5 minutes so the alcohol evaporates.

4. Now pour in the shellfish stock (see p. 142) and let it slowly simmer for 20 minutes.

5. Pour in the cream, add the basil leaves, and let it slowly simmer for 1 minute. Carefully blend the soup with an immersion blender on the lowest level—this gives the soup a more intense flavor. Then, using a ladle, pour the soup through a fine sieve into another pot, squeezing out the carcasses well. Bring

■ **This soup takes its name from the salty, grated biscuits with which it was previously associated. Lobster bisque tastes even better if you start with live lobsters.**

it back to a boil and season with salt and cayenne pepper to taste. Serve the soup in deep bowls and place 1 oz (30 g) of the previously removed lobster pieces in each bowl.

10½ oz (300 g) turbot

10½ oz (300 g) red snapper

1 lb 2 oz (500 g) redfish

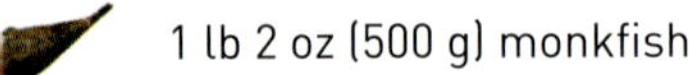
1 lb 2 oz (500 g) monkfish

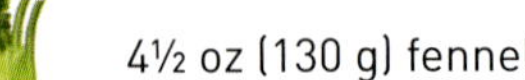
4½ oz (130 g) fennel

5½ oz (150 g) carrots

7 oz (200 g) celery stalks

1 sprig fresh rosemary

3 sprigs fresh thyme

3 bay leaves

1 tsp fennel seeds

1 tsp black peppercorns

⅜ cup (100 ml) extra virgin olive oil

5 garlic cloves

10 saffron threads

1 tbsp tomato paste

⅜ cup (100 ml) dry vermouth

1½ cups (350 ml) white wine

6⅔ cups (1.5 liters) water

1 tsp coarse sea salt

Bouillabaisse Stock Base

1. Remove the fish from the refrigerator, wash, gut, and fillet them, then pull out the small bones with fish-bone tongs, cover, and place the fillets back in the refrigerator for the bouillabaisse. Remove the gills from the fish heads and rinse the heads and bones under running water, until there is no remaining blood. Then drain the fish bones and heads well.

2. Trim the vegetables and cut them in ½-inch (1-cm) pieces. Chop the herbs coarsely, then crush the fennel seeds and peppercorns with the flat side of a knife. Cover the fish bones with the vegetables, herbs, 2 tbsp olive oil, crushed garlic cloves, and saffron threads, and let marinate for about 2 hours.

3. Heat the remaining olive oil in a wide pot, then fry the marinated fish bones and the remaining marinade mix.

4. After 5 minutes, add the tomato paste and pour in the dry vermouth, white wine, and the water. Season with salt. Now reduce the temperature to medium heat and let everything simmer for 20 minutes. Meanwhile, remove the foam with a ladle.

5. First pass the stock through a coarse sieve and press out the fish bones well.

6. Then pass it through a fine sieve. Set the stock aside and use it later for the bouillabaisse.

Makes about 6¾ cups (1.6 liters).

160

■ **Rouille sauce (see p. 52) goes well with bouillabaisse stock.**

2
3
4
5

 7 oz (200 g) red bell peppers

 7 oz (200 g) green bell peppers

 7 oz (200 g) carrots

 7 oz (200 g) fennel

 7 oz (200 g) leeks

 Filleted fish, from the Stock Base (see p. 178)

 ½ tsp salt

 3 sprigs fresh thyme

 4 tbsp extra virgin olive oil

 12 saffron threads

 2 garlic cloves

 1 pinch black pepper

 3 tbsp (50 ml) dry vermouth

 ⅜ cup (100 ml) white wine

 6⅔ cups (1.5 liters) bouillabaisse Stock Base (see p. 178)

 ½ bunch fresh basil

 1½ cups (350 g) rouille sauce (see p. 52)

Bouillabaisse

1. Wash the red and green bell peppers, peel the carrots, and thinly julienne the vegetables (see p. 344). Wash the fennel and leeks, cutting them into thin strips.

2. Marinate the fish fillets with salt, thyme leaves, 2 tbsp olive oil, and half of the saffron threads.

3. Put the rest of the olive oil in a pot and sweat the peeled, finely diced garlic in it, until translucent. Then add the vegetables and sweat them for 5 minutes. Add the rest of the saffron and season with salt and pepper.

4. As soon as the vegetables are done, pour in the dry vermouth and white wine, and cook it down until all the liquid is evaporated. Pour in the stock and let it simmer gently for 10 minutes.

5. Now lay the fish fillets in by hand and bring it back to a boil. Rinse the basil, removing any damaged pieces, cut the leaves in thin ribbons, and add them to the pot. Serve it with rouille sauce. You can also put some of the sauce directly in the soup to bind and thicken it.

■ **Familiar with a different bouillabaisse? There are about 280 different variations. You can make this dish however you like it, using other fish, shellfish, or mussels as well.**

2
3
4
5

Pasta

Contents

184 Types of Pasta
186 Pasta Dough
188 Spinach Pasta Dough
189 Cooking Pasta
190 Cooking Asian Egg Noodles
191 Cooking Asian Rice Noodles
192 Spaetzle Dough
194 Noodle Casserole with Cheese
196 Spaghetti with Aglio Olio
198 Spaghetti with Mussels
200 Tagliolini with Truffles
202 Penne Bolognese
204 Lasagna
206 Ricotta Ravioli with Sage Butter
208 Chicken and Ham Tortellini in Tomato Basil Sauce with Parmesan Cheese
210 Baked Cannelloni with Grilled Vegetables and Mozzarella
212 Cheese Spaetzle with Bacon Strips and Sautéed Onion
214 Shrimp Wontons in Vegetable Broth
216 Fried Noodles with Spicy Beef
218 Rice Noodles with Broccoli and Green Chili Peppers
220 Black Tagliatelli with Squids
222 Tagliatelle in Walnut Gorgonzola Sauce
224 Shanghai-Style Fried Egg Noodles with Chicken
226 Rice Noodles in Red Curry Sauce with Cilantro
228 Fried Glass Noodles in Strawberry Gazpacho

Types of Pasta

Pasta is legendary in Italian cooking, even though many countries have different regional noodle specialties. Spaghetti, tagliolini, and tortellini are different shapes of noodle made with semolina. Rice noodles and vermicelli are made of rice flour and water. They are available in varying sizes and widths. Glass noodles are made from a base of mung bean starch and water. They're thin and almost transparent. There is a variety in Korea made from sweet potato starch.

Gemelli

Rigatoni

Farfalle

Riccioli

Cannaroni lisci

Trulli

Lasagna

Lasagna made with durum wheat

Egg tagliatelle—freshly made

Soup Noodles

Dinosaur-shape pasta

Cavatappi or cellentani

Capellini

Penne

Mafaldine

Thin rice noodles

Spinach tagliolini—freshly made

Black sepia spaghetti

Dried egg tagliatelle

Tagliolini

Whole-grain spiral noodles, eliche or fusilli

 3¼ cups (400 g) all-purpose flour

 1¼ cups (200 g) semolina

 7 eggs

 1 pinch of salt

 3 tbsp extra virgin olive oil

Pasta Dough

1. Mix the flour and semolina in a bowl. Make a well.

2. Add the eggs and salt.

3. Mix some flour into the eggs using a whisk.

4. Add the olive oil and mix with the eggs and the rest of the flour.

5. Put the dough on a flat work surface and knead it vigorously.

6. Knead the dough until the flour is completely worked in and has a firm consistency. Now the dough can be rolled out as desired using a pasta machine.

■ **The pasta dough can be flavored with tomato paste, pureed spinach, porcini powder, finely chopped rosemary or thyme, or truffle paste.**

4

5

6

1

2

3

4

5

Spinach Pasta Dough

1. Remove **1 lb (450 g) spinach leaves** from their stems and rinse well. Cook for 5 to 8 minutes in plenty of salted water until soft. Pour into a sieve, cool under cold water, and firmly push out the water. Puree the dry spinach in a food processor.

2. Separate **6 eggs**. In a bowl, combine the **egg yolks**, **3⅔ cups (450 g) all-purpose flour**, **1¼ cups (200 g) semolina**, **2 tbsp oil**, and **1 pinch of salt**.

3. Add the cooled, pureed spinach.

4. Knead until it makes a smooth dough.

5. Work in more flour as needed to reach the desired consistency. Wrap the spinach pasta dough in plastic and let it set for about 1 hour.

Cooking Pasta

1. Bring plenty of water to a boil in a large pot and add a good amount of salt. Do not add oil to the water, or the pasta will not pick up the sauce well.

2. Add the pasta to the boiling water. The ratio of water to pasta should be 5:1. Cook the pasta according to the packet instructions or according to personal taste.

3. Pour the cooked pasta into a colander and let it drain. If the pasta is going to be eaten immediately, do not rinse in cold water, but put it directly in the sauce.

4. If the pasta is not be used until later, rinse it under cold running water. Then let it drain well.

5. Put it in a sealable container. Drizzle some oil over and mix it up so the pasta does not stick.

Cooking Asian Egg Noodles

1. Asian egg noodles are made from wheat flour and eggs, and resemble thin spaghetti.

2. Put the egg noodles in a pot with plenty of boiling water. Cook the noodles according to the packet instructions.

3. Using a fork, separate the egg noodles while cooking so they don't stick together.

4. Pour into a colander and rinse with cold water.

5. Either use the noodles immediately for a desired dish, or mix with a little oil in a bowl, cover, and store in the refrigerator for later use.

Cooking Asian Rice Noodles

1. Rice noodles are made from rice flour and rolled out into thin strings. When cooked, they are so tender they melt in the mouth.

2. Put the rice noodles in plenty of boiling water. Cook the noodles according to the packet instructions.

3. Pour out and rinse immediately with cold water.

4. Drain well. If the rice noodles are to be stored, as with all noodles, mix in a little oil to keep them from sticking together, cover with plastic wrap, and keep in the refrigerator.

2¾ cups (350 g) all-purpose flour

7 eggs

3 tbsp (50 ml) water

1 pinch of salt
1 pinch of white pepper

1 pinch of freshly grated nutmeg

Spaetzle Dough

1. Put the flour in a bowl, make a well, and add the eggs, some water, and a pinch each of salt, pepper, and freshly grated nutmeg.

2. Mix the eggs and water and, from the middle outward, work the flour in a little at a time.

3. Pour in more water as needed—the dough should have a creamy consistency.

4. Whip the spaetzle dough thoroughly, then let it set for 15 minutes until bubbles appear.

5. Using a rubber spatula, push the spaetzle dough through a colander, directly into a large pot of boiling water.

6. Boil the spaetzle briefly in the water, until it rises to the surface.

7. Take out the spaetzle with a skimmer.

Let it drain in a colander and as desired, either toss with butter and serve it as a side dish, or make cheese spaetzle—layered in a dish with freshly grated cheese, then baked in the oven.

■ **Instead of water, mix the spaetzle dough with 1¾ oz (50 g) spinach or herb puree. This makes the spaetzle a wonderful green and is a feast for the eyes as a side dish with beef or poultry.**

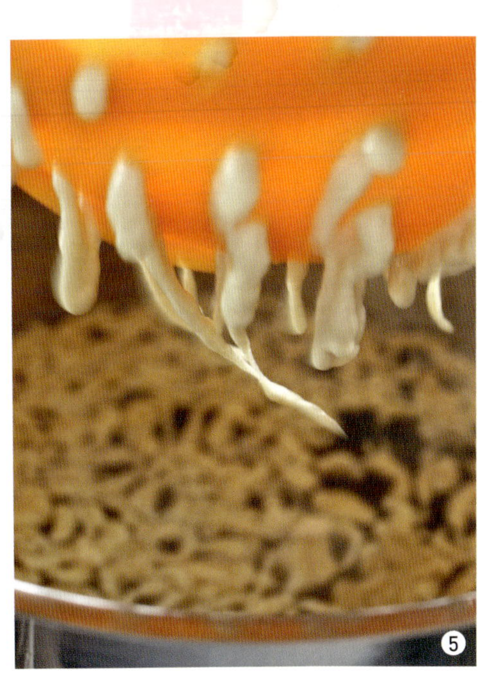
5

6

7

4½ oz (120 g) breadcrumbs

1½ tsp sweet paprika

2 tbsp extra virgin olive oil

1 lb 12 oz (800 g) cooked macaroni or penne

3½ oz (100 g) grated Gouda cheese

3½ oz (100 g) grated cheddar cheese

⅔ cup (150 ml) heavy cream

1 pinch of black pepper

1 tsp butter

1

2

Noodle Casserole with Cheese

1. Mix the breadcrumbs with the paprika and olive oil.

2. Put the macaroni in a large bowl. Add the grated cheese and cream on top and season with freshly ground black pepper.

3. Mix the noodles and the cheese well.

4. Place the noodles in a casserole dish greased with butter.

5. Then sprinkle the seasoned breadcrumbs over the macaroni and put in the oven preheated to 350°F (180°C/ Gas Mark 4) for 30 minutes.

Divide onto plates and serve.

■ **Other types of cheese can be used in this dish if desired, but choose varieties that melt during cooking. Gruyère or Swiss cheese has an especially full flavor and melts nicely.**

3

4

5

 8 garlic cloves

 1 bunch fresh parsley

 1 dried pepper

 3 pepperoncini or chiles

 6 tbsp extra virgin olive oil

 1 lb 2 oz (500 g) spaghetti

 1 pinch of salt

Spaghetti with Aglio Olio

1. Peel the garlic and chop it finely. Rinse the parsley, pick the leaves from the stems, removing any damaged pieces, and chop it finely. Cut both types of pepper into strips.

2. Heat the olive oil in a pot, add the garlic, and brown until golden yellow. Then add the peppers and sauté them to remove some of the heat.

3. In the meantime, cook the pasta until al dente. Pour some of the pasta water into the sauce.

4. Now add the spaghetti and boil until it has completely absorbed the liquid.

5. Sprinkle parsley over it and mix with the pasta. Arrange on plates.

■ **After cutting chiles, do not touch your eyes—thoroughly wash your hands first. This dish tastes just as good with thinner pasta, such as capellini or spaghettini.**

3

4

5

½ bunch fresh parsley

½ bunch fresh basil

2 garlic cloves

7 oz (200 g) cherry tomatoes

2 lb 4 oz (1 kg) mussels

5 tbsp extra virgin olive oil

1 pinch of salt
1 pinch of black pepper

⅔ cup (150 ml) white wine

1 lb 2 oz (500 g) spaghetti

1

2

Spaghetti with Mussels

1. Rinse the parsley and basil, pick the leaves from the stems, and chop finely. Peel the garlic and chop finely. Rinse the cherry tomatoes and cut them in half. Rinse and clean the mussels (see p. 480). Heat the olive oil in a pot, add the garlic, and sauté until golden. Then add the cherry tomatoes, salt, and pepper and sweat for another minute.

2. Drain the mussels well, then add them to the pot and stir.

3. Add the white wine. Cover and steam the mussels for another 2–3 minutes, until they open.

4. Then uncover and remove any unopened mussels.

5. Meanwhile, cook the spaghetti until al dente. Add basil and parsley, folding them in. Add more salt and pepper, and drizzle a little olive oil on the cooked pasta. Next, serve the pasta with the mussels in deep bowls.

■ **The best-tasting mussels are small. You can use them with other mollusks, such as clams, as well. If you add cooked octopus or fried calamari to it, you have frutti di mare spaghetti.**

3

4

5

 1 lb 5 oz (600 g) pasta dough

 ¾ cup (100 g) all-purpose flour

 ⅜ cup (100 ml) cream

 ¼ cup (50 g) butter

 2 tbsp extra virgin olive oil

 1 pinch of salt

 1 pinch of freshly grated nutmeg

 ⅔ oz (20 g) white truffles

Tagliolini with Truffles

1. Put the pasta dough on a floured surface and, with a rolling pin, roll it out to about ½ inch (5 mm) thick. Keep turning the dough and sprinkling it with flour.

2. Then fold the outer edges to the middle to make a square. Add more flour and continue rolling it out evenly.

3. Roll the dough thin enough so you can see the shape of your hands when you pick it up.

4. Now continue to fold both ends toward the middle until it makes a block about 2 inches (5 cm) thick. Meanwhile keep sprinkling with flour.

5. Using a sharp knife, cut the pasta dough into thin strips.

6. Pick up the strips of dough with a meat fork, lift them up, and shake. This separates the pasta.

7. Put the tagliolini in a pot with plenty of boiling salted water and cook for about 1 minute.

8. In the meantime, bring the cream to a boil in another pot. Add the butter and olive oil. Drain the cooked pasta and add it to the sauce. Season with salt and nutmeg, and mix together. Boil it fully again so the pasta takes up the sauce well. Then divide it among plates and shave the cleaned white truffles very thinly over the pasta.

■ A very good butter is required for this dish. Add a few drops of white truffle oil to the cream to enhance the flavor. But use it sparingly, because it has an intense flavor and the actual truffle flavor could overpower the dish.

3
4
5
6
7
8

2½ oz (75 g) grated Gouda cheese

9 oz (250 g) penne pasta

2¼ cups (500 ml) Béchamel sauce (see p. 156)

1 lb 10 oz (750 g) bolognese sauce (see p. 158)

1 pinch of black pepper

3 tbsp olive oil

1

2

Penne Bolognese

1. Grate the Gouda cheese. Cook the penne (see p. 189) until al dente. Then refresh it in cold water and drain. On the bottom of the casserole dish, put a layer of Béchamel sauce (see p. 156), then a layer of penne over it, and then spread a layer of bolognese sauce (see p. 158) on top.

2. Spread part of the Béchamel sauce over the bolognese. Béchamel sauce makes the casserole taste creamy and delicious.

3. Sprinkle the grated cheese over it and follow with another layer of penne and bolognese sauce.

4. Cover with the rest of the cheese and pour the Béchamel sauce over the top. The cheese will melt during baking and combine with the Béchamel sauce.

5. Finish by seasoning with pepper and a drizzle of olive oil, and bake in an oven preheated to 400°F (200°C/Gas Mark 6) for about 20 minutes. Remove the casserole and cool briefly before serving.

■ **This recipe works with other types of pasta, such as macaroni, fusilli, farfalle, or rigatoni. If starting with cooked pasta, use 1 lb 2 oz (500 g).**

3

4

5

2 tbsp (30 g) butter

4½ cups (1 liter) Béchamel sauce, thin

9 oz (250 g) green lasagna sheets

1 lb 10 oz (750 g) bolognese sauce

1 piece of fresh mozzarella cheese

3½ oz (100 g) grated edam cheese

2 tbsp extra virgin olive oil

1

2

Lasagna

1. Grease a rectangular casserole dish with butter and spread around a medium-sized ladleful of Béchamel sauce (see p. 156).

2. Put down a layer of lasagna sheets and another ladleful of Béchamel sauce over it. The sheets will fully absorb the sauce, making the lasagna nice and creamy. Spread a layer of bolognese sauce (see p. 158) on top.

3. Repeat these steps until the casserole dish is full and the top layer of lasagna sheets is covered in Béchamel sauce.

4. Cut the mozzarella into small pieces and along with the grated edam cheese, sprinkle it over the lasagna. Finish by drizzling olive oil over the top and bake in the oven preheated to 350°F (180°C/Gas Mark 4) for about 50 minutes. To prevent the lasagna from getting too brown on top, cover it with aluminum foil and remove the foil 5 minutes before it has finished cooking. Serve the lasagna in the casserole dish.

■ **Homemade green lasagna dough: Roll out and cut the sheet from green pasta dough (see p. 188). Use less Béchamel sauce in this case, because fresh pasta dough does not absorb as much liquid as dry.**

3

4

 9 oz (250 g) ricotta

 3 eggs

 1 tbsp pesto

 1 pinch of salt
1 pinch of black pepper

 1 pinch of freshly grated nutmeg

 1 lb 2 oz (500 g) pasta dough

 ½ cup (100 g) butter

 1 bunch fresh sage

 1¾ oz (50 g) Parmesan cheese

1

2

Ricotta Ravioli with Sage Butter

1. Grate the ricotta into a bowl. Separate 2 eggs and add the 2 egg yolks. Add the pesto, season with salt, black pepper, and nutmeg, and mix everything into a smooth filling.

2. Make the pasta dough (see p. 186) and use a pasta machine several times to roll it thin. Before rolling it out each time, keep sprinkling with flour, and then fold it together. This maintains the desired consistency of the dough. Using a teaspoon, place hazelnut-size portions of the ricotta mix on one sheet of dough, about 2 inches (5 cm) apart.

3. Beat the third egg with 1 tbsp water and brush the edges of the dough with it. Cover the filling with a second sheet of dough, press the edges hard, and seal each ravioli with a small, round pastry cutter.

4. Cut out the raviolis with a round pastry cutter about 2⅓ inches (6 cm) wide, or with pastry cutting wheel, or with a smooth knife, and put them on a flour-covered cookie sheet until ready to use. Cook the ravioli in boiling salted water for about 4 to 5 minutes and then carefully remove them with a skimmer.

■ The remaining uncooked ravioli can be stored on a tray in the freezer. They will be easier to remove from the tray later and can be stored in the freezer in a container or freezer bag for a few weeks. When cooking frozen ravioli, be sure to lengthen the cooking time (which depends on the ravioli size) by about 1–2 minutes.

Meanwhile, heat the butter in a pan until golden. Pick the sage leaves from the stems, add them, and remove the pan from the heat. The butter's temperature is enough to make the sage crisp. Lightly salt the butter. Plate the ravioli, pour sage butter over it, and garnish with Parmesan shavings.

 9 oz (250 g) ground chicken

 2½ oz (75 g) pancetta

 ½ tsp salt
1 pinch of black pepper

 1 sprig fresh rosemary

 1 slice white bread

 ⅜ cup (100 ml) milk

 2¾ oz (80 g) zucchini

 4 tsp (20 g) butter

 1 pinch of freshly grated nutmeg

 ½ bunch fresh parsley

 2 eggs

 2 lb 4 oz (1 kg) pasta dough

 2¼ cups (500 ml) plain tomato sauce (see p. 144)

 ⅛ cup (30 g) butter

 1¾ oz (50 g) Parmesan cheese

 ½ bunch fresh basil

1

2

Chicken and Ham Tortellini in Tomato Basil Sauce with Parmesan Cheese

1. Cut the pancetta into pieces and add them with the ground chicken, salt, black pepper, and the picked rosemary leaves to a food processor. Mix everything until fine.

2. Put the bread slices into a bowl and pour milk over them to soften them. Meanwhile, wash the zucchini and cut into small dice (see p. 344). Melt the butter in a pan, add the zucchini, and season with salt, pepper, and nutmeg. Sweat the zucchini, stirring frequently. Rinse the parsley and basil, pick the leaves from the stems, and chop finely. Add the zucchini and mix. Add 1 egg to the bread slices, then the meat and the zucchini. Mix everything well, and season to taste.

3. Using a pasta machine (level 2), roll the pasta dough out, then sprinkle the pasta sheets with flour. Put 1 tsp of filling at a time on the rolled-out noodles.

4. Cut the pasta dough into 4-inch (10-cm) squares. Separate the second egg and brush the edges of the dough with the white.

5. Fold up the sheets of dough into triangles. Using your fingers, seal the edges closed by pressing them down, to keep the filling in while cooking.

Kitchen doctor: If the pasta sheets tear while you're rolling them out, simply add a little pasta dough to the torn section and carefully roll it out again in the machine. The pasta dough will repair itself.

6. Next, fold the sides of the triangles over a thumb and press them together using your other thumb and index finger.

7. Press that same section together again so that it keeps its shape while cooking.

8. When finished, the tortellini look like little bishop hats. Simmer them lightly in plenty of salted water for about 8 minutes. Heat the tomato sauce (see p. 144) in a pan. Remove the tortellini from the water using a skimmer and put them in the sauce, add butter, and toss. Arrange them on plates and sprinkle with grated Parmesan cheese and basil leaves picked from the stem.

5 ½ oz (150 g) eggplant

5½ oz (150 g) zucchini

1 pinch of salt

½ red bell pepper

½ green bell pepper

1 egg

1¾ oz (50 g) grated Gruyère cheese

1½ cups (80 g) fresh white breadcrumbs

5 tbsp extra virgin olive oil

10 basil leaves

1 pinch of black pepper

10 lasagna sheets

4 tsp (20 g) butter

1⅓ cups (300 ml) Béchamel sauce (see p. 156)

⅞ cup (200 ml) cream

1 piece of fresh mozzarella cheese

1

2

Baked Cannelloni with Grilled Vegetables and Mozzarella

1. Rinse the eggplant and zucchini and cut them in ½-inch (1-cm) slices. Add salt and grill both sides for about 3 minutes on a nonstick grill pan. Then remove them and dice into small pieces. Seed the red and green peppers and dice them.

2. Add the diced vegetables, the egg, grated Gruyère, the white breadcrumbs, and 3 tbsp olive oil to a bowl. Cut the basil into thin ribbons and add half of it to the bowl. Mix everything and season with salt and pepper to taste. In a large pot, bring water to a boil, add salt and cook the lasagna sheets until tender. Remove them and cool them in cold water.

3. Cut the lasagna sheets into squares, divide the filling among them, and, using a knife, lift them up and carefully roll them, jelly-roll style. After greasing a casserole dish with butter, lay the finished rolls next to each other.

4. Combine the Béchamel sauce (see p. 156) with the cream and pour over the cannelloni. Slice the mozzarella and distribute it over the cannelloni. Finally, season with pepper and a drizzle of olive oil, and bake in an oven preheated to 400°F (200°C/Gas Mark 6) for about 20 minutes. Remove it from the oven, sprinkle the remaining basil over it, and serve in the casserole dish.

■ **You can also buy ready-made dry lasagna sheets. When using fresh pasta dough, the lasagna sheets do not need to be precooked. Cannelloni can also be made with other fillings, such as with spinach and ricotta, veal, salmon, or mushrooms.**

3

4

 3 tbsp vegetable oil

 3½ oz (100 g) bacon, cut in strips

 1 lb 5 oz (600 g) boiled spaetzle (see p. 192)

 ½ tsp salt
1 pinch of black pepper

 2 onions

 1¾ cups (200 g) grated cheddar cheese

Cheese Spaetzle with Bacon Strips and Sautéed Onion

1. Heat 2 tbsp vegetable oil in a pan and add the bacon, frying until crisp. Add the spaetzle (see p. 192) and season with salt and black pepper. Fry it lightly for about 10 minutes, tossing frequently.

2. Peel the onions, and cut them in half and then in thin slices. In a second pan, fry them in 1 tbsp vegetable oil until they are light brown and crisp. Blot the onions on paper towels and lightly salt them.

3. Add the grated cheese to the spaetzle and mix well until the cheese has melted.

Plate and garnish with sautéed onions. Serve with a green salad or simply with a favorite beer.

■ For a baked variation, alternate layers of the spaetzle and the cheese, in a casserole dish then pour in ⅞ cup (200 ml) chicken broth and put it in the oven, preheated to 375°F (190°C/Gas Mark 5), baking for 15 minutes. When following this step, put the bacon and onions on top of the spaetzle shortly before serving.

2

3

7 oz (200 g) shrimp

1-inch (2.5-cm) piece of fresh ginger

½ cup (60 g) peas

2 eggs

15 wonton wrappers

1 leek

6⅔ cups (1.5 liters) vegetable stock

2¼ oz (60 g) bean sprouts

2 sprigs fresh cilantro

1

Shrimp Wontons in Vegetable Broth

1. Peel the shrimp and remove the vein. Peel the ginger, and cut it into thin strips. Put the peas (use cooked frozen peas, if necessary), peeled shrimp, and ginger strips in a food processor. Separate the eggs. Add 1 egg white and mix. Then put the mixture in a bowl.

2. Lay out the wonton wrappers on a countertop or cutting board. Put 1 tsp of the pureed shrimp mixture in the middle of each wrapper.

3. Brush the edges of the wonton wrappers with the remaining egg white. Fold the wonton wrappers into triangle.

4. Cut the leek into strips (see p. 350). Bring the vegetable stock to a boil, and add the leeks and bean sprouts. Then add the wontons to the vegetable broth and let them simmer for 1 to 2 minutes. Serve in deep soup bowls and garnish with cilantro leaves.

■ **Shrimp wontons can also be fried in oil instead of boiling them in vegetable broth. You can also use prepeeled shrimp. Serve the fried wontons on a mixed salad with soy dressing.**

2

3

4

 2 limes

 1 red chili pepper

 2 tbsp soy sauce

 2 tbsp jaggery (or brown sugar)

 1 lb 2 oz (500 g) beef tenderloin

 2 sprigs fresh cilantro

 9 oz (250 g) Chinese egg noodles

 6 tbsp vegetable oil

 2 star anise

 4 tbsp hoisin sauce

Fried Noodles with Spicy Beef

1. Juice the limes and add the limes and juice to a bowl. Cut the chili pepper into thin rings and add them to the limes, along with the soy sauce and 1 tbsp jaggery, mixing well together.

2. Using a sharp knife, cut the beef tenderloin into thin strips. In a pot, bring water to a boil and add the beef strips. After 5 seconds, remove them. The water does not need seasoning, because the lime-chili marinade will deliver the flavor.

3. Rinse the cilantro and chop it finely, including the stems. Add the cilantro and beef strips to the lime-chili marinade and mix together.

4. Cook the egg noodles (see p. 190) and rinse in cold water. Heat the vegetable oil in a tall wok, crush the star anise with the back of a knife, and add it along with 1 tbsp of the jaggery.

5. Stir the hoisin sauce with ½ cup (125 ml) water in a glass. Add the boiled egg noodles to the wok, stir, and pour the sauce over it. Continue cooking slowly for about 3 minutes, until the noodles have soaked up the liquid. Then serve on plates, putting the marinated beef strips in the middle.

■ **The beef strips can also be cooked in beef broth. Then you can serve the dish as a soup with fresh Asian herbs and soy sprouts.**

3

4

5

 9 oz (250 g) broccoli

 1 green bell pepper

 1 garlic clove

 9 oz (250 g) rice noodles

 2 large green chili peppers

 5 tbsp vegetable oil

 2 tbsp Thai fish sauce

 2 tbsp soy sauce

 1 tbsp sugar

 2 eggs

 1 tbsp toasted sesame seeds

Rice Noodles with Broccoli and Green Chili Peppers

1. Rinse the broccoli and cut off the florets. Rinse the green bell pepper, seed, and cut into thin, 2-inch (5-cm) long strips. Peel the garlic and chop finely.

2. Boil the rice noodles (see p. 191), shock them under cold water, and drain. Cut the chili peppers into thin rings.

3. Heat a large wok. Add 3 tbsp vegetable oil and fry the broccoli florets for about 5 minutes. Stir frequently and add the Thai fish sauce. Then remove them and set aside.

4. Add the remaining vegetable oil to the wok and fry first the garlic, then the rice noodles and finally the bell pepper strips. Add soy sauce and sprinkle sugar over everything.

5. Add the fried broccoli florets back, mixing everything together. Put the eggs in a bowl, and whisk them. Let the eggs run onto the sides of the wok and stir in. Finish by mixing in the chili pepper rings. Put in bowls and sprinkle with sesame seeds before serving.

■ **Fresh herbs complement this dish as well, such as chives, Thai basil, cilantro, or fresh bean sprouts. Just sprinkle over the finished dish and serve.**

3

4

5

2 squid

9 oz (250 g) cherry tomatoes

1 garlic clove

1 white onion

5 tbsp extra virgin olive oil

1 pinch of salt
1 pinch of black pepper

1 lb 2 oz (500 g) fresh black tagliatelle

½ bunch fresh basil

Black Tagliatelli with Squid

1. Wash the squid, clean them, and let them dry. Cut the bodies into strips, leaving the heads whole.

2. Set a pot of water on the stove and bring it to a boil. Add the cherry tomatoes for 5 seconds and immediately use a skimmer to lift them into ice cold water. Cut into the tomato skins with a small knife and pull them off. Peel the garlic and the onion, and dice them both finely.

3. Heat 2 tbsp olive oil in a nonstick pan and sear the squid. Then add the onion and the garlic and continue frying. Now add the peeled cherry tomatoes and season with salt and freshly ground pepper. Bring a pot of salted water to a boil and cook the black tagliatelle for about 2 minutes.

4. Remove the basil leaves from the stems, rinse, and keep a few leaves for a garnish, cutting the rest into thin ribbons. Drain the black tagliatelle and add it to the pan. Then add the basil strips and the remaining olive oil. Toss everything together, divide onto 4 plates, and garnish with basil leaves.

■ **Multihued cherry tomatoes make this a colorful dish.**

3

4

2 tbsp oil

1 tbsp butter

2¾ oz (80 g) chopped walnuts

Chopped garlic to taste

3½ oz (100 g) fresh spinach

⅞ cup (200 ml) cream

1 pinch of salt
1 pinch of black pepper

1 pinch of freshly grated nutmeg

14 oz (400 g) tagliatelle

4½ oz (120 g) Gorgonzola cheese

Tagliatelle in Walnut Gorgonzola Sauce

1. Put the oil and butter into a pan and sweat the chopped walnuts and the garlic.

2. Rinse the spinach leaves, removing the stems, add them to the pan and sweat briefly.

3. Pour in the cream, stir it in and simmer. Season with salt, pepper, and freshly grated nutmeg to taste.

4. Cook the tagliatelle in salted water before adding it to the pan, then mix well with the sauce.

5. Before serving, sprinkle diced Gorgonzola cheese over it, letting it melt slightly, then serve immediately.

■ **To make it milder, substitute mascarpone cheese for half the Gorgonzola cheese. This makes the tagliatelle taste especially creamy.**

3

4

5

 10½ oz (300 g) cooked egg noodles

 5 tbsp vegetable oil

 6 dried chili peppers

 2 carrots

 7 oz (200 g) broccoli

 2 skinless chicken breasts

 2 tbsp black bean paste

 3½ oz (100 g) bean sprouts

Shanghai-Style Fried Egg Noodles with Chicken

1. Boil the egg noodles (see p. 190). Heat the vegetable oil in a wok and lightly brown the dried chili peppers. This takes a little of the heat out of them.

2. Cut the peeled carrots in half and slice them on a diagonal. Cut the broccoli into florets. Add the carrots and broccoli florets to the wok and fry for 3 minutes. Turn them frequently.

3. Cut the chicken breast into thin strips and add it to the wok. Add the bean paste, mix, and continue stirring.

4. Finally, add the cooked egg noodles and bean sprouts to the wok, stir, and continue frying.

Divide onto plates and serve immediately.

■ **Other vegetables that go well with this dish are green asparagus, bell peppers, and Chinese cabbage.**

10½ oz (300 g) cooked rice noodles

1 tbsp vegetable oil

1 tsp red curry paste

2 tbsp soy sauce

1¾ cups (400 ml) coconut milk

3½ oz (100 g) cherry tomatoes

½ bunch fresh cilantro

Rice Noodles in Red Curry Sauce with Cilantro

1. Boil the rice noodles (see p. 191). Heat the vegetable oil in a pan and lightly toast the curry paste until it melts.

2. Add the soy sauce and let it cook off.

3. Pour in 3 tbsp (50 ml) coconut milk and simmer a few minutes.

4. Pour in the remaining coconut milk. Add the cherry tomatoes whole and simmer another 5 minutes.

5. Heat the cooked rice noodles in the pan and add the coarsely chopped cilantro.

Serve in soup bowls.

■ You can also try this dish with yellow or green curry sauces (see p. 146) and add baby corn, snow peas, water chestnuts, or bamboo shoots.

3

4

5

 1 lb 2 oz (500 g) strawberries

 10 mint leaves

 ½ tsp green peppercorns

 3 tbsp confectioners' sugar

 2⅔ cups (600 ml) mineral water

 4½ cups (1 liter) vegetable oil

 9 oz (250 g) glass noodles

Fried Glass Noodles in Strawberry Gazpacho

1. Cut the stems off the strawberries and rinse them briefly. Then cut them in half. Add mint leaves, picked from the stems, as well as the green peppercorns.

2. Sweeten with 2 tbsp of the confectioners' sugar.

3. Pour in the cold mineral water and mix, then puree everything in a food processor set on high speed until smooth. Put it in a bowl and let it thoroughly chill in the refrigerator for about 1 hour. If desired, the strawberry gazpacho can be flavored with 4 tsp (20 ml) triple sec to taste.

4. Heat the oil to 325°F (160°C) in a small pot about 8 inches (20 cm) wide. Using scissors, cut the glass noodles into four parts, and fry them in the pot one batch at a time. The pot should be filled only about halfway with oil, because the glass noodles will increase their volume five times.

5. Frying them takes only a few seconds. Let the fried noodles drain on paper towels and sprinkle them with the remaining confectioners' sugar while still warm. Pour the strawberry gazpacho in deep, chilled bowls and add the glass noodles to the top. Serve immediately before the glass noodles absorb the liquid, losing their crispiness.

■ **Watermelon, flavored with a little vodka, can be used instead of strawberries.**

3

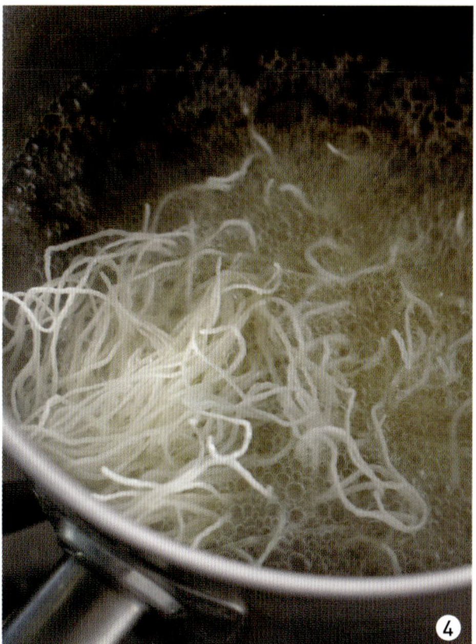
4

5

Rice

Contents

232 Types of Rice
234 Cooking Basmati or Aromatic Rice
235 Cooking Sushi Rice
236 Steaming Long-Grain and Partially Polished Brown Rice
238 Cooking Partially Polished Brown Rice
239 Cooking Long-Grain Rice
240 Boiled Rice with Turmeric
240 Boiled Rice with Spinach
240 Boiled Rice with Tomatoes
240 Boiled Rice with Herbs
240 Boiled Rice with Paprika
242 Nigiri Sushi
244 Spanish Paella
246 Parmesan Risotto
248 Tomato and Artichoke Risotto
250 Brown Rice Risotto with Kabocha Squash and Lime
252 Hungarian Paprikash with Corn
254 Biryani Rice with Lamb
256 Fried Rice Curry with Leeks
258 Fried Rice
260 Indian Curry Rice with Raisins and Cardamom
262 Mexican Brown Rice
264 Rice Pudding with Cinnamon

Types of Rice

Rice is an important staple food in Asia and other parts of the world. There are thousands of varieties, distinguished by color and the size of the grain.

1. Long-grain rice / aromatic rice

Is at least ¼ inch (6 mm) long. It remains granular after boiling. An indigestible casing, or husk, has been removed in a mill.

Aromatic rices include Indian basmati and jasmine rice.

2. Partially polished brown rice

Not entirely whole grains of rice. This brown rice is not completely polished, and therefore still has a sliver of protective skin and also contains more vitamins and micronutrients. It has to be cooked somewhat longer than traditional rice.

3. White rice

Loses a lot of nourishment through milling and polishing. It is buffed with a magnesium silicate or a glucose or talc powder to make it shine.

4. Brown parboiled rice

Processed the same way as white rice, only with the bran and germ retained.

5. Risotto rice

A white short-grain rice. This high-class rice can absorb a lot of liquid. This is why it is used in risottos.

6. Medium-grain rice

Is about ¼ inch (5–6 mm) long with a width of around 1⁄12 inch (1.5–2.5 mm). It remains granular after boiling, but sticks together when cooled.

7. Short-grain rice

Shorter than ¼ inch (5 mm), it usually remains sticky after boiling.

8. Wild rice

The actual grain is white, only the bran under the husk is black. It has to be boiled for 45 minutes. It is not actually rice, but an aquatic grass

9. Forbidden rice

The husk is removed but not the outer layer of the rice grain. It can contain green, unripe grains and is also called "black rice." It has a nutty flavor.

1
2
8
7
9
3
4
6
5

Cooking Basmati or Aromatic Rice

1. Put the rice in a sieve and rinse it well under cold running water; then let it drain.

2. For two servings, put 1 cup rice and 1½ cups water into a pot.

3. A few cardamom pods elevate the flavor of the rice and lend it an Asian note.

4. Bring the rice to a boil, stirring frequently, then cover the pot. Turn off the burner and let the rice soak for about 15 minutes.

5. Remove the rice with a wooden spoon and serve it with Asian or curry dishes (see Boiled Rice with Turmeric p. 240).

Cooking Sushi Rice

1. To make sushi, use a Japanese short-grain rice, which is unpolished and sticks together when cooked.

2. Rinse the rice well under cold running water and let it drain.

3. Put the rice and water, in a ratio of 1:2, in a pot and, while stirring frequently, bring it to a boil.

4. Boil the rice gently for about 15 minutes, stirring, so it doesn't stick to the bottom of the pot.

5. Put the rice in a bowl, spreading it around so it can cool faster. Depending on whether you want to make savory or sweet sushi, mix in mirin (rice wine) and vinegar, or ginger syrup and sugar, then let it cool down.

 1 cup long-grain or partially polished brown rice

 4 tsp butter

 1 bay leaf

 2 cloves

 1 small onion

 1 pinch of salt

1

2

Steaming Long-Grain and Partially Polished Brown Rice

1. Put the rice in the butter and lightly cook.

2. Add a small onion studded with the bay leaf and the cloves and stir.

3. Pour in 1½ cups water and stir to keep the rice from sticking.

4. Lightly salt the rice and stir.

5. Cover the pot with a lid and bring the temperature to the lowest setting. Steam the rice for about 15 minutes. Fluff the rice with a fork. Both types of rice go with poultry and fish, or can be used in salads.

■ **With rice, it is important to pay special attention to quality. The rice grains should be large, not broken at the ends, and should have uniform shape.**

3

4

5

Cooking Partially Polished Brown Rice

1. Heat 2 tbsp olive oil in a pot.

2. Add 1 cup partially polished brown rice and lightly cook.

3. Add 2½ cups water.

4. Salt lightly and stir to keep the rice from sticking to the bottom.

5. Cover with a lid, leaving in a spoon to create a gap, then boil the rice for about 20 minutes. Stir as necessary.

6. If the liquid has evaporated, the rice should be done. This rice goes with dishes that have spicy sauces.

Cooking Long-Grain Rice

1. In a pot, bring plenty of water to a boil and add salt.

2. Add the long-grain rice to the water and stir. Add only 10½ oz (300 g) rice to 8 cups (2 liters) water.

3. Boil the rice over medium heat for about 15 minutes.

4. Pour the rice into a sieve.

5. Rinse the rice under cold running water and store it in a bowl for later use.

1. Boiled Rice with Turmeric

Put **1 tsp turmeric** and **1 tsp curry powder** in a pot with **2 tsp (10 g) melted butter**, stir, and season with **1 pinch of salt** and **1 pinch of freshly ground black pepper**. Mix in **14 oz (400 g) boiled rice** and heat.

■ **Serve the curry rice with Indian curries, vegetable dishes, or lamb stews.**

2. Boiled Rice with Spinach

Put **2 tbsp creamed spinach** (see p. 362) in a pot with **2 tsp (10 g) melted butter**, stir, and season with **1 pinch of salt** and **1 pinch of freshly ground black pepper**. Mix in **14 oz (400 g) boiled rice** and heat.

■ **Spinach rice goes well with practically every fish dish, but also with roasted fowl breast in a mushroom sauce, or with rabbit in a mustard cream sauce.**

3. Boiled Rice with Tomatoes

Add **1 tbsp tomato paste** and **3/8 cup (100 ml) tomato juice** to a pot with **2 tsp (10 g) melted butter**, stir and season with **1 pinch of salt** and **1 pinch of freshly ground black pepper**. Mix in **14 oz (400 g) boiled rice** and heat.

4. Boiled Rice with Herbs

Rinse **½ bunch chives** and **½ bunch parsley**, removing any damaged pieces and chopping finely. Melt **2 tsp (10 g) butter** in a pot, add **14 oz (400 g) boiled rice**, add the herbs, and stir. Season with **1 pinch of salt** and **1 pinch of freshly ground black pepper**, and heat.

■ **Serve the herb rice with chicken fricassee, sautéed fish, or other dishes with a lot of sauce.**

5. Boiled Rice with Paprika

Put **1 tbsp sweet paprika** in a pot with **2 tsp (10 g) melted butter**, stir, and season with **1 pinch of salt** and **1 pinch of freshly ground black pepper**. Mix in **14 oz (400 g) boiled rice** and heat.

■ **Paprika rice can be made with a finely diced bell pepper, sweated in butter. It goes well with roast beef, roast chicken, and Hungarian dishes.**

1
2
5
3
4

 10½ oz (300 g) sushi rice

 1⅔ cups (380 ml) water

 4 tbsp rice vinegar

 1 tbsp sugar

 1 pinch of salt

 3½ oz (100 g) surimi

 1 cucumber

 4 nori sheets

 1 tsp wasabi

 4 tsp mayonnaise

 ½ cup (125 ml) soy sauce

 2 tbsp sliced pickled ginger

Nigiri Sushi

1. Soak the rice in cold water for 30 minutes. Then rinse it in a sieve and let it drain well. Put the rice and the water in a pot and, while stirring carefully, bring to a boil. Cover with a lid, turn off the burner, and let the rice cook with the residual heat for 15 minutes. Fill a wide bowl with the rice and pour in the rice vinegar.

2. Sprinkle with the sugar and salt and stir carefully using a wooden spatula, so the grains do not get damaged. Then let the rice cool.

3. Cut the surimi—imitation crabmeat from Japan made of pure fish meat—in half lengthwise. Peel the cucumber, cut off both ends, and cut into quarters. Then cut out the cores.

4. Lay a sheet of nori on a bamboo mat. Spread about 3 tbsp sushi rice over the bottom third, and add a layer of wasabi on top of it.

5. Then lay two surimi halves on top and spread 1 tsp mayonnaise along the surimi.

6. Cut the cucumber pieces to fit and add them.

7. Lift the nori leaves from the bottom end to wind the rice around the filling.

8. Using the bamboo mat, form a roll and squeeze it together lightly to keep it from unraveling later.

■ Use Nishiki rice, a rice of the best quality that is particularly white and flavorful. Nigiri sushi can also be made without nori, but then it should be rolled in sesame seeds or fish roe before cutting. This variety is called a California roll.

9. Cut each roll in six slices and put them on serving plates or on Japanese plates. Serve with soy sauce, wasabi, and a little bit of pickled ginger.

1 lb 10 oz (750 g) fresh pea pods

2 red bell peppers, diced

2 green bell peppers, diced

5 tbsp extra virgin olive oil

2 lb 4 oz (1 kg) short-grain rice

⅞ cup (200 ml) white wine

1 pinch of salt
1 pinch of pepper

1 dash of ground saffron

4 lb 8 oz (2 kg) fish and seafood

8 cups (2 liters) chicken stock

1

2

Spanish Paella

1. Using finger pressure on the center, open the pea pods and slide out the peas.

2. Heat the oil in a paella pan and sweat the diced peppers and the rice. Add the white wine and season with salt and pepper. Sprinkle with the ground saffron.

3. Add the cleaned and rinsed fish and seafood to the rice.

4. Pour in the stock, add the peas, and cook the paella for about 20 minutes. Serve from the paella pan on the table.

This paella is enough for 6–8 people.

■ **Use Spanish short-grain rice for best results. Italian short-grain rice could make the dish overly thick and become too rich. Other seafoods, shellfish, chicken, or rabbit meat can be used as supplements in paella.**

3

4

 1 shallot

 ½ garlic clove

 ⅓ cup (80 g) butter

 1 tbsp olive oil

 9 oz (250 g) Arborio rice

 1 pinch of salt
1 pinch of black pepper

 ⅔ cup (150 ml) white wine

 3⅓ cups (750 ml) chicken stock

 3¼ oz (90 g) Parmesan cheese

 1 tsp chopped parsley

 1 tbsp whipped cream

Parmesan Risotto

1. Peel the shallot and garlic, and dice finely. Cut ¼ cup (60 g) butter into thin slices and put it back in the refrigerator. Heat 4 tsp (20 g) butter and the olive oil in a nonstick chef's pan until it foams. Add the garlic and shallot and sweat them for about 1 minute, until translucent.

2. Add the Arborio rice, cook briefly, and add the white wine. Add salt and pepper to taste.

3. Let the white wine cook away, and stir the rice with a wooden spoon.

4. Add enough hot stock to keep the risotto rice covered in liquid. The risotto should now no longer be stirred with a wooden spoon, but should only be tossed, to achieve a creamier texture.

5. Cook the risotto for about 15 to 18 minutes, continually adding hot stock. Grate the Parmesan cheese, add the remaining butter from the refrigerator, and toss in the risotto. Finish by adding the parsley and whipped cream. Serve the risotto as a side dish, or as a main dish with Parmesan shavings.

■ **Making saffron risotto follows the basic risotto recipe, except that 12 (1 g) saffron threads are added to the sweating shallots and garlic. Saffron risotto is traditionally served with osso bucco. In this case, bone marrow can be substituted for olive oil.**

3
4
5

 1 oz (30 g) bacon

 9 oz (250 g) tomatoes

 1 garlic clove

 1 shallot

 6 medium artichoke hearts

 ⅓ cup (80 g) butter

 4 tbsp olive oil

 1 pinch of sugar

 1 pinch of salt
1 pinch of black pepper

 9 oz (250 g) Arborio rice

 3⅓ cups (750 ml) chicken stock

 2 sprigs fresh rosemary

 3¼ oz (90 g) grated Parmesan cheese

 1 sprig fresh flat-leaf parsley

1

2

Tomato and Artichoke Risotto

1. Cut the bacon into ½-inch (1-cm) strips. Peel the tomatoes (see p. 346) and cut them into ½-inch (1-cm) dice. Peel the garlic and chop finely. Peel and finely dice the shallot. Rinse and trim the artichoke hearts (see p. 356). Heat 4 tsp butter and 5 tsp olive oil in a nonstick chef's pan until it foams, add the shallot and garlic, and sweat them until translucent. Add the tomatoes, sugar, salt, and pepper, and slowly simmer for about 2 minutes. Add the Arborio rice and stir with a wooden spoon.

2. Add the hot stock until the rice is practically covered. The risotto should only be tossed from now on, not stirred (see Parmesan Risotto on p. 246). Simmer the risotto about 15 to 18 minutes, continuously adding hot broth.

3. Meanwhile, cut the artichoke hearts into sixths. Heat the remaining olive oil in a nonstick pan, add the artichokes, rosemary, salt, and pepper, and slowly sauté for about 5 minutes. Toss them back and forth.

4. Add the bacon, frying until crisp. Then remove the sprigs of rosemary and add the artichokes, along with the parsley, to the risotto. Add the Parmesan cheese and cold butter and toss. Serve on plates and garnish with parsley.

■ Mushroom risotto: clean 9 oz (250 g) mushrooms and, depending on the size, cut into quarters or sixths. Heat 2 tbsp vegetable oil in a nonstick pan, add the mushrooms and sauté until light brown for 5 minutes. Add salt and pepper. Peel ½ a garlic clove and chop finely. Rinse ½ bunch parsley, pick off the leaves, and chop finely. Add them to the garlic and mushrooms. Drizzle the juice from half a lemon, toss, and then toss into the Parmesan risotto.

3

4

 12 oz (350 g) kabocha squash

 ½ onion

 4 tbsp extra virgin olive oil

 1 tbsp butter

 4½ cups (1 liter) vegetable stock

 7 oz (200 g) partially polished brown rice

 1 lime

 1 pinch of salt
1 pinch of black pepper

 1 pinch of nutmeg

 1 cup (120 g) grated Parmesan cheese

Brown Rice Risotto with Kabocha Squash and Lime

1. Dice the squash and cut the onion into strips; then sweat them in the oil and butter.

2. Pour in some stock and let simmer.

3. Slice the lime, then add it and the rice to the pan and stir. Season with salt, pepper, and nutmeg.

4. Add some stock and let it cook off, stirring frequently. In the same way, keep adding stock a little at a time and let it cook off. Stop stirring now and begin only to toss the risotto.

5. The rice is done when it has a creamy consistency, but still has some bite to it. Stir in the grated Parmesan cheese.

Divide onto plates and serve.

■ Before making the risotto, wash the lime well with hot water so the risotto has no unpleasant bitter taste. Carrots and bell peppers can add to the kobacha squash flavor.

3

4

5

5½ oz (150 g) onion

14 oz (400 g) beef round

4 tbsp vegetable oil

1 dried pepper

1 pinch of salt
1 pinch of black pepper

3 tbsp sweet paprika

1 tbsp tomato paste

10½ oz (300 g) long-grain rice

5½ oz (150 g) corn kernels

Hungarian Paprikash with Corn

1. Peel the onion, cut it in half, and then thinly slice (see p. 349). First slice the meat, then cut it into strips. Heat the vegetable oil in a pot over medium heat; add the onions and sweat until translucent. Add the pepper whole.

2. Add the meat, salt, and pepper, sprinkle with paprika, and sauté lightly. Then push the meat aside, add the tomato paste, and sauté it lightly to reduce the acidity.

3. Add the long-grain rice, mix well, and sweat lightly.

4. Drain the corn in a sieve and add it to the rice. Add water, bring it to a boil, cover, and let it cook about 25 minutes over medium heat. Stir occasionally, adding more liquid as necessary.

5. The dish is finished when the rice has completely absorbed the liquids. Serve on plates and sprinkle with paprika.

■ **Beef stock can be used as a substitute for water, making the dish more flavorful. Red and yellow bell peppers, cut into strips, can also be added.**

3

4

5

2 lb 4 oz (1 kg) lamb shoulder

1 pinch of salt
1 pinch of black pepper

5 garlic cloves

12 oz (350 g) onions

¼ cup (50 ml) vegetable oil

2 cinnamon sticks

6 star anise

½ tsp curry powder

1 tsp ground cumin

2 tbsp tomato paste

1 lb 5 oz (600 g) canned peeled tomatoes

9 oz (250 g) basmati rice

12 saffron threads

1

2

Biryani Rice with Lamb

1. Cut the lamb into 1¼ x 1¼-inch (3 x 3-cm) pieces, and add salt and pepper. Peel the garlic and cut into thin slices. Peel the onions, cut them in half, and then cut thin slices (see p. 349). Heat the vegetable oil in a wide pot. Add the garlic, cinnamon sticks, star anise, and onions, sweating them for 5 minutes, until translucent. Season with salt.

2. Add the lamb, browning it, then sprinkle the lamb with the curry powder and ground cumin. Continue to brown lightly for 10 minutes, making sure the spices don't toast too long because they can get bitter.

3. After 5 minutes, shove the meat to the side and add the tomato paste to the pot, sautéing it briefly. Then add the peeled tomatoes along with the juice, bring to a boil, cover, and cook for about 40 minutes over medium heat. Steam the basmati rice (see p. 236).

4. Use a fork to test whether the lamb is done. Now remove the cinnamon sticks and the star anise from the lamb mixture and reserve them for decoration.

5. Let the saffron threads soak in 3 tbsp (50 ml) water and then cook off the liquid to half the volume. Spread the rice over the lamb, drizzle the saffron water over it, cover, and heat for 5 minutes.

■ **Sprinkle with freshly cut mint and serve with plain yogurt. Indian restaurants sometimes lay a few pieces of gold leaf on top of this dish.**

3

4

5

 1 lb 2 oz (500 g) long-grain rice

 7 oz (200 g) leeks, green parts only

 3 eggs

 3 tbsp soy sauce

 1 tsp curry powder

 3 tbsp vegetable oil

Fried Rice Curry with Leeks

1. Steam the long-grain rice (see p. 236). Cut the green parts of the leeks lengthwise into strips.

2. Beat the eggs in a bowl with the soy sauce and curry powder.

3. In a wok, heat 3 tbsp vegetable oil and fry the leeks in it.

4. Add the rice and fry it with the leeks. Push it to the sides and add the eggs to the middle.

5. Mix the eggs with the rice and let them coagulate.

Divide into bowls and sprinkle with a little curry powder.

■ This dish tastes even more authentic with steamed basmati or aromatic rice. Mix in other vegetables, such as spinach, bok choy, scallions, or carrot strips, and finely chopped meat or leftover chicken.

3

4

5

 9 oz (250 g) chicken legs

 1 bunch fresh cilantro

 3½ oz (100 g) green bell peppers

 3½ oz (100 g) red bell peppers

 2¾ oz (80 g) leek

 4 garlic cloves

 14 oz (400 g) long-grain rice

 5 tbsp vegetable oil

 1 tbsp sugar

 4 tbsp soy sauce

 2 tbsp brown rice vinegar

 3½ oz (100 g) peeled, boiled shrimp

 2 eggs

Fried Rice

1. Using a knife, remove the bones from the chicken and cut the meat, with the skin, into strips. Rinse the cilantro and chop it coarsely. Seed the peppers, rinse, and cut them in quarters. Cut the leek in thin strips lengthwise. Peel the garlic and cut into thin slices. Boil the long-grain rice (see p. 239). Heat the oil in a nonstick wok, add the chicken strips, and brown. As soon as the meat takes on a nice brown color, remove it from the wok, but leave the oil.

2. Add the garlic to the wok, sauté until golden, add the pepper, mix everything together, and let it sweat for 2 to 3 minutes.

3. Add the leek and chicken, season with the sugar, soy sauce, and rice vinegar, and mix well. Cook everything for 1 minute, stirring continuously.

4. Add the rice and the shrimp, and fry in the wok for 3 minutes.

5. Beat the eggs in a bowl and stir with a fork. Push the rice to the walls of the wok. Put the eggs in the space left in the middle of the wok and let them set like scrambled eggs, carefully stirring as they do. Combine the scrambled eggs with the rice mixture.

6. Add the cilantro and mix it in well with the rice. Finish by drizzling brown rice vinegar over the rice. Serve the finished dish on plates and garnish with more cilantro.

■ Basmati rice can be used instead of long-grain rice. Other good vegetables for this dish are bean sprouts, small broccoli florets, snow peas, baby corn, bok choy, and Chinese cabbage.

3

4

5

6

 ⅛ cup (30 g) butter

 10 green cardamom pods

 5 cloves

 ⅓ cup (50 g) raisins

 2½ oz (70 g) almonds, slivered

 1 cinnamon stick

 1 tsp curry

 ½ tsp turmeric

 9 oz (250 g) basmati rice

 1 pinch of salt

 2⅔ cups (600 ml) water

 about ¼ cup (50 ml) sunflower oil

 ⅜ cup (100 g) yogurt

 1 sprig fresh mint

Indian Curry Rice with Raisins and Cardamom

1. Let the butter foam in a pot over medium heat. Add the cardamom pods, cloves, raisins, slivered almonds, cinnamon, curry, and turmeric, and toast, stirring continuously.

2. After a minute, add the rinsed basmati rice and salt, then briefly sweat.

3. Add the water, bring to a boil, and cover; let simmer for 12 minutes over low heat.

4. In another pot, heat the sunflower oil over high heat and immediately pour it over the rice. The rice should hiss during this step. This gives it an intense nutty flavor. Finish by serving the rice in a bowl, and garnish with yogurt and mint leaves.

■ **This rice is outstanding with Indian curries, roasted lamb cutlets, or grilled fish steaks.**

2
3
4

 1¾ oz (50 g) almonds, skinned

 1 rabbit (1 lb 12 oz/ 800 g)

 1 pinch of salt
1 tsp coarsely ground black pepper

 4 tbsp vegetable oil

 4 spicy chorizo sausages

 4 tbsp black bean paste

 8 oz (220 g) long-grain rice

 3½ cups (800 ml) rabbit or chicken stock

 1 oz (30 g) bittersweet chocolate

Mexican Brown Rice

1. Put the almonds in a food processor and grind until fine. Cut the rabbit meat into pieces, add salt, and sprinkle with the coarsely ground black pepper. Heat the oil in a pot, add the meat, and brown all sides for about 5 minutes.

2. Cut the chorizo sausages in half and add them to the pot. Brown for another 5 minutes. Then sprinkle the almonds over the rabbit meat, mix everything together, and continue browning until the almonds are also golden brown.

3. Add the bean paste on top of the meat, and carefully turn the meat over. Continue cooking, making sure the almonds and bean paste don't brown too much.

4. Spread the long-grain rice evenly over the meat, adding rabbit or chicken stock.

5. Bring it to a boil, and over low heat, cover and let simmer about 25 minutes. Serve the finished rice on plates and sprinkle with coarsely chopped bittersweet chocolate.

■ **After the liquids have completely cooked away, let the rice sit on the stove briefly. The rice cooks a little further on the bottom, intensifying the flavor.**

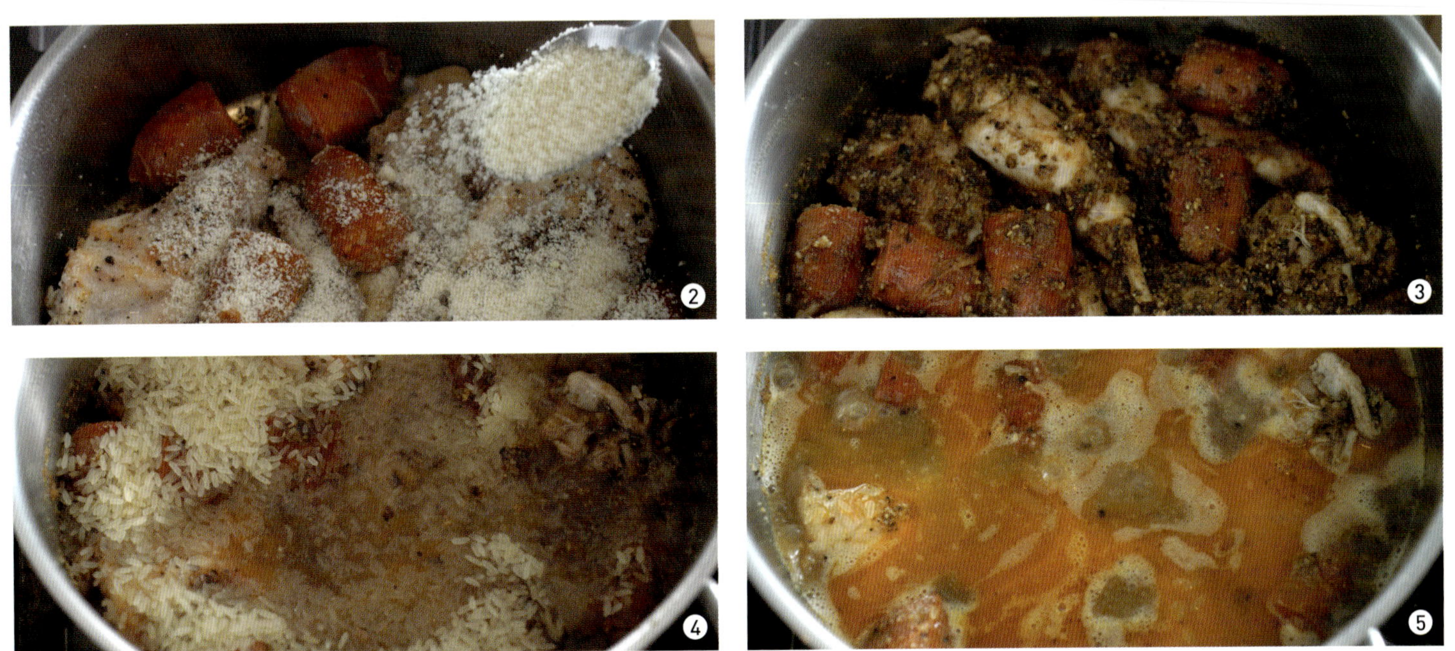
2
3
4
5

 1 orange

 1 lemon

 4½ cups (1 liter) milk

 4 tbsp sugar

 ½ cinnamon stick

 8 oz (220 g) short-grain white rice

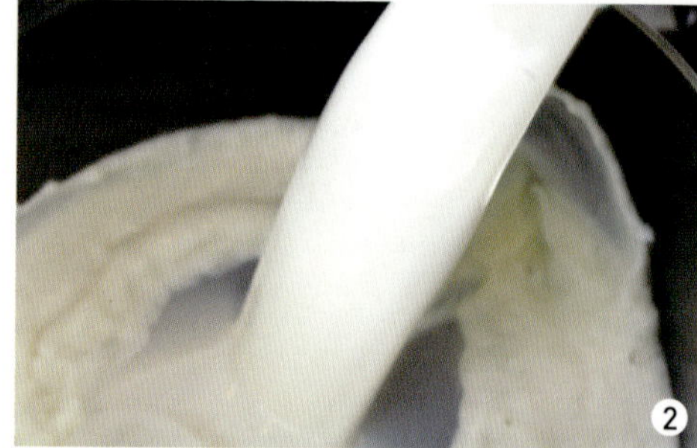

Rice Pudding with Cinnamon

1. Wash the citrus fruits. Using a vegetable peeler, peel 1 thin strip of rind each from the orange and lemon.

2. Pour the milk into a pot.

3. Pour in the sugar.

4. Add the cinnamon, as well as the orange and lemon zests, to the milk.

5. Pour in the rice and bring to a slow boil.

6. Stir the rice continuously to keep it from burning. Let it simmer gently for about 20 minutes.

Remove the lemon and orange peels and cinnamon stick, before serving.

■ Rice pudding tastes best when served warm, sprinkled with cinnamon sugar, with a few butter pats. Serving it with apricot or cherry compote makes an exciting dessert for kids.

4
5
6

Grains & Legumes

Contents

268 Grains & Legumes
268 Cooking Chart
270 Making Couscous
271 Making Bulgur
272 Cooking Green Lentils
273 Cooking Brown Lentils
274 Cooking Millet
275 Cooking Quinoa
276 Bulgur Mint Salad with Yogurt and Tomatoes
278 Couscous Salad on Guacamole and Tomatoes
280 Millet Patties with Cilantro and Orange Zest
282 Cooking White Beans
283 Cooking Pinto Beans
284 Tomato Bean Stew with Spicy Lamb Sausage
286 Mexican Chili with Chipotle Peppers
288 Pinto Bean Ragout with Roast Duck Breast
290 Indian Chickpea Curry with Cinnamon, Yogurt, and Mint
292 Vegetable Lentil Stew with Italian Sausage
294 Sour Vegetable and Lentil Stew
296 Cooking Cornmeal
298 Broiled Cornmeal with Tomatoes and Gorgonzola Cheese

Grains & Legumes

Grain and legumes are important staple foods in many parts of the world. In Europe and the United States, however, they have been pushed aside by corn and potatoes.

Cooking Chart

Product	Amount	Liquid Amount	Temperature	Time	Notes
Couscous	1 unit	2.4 units of liquid	Pour over boiling water	Let it absorb for 30 minutes	
Bulgur	1 unit	2 units of liquid	Pour over boiling water	Let it absorb for 1 hour	
Green Lentils	1 unit	4 units of water	Medium heat	6–8 minutes	Soak for 1 hour in cold water before cooking
Green Lentils	1 unit	5 units of water	Medium heat	15 minutes	No soaking
Brown Lentils	1 unit	4 units of water	Low heat	10 minutes	Rinse under water first
Long-Grain Rice	1 unit	4 units of water	Low heat	15–18 minutes	Boil
Millet	1 unit	2.5 units of water	Low heat	Let it absorb for 35 minutes	Cover and steam
Quinoa	1 unit	2.2 units of water	Low heat	20 minutes	Wash off with lukewarm water
White Beans	1 unit	3 units of water	Low heat	1 hour	Soak for 2 hours in cold water
Borlotti Beans	1 unit	3 units of water	Low heat	45 minutes	Soak for 2 hours in cold water
Partially Polished Brown Rice	1 unit	2.5 units of water	Low heat	20–25 minutes	Cover and steam
Azuki Beans	1 unit	3 units of water	Low heat	25–30 minutes	Soak for 1 hour in cold water
Chickpeas	1 unit	3 units of water	Medium heat	25–30 minutes	Soak for 2 hours in cold water
Cornmeal	1 unit	2.8 units of liquid	Boil	10 minutes	Firm cornmeal for grilling
Cornmeal	1 unit	3.5 units of liquid	Boil	30 minutes	Moist cornmeal, as a dish

Pinto beans

Green lentils

Brown or red lentils

Making Couscous

1. Pour **2⅔ cups (600 ml)** boiling **vegetable stock** over **9 oz (250 g) couscous**. Season with **salt** and **black pepper**.

2. Sprinkle with a few **saffron threads** and mix them into the couscous. Leave to soak for about 30 minutes. Stir frequently.

3. Finally, round it off with **2 tbsp olive oil** and **1 tsp butter** and serve warm as a side with beef or fish. Use cold for salads.

Making Bulgur

1. Bring **2¼ cups (500 ml) vegetable stock** and **3 tbsp olive oil** to a boil.

2. Put **9 oz (250 g) bulgur** in a bowl and pour hot vegetable stock over it.

3. Stir well and let soak for 1 to 2 hours, depending on how soft you want the bulgur.

4. Use the soaked bulgur for salads, as a side dish, or in fillings.

Cooking Green Lentils

1. The tablespoon on the left holds traditional green lentils, seen here with a light color, on the right are the smaller and darker brown lentils. They have a more aromatic flavor.

2. Stud an **onion** or a **shallot** by taking **1 bay leaf** and securing it to the onion or shallot using **2 cloves**.

3. Bring plenty of water to a boil and add salt. Add **1 carrot, 1 unpeeled garlic clove** cut in half, and the studded shallot, and sprinkle in **1 lb 2 oz (500 g) green lentils**.

4. Bring the water with the lentils back to a boil and cook for about 15 minutes. Cooking time depends on lentil size.

5. Lentils are done when they begin to split open on the edges.

6. Drain the lentils in a sieve and rinse briefly with cold water. Let them drain and use in salads, lentil patties, or soups.

Cooking Brown Lentils

1. Bring plenty of water to a boil and add salt. Rinse **1 lb 2 oz (500 g) brown lentils** in cold water and then add them to the boiling water.

2. Bring the water with the lentils back to a boil.

3. Now add **1 sprig rosemary** and **1 bay leaf** and cook the lentils for about 10 minutes.

4. Pour into a sieve and shock with cold water.

5. Store in the refrigerator until later use. Use the lentils for dishes such as salad, or serve as a vegetable lentil stew with fish.

Cooking Millet

1. Heat **2 tbsp vegetable oil** in a pot and sweat **9 oz (250 g) millet**.

2. Use **2⅞ cups (650 ml) water** in total. Now pour in a quarter of the water until the millet is just covered.

3. Let the water cook off almost completely. Repeat this step three times; then the millet is done. This takes about 35 minutes total.

4. Finish by stirring **1 tbsp butter** into the millet. Serve it as a side dish with hot meals, in salads, or use it in patties.

Cooking Quinoa

1. Quinoa is rich in magnesium, iron, and especially unsaturated fatty acids.

2. Rinse **9 oz (250 g) quinoa** under running water, add it to the pot without any fats, and toast until dry, stirring frequently.

3. Use **2⅔ cups (600 ml) water** in total. Add some cold water. The quinoa should be just covered.

4. Add **1 star anise** and simmer gently for about 20 minutes, stirring frequently.

5. Continue adding water again and again to let the quinoa soak.

6. Quinoa is finished when the grains are slightly translucent and a white dot is easily visible in the middle of each.

2 ripe tomatoes

1 white onion

½ bunch fresh mint leaves

1 tsp parsley, chopped

10½ oz (300 g) cooked bulgur (see p. 271)

Juice of 1 lemon

1 container of plain yogurt

1 pinch of salt
1 pinch of black pepper

4 tbsp olive oil

Bulgur Mint Salad with Yogurt and Tomatoes

1. Dice the tomatoes and the onion.

2. Add the tomatoes and onion, the mint cut in ribbons, and the parsley to the bulgur (see p. 271). Squeeze the juice of a lemon over it through a sieve.

3. Add the yogurt to the salad.

4. Add salt, pepper, and the olive oil.

5. Now carefully combine everything and let it marinate for 30 minutes for best results. Then serve, decorating it with mint leaves.

■ This recipe can also be made with couscous. Mix in fresh cucumbers and a few cooked chickpeas. Finally, season with a pinch of curry powder and some ground cumin. This variation can also be served as a side dish with Indian curries.

2
3
4
5

 3 ripe tomatoes

 1 onion

 ½ garlic clove

 2 avocados

 1 pinch of salt
1 pinch of white pepper

 1 lime

 3 tbsp oil

 1 tbsp vinegar

 ½ bunch fresh mint

 7 oz (200 g) cooked couscous (see p. 270)

 bowl of onion sprouts

Couscous Salad on Guacamole and Tomatoes

1. Rinse, pare, and finely dice the tomatoes. Peel and dice the onion. Peel and finely chop the garlic.

2. Use a spoon to remove the avocado from the shell.

3. Season the avocado with salt and pepper and drizzle the juice of a lime over it.

4. Using a fork, mash it together until uniform throughout.

5. Put the tomatoes, onions, and garlic in a bowl and dress with oil, vinegar, pepper, and salt. Mix in finely chopped mint leaves.

Put the tomato salad on plates, adding guacamole on top, and crown it with a couscous peak. Garnish with onion sprouts.

■ **Cut the avocados in half, separate the halves from each other with a slight twist, and remove the pit.**

2
3
4
5

 ½ bunch fresh cilantro

 1 orange

 10½ oz (300 g) cooked millet

 1 egg

 ½ cup (120 ml) cream

 2 tbsp breadcrumbs

 1 pinch of salt

 1 pinch of white pepper

 2 tbsp olive oil

Millet Patties with Cilantro and Orange Zest

1. Rinse the cilantro and chop coarsely. Using a vegetable peeler, peel off two strips from the orange and add the peel to boiling salted water for 1 minute. Rinse the strips and cut them into thin strips.

2. Combine the cooked millet (see p. 274), egg, cream, and breadcrumbs in a bowl.

3. Now add the orange peel and the cilantro. Season with salt and pepper to taste.

4. Carefully mix it together and, with moist hands, form small patties. Press them together well so they don't fall apart when frying.

5. In a pan with a little olive oil, fry them on both sides until golden brown.

Put on plates and serve with a green salad and orange slices.

■ **Couscous or quinoa can be used instead of millet. Grate the orange peel and add some fresh ginger to the mix. Then form the patties and fry as described above.**

2
3
4
5

Cooking White Beans

1. Soak **1 lb 2 oz (500 g) white beans** in a covered pot with water—for at least 2 hours, though overnight is best. Then drain the water.

2. In a pot, sweat **1 slice of bacon** and **1 pressed garlic clove** in some oil, then add the beans.

3. Sweat the beans a little, adding salt and pepper. Cover with **water** and simmer for about 1 hour, until cooked through.

Cooking Pinto Beans

1. Soak **1 lb 2 oz (500 g) pinto beans** in a covered pot with water—for at least 2 hours, though overnight is best. Then drain the water.

2. In a pot, heat some olive oil, **1 sprig rosemary**, and the drained beans. Sweat briefly, adding salt and pepper.

3. Pour **6⅔ cups (1.5 liters) water** or stock over the beans—stock makes them more flavorful. Simmer them gently for about 45 minutes, making sure the beans are always covered with water.

 10 spicy lamb sausages

 2 tbsp vegetable oil

 1 garlic clove

 2 onions

 2 sprigs fresh rosemary

 2 bay leaves

 10½ oz (300 g) white beans, soaked overnight

 1 tsp tomato paste

 14 oz (400 g) canned peeled tomatoes

 1 pinch of salt
1 pinch of black pepper

Tomato Bean Stew with Spicy Lamb Sausage

1. In a pot, brown the lamb sausages on all sides in the oil. Add the sliced garlic.

2. After the garlic is toasted, remove the sausages and set them aside. Peel and cut the onions in half, then slice and sweat them in the pot with the rosemary and bay leaves until translucent. Push them to the side of the pot.

3. Pour the beans into a sieve, drain well, then add them to the pot.

4. Add the canned tomatoes with their juices and crush them with a wooden spoon. Add salt and black pepper to taste.

5. Pour cold water over the beans until they are covered. Add the sausages back in, cover, and simmer gently for 1 hour. Stir frequently and add water as necessary to keep the beans slightly covered, so they can cook completely.

Fill plates with the bean stew, with the lamb sausages on top.

+ 12 hours soaking time

■ Stew 2 fried duck legs, 1 piece of bacon, and a few pieces of lamb with the beans and you have a wonderful cassoulet.

2

3

4

5

 1 lb 2 oz (500 g) black beans

 14 oz (400 g) canned peeled tomatoes

 7 oz (200 g) onions

 4 garlic cloves

 3 dried peppers

 4 tbsp vegetable oil

 1 tsp salt
1 pinch of black pepper

 2 tbsp brown sugar

 1 tbsp tomato paste

 2 chipotle peppers in adobo (marinade)

 4½ cups (1 liter) chicken stock

Mexican Chili with Chipotle Peppers

1. Soak the black beans in cold water for at least 2 hours. Chop the tomatoes finely. Peel the onions and dice them finely. Peel the garlic and chop finely. Remove the stems from the dried peppers and cut them into thin strips.

2. In a pot, heat the vegetable oil over medium heat and add the onions and garlic, sweating until translucent. Add the dried peppers, salt, pepper, and sugar, and sweat another 5 minutes.

3. Push the onions and peppers to the side of the pot, add the tomato paste to the free space, and toast to reduce the acidity.

4. Drain the beans and add them. Mix everything together and sauté it lightly for 5 minutes.

5. Add the whole chipotle peppers to the beans. If a milder chili is desired, serve the chipotle peppers separately. For an especially spicy chili, chop the chipotle peppers and mix them in.

6. Add the tomatoes, pour the chicken stock over everything, cover, and let simmer gently over medium heat for 1½ hours. Stir as necessary to keep the beans from burning on the bottom of the pot. Put the beans on plates and serve with fried eggs.

+ 2 hours of soaking time

■ It is best to soak the beans overnight—to keep their shape while cooking. This dish goes well with broiled meat, such as pork chops, spareribs, and fried chicken legs. In South America, it is served for breakfast with fried eggs and bacon.

2
3
4
5
6

 1 lb 2 oz (500 g) pinto beans

 2¾ oz (80 g) carrots

 2¾ oz (80 g) celeriac

 2 garlic cloves

 2¾ oz (80 g) onions

 2 tbsp olive oil

 4 sprigs fresh rosemary

 3 bay leaves

 1 tsp fennel seeds

 1 tbsp tomato paste

 ⅞ cup (200 ml) white wine

 1 pinch of salt
1 pinch of black pepper

 8 cups (2 liters) chicken stock

 2 duck breasts

Pinto Bean Ragout with Roast Duck Breast

1. Soak the beans for at least 2 hours. Peel the carrot and celeriac and cut into ¼-inch (5-mm) cubes. Crush the garlic cloves into a bowl, then peel and dice the onions. In a wide pot, heat 2 tbsp olive oil, add the onions, carrot, and celeriac, and sweat them slowly for 10 minutes.

2. Add the sprigs of rosemary, bay leaves, chopped fennel seeds, and crushed garlic, lightly toasting them.

3. Push the vegetables to one side of the pot. Add the tomato paste to the empty space and toast it, so it loses acidity. Add white wine, letting the liquid boil down. Drain the beans in a sieve.

4. Add the beans, toasting for another 2 minutes. Add salt and pepper, pour in the chicken stock, and let it simmer slowly for 50 minutes. Stir as necessary to keep the beans from burning and sticking to the bottom of the pot. Stir the beans carefully to avoid crushing them. Add water if necessary.

Cook the duck breasts (see p. 534). Cut the duck breasts into slices and arrange on top of the beans.

+ 2 hours soaking time

80

■ **Fennel seeds are easier to chop if you drizzle them with a little oil beforehand to keep them from jumping. The pinto bean ragout also goes well with sausages or stuffed pigs feet.**

2
3
4

 1 lb 2 oz (500 g) chickpeas

 8 oz (220 g) onions

 7 oz (200 g) eggplant

 3 garlic cloves

 7 oz (200 g) tomatoes

 5 tbsp sunflower oil

 1 tbsp anise seeds

 6 cardamom pods

 8 cloves

 1 cinnamon stick

 1 pinch of salt
1 pinch of black pepper

 1 tsp ground coriander

 1 tsp turmeric

 6⅔ cups (1.5 liters) water or vegetable stock

 ¾ cup (200 g) plain yogurt

 1 dash of cinnamon

 A few drops of lemon juice

 2 sprigs fresh mint

+ 2 hours soaking time

100

Indian Chickpea Curry with Cinnamon, Yogurt, and Mint

1. Soak the chickpeas in cold water for at least 2 hours. Peel the onions, cut them in half, and dice finely. Cut the eggplant into ¾-inch (2-cm) cubes. Peel the garlic and cut into thin strips. Skin and cut the tomatoes into quarters (see p. 347). Heat the oil in a pot over medium heat and add the garlic, sweating until golden brown. Add the anise seeds, cardamom pods, cloves, and cinnamon stick, and toast them together for a more intense flavor.

2. Add the onions, sweat until translucent, and push them to one side of the pot. Put the eggplant in the open space. Add salt and pepper to everything and fry for 5 minutes.

3. Sprinkle with the ground coriander and turmeric and sweat for 5 minutes until the onion and eggplant are slightly mushy. Pour the soaked chickpeas in a sieve to drain.

4. Add the chickpeas and briefly sweat everything together. Then add the quartered tomatoes and the water or vegetable broth.

5. The chickpeas should remain covered in liquid. Cover with a lid and simmer in the pot over medium heat for 70 minutes. Finish by mixing the yogurt with the cinnamon, lemon juice, and mint, cut into ribbons. Put the chickpeas on plates and serve the yogurt on the side.

■ **If possible, begin soaking the chickpeas the day before, or overnight. This makes them soften faster while cooking. This dish can also be served with roast beef or fried eggs.**

2
3
4
5

 1 lb 2 oz (500 g) small lentils

 2½ oz (75 g) carrots

 2½ oz (75 g) celery stalk

 1¾ oz (50 g) bacon

 3 oz (85 g) leeks

 2 shallots

 2 garlic cloves

 4 tsp (20 g) butter

 6 tbsp olive oil

 1 sprig fresh rosemary

 2 bay leaves

 1 pinch of salt
1 pinch of black pepper

 1 tbsp tomato paste

 2 cloves

 ⅞ cup (200 ml) red wine

 4½ cups (1 liter) chicken stock

 1 bunch fresh parsley

 2 tbsp medium-hot mustard

 ½ tsp lemon zest

 ½ tsp orange zest

 1 tsp balsamic vinegar

 8 Italian sausages

Vegetable Lentil Stew with Italian Sausage

1. Add the lentils to boiling salted water and bring it to a boil. Then shake them into a sieve, cool under cold running water, and drain.

2. Finely dice the carrot, celery, bacon, leeks, and shallots. Crush the garlic in its skin. Heat the butter and 4 tbsp oil in a pot over medium heat. Add the shallots and bacon and sweat for about 2 minutes. Add the celery, carrot, garlic, rosemary, bay leaves, salt, and pepper, and fry until translucent, about 5 minutes.

3. Push the vegetables to one side of the pot. Add the tomato paste to the empty space and toast it, so it loses acidity. Mix everything together and continue toasting briefly.

4. Add the drained lentils and the cloves and fry them for 2 to 3 minutes.

5. Add the red wine and cook until the liquid has evaporated, stirring frequently.

6. Add the chicken stock, making sure the lentils are covered in liquid.

■ **Lentils can also be seasoned with the following ingredients: fresh marjoram, freshly grated nutmeg, whipped cream, finely chopped anchovies, finely chopped capers, or pickle juice.**

7. Add a bunch of parsley tied with kitchen twine. Bring the lentils to a boil and let them simmer slowly for 20 minutes. Stir carefully while simmering.

8. Finish by seasoning with mustard, grated lemon and orange zests, and a splash of balsamic vinegar.

9. Heat the remaining oil in a nonstick pan over a medium heat and fry the sausages for 5 minutes on both sides. Plate the lentils, lay the sausages on top, and pour a little of the frying juices over everything.

 1 carrot

 2 celery stalks

 1 leek

 1 onion

 2 tbsp oil

 1 tbsp butter

 1 tbsp tomato paste

 9 oz (250 g) red lentils

 ⅔ cup (150 ml) white wine

 2¼ cups (500 ml) stock

  1 pinch of salt
1 pinch of black pepper

 ½ tsp dried marjoram

 2 tbsp vinegar

 2 tsp Dijon mustard

 2 sprigs fresh parsley, to garnish

Sour Vegetable and Lentil Stew

1. Rinse and trim the carrot, celery, and leek, and dice them finely. Peel the onion and dice it.

2. Sauté the vegetables in hot oil and butter, then add the tomato paste and stir.

3. Add the rinsed lentils to the vegetables and sauté.

4. Add the white wine to the vegetable lentil mixture and bring to a boil. Add the stock and simmer for about 20 minutes.

5. Finally, add salt and pepper to taste, and stir in the marjoram. Season with vinegar and mustard.

Serve sprinkled with parsley and celery leaves.

■ **This is an outstanding side dish with broiled fish or roasted whole squab, or serve it with just a few crispy strips of bacon. The lentils can also be rounded off with finely chopped anchovies, capers, pickles, or even a little whipped cream.**

2
3
4
5

Cooking Cornmeal

1. Put **1⅛ cups (250 ml) water** and **2¼ cups (500 ml) milk** in a pot and bring to a boil.

2. Add **1 tbsp butter**, **salt**, and a **pinch of nutmeg**.

3. Stir **6 oz (180 g) cornmeal** into the boiling liquid, then reduce the heat by half.

4. Continue cooking, stirring frequently.

5. After 30–45 minutes, the cornmeal will become thick. Stir vigorously to keep it from burning in the pot.

6. Put the cornmeal on a surface covered with parchment paper, scraping the pot well.

7. Spread the mixture to about ¾ inch (3 cm) thick.

8. Cover with parchment paper to keep the cornmeal from drying out, and let it cool down. Then the cornmeal can be cut into pieces for grilling or for using in oven-baked dishes.

6

7

 10½ oz (300 g) cooked cornmeal (see p. 296)

 3 tbsp olive oil

 10½ oz (300 g) Gorgonzola cheese

 10½ oz (300 g) small vine tomatoes

 1 pinch of salt
1 pinch of black pepper

 1 tsp fresh oregano

Broiled Cornmeal with Tomatoes and Gorgonzola Cheese

1. Cut the cornmeal into 6 x 3-inch (15 x 8-cm) rectangles. Brush both sides with olive oil.

2. Using a broiler pan, fry both sides of the cornmeal pieces.

3. Meanwhile, cut the Gorgonzola cheese into small pieces.

4. Cut the stems out of the vine tomatoes and depending on size, cut them into quarters. Put the cornmeal slices in a flat casserole dish greased with oil and cover them with the tomatoes and pieces of Gorgonzola cheese. Salt lightly and pepper vigorously.

Put it under the broiler for about 3–5 minutes. Serve with fresh oregano leaves.

■ **Broiled cornmeal tastes just as delicious with lightly sautéed spinach and with Gorgonzola cheese melted over the top. Another delicious combination is broiled eggplant with a thick tomato sauce and mozzarella. Lastly, garnish with basil.**

2

3

4

Potatoes

Contents

302 Potato Varieties
302 Cooking Chart
304 Potato Cuts
306 Cooking Gnocchi
307 Cooking Potatoes in their Skins
308 Cooking Sweet Potatoes
309 Caraway Potatoes
310 Deep-Fried Potatoes
312 Potatoes en Papillote with Fresh Herb Yogurt
314 Potatoes au Gratin
316 Potato Gnocchi
318 Potato Gnocchi with Cherry Tomatoes and Arugula
320 Baked Gnocchi in Tandoori Yogurt Sauce
322 Potato Finger Noodles with Sage and Salami
324 French Fries
326 Golden Potato Cake
326 Roasted Potatoes
326 Hash Browns
328 Sautéed Potatoes
330 Macaire Potatoes
332 Indian Saffron Potatoes in Coconut Milk
334 Sweet Potato Balls with Crisp Basmati Rice Coating
336 Homemade Mashed Potatoes
338 Swedish Potatoes with Chives

Potato Varieties

There are numerous varieties of potato available for every conceivable purpose—from French fries to soups, casseroles, and salads. Colors and shapes vary, but avoid potatoes that feel soft or that have been damaged by harvesting equipment. Their skins should be clean and smooth, and not too dry.

There are about 3,000 potato varieties in total worldwide, with just a few examples shown here. At least 100–150 varieties still reach our markets. They are classified according to when they are harvested. Potatoes must always be cooked before they are consumed and are very versatile. They can be boiled, mashed, steamed, baked, deep-fried, or even microwaved.

In the kitchen, it is important to make a further distinction because potatoes in the United States are divided into four groups—russet, long white, round red, and round white—and these are suitable for different cooking methods. Russets are floury potatoes that are very starchy. They have brown skin, a lot of eyes, and white flesh; these are best suited for mashing, baking, and frying. Although long white potatoes are similar in shape to the elliptical russets, their skin is gray-brown and has hard-to-see eyes. Long whites are suitable for baking, broiling, and frying. Round red and round white potatoes, also called boiling potatoes, are a medium size and waxy. These potatoes are firm but moist and are suitable for boiling, frying, and roasting.

Potatoes from the supermarket should be taken out of the plastic bag they come in. Otherwise, they will quickly become moldy and rotten. For best results, store potatoes in a wooden box or a basket in a cool, dark, dry environment.

Cooking Chart

Product	Form	Method	Temperature	Time	Notes
Potatoes	Whole	Saucepan	Boiling	20 minutes	
Potatoes	In quarters	Saucepan	Boiling	12–14 minutes	
Potatoes	French fries	Saucepan	Deep-fry at 350°F (180°C)	3 minutes	Precook or deep-fry in advance
Potatoes, raw	Sliced	Skillet	Low to medium heat	15–20 minutes	
Potatoes, cooked	Whole	Skillet	Medium heat	8–10 minutes	
Sweet potatoes	Whole	Saucepan	Medium heat	25 minutes	
Sweet potatoes	Sliced	Skillet	Medium heat	20 minutes	

Kennebec

Charlotte

Monalisa

BF 15

Bintje

Agria

Black asparges

King Edward

Red

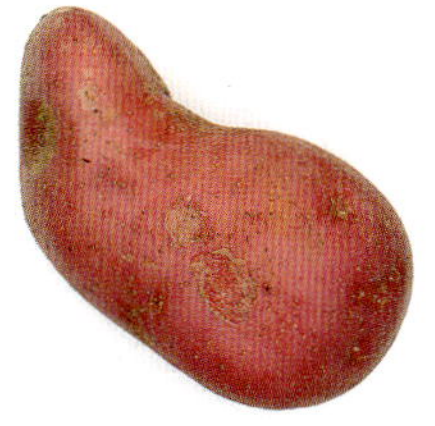

Roseval

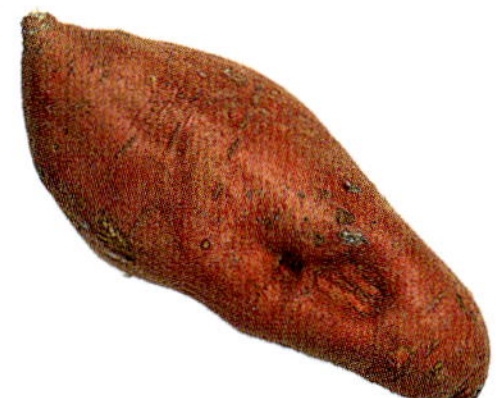

Sweet potato

Vitelotte

Potato Cuts

Thin potato disks are used for Potatoes au Gratin or Potatoes Boulangère. The latter are layered in an ovenproof dish like Potatoes au Gratin, sprinkled with gently sautéed onion slices, and covered with broth. They are cooked in the same way as Potatoes au Gratin.

Turned potatoes are potatoes that are cut (turned) into a specific shape. Thus, they are evenly sized and can be used for parsley potatoes or stewed potatoes.

Soufflé potatoes are 1/16-inch (1-mm) thick potato disks that are used to make chips. First, they are deep-fried in hot fat at a temperature of 275°F (140°C) and then once more at 350°F (180°C), so they rise like a soufflé. Soufflé potatoes go well with roast meat and poultry.

Potatoes à la Lyonnaise consist of approximately 1/8-inch (3-mm) thick disks and are prepared like fried potatoes. Thus, they are placed raw in a nonstick skillet, browned slowly and evenly on all sides, and finally mixed with diced onion.

For **diced potatoes**, cut potatoes into ½-inch (1-cm) cubes, briefly plunge them into boiling water, cool them by immersing them in cold water, and let them drain. Fry them in a skillet with a generous amount of oil until they are golden. Then, discard the oil, fry the cubes in butter, and season them with salt. They are delicious on corn salad or with steak, rose veal kidney, or liver.

French fries are approximately 2½ inches (6 cm) long and approximately ¼ inch (5 mm) thick. This is how the classic "fry" looks.

Matchstick potatoes—their name refers to their shape and size. They are prepared like French Fries and are nice when added to salads as a crisp ingredient. Formerly, matchstick potatoes were a classic accompaniment to Parisian pepper steak, but they are not easy to eat with a fork.

Straw potatoes are even finer than matchstick potatoes. Like French fries, they are cooked until golden and are mostly used to garnish large roasts or other pieces of meat. Try them also with carrots, celery, or leeks.

Pont Neuf potatoes are approximately 3¼ inches (8 cm) long and approximately ¾ inch (2 cm) thick. Cook them first in salted water for 2 minutes, then chill them in cold water and put them on a baking sheet. Brush them with melted butter and bake them for 20 minutes in the oven. Shortly before they are done, brush them with veal sauce. They can be served with roast meats, roast poultry, or T-bone steaks.

Parisian potatoes are small and round and shaped with a special scoop or potato baller. They can be used to make boiled potatoes or be sautéed until golden by constant tossing in a skillet.

The leftover potato can be used for soup or potato cakes.

Potato wedges are small or new potatoes that are not peeled, just washed well and cut lengthwise into sixths. Put them into a casserole dish, season them with salt and pepper, and drizzle them with olive oil. Bake them in the oven for approximately 20 minutes at 400°F (200°C), until they are golden. They can also be mixed with crushed garlic cloves and baked; this method will add a French touch to the potatoes. They are delicious with roast chicken.

Cooking Gnocchi

1. Add the potato gnocchi to simmering salted water.

2. Simmer gently for approximately 1 minute.

3. Stir them carefully with a skimmer and loosen any gnocchi that are sticking to the bottom of the saucepan.

4. Strain them carefully in a colander.

5. Rinse the gnocchi with cold water, until they are cold. Let them drain well and use them as you prefer.

Cooking Potatoes in their Skins

1. Wash starchy potatoes well and place them in a saucepan with an ample quantity of salted water.

2. Add 1 tsp of caraway seeds to the water and bring it to a boil.

3. Cook the potatoes for approximately 25 minutes, depending on their size.

4. Check for doneness by pricking the potatoes with a fork. You can also tell that they are done if their skins come off easily.

Cooking Sweet Potatoes

1. Wash the sweet potatoes and cover them with water in a saucepan. Add salt and 2–3 cloves and bring to a boil.

2. Let the sweet potatoes cook for approximately 30 minutes and check for doneness by pricking them with a fork.

3. Drain the sweet potatoes and let them rest in the pan for 10 more minutes to let the moisture evaporate.

4. Peel them carefully and remove brown spots with a knife. Cover them and set them aside to cool until they are needed.

Caraway Potatoes

1. Select **1 lb 12 oz (800 g) golden yellow-skinned potatoes**. Wash them well and clean off any dirt with a brush. Cut the potatoes in half and put them in a bowl. Combine with **1 tsp of salt, a pinch of black pepper, 1 tsp of caraway seeds,** and **3 tbsp of vegetable oil**.

2. Put the potatoes in a nonstick roasting pan and bake them in the oven at 350°F (180°C) for approximately 35 minutes, until golden. Turn them frequently so that they don't stick. Shortly before they are done, add **¾ oz (20 g) butter** and continue to roast them. Serve the caraway potatoes with roast pork or simply with buttermilk for a light evening meal.

■ **The most suitable varieties for this recipe are firm-fleshed potatoes.**

1 lb 2 oz (500 g) potatoes, boiled in their skins

8 cups (2 liters) vegetable oil for deep-frying

3 unpeeled garlic cloves

1 tsp salt

Deep-Fried Potatoes

1. Peel the boiled potatoes (see p. 307) and cut into ¾-inch (2-cm) pieces.

2. Add the oil to a large saucepan, heat it to 325°F (160°C), and deep-fry the unpeeled garlic.

3. Add the potato pieces to the hot oil and fry them for approximately 3 minutes, until they are golden. Lift the potatoes out with a skimmer.

4. Put them on paper towels to drain and sprinkle with salt. Arrange them on plates and serve them with a spicy tomato sauce (Salsa Brava) for dipping.

■ They are delicious as a snack with wine or beer.

3

4

 4 large potatoes

 1 tsp caraway seeds

 1 pinch of salt

 4 tsp (20 g) butter

 14 oz (400 g) Greek-style yogurt

 1 bunch mixed fresh herbs

 1 scallion

 1 pinch of black pepper

 3 tbsp olive oil

 Juice of ½ lemon

Potatoes en Papillote with Fresh Herb Yogurt

1. Wash the potatoes and cook them with the caraway seeds in salted water for 10 minutes. Then, drain the potatoes and let the moisture evaporate.

2. Cut a sheet of aluminum foil into pieces large enough to wrap around a potato, and use a brush to coat these with butter. Season them with salt, and sprinkle with some caraway seeds.

3. Preheat the oven to 400°F (200°C/ Gas Mark 6). Wrap each potato in foil and bake them for 50 minutes. Turn the potatoes occasionally.

4. In the meantime, mix the yogurt with the cleaned, finely chopped herbs, diced scallion, salt, black pepper, and olive oil. Season to taste with lemon juice. Open the aluminum-foil envelopes, cut halfway through the potatoes, and spoon the yogurt mixture on top.

■ **These potatoes are just as tasty when they are cooked on the grill instead of in the oven. In that case, however, turn them more often.**

2

3

4

1 cup (250 g) cream

1⅛ cups (250 ml) milk

1½ tsp salt
1 pinch of black pepper

1 pinch of nutmeg, freshly grated

2 garlic cloves

1 lb 14 oz (850 g) potatoes

2 tsp (10 g) butter

Potatoes au Gratin

1. Put the cream and milk in a saucepan to boil and season with salt, pepper, and freshly grated nutmeg. Add the unpeeled, crushed garlic cloves and let them steep for 10 minutes.Then, pass the mixture through a fine strainer.

2. Cut the potatoes into 1/16-inch (1-mm) slices or use a vegetable slicer or a mandoline. Butter a casserole dish.

3. Spread the potatoes in layers in the casserole dish and pour the cooked cream-milk mixture over them.

4. Dot the top evenly with butter.

5. Cover the dish with aluminum foil and use the tip of a knife to poke small holes in it. Bake the dish in a preheated convection oven at 375°F (190°C/Gas Mark 5) for approximately 20 minutes. Remove the aluminum foil for the last 10 minutes, so that the gratin cooks to a golden color. You can also use Gruyère cheese or Swiss cheese in this dish.

■ **For a potato-leek gratin, gently sauté 7 oz (200 g) leek strips (see p. 350) in ¾ oz (20 g) butter. Butter the casserole dish and put a layer of leeks on the bottom. Then follow the instructions for the Potatoes au Gratin.**

2
3
4
5

1 lb 12 oz (800 g) starchy potatoes

1 cup (150 g) cake flour

4½ oz (120 g) durum wheat semolina

1 egg

1 pinch of salt

1 pinch of nutmeg, freshly grated

1 tbsp oil

Potato Gnocchi

1. Cook the potatoes, let them cool down, and grate them finely.

2. Spread the grated potatoes out on a work surface. Sprinkle with the flour and semolina. Add the egg to the potatoes and season them with salt and freshly grated nutmeg.

3. Knead the potatoes with your hands to form a dough.

4. Divide the dough into 7-oz (200-g) pieces, dust with flour, and roll out into ½-inch (1-cm) thick logs. Cut the logs into ½-inch (1-cm) long pieces with a knife. Cook them in salted water (see p. 306) and let them cool in cold water. Drain them and drizzle a little oil on them. Store them in the refrigerator for future use.

■ **You can either lightly press on the gnocchi with the tines of a fork, or shape them into finger noodles by rolling them in your hands.**

2
3
4

 1 lb 2 oz (500 g) potato gnocchi

 7 oz (200 g) cherry tomatoes

 2 garlic cloves

 3 tbsp olive oil

 1 pinch of salt
1 pinch of black pepper

 1 pinch of sugar

 ½ bunch arugula

Potato Gnocchi with Cherry Tomatoes and Arugula

1. Cook the gnocchi in a large quantity of salted water (see p. 306). Halve the cherry tomatoes; peel the garlic and slice it thinly.

2. In a skillet, sauté the sliced garlic in the olive oil.

3. Add the cherry tomatoes, and sprinkle them with salt, pepper, and a little sugar. Toss them in the skillet for 2–3 minutes, until they soften slightly.

4. Add the cooked potato gnocchi and mix them with the tomatoes.

5. Add the clean, washed arugula to the gnocchi.

6. Toss the mixture in the skillet, until the arugula is slightly wilted.

Arrange it on plates and serve immediately. Garnish the dish with some fresh arugula leaves.

■ **This is also delicious if you use yellow cherry tomatoes or sliced large tomatoes. Mix them with fresh basil or baby spinach.**

4

5

6

 14 oz (400 g) potato gnocchi

 1½ cups (350 g) plain low-fat yogurt

 2 tsp tandoori seasoning

 Juice of ½ lemon

 1 pinch of salt
1 pinch of black pepper

 1⅛ cups (250 ml) milk

 1 tbsp butter

 3½ oz (100 g) drained, crumbled feta cheese

 3 sprigs fresh cilantro, to garnish

1

2

Baked Gnocchi in Tandoori Yogurt Sauce

1. Cook the gnocchi (see p. 306). Put the yogurt into a tall container and sprinkle it with the tandoori seasoning.

2. Add the lemon juice to the yogurt.

3. Season with salt and freshly ground black pepper.

4. Pour in the milk and stir well with a fork.

5. Arrange the gnocchi in the bottom of a buttered casserole dish and cover them with the tandoori sauce.

6. Sprinkle them evenly with the feta cheese and put them into the preheated oven.

7. Bake for approximately 25 minutes at 350°F (180°C/Gas Mark 4). The gnocchi are done when the cheese has turned a light golden color.

Serve them in the casserole dish, garnished with the cilantro leaves.

■ **Curry or garam masala spices can also be used instead of tandoori seasoning.**

3
4
5
6
7

 14 oz (400 g) Gnocchi Dough

 1 pinch of salt

 1 tbsp butter

 ½ bunch sage

 3 ½ oz (100 g) spicy salami

 1 pinch of black pepper

Potato Finger Noodles with Sage and Salami

1. Make small finger noodles with the gnocchi dough (see p. 316) and boil them in salted water until they rise to the top; drain them.

2. Melt the butter in a skillet until it foams, and then add the plucked sage leaves.

3. Slice the salami, add it to the skillet, and sauté gently so that the flavor can develop.

4. Put the drained finger noodles into the skillet and stir them.

5. Continue sautéing for another 5 minutes, and season with salt and freshly ground black pepper.

Arrange them on plates and serve.

■ This dish can also be made with store-bought gnocchi. Sauerkraut and bacon can be added.

4

5

 3 lb 5 oz (1.5 kg) potatoes

 3⅛ quarts (3 liters) vegetable oil

 1 tsp salt

French Fries

1. Peel the potatoes and cut into large wedges. Remove the corners to even out the sides.

2. Cut the wedges into ½-inch (1-cm) thick strips and wash them thoroughly in cold water to remove the starch. This will make the French fries nice and crisp.

3. Dry the potato strips with a kitchen towel before deep-frying them. If the strips are damp, the oil will bubble and splash.

4. Prefry the French fries in vegetable oil at 275°F (140°C) for approximately 1 minute, without browning them.

5. Remove the prefried fries from the pan with a skimmer and let them cool on a baking sheet.

6. Fry the French fries for a second time at 350°F (180°C), until they are crisp and golden yellow.

7. Remove the French fries from the oil and let them drain on paper towels. Sprinkle them with salt and serve them on a plate as a side dish.

■ In Belgium and France, traditional French fries are still deep-fried in suet or horse fat, then dried in preheated fabric napkins and arranged on heated silver platters.

2
3
4
5
6
7

1. Golden Potato Cake

Peel **1 lb 12 oz (800 g) starchy potatoes**, grate coarsely into a bowl, and season with **a pinch of salt** and **a pinch of freshly ground black pepper**. Then, use your hands to squeeze the excess water out of the potato mass. Heat **2 tbsp vegetable oil** in a nonstick skillet. Add the potato mixture and fry for approximately 10 minutes, stirring occasionally. Flatten the potato mass and form it into a pancake. Add another **2 tsp vegetable oil** to the edge of the skillet and cook it for 10 minutes longer. Transfer the potato cake onto a plate and with the browned side facing upward, slide it back into the skillet. Fry it for another 10 minutes, until it is golden brown. Turn it out onto a plate, cut it like you would a cake, and arrange the slices on plates.

■ **Serve it with roast duck, cold-cured salmon, or fresh steak tartare.**

2. Roasted Potatoes

Peel **1 lb 5 oz (600 g) waxy potatoes**, cut them in half lengthwise, then cut them into eighths and boil in salted water for 2 minutes. Crush **4 unpeeled garlic cloves**. Put the potatoes and the garlic into a casserole dish and season with **a pinch of salt** and **a pinch of freshly ground black pepper**. In an oven that has been preheated to 400°F (200°C/Gas Mark 6), roast them for approximately 20 minutes. Just 5 minutes before the end of cooking, pluck off the needles from a **sprig of rosemary** and add them. Do not add them any earlier, otherwise they will burn.

■ **Serve the dish of roasted potatoes as an accompaniment to cutlets, steaks, burgers, or buttered sole.**

3. Hash Browns

Peel **1 lb 2 oz (500 g) starchy potatoes**, add **½ garlic clove**, and finely grate the potatoes into a bowl. Add **1 egg** and **1 tbsp flour** and rub in **½ tsp dried marjoram** by hand. Season with **a pinch of salt** and **a pinch of freshly ground black pepper** and combine everything to form a dough. Heat **4 tsp vegetable oil** in a skillet. Use a small ladle to transfer the potato mixture to the skillet and to form it into small hash browns. Fry on each side for at least 3 minutes, until they are golden.

■ **Serve the hash browns with roast duck, cold-cured salmon, or fresh steak tartare. Variation: Omit the marjoram and garlic and serve them with applesauce.**

1
2
3

 1 lb 12 oz (800 g) potatoes in their skins

 2¼ oz (60 g) onion

 ½ bunch parsley

 3 tbsp vegetable oil

 1 pinch of salt
1 pinch of black pepper

 4 tsp (20 g) butter

Sautéed Potatoes

1. Cook the potatoes in their skins (see p. 307), peel them with a knife and slice them into ¼-inch (5-mm) thick disks. Peel the onion and dice it finely. Wash the parsley, pluck the leaves, and chop them finely.

2. Heat the oil in a nonstick skillet and add the potato disks.

3. Season with salt and pepper. Fry them at medium heat for approximately 10 minutes, tossing frequently and being careful to keep the potatoes as intact as possible.

4. As soon as the potato disks are golden brown and crisp, add the butter and continue to cook them. This will help bring out their flavor.

5. Add the diced onion and cook for another minute, tossing frequently.

6. Add the finely chopped parsley, toss once more thoroughly, and serve immediately. These potatoes go well with cutlets, or alongside creamed spinach with a fried egg. They are also delicious if you top them with sharp cheese and bake them in the oven.

■ **Sautéed potatoes are even tastier if they are cooked in goose fat and seasoned with caraway seeds, bacon strips, or chives.**

2
3
4
5
6

 1 lb 10 oz (750 g) starchy potatoes

 1 bunch chives

 1 egg

 1 tbsp crème fraîche (or sour cream)

 1 pinch of nutmeg, freshly grated

 4 tsp (20 g) butter

 1 pinch of salt

 5 tbsp cornstarch

 ⅓ cup (40 g) all-purpose flour

 1 tbsp vegetable oil

Macaire Potatoes

1. Peel the potatoes, cook them for 20 minutes in salted water, and then press them through a potato ricer. Wash the chives, remove any wilted leaves or stems, and chop the rest finely with a sharp knife.

2. Form a little well in the center of the potatoes. Separate the egg and put the egg yolk, along with the crème fraîche, grated nutmeg, chives, butter, salt, and cornstarch, into the well.

3. Mix with your hands, and shape the mixture into an elongated roll. As you work, dust the roll with flour so it doesn't stick to your hands.

4. Use a floured knife to slice the dough into ½-inch (1.5-cm) thick disks.

5. Toss the disks in flour and shape them into evenly sized cakes.

6. Use paper towels to oil a nonstick skillet, then brown the potato cakes for approximately 3 minutes on each side.

■ **Crisp roasted cubes of ham can be added to the potato mixture. Macaire potatoes go well with roast saddle of venison, haunch of venison, or veal medallions with cream sauce.**

2
3
4
5
6

1 garlic clove

1 lb 5 oz (600 g) waxy potatoes

1-inch (2.5-cm) piece of fresh ginger

3 tbsp vegetable oil

1 tsp fennel seeds

½ tsp turmeric

1 pinch of nutmeg, freshly grated

1 pinch of salt

20 saffron threads

1¾ cups (400 ml) coconut milk

1 sprig fresh mint

Indian Saffron Potatoes in Coconut Milk

1. Peel the garlic and chop it finely. Peel the potatoes, cut them into 1¼-inch (3-cm) cubes, and set them aside in cold water, so they don't turn brown. Peel the ginger and cut it into fine julienne strips. Heat the vegetable oil in a tall saucepan, add the garlic, ginger, turmeric, and fennel seeds, and sauté gently for a short time.

2. Add the potato cubes, season them with nutmeg and salt, and sauté them gently for approximately 1 minute.

3. Then, add the saffron threads and sauté briefly.

4. Pour in the coconut milk, cover the pan, and let the mixture simmer slowly for approximately 20 minutes. Stir occasionally, adding some water, if necessary, so the potatoes don't stick to the pan. Finally, arrange the potatoes in a bowl and sprinkle them with mint leaves.

■ You can also use garam masala, the Indian spice mixture, instead of the various spices listed. Garam masala incorporates many flavors and is easy to use. Or, replace half the potatoes with cooked garbanzo beans. Sprinkle with fresh scallions.

2
3
4

1 lb 2 oz (500 g) sweet potatoes

3½ oz (100 g) cooked basmati rice

1 egg yolk

2 tbsp flour

½ tsp cumin seeds

½ bunch cilantro

1 pinch of salt
1 pinch of black pepper

4 tbsp breadcrumbs

4½ cups (1 liter) vegetable oil for deep-frying

1

Sweet Potato Balls with Crisp Basmati Rice Coating

1. Cook the sweet potatoes (see p. 308), let the moisture evaporate, then grate them finely and put them in a bowl. Cook the basmati rice (see p. 234) and let it cool.

2. Add the egg yolk, flour, and cumin seeds to the sweet potatoes. Wash the cilantro, remove any withered leaves, and finely chop the remaining leaves and stems. Add the cilantro to the bowl and season the mixture with salt and pepper.

3. Add the breadcrumbs and work the mixture into a dough. Add more breadcrumbs, as needed, so that a uniform mixture is created.

4. Moisten your hands, and shape the dough into small balls.

5. Roll the balls in the cooked rice and deep-fry in the heated oil at 350°F (180°C), until they are crisp. Remove the balls with a slotted spoon and let them drain on a kitchen towel.

These sweet potato balls go well with chicken strips and vegetables.

■ **Serve the sweet potato balls as a snack with wine, accompanied by a spicy yogurt dip.**

2
3
4
5

2 lb 4 oz (1 kg) starchy potatoes

1 tbsp salt

⅔ cup (150 g) butter

1⅓ cups (300 ml) milk

1 pinch of nutmeg, freshly grated

Homemade Mashed Potatoes

1. Peel and halve the potatoes. Put them in a saucepan with salted water and bring them to a boil. Cook the potatoes for approximately 25 minutes, until they are completely soft.

2. Discard the water, and return the potatoes to the saucepan. Heat them on the stove for as long as it takes to boil away any remaining liquid and for the potatoes to become very starchy.

3. Mash the soft potatoes with a wooden spoon.

4. Work the potatoes with the wooden spoon until you have an almost glossy mass.

5. Add the sliced, cold butter, and work it in with the aid of the wooden spoon.

6. The butter must be fully absorbed by the mashed potatoes.

7. Heat the milk, and gradually stir it into the mash.

8. Finally, season with freshly grated nutmeg and salt.

9. It is important not to use a wire whisk, because this will make the mashed potatoes dense.

■ **Olive oil can be used, instead of butter, to smooth the mashed potatoes. However, in that case, be sure to use good-quality virgin olive oil.**

5
6
7
8
9

1 lb 2 oz (500 g) potatoes

1 bunch chives

1 tbsp vinegar

4½ cups (1 liter) Béchamel sauce (see p. 156)

Swedish Potatoes with Chives

1. Peel the potatoes with a vegetable peeler, cook whole for 25 minutes, and drain.

2. Wash the chives, shake them dry, and chop them finely with a knife.

3. Drizzle the vinegar onto the cooked potatoes.

4. Pour the hot Béchamel sauce (see p. 156) over the potatoes.

5. To finish, sprinkle them with chives and arrange them on a platter.

■ **For best results, use small, yellow-fleshed potatoes. Chervil or dill may be used instead of chives and mixed with the potatoes. Serve as an accompaniment to boiled fish or meatloaf.**

2
3
4
5

Vegetables

Contents

342 Vegetable Varieties
344 Vegetable Cuts
345 Cooking Chart
346 Peeling and Coring Tomatoes the Quick Way
347 Peeling and Coring Tomatoes the Proper Way
347 Seeding Tomatoes
348 Dicing Onions
348 Preparing Scallions with Green Tops
349 Avoiding Dull Knives When You Work with Onions
349 Cutting Onions into Strips
350 Preparing and Washing Leeks
350 Preparing and Washing Young Leeks
351 Swiss Chard—Separating the Leaves and the Stalks
351 Washing and Sorting Spinach
352 Cutting Pumpkin into Cubes
352 Preparing Zucchini for Stuffing
353 Preparing Carrots
353 Peeling and Seeding Cucumbers
354 String Beans
354 Celery Stalks
355 Preparing Fennel Bulbs
355 Cutting Fennel Bulbs Into Cubes or Strips
356 Preparing Artichoke Hearts
356 Marinating Raw Artichoke Hearts
357 Cooking Artichokes Whole
357 Frying Artichoke Hearts
358 Slicing Eggplants
359 Seeding Bell Peppers
359 Preparing Chili Peppers for Stuffing
360 Button Mushrooms
361 Oyster Mushrooms
361 Shitake Mushrooms
362 Steamed Spinach Leaves
364 Zucchini in a Thyme Batter with Yogurt Sauce
366 Stuffed Eggplant with Goat Cheese and Oregano Filling
368 Tomatoes au Gratin with Rosemary and Mozzarella
370 Peapods Stewed with Lettuce and Ham Strips
372 Fava Beans with Garlic and Onions
374 Vegetable Goulash
376 Fried Red Pine Mushrooms on Whole-Wheat Bread
378 Mushroom Ragout with Nutmeg and Parsley
380 Deep-Fried Beet-Ricotta Pockets
384 Pumpkin au Gratin with Fontina Cheese and Paprika
386 Fluffy Cauliflower Puree
388 Ayurvedic Cauliflower with Tomatoes and Cumin
390 Glazed Carrots
392 Vichy Carrots
394 Quiche Lorraine with Leeks
396 Boiled White Asparagus
396 Boiled Green Asparagus
396 Stir-Fried White Asparagus
398 Sauerkraut with Bacon
400 Ratatouille

Vegetable Varieties

Choose vegetables that appear plump and moist, free of discoloration and decay. Always buy them in season and from a local grower, if possible. Wash gently but thoroughly under running water, using a stiff-bristled brush to remove dirt.

Carrot

Leek

Fennel

Zucchini

Spinach

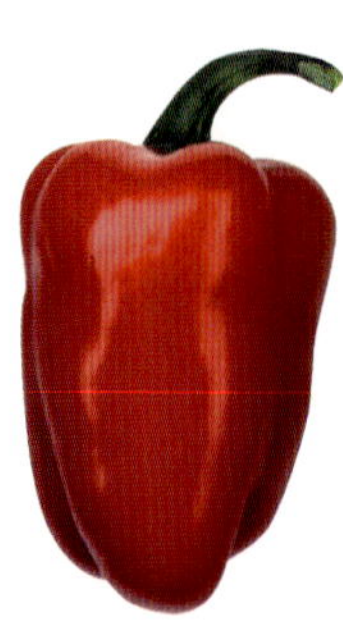

Bell pepper

Tomato

Artichoke

Eggplant

Peas

Fava beans or field beans

Green beans

Garlic

Broccoli

Cabbage

Asparagus

Cucumber

Button mushrooms

Morel

Chanterelles

Porcini

Vegetable Cuts

Bâtonnets: Broad strips, approximately ½ inch (1 cm) wide and 2 inch (5 cm) long, that are used as a garnish for sauces and also as an accompaniment to stewed fish dishes.

Julienne: Thin vegetable strips that are approximately 1/16 inch (1 mm) thick and 2–2¾ inches (5–7 cm) long, and are suitable for potato dishes, for stewing with fish, or as a garnish for soups and sauces.

Brunoise: Delicate 1/16-inch (1-mm) cubes that are used for salad dressings, as a garnish for fish sauces, for dishes with beans and lentils, and for stews. They can also be stewed with whole vegetables.

Small dice ¼-inch (5-mm) cubes that are suitable for soups and stews, and cook in approximately 15 minutes.

Medium dice ½-inch (1-cm) cubes that are suitable for quick-cooking sauces. Ratatouille ingredients can be diced in this manner, as well as vegetables for rustic soups and stews.

Large dice ¾–1¼-inch (2–3-cm) cubes that are braised with roasts and stews or gently fried and added to gravies.

Soup vegetables refers to vegetables that are just cut into quarters or thirds. They are added to soups or stocks that have to cook for a long time, and they don't cook down as fast as the other vegetable cuts.

Small mirepoix: Cut the vegetables into medium-sized pieces. Cut unpeeled garlic cloves in half. Use 2 parts of onions/shallots for 1 part of each of the remaining vegetables (celery, carrots, celeriac, or parsley root). Small mirepoix is used as an addition to shellfish and poultry sauces.

Large mirepoix: Peel the vegetables and cut them into coarse pieces or cubes, measuring approximately 1¼ inches (3 cm). Cut unpeeled garlic cloves in half. The same proportions of vegetables are used for both small and large mirepoix. The large mirepoix is used for meat sauces or vegetable broths, or in marinades for wild game.

Cooking Chart

Product	Form	Method	Temperature	Time
Artichokes	Whole	In water	Boiling	35 minutes
Artichokes	Slices	Skillet	Medium heat	8 minutes
Artichokes	Quarters	Skillet	Medium heat	12 minutes
Asparagus, green	Whole	In water	Boiling	6 minutes
Asparagus, green	Pieces	Skillet	Medium heat	5 minutes
Asparagus, white	Pieces	Skillet	Medium heat	8 minutes
Asparagus, white	Whole	In water	Boiling	10 minutes
Bell peppers	Bâtonnets	Skillet	Medium heat	10 minutes
Bell peppers	Small cubes	Skillet	Medium heat	3 minutes
Broccoli	Florets	Skillet	Medium heat	15 minutes
Broccoli	Whole	In water	Boiling	20 minutes
Button mushrooms	Slices	Skillet	High heat	4 minutes
Cabbage	Quarters	Oven	325°F (160°C/Gas Mark 3)	45 minutes
Cabbage	Shreds	Saucepan with lid	Medium heat	35 minutes
Cabbage	Shreds	Skillet	High heat	10 minutes
Carrots	Julienne strips	In water	Boiling	10 seconds
Carrots	Slices	Skillet	Medium heat	6 minutes
Carrots	Small cubes	In water	Boiling	5 seconds
Cauliflower	Whole	In water	Boiling	25 minutes
Cauliflower	Florets	Skillet	Medium heat	15 minutes
Chanterelles	Whole	Skillet	High heat	3 minutes
Cucumber	Slices	Skillet	Medium heat	6 minutes
Cucumber	Whole	Oven	325°F (160°C/Gas Mark 3)	20 minutes
Eggplant	Slices	Griddle	High heat	10 minutes
Eggplant	Large cubes	Skillet	Medium heat	8 minutes
Fava beans	Whole	In water	Boiling	2 minutes
Fennel	Whole	Oven	325°F (160°C/Gas Mark 3)	50 minutes
Fennel	Bâtonnets	Skillet	Medium heat	2 minutes
Fennel	Small cubes	Skillet	Medium heat	1 minute
Green beans	Whole	In water	Boiling	2 minutes
Leeks	Julienne strips	Skillet	Medium heat	1 minute
Leeks	Slices	Skillet	Medium heat	2 minutes
Leeks	In thirds or quarters	In water	Boiling	20 minutes
Morels	Whole	Skillet	Medium heat	6 minutes
Peas	Shelled	In water	Boiling	2 minutes
Peapods	Whole	Skillet	Medium heat	1 minute
Porcini	Slices	Skillet	High heat	5 minutes
Spinach	Whole	Skillet	Medium heat	5 minutes
Swiss chard	Leaf	Skillet	Medium heat	5 minutes
Swiss chard	Stalk	Skillet	Medium heat	8 minutes
Tomatoes	Whole	Oven	325°F (160°C/Gas Mark 3)	25 minutes
Tomatoes	Small cubes	Skillet	Medium heat	1 minute
Zucchini	Slices	Skillet	Medium heat	6 minutes
Zucchini	Julienne strips	In water	Boiling	10 seconds
Zucchini	Bâtonnets	In water	Boiling	15 seconds
Zucchini	Small cubes	Skillet	Medium heat	15 seconds

Peeling and Coring Tomatoes the Quick Way

1. Cut out the stem of the tomato with a sharp knife.

2. Cut the tomato in quarters.

3. Cut out the core with a knife and scrape out the remaining seeds.

4. Using a sharp knife, cut the flesh off the skins. While you are doing this, tilt the knife at a slight downward angle, so that all of the flesh is loosened from the skin.

5. Cut the tomato quarters into small cubes and use them for sauces, salads, or fillings. The tomato quarters can also be used to garnish fish fillets or can be stuffed with Greek-style yogurt mixed with herbs, or with olive paste.

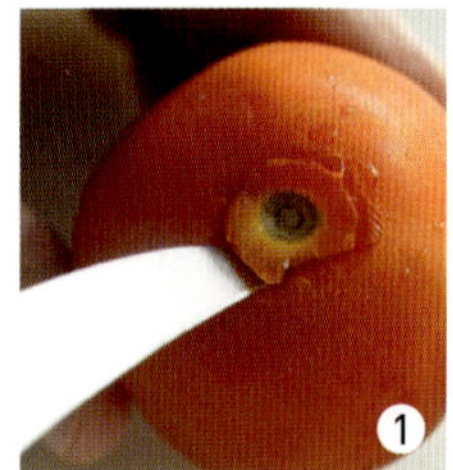

5

Peeling and Coring Tomatoes the Proper Way

1. Cut out the stem of the tomato with a sharp knife. Score the tomato skin crosswise. Bring water to a boil and place the tomatoes in it for 5–10 seconds.

2. As soon as the skin starts to loosen, remove the tomatoes from the water.

3. Put them into a bowl of ice water immediately to interrupt the cooking process.

4. Carefully remove the skin with a small knife.

5. Cut the tomatoes into quarters, cut out the core with a sharp knife, and use the flesh, as desired.

1

2

3

4

5

Seeding Tomatoes

1. Cut the seeds out of the tomatoes; they make salads or sauces watery. The tomato flesh can be cut into cubes or strips and used as a topping for bruschetta or pasta dishes, or for salads.

Use the seeds in sauces or soups.

1

Dicing Onions

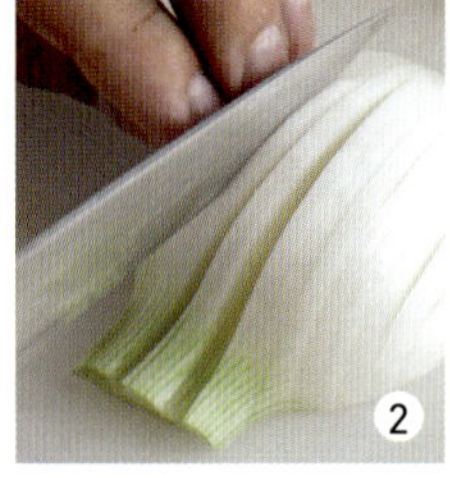
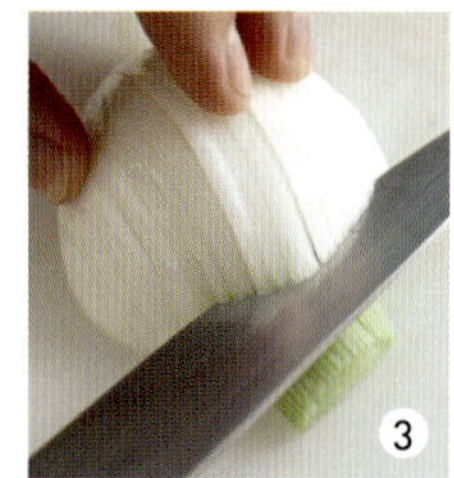

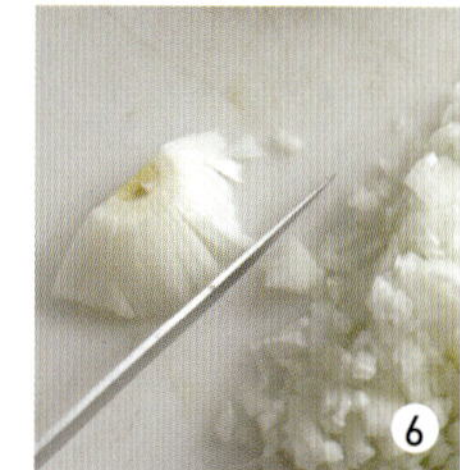

1. Cut the peeled onion in half lengthwise.

2. With a sharp knife, cut the onion halves into slices lengthwise. You should not cut completely through the slices at the stem, so that they hold together and the onion doesn't fall apart.

3. At a right angle to the slices, make a horizontal cut into the lower third of the onion half, almost to the end.

4. Make another cut into the upper third of the onion half.

5. Slice the onion in half to dice it finely. By cutting through the onion half twice, as described above, you will get fine dice.

6. The stem end, which held the slices together, will be left over.

7. Cut as much onion as possible from the stem end to avoid waste.

Preparing Scallions with Green Tops

1. Depending on the size of the scallions, a bunch will consist of three to five scallions.

2. Cut off the upper third of the green tops and discard that part.

3. Cut off the root base.

4. Cut off the remaining green part at the top, which will be used later.

5. Remove the outer scallion skin.

6. Cut off any bad parts of the stem base.

7. Cut the green tops into fine slices and use them for soup or as a garnish for salads.

8. The white part is best suited to be used raw, because young onions are not that hot but are very flavorful.

Avoiding Dull Knives When You Work with Onions

1. If your knife is dull, the onions will be more crushed than cut, and you won't be able to cut thin slices.

2. The onion will disintegrate when it is cut and the danger of cutting yourself will be much greater than when you are using a sharp knife.

3. Furthermore, if a dull knife is used, the result is very irregular, squishy dice and far too much waste.

4. The piece of onion on the left was cut with a dull knife: The edges are translucent, the onion was crushed, and is probably bitter. The onion on the right was cut with a sharp knife: The cut is smooth and the onion is still juicy.

1

2

3

4

Cutting Onions into Strips

1. Cut the onion in half lengthwise.

2. Cut the stem and the root ends off on a slight inward slant.

3. Cut the onion half into thin strips lengthwise. These strips are ideal for stews, and are a good way of thickening sauces.

1

2

3

Preparing and Washing Leeks

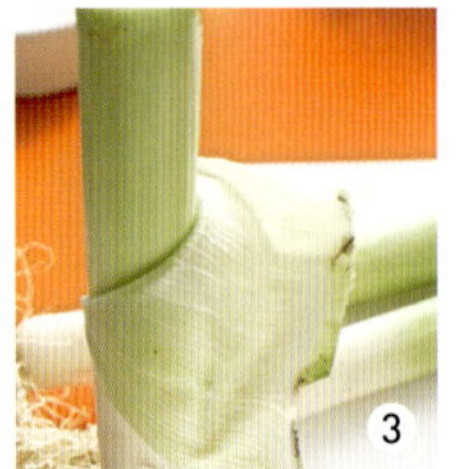

1. Cut approximately ½ inch (1 cm) off the root base.

2. Cut through the stalks at the top.

3. Tear the outer leaves off the leek.

4. You can determine whether the leek is fresh by piercing the stalk. Juice will ooze out at the point of the cut if the leek is fresh. Otherwise, it will be dry and woody.

5. Peel the outer leaves of the green part of the leek off and use only the bright yellow leaves.

6. Rinse the white and light green part of the leek under running water so all of the dirt will be washed away.

7. Wash out the bright green parts of the leek under cold water as well.

Preparing and Washing Young Leeks

1. Cut the upper green leaves off the young leeks.

2. Cut off the root base and remove the first leek leaf, because it is usually limp.

3 Wash the leeks well under running water, because dirt often clings to the leaves.

4. Let them drain well after washing, and either use them immediately or put them in containers, cover them, and store them in the refrigerator.

Swiss Chard—Separating the Leaves and the Stalks

1. Trim the bottom end of the stalk.

2. Cut the stalks off the Swiss chard leaves.

3. Chop the leaves coarsely and prepare the Swiss chard like leaf spinach.

4. Cut the stalks into 2 x ½-inch (5 x 1-cm) pieces. Steam the stalks or use them in stews.

Washing and Sorting Spinach

1. Wash the spinach leaves well in copious amounts of water, several times. Remove any yellow, wilted leaves.

2. Separate the leaves from the stems and set the spinach leaves aside, for future use, in a bowl covered with a damp cloth.

Cutting Pumpkin into Cubes

1. Halve the pumpkin, scrape out the seeds with a spoon, and set them aside.

2. Cut the pumpkin half into quarters and slice them into smaller segments. Use a knife to remove the skin.

3. Use a knife to remove a thin layer of the inner part of the pumpkin.

4. Cut the pieces into even thinner segments. These segments are suitable for breading or for baking in a batter.

5. Cut the pumpkin segments into ½-inch (1-cm) cubes and use them for soups, stews, or gratins.

6. Roast the pumpkin seeds in the oven for approximately 30 minutes at 325°F (160°C/Gas Mark 3), sprinkle them with salt, and munch on them instead of chips.

Preparing Zucchini for Stuffing

1. Cut off the stem ends and the tips of the zucchini.

2. Cut the zucchini into 1¼-inch (3-cm) pieces.

3. Hollow out the zucchini pieces with a small spoon.

4. Scoop out the zucchini flesh, leaving a ½-inch (1-cm) thick base, and fill the cavity with meat, cheese, or bolognese sauce.

Preparing Carrots

1. Cut off both ends of the carrots with a knife.

2. Peel the carrots lengthwise, then cut them into slices, grate them, or use them as part of a selection of vegetables and herbs for soup.

Peeling and Seeding Cucumbers

1. Wash the cucumber and peel it from top to bottom with a vegetable peeler.

2. Cut the cucumber in half lengthwise and then either cut it into slices and use it for salads, or remove the seeds with a teaspoon. Cucumbers can be stuffed with meat or fish, or simply braised as a vegetable in butter and herbs.

String Beans

1. Trim off the ends of the beans with a knife.

2. Remove any bruised or brown spots with a small knife.

3. Cut the beans into ⅛-inch (2-mm) thick, diagonal strips and use them for a delicate bean side dish or for fermented beans with dill.

4. Another variation: Cut the beans into approximately 2-inch (5-cm) pieces, cook them in salted water, and sauté them with onions and bacon.

1

2

3

4

Celery Stalks

1. Cut ½ inch (1 cm) off the stump and the tops of the stalks.

2. Wash the celery stalks well under running water.

3. Divide the head into outer stalks, middle stalks, and the innermost heart stalks. Cut the heart stalks into pieces 3¼ inches (8 cm) long. Serve them with various dips or add them to salads.

4. Remove the fibers from the middle stalks in the lower part of the head.

5. Cut the stalks diagonally into thin slices and use them for meat and vegetable dishes.

6. Use a knife to remove the brown parts from the outer stalks.

7. Cut them into 2-inch (5-cm) pieces and use these for meat or vegetable broths.

1

2

3

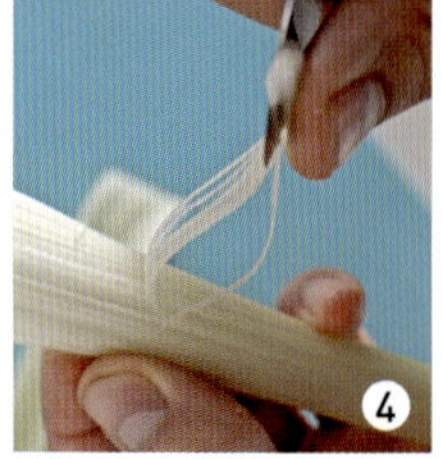

4

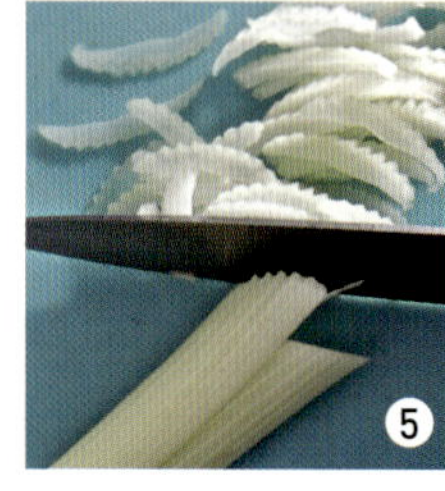

5

6

7

Preparing Fennel Bulbs

1. Wash the fennel bulb well under running water.

2. Cut off the base.

3. Remove the outer layer of the fennel bulb, because it is stained with brown spots.

4. Cut ½ inch (1 cm) off the stalk to remove the brown parts.

5. Remove any remaining brown spots and blemishes under running water once again.

6. The bulb is snow white and can now be used in the preparation of various dishes. Store the green fennel fronds in water or chop them immediately and add them to sauces or soups. Use the cutoff stalks for broth or stock.

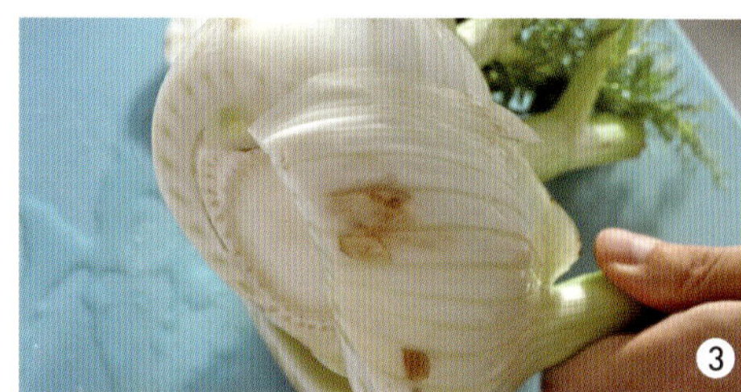

Cutting Fennel Bulbs into Cubes or Strips

1. Cut the fennel bulb in half from the stalk base down to the bottom.

2. Cut it into segments and sauté them or braise them with other vegetables.

3. Cut the fennel bulb into thin slices, marinate these in oil and lemon juice, and serve them as a salad.

4. Dice the fennel bulb and stew it for soups or use it as an ingredient in vegetable dishes.

Preparing Artichoke Hearts

1. Cut the artichoke stem to 1¼ inches (3 cm). Cut off approximately two-thirds of the upper part of the artichoke.

2. Peel off the outer petals until the bright green part is revealed.

3. Peel off the stem and the remaining dark green parts with a small knife.

4. Scrape out the choke (the fibrous core) with a scoop or a small spoon.

5. Store the prepared artichoke hearts in lemon water to prevent browning.

Marinating Raw Artichoke Hearts

1. Cut the artichoke hearts into thin slices.

2. Mix lemon juice, salt, ground fennel seeds, and high-quality olive oil in a bowl and marinate the artichoke slices for approximately 10 minutes.

Cooking Artichokes Whole

1. Remove the stem at the base and cut off the top half with a serrated knife.

2. Put a slice of lemon on the cut surface and fasten it in place with kitchen twine.

3. Reserve this preparation for use with large artichokes.

4. Cook the artichokes with some white wine, peppercorns, a bay leaf, and salt for approximately 35 minutes, and serve lukewarm with an herb sauce.

Frying Artichoke Hearts

1. Cut the artichoke hearts into small segments.

2. Heat olive oil in a skillet and add unpeeled garlic cloves, thyme, and the artichoke pieces.

3. Season them with salt and pepper, fry them until they are golden, and serve them with salad or fish.

Slicing Eggplants

1. Wash the eggplant and cut off the stem with a knife.

2. Remove brown tips or other bruised spots.

3. Cut the eggplant into thin slices lengthwise and put them in a bowl.

4. Lay the last slice flat on the cutting board and cut through it horizontally one more time. Eggplant slices are suitable for broiling, grilling, or for coating with an herb, cheese, and bread-crumb mixture.

4

Seeding Bell Peppers

1. Wash the bell pepper and cut it in half lengthwise from the stem to the tip.

2. Pull the shell apart.

3. Twist the green stem out of one half and cut the bell pepper into quarters.

4. Cut out the white membranes and use the bell pepper quarters as desired.

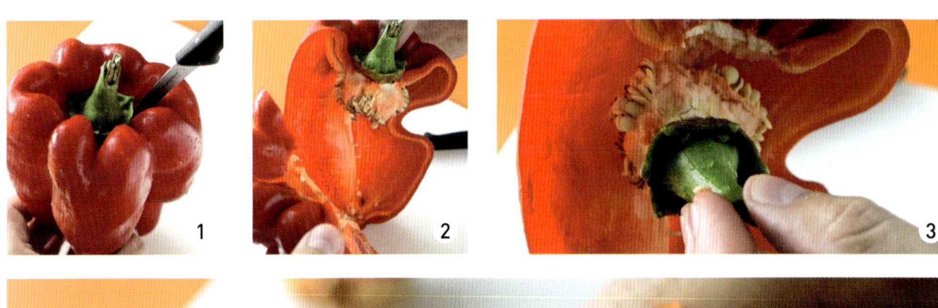

Preparing Chili Peppers for Stuffing

1. Cut out a cone-shaped section to remove the green stem from a chili pepper.

2. Cut out the white membranes and the seeds by inserting a knife as far as you can into the pepper. Then wash the pepper and use it as desired.

Button Mushrooms

1. Cut off the stalk and any soil residue.

2. Rub the cap with paper towels and clean it carefullly.

3. Put the clean mushrooms into a dry bowl.

4. For sauces or omelets, use a long knife to cut the mushrooms into thin slices.

5. For best flavor, the mushroom gills must be light brown and the caps must be tightly closed.

6. Cut the caps into quarters if you want to marinate them as an appetizer or use them for mushroom ragout.

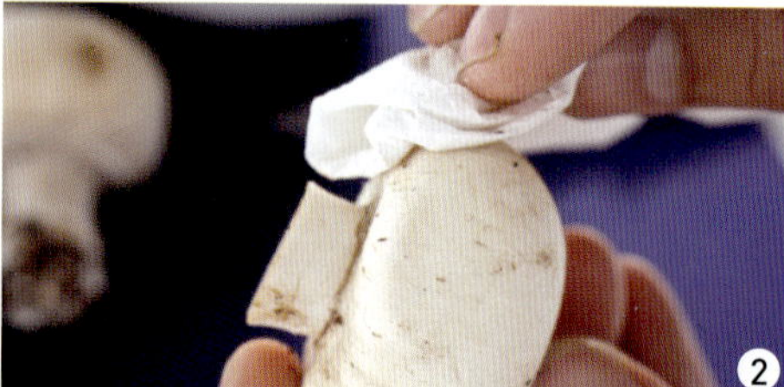

Oyster Mushrooms

1. Cut off the stem of the oyster mushroom even with the cap.

2. Never cut oyster mushrooms, but always tear them by hand along the gills into chunks of the desired size.

3. Store oyster mushrooms in a cool place and use them as quickly as possible.

4. Oyster mushrooms can be broiled or grilled whole or breaded like cutlets.

Shitake Mushrooms

1. Cover dried shitake mushrooms with cold water.

2. Let them soften in cold water for 2 hours. Smaller shitake mushrooms will take a shorter time to soften.

3. Cut off the inedible stems of the shitake mushrooms. Cut the caps into slices and use for stuffing and for Asian dishes.

2 shallots

1 lb 2 oz (500 g) spinach leaves

3 tbsp (40 g) butter

1 pinch of salt
1 pinch of black pepper

1 pinch of nutmeg, freshly grated

1 garlic clove

Steamed Spinach Leaves

1. Peel the shallots and dice them finely. Clean the spinach leaves and remove the stems (see p. 351). Melt the butter in a saucepan, add the shallots, and sweat them briefly.

2. Add the spinach leaves and season with salt, pepper, and freshly grated nutmeg. Steam them for approximately 3 minutes until the liquid has boiled off.

3. Spear the peeled garlic clove with a fork and stir the spinach leaves with it, so that they acquire a subtle garlic flavor. Serve the spinach leaves as an accompaniment to prime boiled beef, broiled sole, or other saltwater fish.

■ Creamed spinach: Pour ⅜ cup (100 ml) cream onto the spinach and let it cook down. Blend the cream and spinach with a handheld blender until smooth. Serve the creamed spinach with fried potatoes, fried eggs, prime boiled beef, or roasted veal medallions, or as an accompaniment to Potatoes en Papillote with roast beef.

2

3

 2¾ cups (350 g) flour

 2 tsp baking powder

 3 eggs

 1¾ cups (400 ml) beer

 ⅔ cup (150 ml) vegetable oil

 ½ tsp salt

 3 zucchini

 4 sprigs thyme

 ¾ cup (200 g) plain yogurt

 ½ lemon

 1 pinch of salt
1 pinch of black pepper

 8 cups (2 liters) peanut oil

Zucchini in a Thyme Batter with Yogurt Sauce

1. Put the flour and the baking powder into a bowl and mix them. Separate the eggs, and add the egg yolks. Pour the beer in slowly and mix everything with a wire whisk until a smooth batter is created. Then, stir in the vegetable oil so that the batter will crisp. Beat the egg whites with salt until semistiff peaks form, and fold them into the batter.

2. Wash the zucchini and cut it into ½-inch (1-cm) slices. Pluck the thyme leaves from the stems and coat them and the zucchini slices with batter. Put the yogurt into a bowl and season with the lemon juice, salt, and pepper to taste, and stir until smooth.

3. Heat the peanut oil to 325°F (160°C) in a wide saucepan and fry the batter-coated zucchini slices until golden on both sides. Then, let them drain on paper towels and sprinkle lightly with salt. Serve the zucchini slices on a platter with the yogurt dip.

■ **The batter can also be prepared with white wine or mineral water. Batter-coated, fried basil or sage leaves provide a delicious snack for your aperitif.**

2

3

9 oz (250 g) mixed ground meat

5½ oz (150 g) goat cheese

1 egg

2 tbsp breadcrumbs

3 scallions

1 tbsp basil strips

½ tsp salt
1 pinch of black pepper

1 tsp dried oregano

2 large eggplants

4 tbsp olive oil

2¼ cups (500 ml) tomato juice

1 tbsp sugar

Stuffed Eggplant with Goat Cheese and Oregano Filling

1. Put the ground meat, coarsely mashed goat cheese, egg, breadcrumbs, sliced scallion rings, basil strips, salt, black pepper, and oregano into a large bowl.

2. Mix the filling with your hands. Do not knead it, however, because the pieces of cheese should remain large.

3. Cut the stems off the eggplants and then cut in half lengthwise, removing a thin slice of the curved base, so they will sit flat in the casserole dish.

4. Scoop out the inside of the eggplants with a teaspoon.

5. Smear a casserole dish with olive oil and put the eggplant halves into it. Fill them with the ground meat mixture, put them into the oven, preheated to 350°F (180°C/Gas Mark 4), and bake for approximately 45 minutes. Meanwhile, add a little water consistently, and baste them with the juice produced. Mix the tomato juice with the sugar, salt, and black pepper, and pour it over the eggplant halves. Bake for 15 minutes longer.

Arrange an eggplant half with sauce on each plate to serve.

■ **Fill zucchini, bell peppers, or cucumbers with the same mixture and braise them in the oven.**

2

3

4

5

1 garlic clove

4 tbsp extra virgin olive oil

1 pinch of salt
1 pinch of black pepper

1 lb (450 g) tomatoes

1 sprig rosemary

4½ oz (125 g) mozzarella cheese

2 slices of toast

Tomatoes au Gratin with Rosemary and Mozzarella Cheese

1. Rub a casserole dish with the garlic clove, drizzle it with 1 tbsp of the olive oil, and season it with salt and pepper.

2. Peel the tomatoes (see p. 347) and cut them into ¼-inch (5-mm) thick disks. Put them into a casserole dish in layers and season them with salt and pepper.

3. Remove the rosemary needles from the stem and chop them finely. Halve the mozzarella and cut it into disks. Cut the crusts off the toasted bread and grate it or put it into the blender to make fine breadcrumbs. Distribute the mozzarella evenly between the tomato slices and sprinkle everything with rosemary.

4. Sprinkle the white breadcrumbs on the gratin and drizzle it with the remaining olive oil. Bake the casserole for approximately 30 minutes in a preheated 375°F (190°C/Gas Mark 5) oven. The tomatoes are ready when the cheese has a brilliant golden hue. Serve in the casserole dish.

■ This tomato casserole goes very well with fried veal cutlets, spring chicken, or a grilled or broiled chicken breast fillet. It can also be served as a main course with toasted garlic bread and a green salad. If you are serving it as a main course, double the quantities of the ingredients.

2

3

4

 1½ oz (40 g) cooked ham

 1 young onion

 4 tsp (20 g) butter

 5½ oz (150 g) peapods

 1 lb (450 g) peas

 1 pinch of salt

 1 pinch of sugar

 1 pinch of white pepper

 ⅔ cup (150 ml) poultry stock

 ½ head of lettuce

 2 sprigs mint

 4 tsp (20 g) chilled butter

Peapods Stewed with Lettuce and Ham Strips

1. Cut the cooked ham into thin strips and finely dice the onion. Let the butter foam in a saucepan, add the cooked ham and the onion, and sauté them gently.

2. Clean the peapods, remove the stems, and cut the pods diagonally, twice. Add the pods to the ham with the peas, mix them, and season them with the salt, sugar, and white pepper.

3. Pour in the poultry stock, cover the pan, and stew them for approximately 5 minutes.

4. Wash the lettuce and cut it into strips. Chop the mint into fine strips. Add the lettuce and the mint to the peas, and mix in the chilled butter. Season them to taste and serve them in bowls.

■ **Fresh peas are the most delicious kind for this recipe. For 1 lb (450 g) shelled peas, you will need at least double the amount of peapods. This dish is very nice when served as an accompaniment to poultry, such as squab or Bresse chicken, and is also delicious with roast veal.**

2
3
4

2 shallots

1 bunch of parsley

1 garlic clove

1 lb 5 oz (600 g) fava beans

3 tbsp (40 g) butter

1 pinch of salt
1 pinch of black pepper

1 pinch of nutmeg, freshly grated

Fava Beans with Garlic and Onions

1. Peel the shallots and dice them finely. Wash the parsley, pluck the leaves, and chop them finely. Peel the garlic and dice it finely as well. Bring water to a boil in a saucepan add the beans, and cook them for 1 minute. Put the beans in a colander and rinse them under cold water to cool.

2. Remove the white skin from the beans with your fingers. Very small beans can also be cooked in their skins.

3. Let the butter foam in a skillet, add the shallots and the garlic, and sauté them gently until they are translucent.

4. Add the beans and season with salt, pepper, and nutmeg.

5. Sauté for 2 to 3 minutes more; then add the parsley, mix, and arrange the beans on plates to serve.

■ For 1 lb 5 oz (600 g) beans, you will need 6 lb 8 oz (3 kg) fresh beans in their pods. This dish can also be prepared with wax beans or a combination of various kinds. However, the beans should be cooked in salted water first until they are al dente.

 2 red bell peppers

 1 green bell pepper

 3 young onions

 1 lb 2 oz (500 g) potatoes

 2 garlic cloves

 Rind of 1 lemon

 ½ tsp caraway seeds

 3 tbsp vegetable oil

 2 tsp ground sweet paprika

 1 pinch of salt
1 pinch of black pepper

 5⅓ cups (1.2 liters) vegetable stock

Vegetable Goulash

1. Halve, seed, and trim the red and green bell peppers. Then cut them into approximately ¾-inch (2-cm) pieces. Peel, halve, and dice the onions coarsely. Peel the potatoes, cut them into ¾-inch (2-cm) pieces, and store them covered with cold water, so that they don't brown. Peel the garlic cloves and chop finely with the lemon rind. Drizzle some oil on the caraway seeds and then chop them.

2. Heat the oil in a stainless steel stockpot and sauté the onions in it. Then pour the potato pieces into a colander and let them drain well. Add the potatoes to the onions and sauté over medium heat for 5 minutes.

3. Sprinkle the garlic, lemon rind, caraway seeds, and ground paprika on the potatoes and onions, and sweat slightly.

4. Add the red and green bell peppers, season with salt and pepper, and sauté them gently for a few minutes over medium heat.

5. Pour in the vegetable stock and let the mixture simmer slowly for about 25 minutes, stirring occasionally. Ladle the goulash into soup plates and serve with rye bread.

■ **Zucchini and whole cherry tomatoes can be used instead of green and red bell peppers.**

2
3
4
5

 2 scallions

 2 sprigs parsley

 14 oz (400 g) red pine mushrooms

 1 garlic clove

 3 tbsp vegetable oil

 ½ tsp salt
1 pinch of black pepper

 ½ tsp caraway seeds

 4 slices whole-wheat bread

Fried Red Pine Mushrooms on Whole-Wheat Bread

1. Wash and trim the scallions and slice them into rings. Wash the parsley, shake it dry, and chop it finely.

2. Clean the mushrooms, remove the stems, and put them in a skillet with the gills facing up.

3. Peel the garlic clove and chop it finely. Pour the oil over the mushrooms and braise them gently.

4. Sprinkle the scallions, garlic, and parsley on top, and season the mushrooms with salt and pepper. Chop the caraway seeds with some oil and add them to the skillet.

Remove the mushrooms with some oil from the skillet and arrange them on the slices of bread.

■ As it is not always possible to obtain red pine mushrooms, button mushrooms, oyster mushrooms, shitake mushrooms, or king oyster mushrooms can also be used for this recipe.

3

4

 1 lb 5 oz (600 g) chanterelles

 2 shallots

 3 tbsp (40 g) butter

 1 pinch of salt
1 pinch of black pepper

 1 pinch of nutmeg, freshly grated

 ½ bunch parsley

 ⅞ cup (200 ml) cream

 2 tbsp crème fraîche (or sour cream)

 Juice of ½ lemon

Mushroom Ragout with Nutmeg and Parsley

1. Remove coarse dirt from the chanterelles with a small knife and wash them in cold water only briefly, so that they do not become saturated. Put them on paper towels to drain.

2. Cut the large chanterelles into ¼-inch (5-mm) slices and leave the small ones whole. Peel the shallots and dice them finely.

3. Melt the butter in a wide saucepan and braise the shallots until they are translucent, stirring them constantly with a wooden spoon.

4. Add the chanterelles, season them with salt, pepper, and freshly grated nutmeg, and sweat them for 2 to 3 minutes. Meanwhile, wash the parsley, pluck the leaves, and chop them finely.

5. Add the cream and the crème fraîche and simmer the ragout slowly for approximately 5 minutes. Finally, season it with the lemon juice, mix with the finely chopped parsley, and serve.

■ **Other wild mushrooms, such as porcini, bay boletus, birch boletus, boletus luridus, or morels can be prepared in the same way. You can also use a mix of different mushrooms, and serve it as a main dish with bread dumplings.**

2
3
4
5

1 medium-sized beet, cooked and peeled

2 eggs

10½ oz (300 g) ricotta cheese

1 pinch of salt
1 pinch of black pepper

1 package egg-roll wrappers

8 cups (2 liters) vegetable oil for deep frying

Deep-Fried Beet-Ricotta Pockets

1. Finely grate the beet.

2. Separate the eggs and add the egg yolks, ricotta cheese, salt, and black pepper to the beet. Set the egg whites aside.

3. Mix the ingredients well and season to taste.

4. Lay the egg-roll wrapper flat on a work surface and fold the right corner nearest you to the center. Brush the outer edge with reserved egg white.

5. Fold the left corner nearest you to the center and place it on top of the right corner. Press it lightly so that the sides stick together.

6. Lift the combined corners to open the pocket created and stuff with 2 tsp of the filling.

7. Press the filling into the corners and paint the upper section with egg white.

»

■ **These pockets can be stuffed with any kind of filling you like. However, the filling must not be too moist, because the pockets would burst open during deep-frying.**

3

4

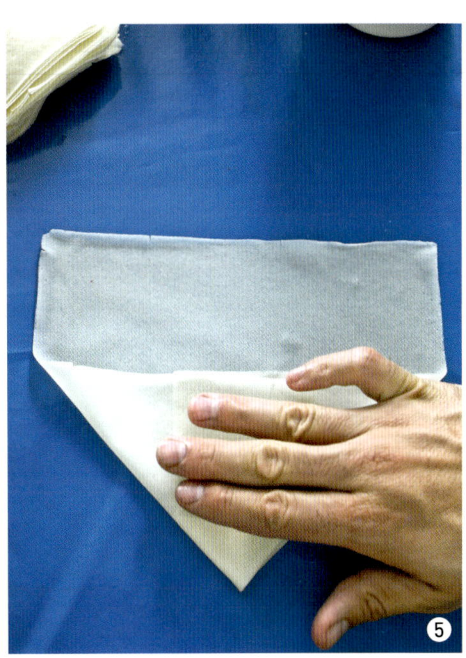
5

6

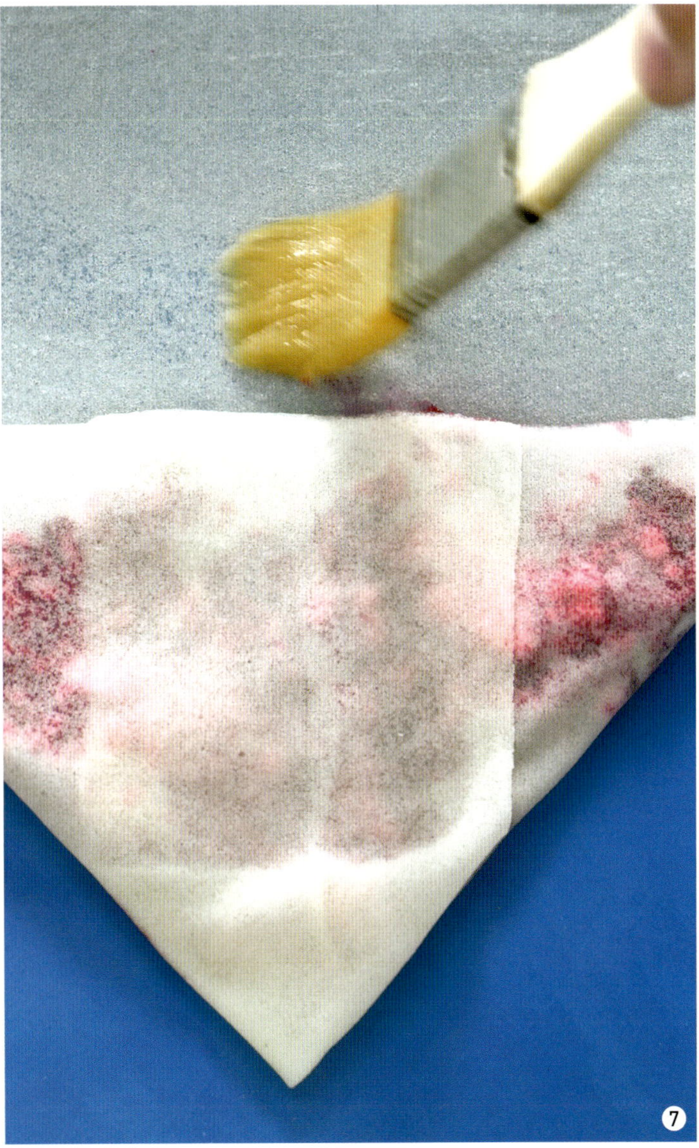
7

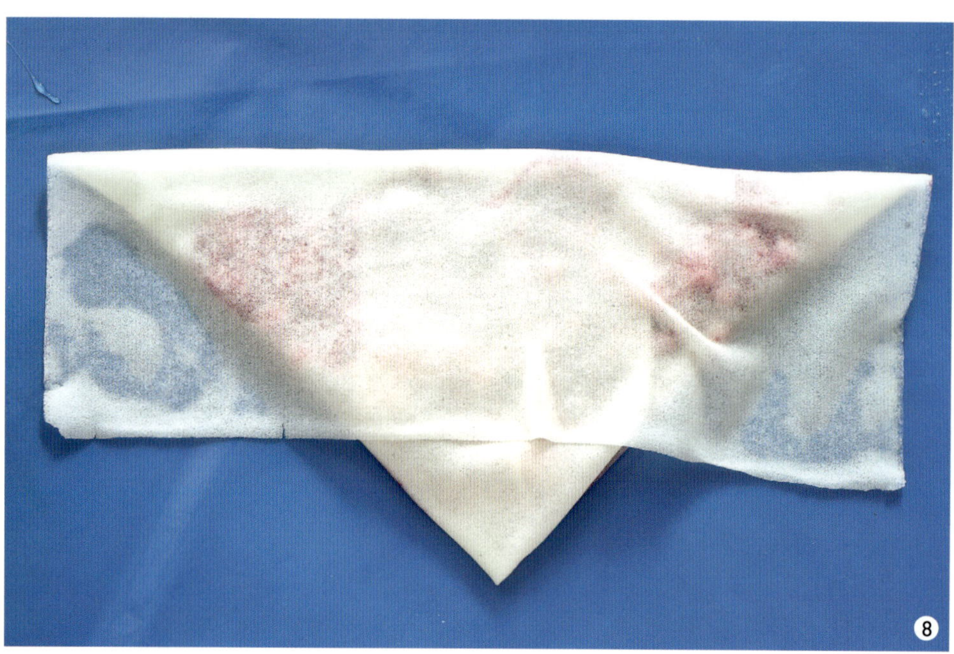

8. Fold the upper half down.

9. Turn the pocket over and paint the protruding corners with egg white.

10. Turn down the ends and seal the pocket well so the filling cannot come out when the pocket is being deep-fried.

11. Heat the oil to 325°F (160°C) in a saucepan and deep-fry the pockets for 3 minutes. Let the pockets drain briefly on paper towels.

Serve as a snack with wine.

■ **These pockets can also be prepared in advance and stored in the freezer.**

9

10

11

6 oz (180 g) carrots

2¾ oz (80 g) celery stalks

2¼ oz (60 g) shallots

1 lb 5 oz (600 g) pumpkin

1-inch (2.5-cm) piece of fresh ginger

⅛ cup (30 g) butter

4 tsp (20 ml) olive oil

1 pinch of salt
1 pinch of black pepper

1 tsp ground sweet paprika

1 pinch of curry powder

1½ oz (40 g) ketchup

1 bay leaf

⅞ cup (200 ml) poultry stock

1⅛ cups (250 ml) cream

1⅛ cups (250 ml) milk

1 pinch of nutmeg, freshly grated

2¾ oz (80 g) fontina cheese

Pumpkin au Gratin with Fontina and Paprika

1. Chop the carrots, celery, and shallots into ¼-inch (5-mm) cubes and the pumpkin into ¾-inch (2-cm) cubes (see p. 352). Peel the ginger and grate it finely.

2. Let the butter and the olive oil foam up in a wide saucepan. Add the shallots and sauté until they are translucent, and then sauté the diced celery and carrots. Add the pumpkin, season the mixture with salt, pepper, grated fresh ginger, ground paprika, and curry powder, and brown it for 5 minutes.

3. Push the whole mixture to the sides of the pan and put the ketchup in the clear space. Brown the ketchup slightly and then mix it with the other ingredients.

4. Add the bay leaf and pour in the poultry stock. Let it simmer for approximately 5 minutes, stirring constantly. Then, pour in the cream and the milk and bring to a boil. Let it simmer gently for 5 more minutes.

5. Remove the bay leaf, season the pumpkin with freshly grated nutmeg, and spread it evenly in a casserole dish. Grate the cheese finely and sprinkle it on top of the pumpkin gratin. Put the casserole dish in the oven, preheated to 375°F (190°C/Gas Mark 5), and bake it for approximately 15 minutes. Make sure the cheese does not brown too much; cover the dish with aluminum foil if necessary.

■ **This gratin can also be served as a main dish. If you are serving it as a main dish, the quantities specified are sufficient for two people. Use either muscat pumpkin or Hokkaido pumpkin for this dish, because they are particularly flavorful.**

2
3
4
5

1 tbsp butter

1 small onion

½ medium-sized cauliflower

1 pinch of salt
1 pinch of black pepper

1 pinch of nutmeg, freshly grated

1⅛ cups (250 ml) vegetable or poultry stock

1¾ cups (400 ml) cream

Fluffy Cauliflower Puree

1. Melt the butter in a saucepan, chop the peeled onion into strips, and sauté it gently in the butter until it is translucent. Cut the cauliflower into florets, wash it well, then cut the florets into slices.

2. Sauté the cauliflower gently for approximately 3 minutes, seasoning it with salt, black pepper and freshly grated nutmeg. Pour in the stock, cover the pan, and steam the cauliflower for 10 minutes.

3. Add the cream and bring the mixture to a boil. Remove the lid and simmer the mixture gently for 5 minutes longer.

4. Put the mixture in a blender and puree it finely. Season it to taste once again.

5. Fill a soda siphon three-quarters full with the mixture and close it. Twist a nitrogen capsule onto the siphon and shake it gently a few times.

Spray the foam into a bowl and serve it immediately as a side dish. It's wonderfully light and delicious.

■ **Serve the cauliflower puree with roast poultry or fish. It's also delicious with boiled potatoes.**

2
3
4
5

1 onion

1 lb 9 oz (700 g) cauliflower

½ bunch cilantro

6 tbsp vegetable oil

1 tsp cumin seeds

6 star anise pods

1 pinch of salt
1 pinch of black pepper

⅔ cup (150 ml) water

6 oz (180 g) cherry tomatoes

1

Ayurvedic Cauliflower with Tomatoes and Cumin

1. Peel the onion and dice it finely. Divide the cauliflower into small florets. Wash the cilantro and chop it coarsely.

2. Heat 4 tsp of the vegetable oil in a long-handled saucepan. Lightly brown the cumin seeds and the star anise in the oil. Cook just until fragrant so the spices do not burn and become bitter.

3. Add the cauliflower and sauté it gently for approximately 5 minutes, then add water and cook for another 5 minutes with the lid closed until the liquid is reduced.

4. Add the whole cherry tomatoes and fry them gently for 5 minutes. Heat the remaining oil in a separate skillet and fry the onions until they are golden. Arrange the cauliflower on plates and put the onions and the cilantro on top.

■ **Serve the cauliflower with a cool, light yogurt-cinnamon sauce. Instead of cauliflower, you can also add a choice of broccoli, kohlrabi, or carrots. When they are prepared in this way, vegetables taste quite different and are particularly spicy.**

 1 lb 5 oz (600 g) carrots

 3 tbsp olive oil

 1 pinch of salt

 1½ tbsp sugar

 1 pinch of black pepper

 2 tbsp balsamic vinegar

Glazed Carrots

1. Peel the carrots, halve them lengthwise, and cut them into ½-inch (1-cm) wide strips.

2. Heat the olive oil in a skillet, add the carrots, season them with salt, sugar, and pepper, and sauté them gently, constantly stirring them. The sugar will brown slightly when you are doing this. If the skillet becomes too hot, add some water.

3. Finally, sprinkle the carrots with the balsamic vinegar. This provides a nice balance for the sugar and lends the carrots a sweet-and-sour character.

■ **These carrots can also be served cold with roasted pine nuts and finely chopped basil as an antipasto. They are a delicious accompaniment to roast chicken or broiled lamb chops.**

Do not fry these carrots at an excessively high temperature, otherwise the sugar will burn.

2

3

1 lb 5 oz (600 g) carrots

⅛ cup (30 g) butter

1 pinch of sugar

1 pinch of white pepper

⅞ cup (200 ml) Vichy mineral water

Vichy Carrots

1. Peel the carrots and cut them into thin disks. The most suitable carrots for this recipe are young carrots with green tops, because they taste fresh and sweet.

2. Let the butter foam in a saucepan, add the carrot slices, season them with sugar and pepper, and sauté briefly. Add the mineral water until the carrots are covered with liquid and bring them to a boil.

3. Steam the carrots for approximately 10 minutes with a closed lid, until almost all of the liquid has evaporated. Continue to stir the carrots occasionally, so that they cook evenly.

■ In this recipe, Vichy mineral water is used as a substitute for salted water. If you like your carrots somewhat saltier, salt can be added to taste. It's important to use carrots with green tops because they are young and have a very delicate flavor. Serve as an accompaniment to small veal cutlets or a roast.

2

3

 1⅔ cups (200 g) flour

 ⅔ cup (140 g) butter

 ½ tsp salt

 4 eggs

 1 tbsp water

 9 oz (250 g) leeks

 3½ oz (100 g) bacon, cut in strips

 1 pinch of black pepper

 ⅔ cup (150 ml) cream

 1 pinch of nutmeg, freshly grated

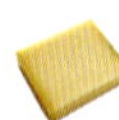 7 oz (200 g) Gruyère cheese

Quiche Lorraine with Leeks

1. Sift the flour onto a work surface. Use your hands to work half of the chilled butter and the salt into the flour. Then add 1 egg and the water, and knead the mixture quickly into a smooth dough, so the butter doesn't become too warm and the dough doesn't puff up when it's baked. Wrap it in plastic wrap and let it rest in the refrigerator for half an hour. Put the dough on a floured surface and roll it out evenly with a rolling pin until it is approximately ⅛ inch (3 mm) thick. As you work, dust the dough with flour, so it doesn't stick to the work surface.

2. Place the oval baking dish on the rolled-out dough to check whether the dough is large enough.

3. Coat the baking dish with 2 tsp (10 g) butter, and unroll the dough that is wrapped around the rolling pin, fitting it into the baking dish so that it doesn't tear.

4. Press the dough on the edge of the dish and cut off the excess. Then, prick the dough with a fork so it doesn't puff up during baking. Put the dish in the refrigerator until needed.

5. Clean the leeks, remove the outer leaves, and cut the stalks into rings. Wash them under running water and let them drain well. Cut the bacon slices into fine strips. Let the rest of the butter foam in a skillet, gently sauté the bacon strips in it briefly, and add the leeks. Season the mixture with salt and pepper to taste and sauté it gently for approximately 5 minutes, until the leeks have wilted and the liquid has boiled off.

+ 30 minutes resting time

■ **Instead of leeks, you can use button or oyster mushrooms. This quiche is also delicious with ratatouille or fennel bulb and bell peppers.**

6. Whisk the cream with the remaining eggs, the salt, the pepper, and the freshly grated nutmeg. Grate the cheese finely and set it aside.

7. Remove the oval baking dish from the refrigerator and spread the leek-bacon filling in the bottom.

8. Spread the grated cheese on top of the filling and cover it with the cream-egg mixture. Bake in the oven, preheated to 350°F (180°C/Gas Mark 4), for 15–20 minutes until the custard is set. Then let it rest briefly, cut it into portions, and arrange them on plates to serve.

Boiled White Asparagus

Peel **1 lb 2 oz (500 g) white asparagus spears** evenly from the tip downward, and cut approximately ½ inch (1 cm) off of the base. Bring **8 cups (2 liters) water** to a boil in a large saucepan and add **1 tbsp of salt**, **1½ tbsp of sugar**, and the juice of **½ lemon**. Add the asparagus to the boiling water and cook it for approximately 6–8 minutes, depending on the size and thickness of the spears. Melt **3 tbsp (40 g) butter** in a skillet. Remove the asparagus from the water, toss it carefully in the skillet, and serve it with chopped parsley.

■ **You can drink the water in which the asparagus was cooked as asparagus broth, or you can save it to use as the basis for asparagus soup.**

Boiled Green Asparagus

Peel the lower half of **1 lb 2 oz (500 g) green asparagus spears** and cut approximately ½ inch (1cm) off the base. Bring **8 cups (2 liters) water**, to which **1½ tsp of salt** has been added, to a boil in a large saucepan. Add the asparagus and cook for approximately 5 minutes, depending on the size and thickness of the spears. You can use the tip of a knife to check whether the end of the spear is soft enough. Grind **2 slices of white bread** in a food processor. Let **¼ cup (50 g) butter** melt in a skillet, add the bread crumbs, and brown them slowly, stirring continuously to prevent them from becoming too dark. Then place the asparagus onto plates and serve them with the toasted bread crumbs sprinkled on top.

Stir-Fried White Asparagus

Peel **1 lb 2 oz (500 g) white asparagus spears** evenly from the tip downward and cut approximately ½ inch (1 cm) off of the base. Cut the spears diagonally into 2-inch (5-cm) lengths. Heat **2 tsp of sunflower oil** in a skillet and add the asparagus. Season it with a **pinch of salt**, a **pinch of freshly ground black pepper**, and **1 tsp sugar**, and sauté it gently. Wash **2 oranges**, peel off strips of zest with a vegetable peeler, and cut them into very narrow strips with a sharp knife. Sprinkle these strips on the asparagus spears. Squeeze the oranges and strain the juice through a fine sieve to remove the pulp. Pour the orange juice on the asparagus spears and cook them for 6–8 minutes. This dish is ready when the orange juice has cooked down and the asparagus is golden yellow.

■ **This side dish goes very well with roast breast of duck, baked salmon fillet, or veal medallions with Hollandaise sauce.**

 10½ oz (300 g) onions

 2 tbsp sugar

 ⅜ cup (100 ml) water

 2¼ oz (60 g) bacon cut in strips

 3 tbsp vegetable oil

 2 bay leaves

 3 cloves

 1 garlic clove

 10 whole black peppercorns

 5 juniper berries

 ⅔ cup (150 ml) white wine

 1 lb 12 oz (800 g) fresh sauerkraut

 3⅓ cups (750 ml) poultry stock

 ½ tsp salt

 ½ potato

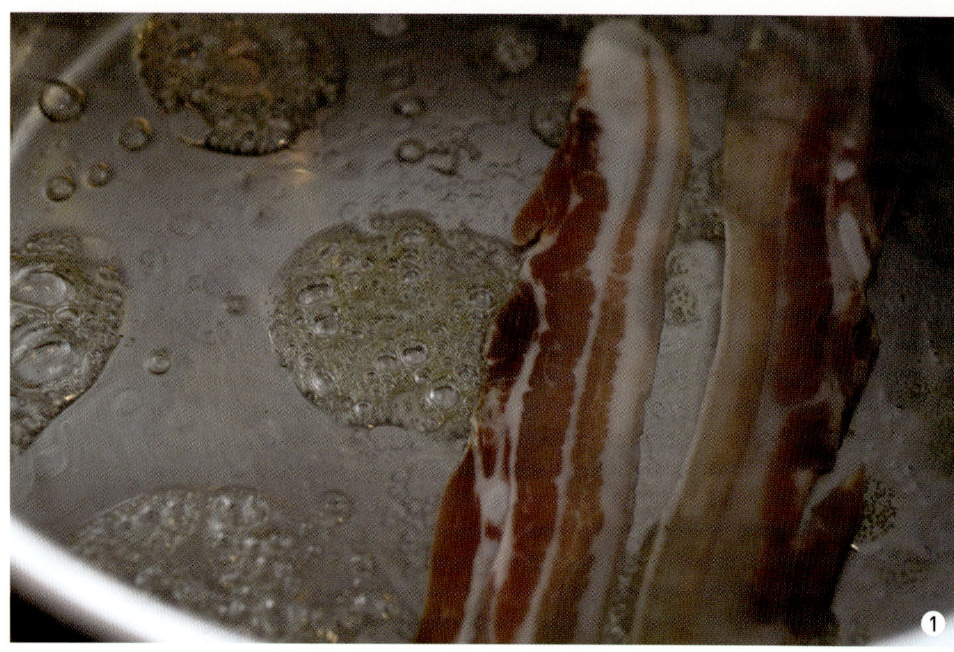
1

Sauerkraut with Bacon

1. Peel and halve the onions and cut them into thin strips. Boil the sugar in a saucepan with the water and heat it until it turns a bright golden color and caramelizes.

2. Place the bacon in the caramel, add the vegetable oil, and brown them slightly. Turn the bacon after a few minutes and add the onions.

3. Add the bay leaves, cloves, garlic, peppercorns, and juniper berries, and sauté them gently until the onions are translucent.

4. As soon as the onions are translucent, add the white wine and let it boil away completely. Loosen the drippings with a wooden spoon.

5. Add the sauerkraut and spread it around the pan, pour in the poultry stock, and season it with salt. Cover the pan and let the mixture simmer gently at a moderate temperature for approximately 40 minutes. About 5 minutes before the end of cooking, grate the ½ potato finely and mix it with the sauerkraut. The potato starch will bind the sauerkraut, so that it is nice and shiny at the end. Remove the peppercorns before serving the sauerkraut.

■ Sauerkraut goes well with loin ribs and bratwurst. Depending on the use, you can add goose or pork fat instead of oil. The spices are easier to remove from the sauerkraut later if you put them into a little cheesecloth bag before adding them.

2
3
4
5

 10½ oz (300 g) eggplant

 10½ oz (300 g) zucchini

 3½ oz (100 g) onion

 2 green bell peppers

 1 red bell pepper

 8 oz (220 g) fennel bulb

 4 garlic cloves

 ½ tsp fennel seeds

 5 tbsp olive oil

 3 sprigs thyme

 3 sprigs rosemary

 1 pinch of salt

 1 bay leaf

 1 pinch of black pepper

 14 oz (400 g) canned peeled tomatoes

 1 sprig basil

Ratatouille

1. Cut all of the vegetables into ¾-inch (2-cm) cubes. Peel the garlic and chop finely. Drizzle some olive oil on the fennel seeds and chop finely. Pluck the thyme leaves and the rosemary needles from their stems. Heat the remaining olive oil in a large saucepan. Add the eggplant, season with salt, and brown for approximately 5 minutes.

2. Move the eggplant to one side of the pot. Add the garlic to the free space created and sauté it gently, until it is golden brown.

3. Add the rest of the vegetables to this clear space also, and sauté them gently for approximately 2 minutes.

4. Add the bay leaf, thyme, coarsely chopped rosemary needles, and chopped fennel seeds. Mix well, season with salt and pepper, and sauté gently for another 5 minutes.

5. Clear a space in the center of the pot and add the peeled tomatoes with the salt, and cook them at a low heat for another 15 minutes. Stir them frequently, so that the vegetables don't brown. Add a little water occasionally. Garnish the ratatouille with basil leaves.

■ **The vegetables can also be combined in different proportions to suit your taste. If the vegetables are diced into small ¼-inch (5-mm) cubes, you can use large spoons to make piles of this ratatouille and arrange them attractively for serving.**

2
3
4
5

Plant Proteins

Contents

404 Plant Proteins
406 Miso Soup with Spinach and Tofu
408 Fried Tempeh with Dips
410 Tofu in Hot Curry Sauce with Thai Basil and Baby Corn
412 Corn Fusilli Pasta with Cauliflower and Anchovies
414 Yuba Pockets Filled with Chinese Cabbage and Sweet Soy Sauce
416 Vegetarian Goulash with Potatoes and Paprika
418 Broccoli with Asparagus and Seitan

Plant Proteins

If you have never explored vegetarian cuisine, you may have never tried plant proteins. Some of the most important basic ingredients in a vegetarian diet are tofu, soy milk, seitan, tempeh, and yuba. Most of the exotic-sounding ingredients originate from Asia.

Tempeh

Tempeh likely originated in Indonesia. It is made from fermented soybeans. However, there are varieties that are made of kidney beans or peanuts. It has a strong flavor. Don't worry about gray or black speckles. However, beware of tempeh that is speckled pink, yellow, or blue or that has a foul odor—this is an indication that it was not fermented properly.

Seitan

Seitan is made from gluten-rich wheat flour and water. Its texture is very similar to that of meat. It is believed to have originated in Chinese cuisine. It is a popular meat substitute used in many parts of Asia and around the world.

Yuba pockets

Yuba is a meat substitute from Japan with a nutty flavor. Yuba is the skin that forms when soymilk is boiled. Despite its strong flavor, soymilk is used just like cow's milk. Yuba is a by-product of the tofu-making process.

Miso

Miso is a seasoning produced by fermenting soybeans. Dark miso is typically more salty and the lighter kind is more sweet in flavor.

Tofu

Tofu is coagulated soymilk. It has very little flavor of its own, so it can be used with a variety of ingredients. In addition, smoked tofu and tofu flavored with herbs are available.

 3½ oz (100 g) spinach leaves

 2¾ oz (80 g) tofu

 4½ cups (1 liter) water

 1 sheet kombu seaweed, dried

 1 tbsp miso paste

 1 tbsp sesame oil

1

2

Miso Soup with Spinach and Tofu

1. Wash the spinach leaves and separate them. Cut into ¼-inch (5-mm) wide strips. Cut the tofu, which should be soft and fresh, into ½-inch (1-cm) large cubes and set aside for later.

2. Put the water, the kombu, and the miso paste together into a saucepan and simmer slowly for about 10 minutes.

3. Remove the kombu.

4. Add the spinach strips and tofu cubes and bring to a boil. Serve in soup bowls. If you like, sprinkle with sesame oil.

■ The high glutamic acid content of the miso paste enhances the soup's flavor and provides just the right amount of savoriness.

3

4

 1 red bell pepper

 ¾ cup (200 g) yogurt

 1 pinch of salt
1 pinch of black pepper

 Juice of ½ lemon

 1 tsp miso paste

 ⅓ cup (70 g) sugar

 ⅜ cup (100 ml) red wine vinegar

 14 oz (400 g) tempeh

 4½ cups (1 liter) peanut oil

Fried Tempeh with Dips

1. Cut the red bell pepper into quarters, seed it, and puree it in a food processor.

2. Put the yogurt in a bowl. Mix with the salt, pepper, lemon juice, and miso paste. Cover and place in the refrigerator until ready to use. Put the sugar and red wine vinegar in a small saucepan and boil.

3. Add the pureed bell pepper and slowly simmer for about 15 minutes, until it thickens to a pastelike consistency. Cool, transfer to serving bowls, and set aside.

4. Cut the tempeh into 1½-inch (4-cm) cubes, and fry for about 3 minutes in peanut oil preheated to 340°F (170°C). This gives the tempeh a strong, nutty flavor.

5. Remove the tempeh from the oil with a skimmer and let it drain on paper towels. Divide in small bowls and serve as an appetizer alongside the yogurt and pepper dips.

■ **Fried tempeh is also delicious on a salad of bean sprouts and carrots with various spicy sauces.**

2
3
4
5

9 oz (250 g) red cherry tomatoes

1¾ oz (50 g) yellow cherry tomatoes

1 lb 2 oz (500 g) tofu

½ bunch fresh Thai basil

5½ oz (150 g) baby corn

2 tbsp peanut oil

1 tbsp brown sugar

1 tsp red curry paste

2⅔ cups (600 ml) coconut milk

3 tbsp soy sauce

Tofu in Hot Curry Sauce with Thai Basil and Baby Corn

1. Wash the cherry tomatoes. Cut the tofu into 1¼-inch (3-cm) cubes. Wash the Thai basil and pluck the leaves. Wash the baby corn and cut each piece twice diagonally.

2. Heat the oil in a saucepan. Caramelize the sugar and red curry paste, and then add the coconut milk. Season with the soy sauce and simmer for an additional 3 minutes.

3. Add the tofu cubes, cherry tomatoes, and baby corn, and simmer for another 3 minutes while stirring.

4. Mix in nearly all of the uncut basil leaves. Serve the curry in bowls, and garnish with the remainder of the basil leaves.

■ **For anyone who enjoys more of a fruity curry, adding fresh pineapple or mango cut into small cubes does the trick. You can also substitute the Thai basil with cilantro. For additional ingredients, try beans and eggplant.**

2
3

4

14 oz (400 g) tofu

2 garlic cloves

10 anchovies

1 lb 2 oz (500 g) cauliflower

3 tbsp oil

1 pinch of salt
1 pinch of black pepper

1 lb 2 oz (500g) cooked corn fusilli pasta

2 tbsp parsley, chopped

Corn Fusilli Pasta with Cauliflower and Anchovies

1. Cube the tofu; peel and slice the garlic cloves. Remove the anchovies from the oil and drain. Wash the cauliflower and separate it into florets.

2. Sauté the tofu, garlic, anchovies, and cauliflower in the oil.

3. Season with freshly ground salt and pepper, and continue sautéing while stirring until the anchovies become creamy.

4. Add the corn fusilli pasta and mix with the tofu and vegetables.

5. Mix well; reheat until the noodles are hot.

Serve on plates and garnish with parsley leaves.

■ **This dish is very tasty with smoked tofu or seitan roasted over medium heat. To add a splash of color, mix the cauliflower with broccoli or romanesco. The broccoli has a more assertive flavor. This dish is also delicious when made with other kinds of pasta, such as penne, farfalle, or rigatoni.**

2
3
4
5

1 red chili pepper

1 bunch fresh mint

7 oz (200 g) Chinese cabbage

4 tbsp Thai fish sauce

4 tbsp sweet soy sauce (or Ketjap Manis)

12 fried yuba pockets

Yuba Pockets Filled with Chinese Cabbage and Sweet Soy Sauce

1. Finely slice the red chili pepper. Wash the mint, remove the leaves, and finely slice them. Wash the Chinese cabbage, drain, and finely slice it.

2. Pour the Thai fish sauce into a bowl. First add the chili pepper, and then the sliced Chinese cabbage. Marinate for about 5 minutes.

3. Add the mint and 2 tbsp sweet soy sauce and mix well.

4. Carefully open the fried Yuba pockets and fill with the Chinese cabbage salad. Then arrange them on plates and sprinkle with a few drops of sweet soy sauce. Serve as an appetizer with chilled beer.

■ **You can find fried Yuba pockets in any well-stocked Asian specialty store. Yuba is rich in protein and has a creamy, nutty, and sweet flavor when fried.**

2
3
4

 ½ tsp caraway seeds

 4½ tbsp oil

 1 lb 2 oz (500 g) seitan

 1 garlic clove

 1 tsp marjoram

 1 pinch of salt
1 pinch of black pepper

 3 onions

 1 lb 2 oz (500 g) starchy potatoes

 2 tbsp sweet paprika

 4½ cups (1 liter) vegetable broth

 1 tsp freshly snipped chives

Vegetarian Goulash with Potatoes and Paprika

1. Finely chop the caraway seeds in ½ tbsp of the oil. The oil helps the caraway seeds to stay on the cutting board while chopping.

2. Cube the seitan and marinate for 10 minutes with the chopped garlic, the caraway seeds, the marjoram, the pepper, and the salt.

3. Peel the onions, cut into strips, and sauté in 4 tbsp oil. Add the peeled and cubed potatoes.

4. Dust with the paprika and stir well.

5. Add the marinated cubes of seitan to the potatoes and mix.

6. Add the broth and let it simmer together for about 30 minutes.

Place on plates and sprinkle with chives.

■ Adding other vegetables such as red and yellow bell peppers, zucchini, and pieces of tomatoes, adds additional zest to the goulash. They give it a fruitier and fresher flavor. Seitan is a flavorful substitute for beef or pork. If you like goulash really hot, then substitute hot paprika for half the sweet paprika.

2
3
4
5
6

½ tsp Thai red curry paste

2 tbsp oyster sauce

9 oz (250 g) seitan

9 oz (250 g) green asparagus

1 lb 2 oz (500 g) broccoli

3 tbsp oil

1

2

Broccoli with Asparagus and Seitan

1. Place the curry paste in a small bowl and mix together with the oyster sauce to make a marinade.

2. Cut the seitan into finger-sized strips. Wash the asparagus, cut off the ends, and cut the asparagus into 2-inch (5-cm) pieces. Trim the broccoli, wash it, and cut into small florets.

3. Marinate the seitan for about 15 minutes.

4. Heat the oil in a skillet. First, sauté the broccoli; then add the asparagus pieces and sauté together.

5. Finally, add the marinated seitan strips and mix well in the pan.

Serve in small bowls.

■ This dish is also delicious with Swiss chard, bean sprouts, leeks, scallions, and various Asian herbs. Thai basil and cilantro go especially well together. In addition, many varieties of rice can be mixed with this dish.

3

4

5

Freshwater Fish

Contents

422 Types of Fish
422 Cooking Chart
424 Cleaning and Scaling Fish
425 How to Fillet Fish
426 Trout Meunière
426 Trout Amandine
428 Catfish in Root Vegetable Stock
429 Catfish in Paprika Sauce
430 Salmon Steaks with Horseradish Butter and Cooked Cucumbers with Dill
432 Potato Pancakes with Cured Salmon
434 Carp Fried in Breadcrumbs
436 Slow-Roasted Salmon
438 Poached Tilapia in Red Wine Butter Sauce

Types of Fish

If you are looking for excellent quality fish, you should buy it whole at a seafood market or fish store. There, they will gut, scale, and fillet the fish. It is best to eat the fish within the next two hours or at least on the day of purchase. Otherwise, it will oxidize and become unsavory. Fish can be frozen; however, in most cases the fish loses flavor noticeably when frozen.

Carp: Live in rivers, lakes, and ponds. The flesh often tastes a bit musty. Tip: Place the gutted and scaled carp in water with some vinegar for 1–2 hours to improve the taste. The water must be changed frequently. It is difficult to remove the scales from a carp: scaling is a lot easier if you briefly place the fish in boiling water. You can use nearly every part of a carp. Even its tongue, lips, and cheeks are delicious.

Tilapia: A type of cichlid fish, tilapia generally comes from fish farms. The quality of the meat varies greatly depending on the farming conditions. In this country, you can often get tilapia fillets in supermarkets.

Salmon: The Atlantic salmon or Ouananiche is a type of salmon found in lakes and rivers. It is smaller than other salmon and can be prepared like trout.

Trout: Live in lakes, rivers, and also the sea. Species of trout include the salmon trout, the rainbow trout, the arctic char, the brook trout, the American arctic char, and the grayling. The various species of trout vary in size and flavor. Trout from clean water tastes best. If the water quality is poor, they can taste a bit brackish. Trout need no scaling, and filleting is easy.

Catfish: They are either net- or line-caught. They are served fried or baked.

Cooking Chart

Product	Weight	Method	Temperature	Time	Notes
Trout	9–10½ oz (250–300 g)	Pan	Medium heat	10–14 minutes	
Pike	9 oz (250 g)	Oven	320°F (160°C/Gas Mark 3)	20–25 minutes	
Carp	7 oz (200 g)	Pan	Medium heat	8 minutes	
Salmon steak	7 oz (200 g)	Pan	Medium heat	6 minutes	
Salmon (frozen)	7 oz (200 g)	Oven	185°F (85°C)	45 minutes	
Tilapia	5½ oz (160 g)	Pan	Medium heat	6 minutes	
Catfish	approx. 5½ oz (150 g)	Pot	Medium heat	8–10 minutes	In root vegetable stock
Walleye or pike-perch fillet	10½ oz (300 g)	Pan	Medium heat	8–10 minutes	Fry with the scales on

Carp

Tilapia

Salmon

Trout

Grayling

Walleye or pike-perch

Eel

Pike

Catfish

Cleaning and Scaling Fish

It is best to ask the fish dealer to gut the fish and cut the gills. If you do it yourself, follow the instructions for sea bass (see p. 444).

Take sharp kitchen scissors and cut off the pectoral fins.

Cut off the ventral fin with scissors.

Trim the tail fin by half, otherwise it could burn during pan-frying.

Use a small kitchen knife to scale the fish.

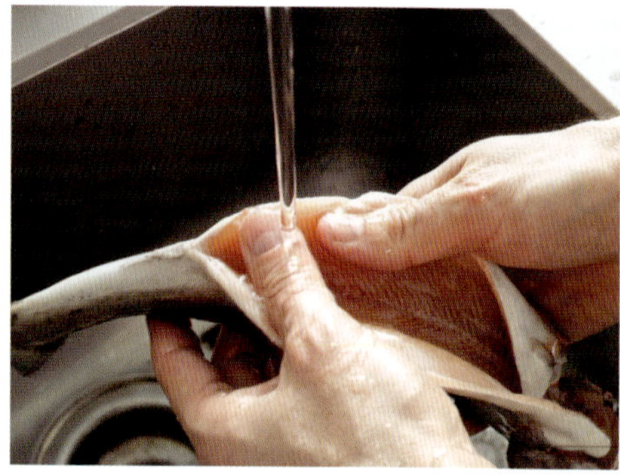

Rinse well under running water and wash off any blood and other pieces of skin.

If you scale the fish under running water, the scales will be rinsed off by the water rather than flying all over the kitchen.

Remove the excess water by hand.

Put the fish on paper towels and make a small slit in the skin from the head to the tail fin.
It is easier to get the knife under the meat to fillet the fish this way, and it prevents the skin from tearing irregularly during frying.

How to Fillet Fish

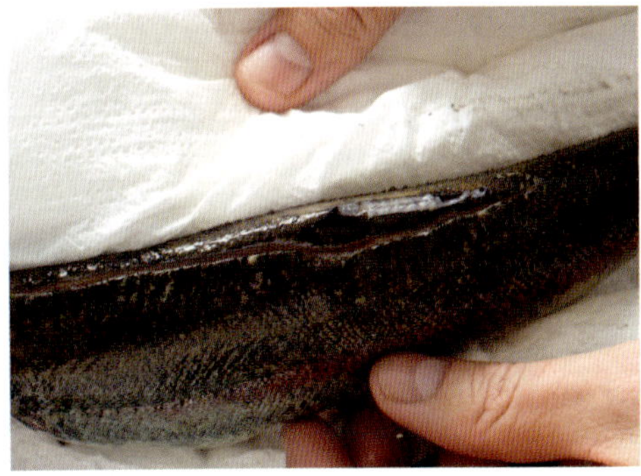

Place the fish on a cutting board to fillet it. Using a knife, cut at an angle from the head to the backbone.

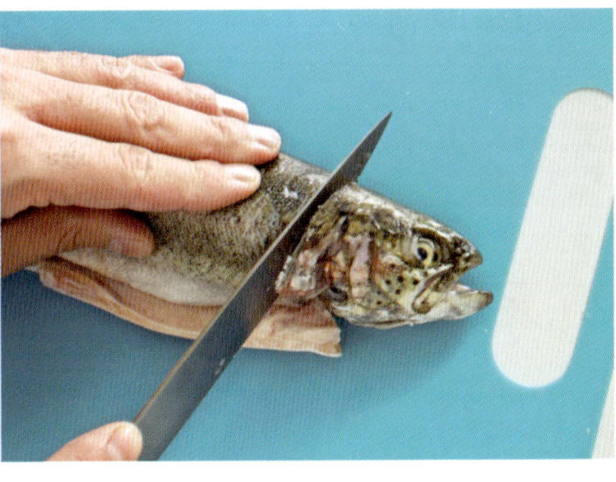

Turn the blade toward the tail fin and make a small cut.

Push the knife along the backbone and cut off the fillet. Make sure that the top fillet is always stretched, because it makes the job easier.

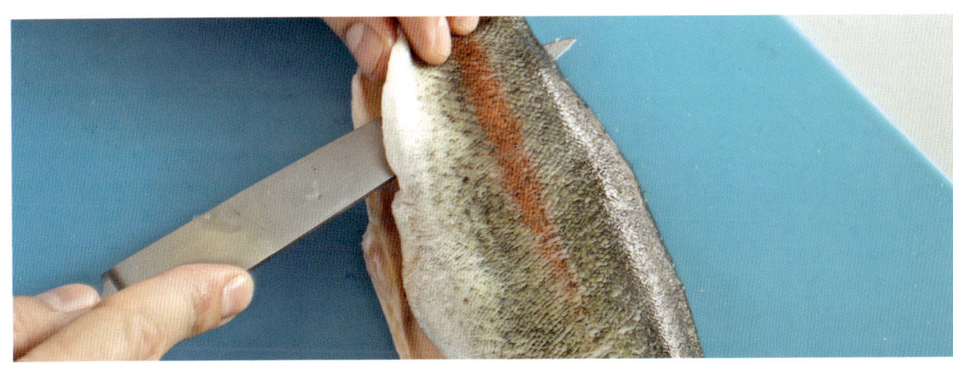

Remove the fillet with the knife all the way to the tail fin. Turn the fish over and remove the bottom fillet.

Remove the rib cage without cutting away too much meat and put the cuttings aside.

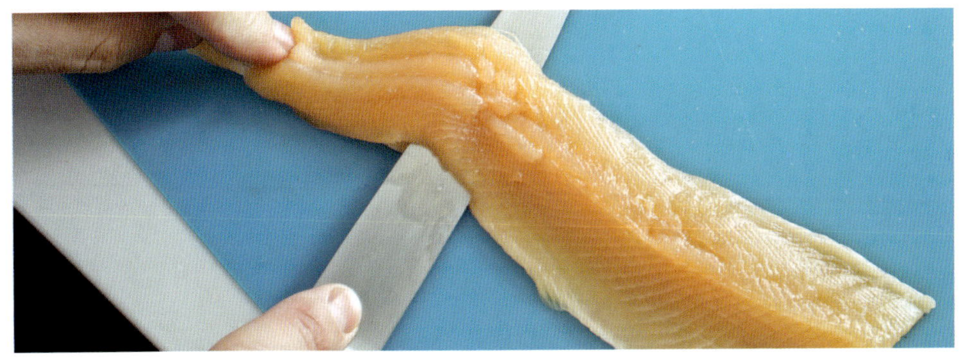

Separate the fillet from the skin. Hold the skin with your left hand and with the other hand remove the fillet with your knife.

Remove the small bones with fish pliers.

The leftovers from filleting are perfect to prepare fish stock later. Stock from freshwater fish is sometimes a bit cloudy and does not have the distinct flavor of saltwater fish.

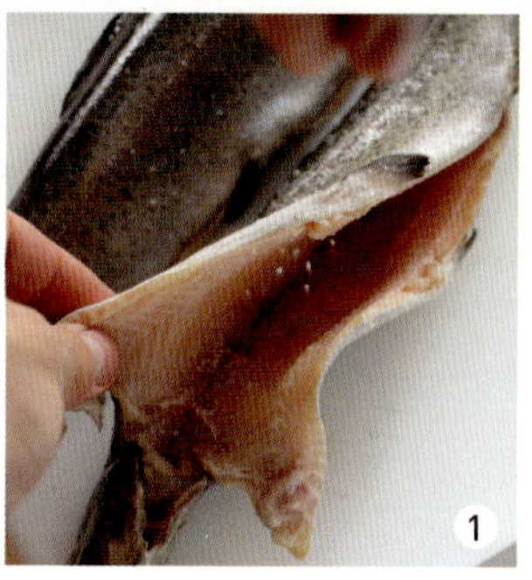

Trout Meunière

 4 trout, 9 oz (250 g) each

 1 pinch of salt

 ⅓ cup (50 g) flour

 4 tbsp vegetable oil

 ⅓ cup (80 g) butter

 1 bunch fresh parsley

 1 lemon

1. Gut the trout and scale, clean, and drain them (see p. 424). Season both the insides and outsides of the fish with salt and dust them lightly with flour.

2. Heat the oil in an oval skillet; place the trout in the pan and pan-fry for about 5–7 minutes on each side. After each trout is golden brown on both sides, remove the oil from the pan using a tablespoon.

3. Add the butter, sprinkle with washed, finely chopped parsley, and sauté. Finally, add the juice of a lemon, put the fish on a serving plate, and serve with parsley potatoes.

Trout Amandine

 4 trout, 9 oz (250 g) each

 1 pinch of salt

 ⅓ cup (50 g) flour

 4 tbsp vegetable oil

 ⅓ cup (80 g) butter

 2¼ oz (60 g) slivered almonds

1 lemon

1. Gut the trout and scale, clean, and drain them (see p. 424). Season both the insides and outsides of the fish with salt and dust them lightly with flour.

2. Heat the oil in an oval skillet; place the trout in the pan and pan-fry for about 5–7 minutes on each side. After each trout is golden brown in color on both sides, remove the oil from the pan using a tablespoon.

3. Add the butter and the almonds to the pan and sauté. The almonds should be light golden brown. Add the juice of the lemon, put the fish on a serving plate, and serve with parsley potatoes.

 4 catfish fillets, 5–5½ oz (140–160 g) each

 2¾ oz (80 g) leeks

 2¾ oz (80 g) carrots

 ¼ celeriac

 3⅓ cups (750 ml) water

 3 tbsp salt

 3 tbsp white vine or cider vinegar

 1 onion

 1 bay leaf

 1 clove

 ⅔ cup (150 ml) fish stock

 ¼ cup (50 g) butter, cold

 ½ bunch fresh chives

 ½ horseradish root

Catfish in Root Vegetable Stock

1. With a knife, trim the skinned catfish fillets and cut them in half. Slice the leeks, carrots, and celeriac into long thin strips (julienne-style, see p. 354). Put the water in a pot and add 2 tbsp salt and the vinegar. Stud the onion with the bay leaf and clove, and place it in the pot. Bring to a boil and let it simmer for 5 minutes. Place the catfish in this stock, take it off the burner, and let it sit for 8–10 minutes. In the meantime, cook the julienned vegetables in salt water for about 1 minute, and then shock them with cold water.

2. Combine the fish stock with ⅞ cup (200 ml) stock from the catfish, strain into a saucepan, and reduce the liquid for 5 minutes. Add the cold butter using a wire whisk to blend the stock well. Wash the chives and finely chop them.

3. Place the parboiled strips of vegetables in the stock. Place the catfish fillets in the stock and bring to a boil. Serve in soup plates and garnish by sprinkling the chives and finely grated fresh horseradish over it. Serve with vegetable rice or parsley potatoes.

■ **Cod fillets can be prepared the same way. However, increase the cooking time to 8 minutes and add 1 tsp mustard to the stock. This makes it more flavorful.**

4 catfish fillets, 5–5½ oz (140–160 g) each

1 lemon

1 pinch of salt
1 pinch of white pepper

1 tsp sweet paprika

1 tbsp extra virgin olive oil

3⅓ cups (750 ml) paprika cream sauce (see p. 150)

2 tbsp heavy cream, whipped

Catfish in Paprika Sauce

1. With a knife, trim the skinned catfish fillets and cut into ¾-inch (2-cm) strips. Place in a bowl and sprinkle with the juice of 1 lemon. Season to taste with salt, pepper, and paprika. Add the olive oil and mix. Marinate for about 10 minutes.

2. Pour the paprika cream sauce in a saucepan and bring to a boil. Place the marinated strips of catfish in it and reheat slowly for about 3 minutes. Do not boil it. This would make the fillets tough. Add the whipped cream, mix, and arrange on plates. Serve with parsley potatoes or steamed rice.

■ **Catfish is typically associated with traditional Deep South cooking. Pan-fried, grilled, broiled or baked catfish with blackening seasoning is called Catfish Creole, Cajun-style, or Blackened Catfish. Catfish gumbo (okra, tomatoes, and seasonings) is a traditional Louisiana dish.**

1 bunch fresh dill

3 cucumbers

1 lb 12 oz (800 g) salmon fillets, skinned

½ horseradish root

1 lemon

¼ cup (60 g) butter

1 pinch of salt
1 pinch of white pepper

1 pinch of sugar

⅞ cup (200 ml) fish stock

⅜ cup (100 ml) heavy cream

3½ oz (100 g) crème fraîche (or sour cream)

2 tbsp heavy cream, whipped

1

Salmon Steaks with Horseradish Butter and Cooked Cucumbers with Dill

1. Wash the dill, then set it aside. Peel the cucumbers, halve them lengthwise, and remove the seeds with a small spoon. Then, cut the cucumbers diagonally into ½-inch (1-cm) thick slices.

2. Trim the salmon, remove any bones with fish pliers, and cut the fillet into four equal portions. Marinate the fillets with freshly grated horseradish and the juice of half a lemon. Cut the other half of the lemon into thin slices.

3. Melt 4 tsp (20 g) butter in a wide pot and add the cucumber slices. Season with salt, white pepper, and sugar and sauté briefly. Add the fish stock and simmer for about 5 minutes, until the liquid is reduced by half.

4. Add the cream and the crème fraîche (or sour cream) and let it simmer for 1 minute. Mince the dill, combine with the whipped cream, and add the mixture to the cucumbers.

5. In the meantime, melt the remaining piece of butter in a nonstick skillet. Season the marinated salmon steaks and place in the skillet. Sauté slowly on both sides for about 3 minutes, while basting with butter. Arrange the cooked cucumbers on plates, place one piece of salmon on each plate, and garnish with a slice of lemon.

■ You can prepare a horseradish crust for the salmon pieces by beating ¼ cup (60 g) butter until creamy, then adding 2 egg yolks, 2 tbsp grated horseradish, and 2¾ oz (80 g) white breadcrumbs. Mix the ingredients and season with salt and pepper to taste. Pour the mixture over the raw pieces of salmon and place them in a buttered soufflé dish. Pour ⅜ cup (100 ml) white wine over it and bake for 15 minutes at 340°F (170°C/Gas Mark 3½) until golden brown.

2
3
4
5

 4 tbsp salt

 3 bay leaves

 1 tsp anise

 1 tbsp black peppercorns

 1 tbsp juniper berries

 1 tsp fennel seeds

 5 tbsp sugar

 1 bunch fresh dill

 1 lemon

 1 orange

 2 lb 4 oz (1 kg) salmon fillet

 12 potato pancakes (see p. 326)

Potato Pancakes with Cured Salmon

1. In the food processor, grind the salt, bay leaves, anise, peppercorns, juniper berries, and fennel seeds. Put the herbal mixture in a bowl, add the sugar, and mix.

2. Wash the dill and chop it. Peel the lemon and orange with a paring knife and slice the peel in fine strips. Place the salmon in a soufflé dish, with its cleaned skin facing the bottom. Arrange the dill together with the orange and lemon rinds over it, distributing them evenly.

3. Sprinkle the salt-sugar-herb mixture over the top and pat down lightly. Cover with plastic wrap and refrigerate in the marinade for about 24 hours.

4. After 12 hours, turn the salmon over and place it back in the refrigerator for an additional 12 hours, covered in plastic wrap. Remove the salmon from the marinade and cut the salmon into thin, diagonal slices with a long, sharp kitchen knife. Place them on the finished potato pancakes and garnish with dill and lemon slices.

+ 24 hours to marinate

■ **Serve crème fraîche or sour cream with a little lemon juice or a mustard-dill sauce as a dip.**

2
3
4

 2 carp fillets

 1 pinch of salt
1 pinch of black pepper

 2 lemons

 2 eggs

 ¾ cup (100 g) flour

 1 lb 2 oz (500 g) breadcrumbs

 4 tbsp oil

 ¼ cup (60 g) butter

Carp Fried in Breadcrumbs

1. Scale the carp fillets and clean with paper towels. Hold the fish with one hand while carefully removing the bones with fish pliers.

2. Cut the fillets into 1¼-inch (3-cm) wide strips and check with your fingers for bones. If necessary, use the fish pliers again.

3. Season the carp strips with salt and pepper, and rub them on both sides with the halved lemon. Slice the other lemon into small wedges and save for garnish.

4. Beat the eggs in a shallow dish. Dip the carp strips into the flour on both sides. Dip them in the egg mixture, then turn them in the breadcrumbs. Slightly pat the coating.

5. In a large skillet, melt the oil and butter and fry the carp pieces on both sides for about 8 minutes, until golden brown. Place them on paper towels to drain.

Potato-vegetable salad is a good side dish for this meal.

■ Carp is predominantly used in "Gefilte Fish," or stuffed fish, which is a Jewish tradition. If you use a large carp, remove the skin with a long sharp kitchen knife to avoid the dish becoming too fatty. It is best to use a carp that weighs approximately 2 lb 4 oz–3 lb 5 oz (1–1.5 kg).

2
3
4
5

⅔ cup (150 g) butter

2 tbsp chopped dill

1 tbsp chopped parsley

1 egg yolk

1 pinch of salt
1 pinch of white pepper

2 tbsp breadcrumbs

4 portions of salmon, 7 oz (200 g) each, skinned

⅜ cup (100 ml) dry white wine

4 slices lemon

Slow-Roasted Salmon

1. Use a small mixing bowl to beat the butter until creamy. Wash and finely chop the dill and the parsley and mix into the butter. Separate the egg white from the yolk and mix in the yolk. Season with salt and white pepper to taste. Mix in the breadcrumbs and season to taste.

2. Season the drained and cleaned salmon portions with salt, place each in an individual buttered soufflé dish, and spread on the herb butter.

3. Pour the white wine over the fillets. Slice the lemon and add 1 slice to each portion.

4. Cook the salmon in the oven, preheated to 185°F (85°C), for about 45 minutes. Remove and serve with white bread or rice. Cooking at such a low temperature makes the meat of the fish very tender and the herbal butter makes it juicy.

■ **A fresh alternative for this salmon dish is mincing the herbs together with 1 tbsp ginger and 1 bunch fresh cilantro before adding to the butter. Then continue as described above.**

2
3
4

 1⅛ cups (250 ml) red wine

 ⅜ cup (100 ml) port

 1 pinch of sugar

 ⅔ cup (150 ml) heavy cream

 1 pinch of salt
1 pinch of black pepper

 ½ cup (100 g) butter

 14 oz (400 g) spinach leaves

 1 pinch of nutmeg, freshly grated

 4 tilapia fillets, 5–5½ oz (140–160 g) each

 Juice of ½ lemon

 2 tbsp vegetable oil

 8 sprigs fresh lemon thyme

Poached Tilapia in Red Wine Butter Sauce

1. Combine the red wine and port with the sugar in a saucepan and reduce the liquid to about a sixth of its volume.

2. Add 3 tbsp (50 ml) heavy cream and bring it to a boil. Season with salt and pepper.

3. Cut ¼ cup (60 g) of the butter into thin slices and place in the red wine reduction to bind it. Set the sauce aside.

4. Thoroughly drain the washed spinach leaves. Melt 4 tsp (20 g) of the butter in a saucepan until it foams, add the spinach leaves, and let them wilt. Season with salt, pepper, and freshly grated nutmeg to taste. Add the remaining heavy cream and slowly simmer for an additional 2 minutes.

5. With a kitchen knife, cut the tilapia fillets into a nice shape, sprinkle the lemon juice over them, and season with salt on both sides. Heat the remaining butter and the oil in a nonstick saucepan. Place the fillets in it and top each with a sprig of lemon thyme. Baste with butter occasionally and sauté slowly for about 3 minutes on each side until lightly colored. Arrange the spinach in the middle of the serving plate, and place the sautéed tilapia fillet on top. Garnish with a sprig of lemon thyme.

■ A good red wine is an absolute must for a flavorful red wine butter sauce. This recipe can also be prepared with turbot, haddock, flounder, or pike instead of the tilapia. Leeks or Swiss chard can be substituted for spinach.

2
3
4
5

Saltwater Fish

Contents

442 Types of Fish
442 Cooking Chart
444 Gutting and Preparing Sea Bass
446 How to Prepare Turbot
447 How to Prepare Sole
448 Sea Bass Baked in Puff Pastry
452 Flounder Steamed in Swissh Chard Served in Tomato Sauce with Pesto Oil
454 Turbot Fillet Fried on the Bone
456 Sole in Sage Butter
458 Stuffed Sole Garnished with Potato Scales
460 Porgy Baked in Salt Crust
462 Sautéed Porgy Fillets in White Wine with Button Mushrooms
464 Salmon in Batter
466 Fried Sardines
468 Tuna Steak
470 Sesame-Coated Tuna Fish Sticks
472 Monkfish Medallions on a Ragout of Tomatoes with Capers
474 Hake Poached in Spiced Milk

Types of Fish

Fish must be fresh. Despite this, fish are sometimes as much as 14 days old when they are sold at the market, especially if they were not caught close to the coast. Large fishing boats stay out at sea for a week or more. Then the fish is delivered to the fish market, where wholesalers buy it. The wholesalers in turn sell it to small fish dealers or seafood markets.

In general, fish should always have bright, often protruding eyes. Its flesh must be firm to the touch and its gills bright pink or red. When you buy at a fish store or market, have them gut, scale, and fillet the fish. It is best to use the fish within the next two hours, or at least on the same day. Otherwise, the fish oxidizes and becomes bland.

Cooking Chart

Product	Weight	Method	Temperature	Time	Notes
Plaice fillet	4–5 oz (120–140 g)	Pan	Medium heat	4 minutes	
Atlantic catfish	1 lb 5 oz–1 lb 12 oz (600–800 g)	Pan	Medium heat	16–18 minutes	Fry
Tuna	7 oz (200 g)	Grill pan	High heat	4 minutes	Grill
Monkfish	Medallions of 1¾ oz (50 g)	Pan	High heat	3 minutes	Deep fry
Turbot	7 oz (200 g) each	Pan	Medium heat	10 minutes	Fry
Sole	1 lb 2 oz (500 g)	Pan	Medium heat	10 minutes	Fry
Porgy	1 lb 5 oz–1 lb 12 oz (600–800 g)	Oven	450°F (230°C/Gas Mark 8)	35 minutes	Bake
Hake	Pieces of 5½ oz (150 g) each	Pan	Low heat	10 minutes	In stock or spiced milk
Flounder	Portion size 5½ oz (150 g) each	Oven	325°F (160°C/Gas Mark 3)	12 minutes	Poach
Sardines	1 lb 2 oz (500 g)	Pot	High heat	2 minutes	Fry in oil
Salmon	Pieces of 7 oz (200 g) each	Pot	Medium heat	12 minutes	Pan-fry or fry in batter for 5 minutes

Sardine

Monkfish

John Dory

Sole

Porgy

Sea bass (Loup de Mer)

Turbot

Hake

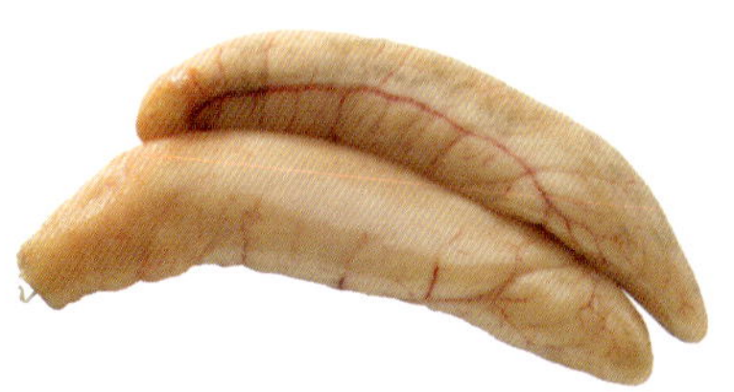

Hake roe

Tuna

Redfish

Gurnard (soup fish)

Gutting and Preparing Sea Bass

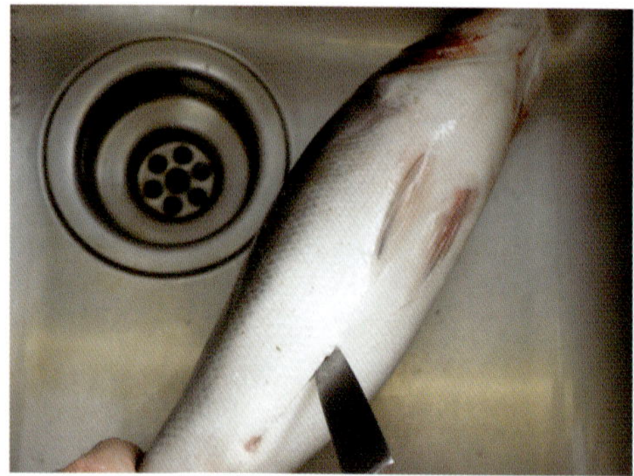

Carefully slit open the underside from the anus to the gills to avoid damaging the organs.

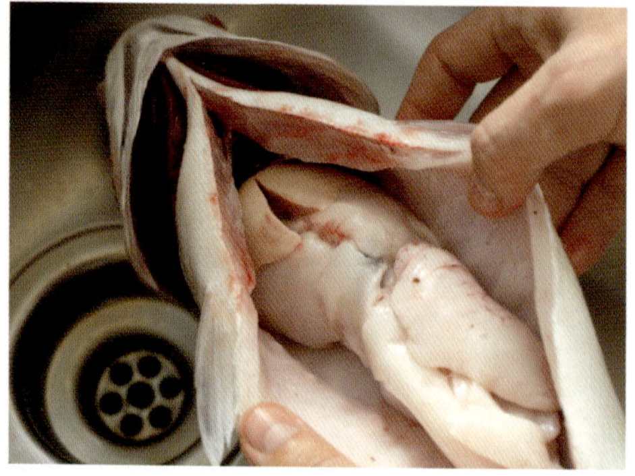

Carefully remove the innards.

Wash the fish thoroughly under running water.

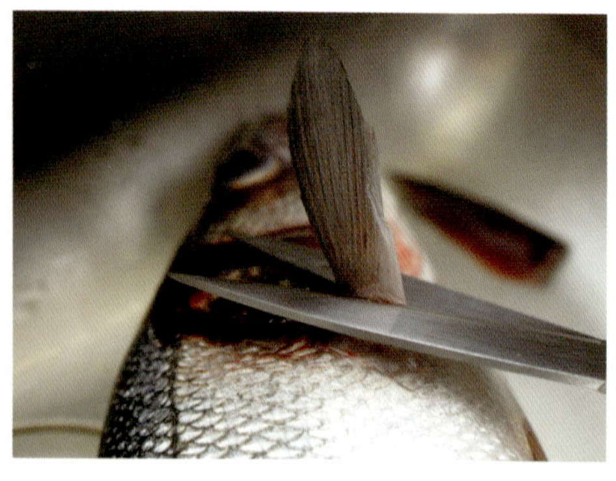

To prevent injury during further processing, use scissors to cut off all fins.

The dorsal fin is especially sharp and dangerous.

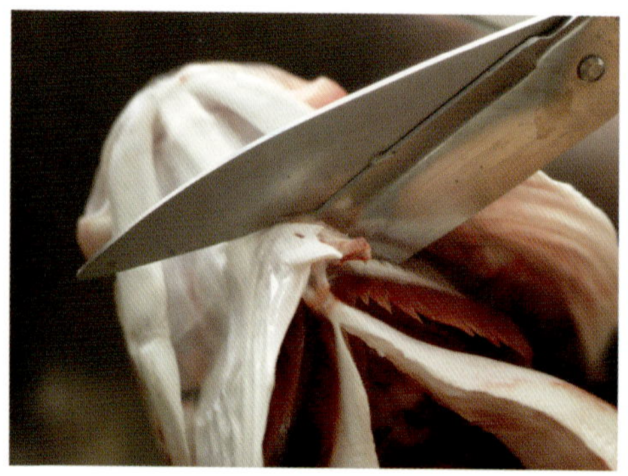

Cut into the sides of the gills with scissors.

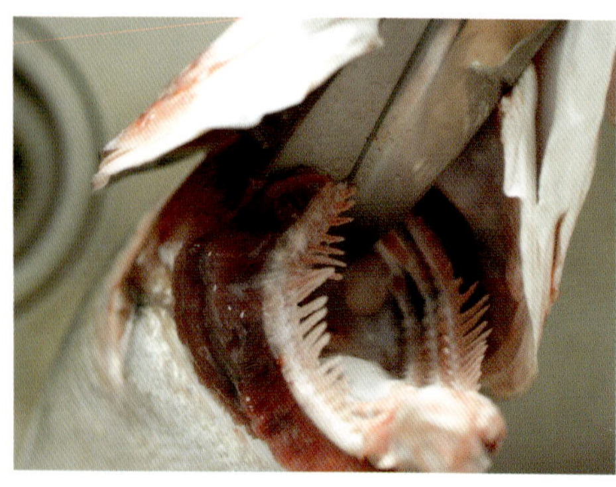

Remove the gills from the inside and cut them out. Wash the fish thoroughly.

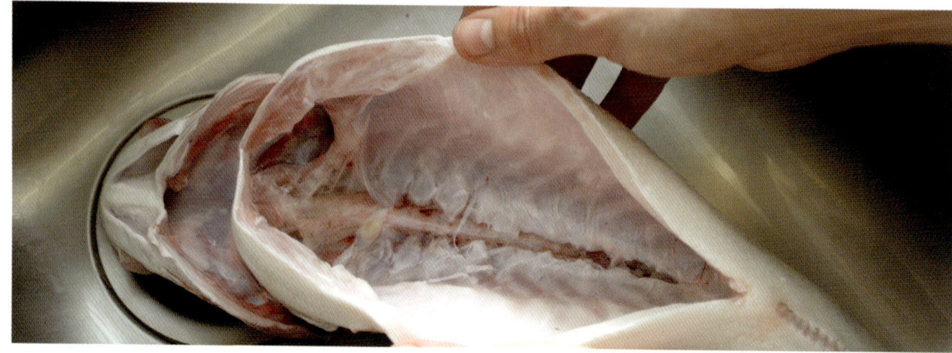

Take a knife and slit the underside of the backbone under running water, and remove the last remaining blood with a small spoon, or wash it out. The result is a completely gutted and cleaned sea bass.

You can check the freshness of fish by its protruding eyes. When the fish is fresh, it can be kept in the refrigerator for 3–4 days. However, before you store fish, you must gut it, as described previously.

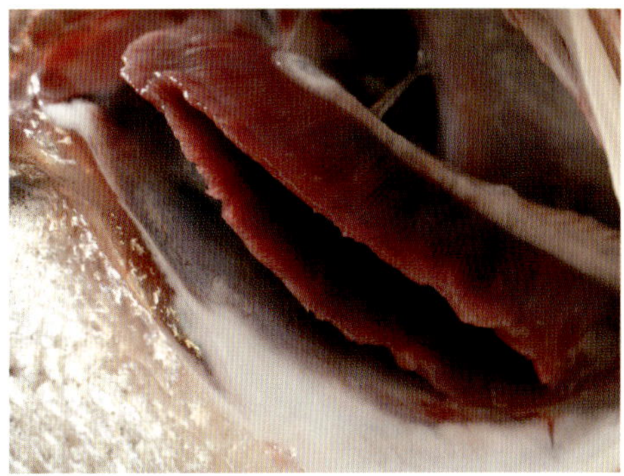

The gills must be bright red and preferably without slime. You can quickly smell whether a fish is fresh. It is fresh if it smells like the sea or relatively neutral.

Kitchen doctor: Innards and gills are the first parts of the fish to emit odors. By removing them, you can increase the fish's shelf life.

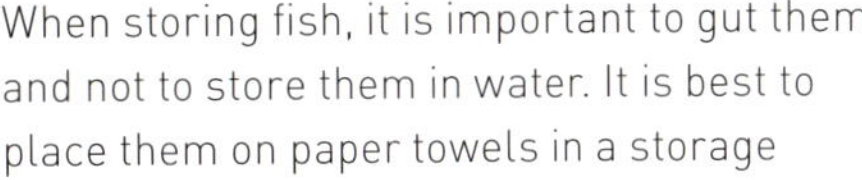

When storing fish, it is important to gut them and not to store them in water. It is best to place them on paper towels in a storage container and cover it with plastic wrap. Keep it refrigerated at about 39°F (4°C).

How to Prepare Turbot

1. Wash the turbot, remove the innards from its underside, and drain the fish.

2. With the kitchen scissors, cut off the tail fin, the ventral fins, and the dorsal fins.

3. Use a sharp knife to cut above the backbone.

4. Make a cut below the backbone. Turn the turbot over and repeat this step.

5. Cut out the fillets along the center bone using a serrated knife.

6. Use the head, and the center bone, for fish stock. The turbot portions are fried whole with the bones. This retains more flavor and they are juicier.

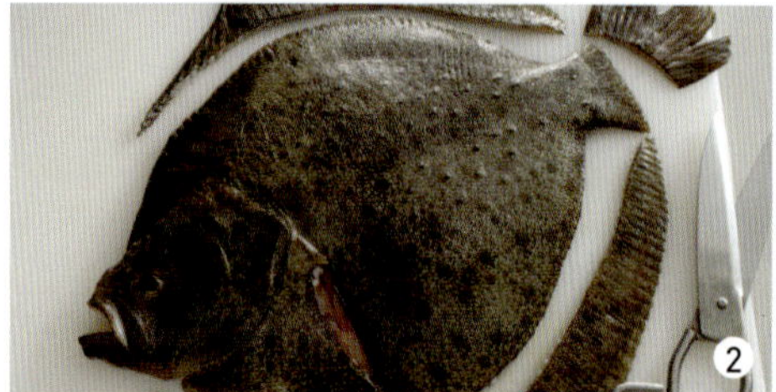

6

How to Prepare Sole

1. With a knife, make a slit in the skin at the center of the tail fin and lightly peel in order to get a better grip.

2. Grab the skin with paper towels, so it does not slip out of your hands.

3. Pull off only the dark skin over the head. Leave the white skin and scale it.

4. With kitchen scissors cut off the fins.

5. Make a cut along the underside and remove the innards and remaining blood.

6. Wash the finished sole under running water and pat dry with paper towels. Keep covered in the refrigerator until ready to use. Either pan-fry it whole or remove the fillets with a knife.

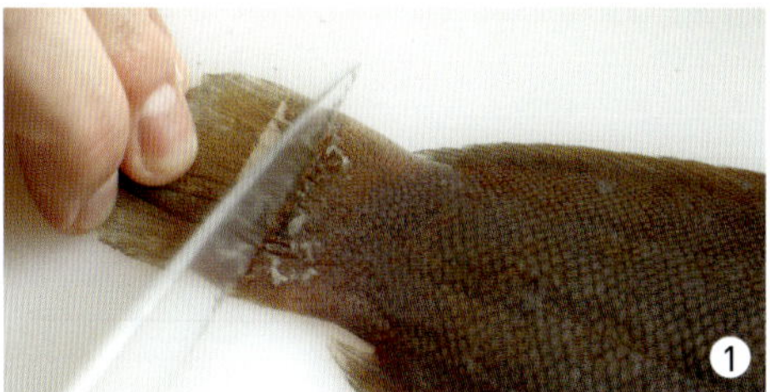

6

 1 sea bass, 4 lb 8 oz (2 kg)

 12 oz (350 g) shrimp

 ½ bunch fresh dill

 3 eggs

 2 tbsp heavy cream

 1 tsp salt

 ⅔ cup (150 g) crème fraîche (or sour cream)

 1 pinch of cayenne pepper

 juice of ½ lemon

 2 tbsp flour

 1 lb 10 oz (750 g) puff pastry dough

 2¼ cups (500 ml) Crustacean Cream Sauce (see p. 143)

Sea Bass Baked in Puff Pastry

1. Gut the sea bass (see p. 444), clean, and pat dry. Peel the shrimp and, after deveining, refrigerate them. Wash the dill, then mince. Separate 2 eggs and combine the yolks with the heavy cream. Refrigerate the egg-cream mixture. With a sharp, long, thin knife, cut open the fish starting at the backbone, and cut off the tail fin. Turn the fish over and repeat the previous step, so that the fillets are connected only at the head. With scissors, remove the entire backbone and cut the bones away close to the underside. Remove any remaining bones with fish pliers.

2. With a knife, cut the skin from the fillet. Hold the blade diagonally toward the bottom skin and separate it from the fillet starting at the tail. With your other hand, hold the skin, applying light tension. Refrigerate the sea bass.

3. Mix the shrimp with 1 egg and ½ tsp salt in the food processor for 1 minute and then pour the mixture in a bowl.

4. Add the minced dill, crème fraîche, and cayenne pepper to the shrimp. Mix with the juice of half a lemon, and place it in the refrigerator until further processing.

5. Season the sea bass with salt, carefully turning it over. Then spread the shrimp mixture on top of the bottom fillet and place the top fillet over it, pressing down lightly to avoid any air spaces.

»

■ **Take your time for the preparations, especially for deboning.**

2
3

4

6

7

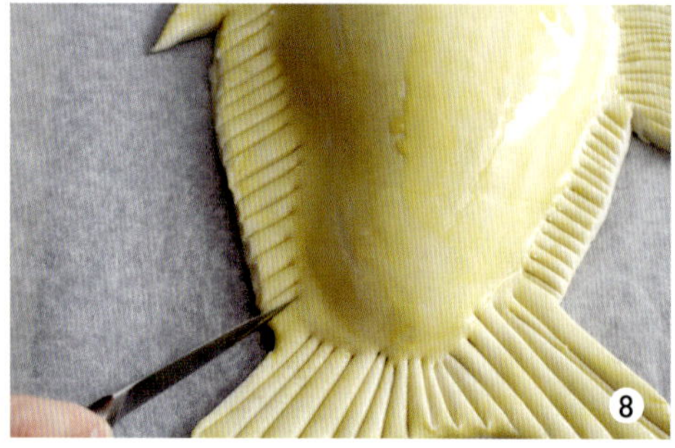

8

9

6. Dust the work surface with flour, halve the pastry dough, and roll each piece out to a thickness of about ¼ inch (5 mm). Brush some of the egg-cream mixture on one piece of the dough. This helps the puff pastry cover to close more easily. Place the stuffed fish carefully on top of the dough and cover with the second portion of the dough.

7. Press the edges of the dough together so they stick. Take a knife and cut out the shape of a fish, and set aside the remaining dough. Brush more egg-cream mixture on the dough fish.

8. Then place the dough fish on a cookie sheet covered with parchment paper, and with the back of a knife press a fin pattern in the dough.

9. Then take a round object, such as a liqueur glass, and mimic scales. Use a strip of dough to mark the head. Then brush on more egg-cream mixture.

10. Cut a small hole in the pastry at the head to prevent enclosed air from tearing the dough during baking.

11. Preheat the oven to 350°F (180°C/Gas Mark 4), place the fish in it, and bake for about 40 minutes. After a few minutes, cover the head, tail, and edges with aluminum foil. This prevents the puff pastry from turning too dark on those places. After 20 minutes, reduce the temperature to 325°F (160°C/Gas Mark 3).

12. Remove the baked sea bass from the oven, then use a serrated knife to cut it into 1¼-inch (3-cm) portions. In the meantime, pour the reheated Crustacean Cream Sauce on the plates and carefully place one portion of sea bass on each.

■ **This recipe is suitable for special occasions and can be adapted to suit any taste. Try filling the pastry with spinach and vegetables or lobster and truffles. Serve with well-chilled champagne.**

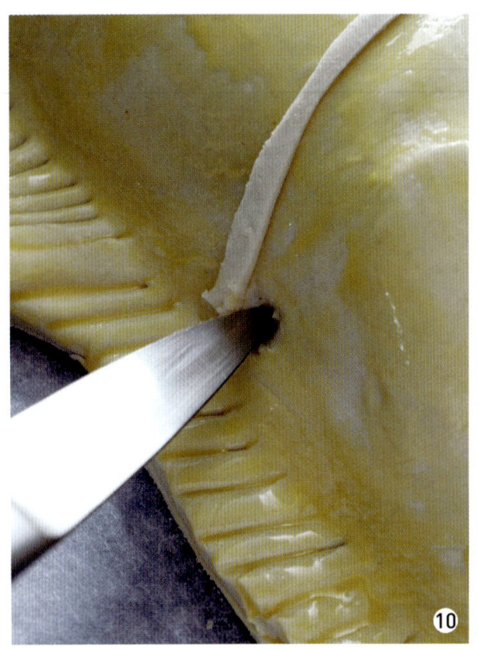
10

11

12

 10 ½ oz (300 g) salmon fillet

 1 pinch of salt

 ¼ cup (60 g) heavy cream

 1 egg

 Juice of ½ lemon

 1 pinch of cayenne pepper

 3 tbsp (40 ml) dry vermouth

 8 Swiss chard leaves

 1 lb 5 oz (600 g) flounder fillets

 4 tsp (20 g) butter

 3 tbsp extra virgin olive oil

 2 tbsp pesto (see p. 60)

 1¾ cups (400 ml) Easy Tomato Sauce (see p. 144)

Flounder Steamed in Swiss Chard Served in Tomato Sauce with Pesto Oil

1. Cut the skinned salmon fillet into ¾-inch (2-cm) pieces and put them in the food processor. Add 3 crushed ice cubes. Season with salt and add the heavy cream. Separate the egg and add the egg white.

2. Mix well for about 1 minute. Season with the lemon juice, cayenne pepper, and some dry vermouth. Use a rubber spatula to push the mixture through a fine strainer into a bowl, cover, and refrigerate to be used later.

3. Boil water in a pot, season with salt, and add the Swiss chard leaves. Cook for only 15 seconds. Place in a bowl with water and ice cubes to chill, stopping the cooking process. Remove the Swiss chard leaves and place them on paper towels to drain.

4. Place 2 Swiss chard leaves on top of each other and spread 1 tbsp of salmon mixture on top. Cut the flounder fillets into 4 equal portions, season with salt, and place in the center of the Swiss chard leaves. Fold the sides over and roll up like a package.

■ Cut off the Swiss chard stems so the leaves roll more easily. Other types of fish, such as turbot, salmon, or pike, also taste delicious when wrapped in Swiss chard.

5. Coat a baking dish with butter and pour in the remaining vermouth. Smear a little butter on the top side of each package and season with salt. Preheat the oven to 325°F (160°C/Gas Mark 3). Mix the olive oil with the pesto and heat the tomato sauce in a saucepan.

6. Cover the baking dish with parchment paper and cook in the oven for about 12 minutes. Spoon the tomato sauce onto the serving plates. Cut the Swiss chard parcels in half and place them with the cut side up on the tomato sauce. Sprinkle with pesto oil and serve.

2 turbots, about 1 lb 12 oz (800 g) each

1 pinch of salt
1 pinch of white pepper

¼ cup (30 g) flour

4 tbsp vegetable oil

¼ cup (60 g) butter

½ bunch fresh parsley

Juice of ½ lemon

Turbot Fillet Fried on the Bone

1. Fillet the turbot along the bone (see p. 444). Season both sides of the turbot fillets with salt and pepper and lightly dust with flour. Shake off the excess flour. Heat the oil in a large oval skillet (fish pan), fry the turbot with its dark side down, basting with the oil. Turn over after about 5 minutes and pan-fry for another 5 minutes.

2. With a spoon, remove the oil from the pan. Add the butter, and slowly sweat the turbot at low heat for 2 minutes. Make sure the butter is not getting too dark.

3. Remove the dark skin of the turbot while still in the pan. It is easily removed after the turbot is cooked. Season with salt to taste.

4. Wash, trim, and mince the parsley and add it to the pan with the lemon juice. Slightly tilt the pan and keep pouring butter from the pan over the turbot. Place the turbot on a serving plate and pour the parsley butter over it. Serve with mashed potatoes (see p. 336).

■ As an alternative, you can prepare one 10½ oz (300 g) turbot fillet per person. Tarragon, basil, and chives can be substituted for the parsley.

2
3
4

½ bunch fresh sage

1 bunch fresh parsley

1 lb 2 oz (500 g) small firm-fleshed potatoes

4 sole fillets

1 pinch of salt

1 lemon

4 tbsp flour

½ cup (125 ml) safflower oil

½ cup (100 g) butter

1

Sole in Sage Butter

1. Wash the sage and set aside the leaves. Wash the parsley and mince. Peel the potatoes and cook in salted water. Slit the fish on both sides along the backbone. This makes it easier to remove the bones later. Season with salt and sprinkle some lemon juice over it. Dust with flour and remove any excess flour. Heat an oval skillet over medium heat, add the safflower oil, and fry the fish with the white side of its skin on the bottom for 5 minutes, until golden brown. Then turn it over and fry for an additional 5 minutes. Spoon out the oil, add 3/8 cup (80 g) butter, and let it froth.

2. Refry the fish in the butter and occasionally baste with the butter. Drain the potatoes. Use the remaining butter and the parsley for the potatoes, mix, and season with salt to taste.

3. Add the sage leaves to the sole and continue to baste the sole until the sage leaves are crisp. Arrange the cooked potatoes on serving plates. Place the whole fish on the serving plate and pour the sage butter over it.

■ **The bones of a fried sole can be carefully removed with a spoon. Serve with fresh spinach or white wine sauce.**

 2 sole fillets

 1 pinch of salt

 7 oz (200 g) white fish fillet

 3 tbsp (50 ml) heavy cream

 1 pinch of cayenne pepper

 1 bunch fresh parsley

 10 basil leaves

 2 sprigs fresh tarragon

 ½ bunch fresh chives

 10 ½ oz (300 g) potatoes

 ⅔ cup (150 ml) butter, clarified (see p. 34)

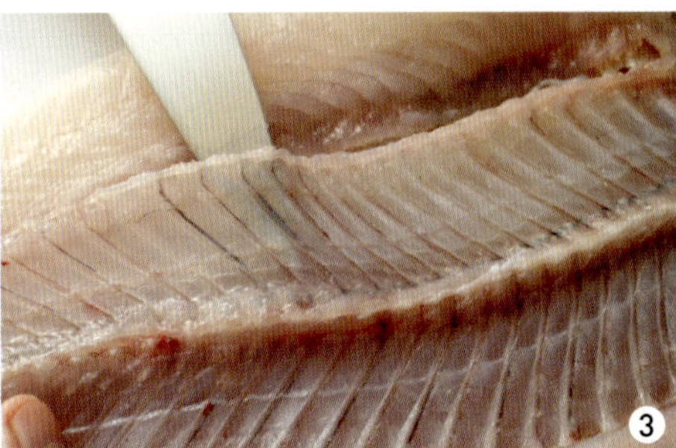

Stuffed Sole Garnished with Potato Scales

1. Use a sharp, flexible knife to cut the prepared sole (see p. 444) along their backbone. Slowly loosen the fillet until the center bone is clearly visible, but the fillets are still attached to the sole.

2. Separate the outside of the center bone, starting from the fish's tail, using kitchen scissors.

3. With the knife, cut along the center bone to loosen it.

4. Bend the center bone, which now is only attached at one point, from the tail end up and gradually pull out. Season the sole on the inside and outside with salt.

5. Dice the white fish fillet and place in the freezer for 5 minutes. Place the frozen cubes in the food processor, add the heavy cream, and mix until smooth. Season with salt and cayenne pepper. Wash the herbs, trim, mince, and add to the mixture. Spread the herb filling on the open sole.

6. Close the fillets. This brings your sole back to its original shape.

7. Peel the potatoes and slice paper thin. Place three slices on top of each other and cut out ¾-inch (2-cm) circles with a cookie cutter.

■ You can also prepare the herb filling with watercress or dill. In addition, you can coat the unfilled sole with breadcrumbs like veal scallops or Wiener schnitzel and bake it in butter and oil until golden brown. Then put the herb or tomato butter inside and let it melt.

8. Overlap the potato slices like scales on the sole and generously brush on the clarified butter; then season with salt.

9. Place the sole for 3 minutes in the freezer, so the butter solidifies, and the sole can be placed in a skillet without the potato scales moving around. Use a nonstick skillet at medium heat and slowly sauté the fish with the scales on the bottom. Tilt the pan occasionally and use the liquid in the pan to pour over the sole with a spoon. Carefully turn it over after 5 minutes and sauté for an additional 5 minutes.

4 lb 8 oz (2 kg) coarse sea salt

1 porgy, about 2 lb 4 oz (1kg), unscaled

1 slice of fennel

1 slice of lime

10 white peppercorns

1 sprig fresh rosemary

Some fennel greens

Porgy Baked in Salt Crust

1. Moisten the coarse sea salt with a bit of water and mix to form a paste.

2. Stuff the prepared but unscaled porgy with the slice of fennel, the slice of lime, the white peppercorns, the rosemary sprig, and the fennel green. Then close the fish up, so that no salt from the salt crust can get inside.

3. Place a piece of parchment paper on a cookie sheet and add a ½-inch (1-cm) thick layer of salt. Place the porgy on top and cover with the rest of the salt.

4. Pat down the salt around the fish to form the shape of a fish.

5. Put the fish in a preheated oven and cook for about 35 minutes at 450°F (230°C/Gas Mark 8). Break open the salt crust to free the fish.

6. Cut the skin along the backbone, and then use a spoon and a knife to skin the fish.

7. Carefully remove the fillets. Make sure the fish does not come in contact with the salt crust. Place the fillets on a serving plate and put them back together. Sprinkle tomato vinaigrette (see below) over the fish. Serve with fresh bread or rosemary potatoes.

■ Prepare a light vinaigrette using diced tomatoes, olive oil, lemon juice, fennel greens, salt, and pepper. Pour it over the fish fillets.

4
5
6
7

 ½ leek

 5 button mushrooms

 3 tbsp (40 g) butter

 4 porgy fillets, 6 oz (180 g) each, skinned

 1 pinch of salt

 1 pinch of white pepper

 3 tbsp (40 ml) vermouth

 ⅔ cup (150 ml) good-quality white wine

 1 tbsp basil leaves

Sautéed Porgy Fillets in White Wine with Button Mushrooms

1. Cut the leek lengthwise in half and slice into thin strips. Clean the mushrooms and cut into thin slices. Sauté both in the pan with 2 tbsp frothing butter and season with a bit of salt.

2. Pat the porgy fillets dry with paper towels and season with salt and white pepper. Put them in the skillet over the vegetables.

3. Add the vermouth and the white wine. Reduce the heat to about one third.

4. Sprinkle with basil leaves and cover with a lid. Steam for about 5 minutes. Add the rest of the cold butter.

Serve with potatoes or rice.

■ **Try this dish with Atlantic catfish, turbot, or halibut fillets instead of the porgy, and serve with white wine or butter sauce.**

2
3
4

 3 eggs

 2⅓ cups (300 g) flour

 1 tsp baking powder

 1 tsp salt

 1½ cups (360 ml) beer

 1 lb 5 oz (600 g) salmon fillet

 1 pinch of white pepper

 Juice of ½ lemon

 2 quarts (2 liters) vegetable oil for frying

Salmon in Batter

1. Separate the eggs and refrigerate the egg whites. Put the flour in a mixing bowl. Add the egg yolks, the baking powder, and 1 pinch of salt.

2. Gradually add the beer and beat until the batter is smooth.

3. Add a few drops of vegetable oil to make the batter crispy. Beat the egg whites with 1 pinch of salt into soft peaks, and carefully fold into the batter.

4. Cut the salmon fillets into 1½-oz (40-g) pieces, season with salt and pepper, sprinkle some lemon juice over them, and carefully dip them in the batter.

5. Place the salmon pieces in the oil heated to 325°F (160°C), fry for about 5 minutes, or until cooked and remove them. Drain on paper towels.

Serve with French fries or potato salad and garnish with lemon wedges.

35

■ **To prevent the fat from splattering, it is best to use a pot with high sides.**

2
3

4

5

 9 oz (250 g) sardines

 2 tbsp flour

 2 quarts (2 liters) vegetable oil for frying

 ½ tsp salt

 1 lemon

Fried Sardines

1. Clean the sardines under running water. Slowly break away the head with an upward motion and pull out the innards.

2. Open the stomach with your thumb and wash it thoroughly. After removing the head you can loosen the backbone and remove it completely.

3. Place the sardines in a sieve, pat dry, and sprinkle with flour.

4. Then place the sieve over the sink to remove any excess flour.

5. Heat the oil in a wide pot to 340°F (170°C). Fry whole sardines for 2 minutes, sardine fillets for 1 minute. Remove from oil and drain on paper towels. Serve with a lemon wedge as a snack with beer.

■ Sardines prepared the Italian way means they are marinated in balsamic vinegar and olive oil and served cold with white bread.

2
3
4
5

 1 eggplant

 1 pinch of salt

 6 tbsp extra virgin olive oil

 1 tsp tandoori powder

 2 red onions

 3 tomatoes, peeled

 10 basil leaves

 1-inch (2.5-cm) piece of fresh ginger

 4 limes

 1 pinch of black pepper

 1 lb 12 oz (800 g) tuna fillet

Tuna Steak

1. Cut the eggplant into ½-inch (1-cm) slices, season with salt to taste, and sauté on both sides in a skillet using 2 tbsp olive oil. Mix the tandoori powder with 2 tbsp olive oil in a small bowl and season lightly with salt.

2. Peel and dice the onions. Seed the peeled tomatoes (see p. 346). Mince the basil leaves, peel the ginger, and finely grate. Combine in a bowl with the juice of 2 limes. Season with salt and pepper.

3. Cut the tuna fillet into 1¼-inch (3-cm) thick steaks, spread the remainder of the olive oil over them, and season with salt. Cut the remaining limes in half.

4. Grill the tuna steaks in a nonstick griddle for 2 minutes on each side. Pour the tomato-onion sauce on the serving plates and arrange the fried eggplant slices and tuna steaks over it. Garnish with tandoori oil and the lime halves, and serve.

■ **Tuna remains fresh longer if sliced shortly before cooking.**

2
3

4

- 1 lb 5 oz (600 g) tuna fillet
- 1 tsp roasted sesame oil
- 2¾ oz (80 g) black sesame seeds
- 2¾ oz (80 g) white sesame seeds
- 1 lemon
- 3 tsp chili oil
- 3 tsp soy sauce

Sesame-Coated Tuna Fish Sticks

1. Pat dry the tuna fillet, remove any tendons, and cut into ½-inch (1-cm) slices.

2. Cut the slices into ¾-inch (2-cm) strips.

3. Sprinkle the roasted sesame oil over the strips and turn them to coat.

4. Place the tuna pieces on a baking sheet with the mixed black and white sesame seeds and turn them to cover them on all sides with the seeds.

5. Fry them in a nonstick pan without oil for about 1 minute. The tuna should be slightly raw on the inside. If you like the fish well done, then double the cooking time.

Arrange the fish sticks on a serving plate, add the lemon slices, sprinkle a bit of chili oil over them, serve with soy sauce. Serve cooked rice or steamed spinach as a side dish.

■ **The sesame seeds can be mixed with chopped fennel seeds, coriander seeds, or a few Sichuan peppercorns. This gives the tuna fish sticks more zest and aroma.**

3

4

5

 2 shallots

 1 lb 10 oz (750 g) cherry tomatoes of various colors

 1 tbsp capers

 1 garlic clove

 ½ bunch fresh basil

 3 lb 5 oz (1.5 kg) monkfish

 1 sprig fresh thyme

 ⅛ cup (30 g) butter

 2 tbsp extra virgin olive oil

 1 pinch of salt

 1 tsp sugar

 1 pinch of black pepper

 2¼ cups (500 ml) fish stock

 2 tbsp safflower oil

 1 pinch of sea salt

 1 tbsp coarse mustard

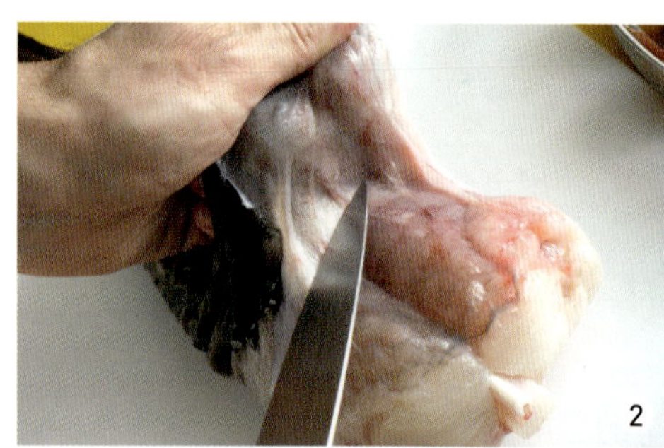

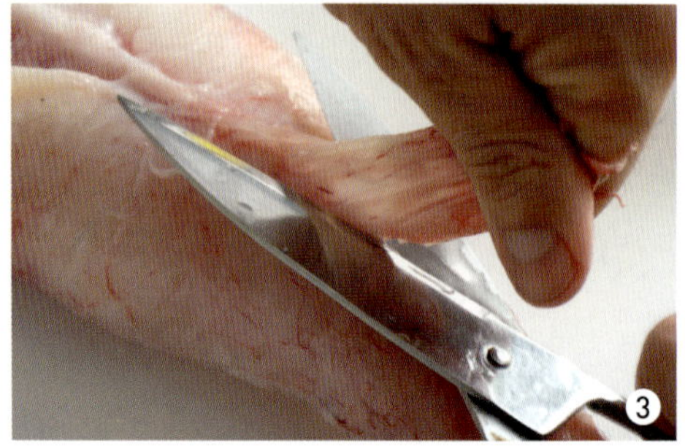

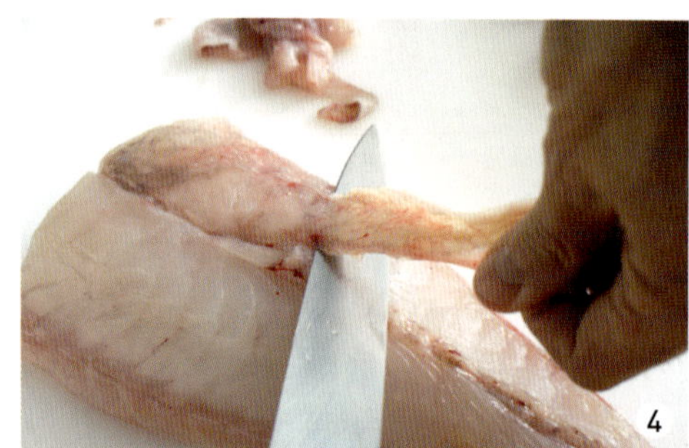

Monkfish Medallions on a Ragout of Tomatoes with Capers

1. Peel the shallots and dice. Wash and hull the cherry tomatoes. Chop the capers. Peel the garlic and dice. Wash the basil and cut into fine strips.

2. Prepare the monkfish. First, remove the skin by stretching it with the left hand and cutting it with the tip of the knife. Just pull off the last 4 inches (10 cm) of the skin.

3. Cut off the dorsal and ventral fins with scissors.

4. Remove the top layer of the skin and all bloody skin layers carefully with a sharp knife. Cut the fish into 1¼-inch (3-cm) slices.

5. Sprinkle the thyme leaves over the monkfish.

6. Melt 2 tsp (10 g) butter with the olive oil in a saucepan over medium heat and brown the garlic with the shallots. Add the cherry tomatoes and season with regular salt, sugar, and freshly ground black pepper. Reduce the temperature to low heat. Pour in the fish stock and simmer for 7 minutes.

■ The tomato varieties not only add color to the ragout, but they also add varied flavors.

7. Pour the safflower oil in a skillet and sauté the monkfish on both sides for 2–3 minutes at medium to high heat. Season with sea salt.

8. Add the capers, the basil, the mustard, and 4 tsp (20 g) butter to the tomatoes and lightly toss in the pan. Spoon the finished tomato ragout onto serving plates and place the sautéed monkfish medallions on top of it.

 2 lb 12 oz (1.2 kg) hake

 1 lb 5 oz (600 g) steamed rice (see p. 236)

 2 tbsp safflower oil

 1 tsp hot paprika

 2 quarts (2 liters) milk

 4 shallots

 5 garlic cloves

 1 tbsp salt

 3 bay leaves

 3 sprigs fresh thyme

 3 dried jalapeño peppers

 5 cloves

 10 juniper berries

 1 tsp fennel seeds

 ½ tsp white peppercorns

 4 tsp paprika oil

Hake Poached in Spiced Milk

1. Prepare the hake like a sea bass (see p. 444) and gut. Cut off the dorsal, ventral, and pectoral fins.

2. Cut out the skin of the abdominal cavity and rinse the fish thoroughly. Scale the hake and rinse again.

3. Cut into 1½-inch (4-cm) portions and set aside. Prepare the steamed rice. Mix the safflower oil with the hot paprika.

4. Pour the milk into a wide cooking pot. Slice the shallots, crush the garlic cloves in their skins, and add them with the salt and all the herbs and spices. Bring to a boil and reduce the heat.

5. Place the hake pieces in the milk and let sit for about 10 minutes. Spoon the rice onto the serving plates and place the hake directly from the spiced milk on top of the rice. Sprinkle with some hot paprika oil and serve.

■ **Small whiting and hake can be cooked whole in the milk. They make a delicious meal.**

2
3
4
5

Crustaceans & Shellfish

Contents

478 Crustaceans and Shellfish
478 Cooking Chart
480 Cleaning Mussels
480 How to Open an Oyster
481 How to Open Razor Shells
482 Cracking a Cooked Lobster
484 Peeling Shrimp
486 Defrosting Crustaceans and Shellfish
488 Shrimp Cocktail with Cocktail Sauce
490 Sautéed Sesame-Coated Shrimp
492 Garlic Shrimp
494 Boiled Lobster with Corn and Melted Butter
496 Crispy Crab Cakes
498 Crayfish in Dill Stock
500 Oysters on Ice
501 Baked Oysters
502 Octopus with Lemon Dressing
504 Mussels Steamed in White Wine
506 Mussels in Herb Marinade
508 Razor Shells with Herbs and Soy Sauce
510 Fried Scallops Wrapped in Bacon
512 Grilled Cuttlefish

Crustaceans and Shellfish

Whether lobster or crayfish, crustaceans should be bought alive and consumed on the same day. The so-called noble crustaceans, such as lobster and crayfish, have little flavor after being frozen. Don't buy precooked crustaceans at the store. You don't really know how long they have lived in the tank, and you don't know whether the dealer has kept the right cooking time. Two additional rules make it a little easier to shop for lobsters and crayfish: just like with fish, crustaceans from tropical waters are less noble than their cousins from the cold arctic seas. And just like with poultry, beef, pork, or venison, female animals taste better than their male counterparts. If you don't feel good about placing a live lobster in the cooking pot, let it rest in the refrigerator for a few hours; then the lobster will be a bit dazed and sleep deeply.

Even mussels should be bought fresh. Do not eat any mussels that open easily and without resistance. Wrap live clams firmly in a moist towel to prevent them from opening.

Cooking Chart

Product	Weight/Size	Method	Temperature	Time	Notes
Crayfish	2 lb 4 oz (1 kg)	Cooking pot	Boil	3 minutes	
Oysters	Belon 00 or Fines de Claire	Oven	425°F (220°C/Gas Mark 7)	2–3 minutes	Bake with sauce
Lobster	1 lb 4 oz (550 g)	Cooking pot	Low heat	10 minutes	Put in boiling water to kill the lobster, then let it simmer and cook
Shrimp	Medium-sized without shell	Saucepan	Medium heat	2 minutes	
Octopus	Approx. 1 lb 4 oz (600 g)	Large pot	Medium heat	40 minutes	
Mussels		Large pot	High heat	3–5 minutes	Depending on size
Razor shells		Oven	425°F (220°C/Gas Mark 7)	8 minutes	Baked
Scallops	Muscle only	Skillet	High heat	1–2 minutes	Taste delicious when eaten raw or only fried on one side
Cuttlefish	Approx. 5 ½ oz (150 g)	Grill pan	High heat	4–6 minutes	

Shrimp
Lobster
Spiny lobster
Shrimp scampi, Norway lobster
Mussel
Scallop
Oyster
Clams
Crayfish
Cuttlefish
Calamari
Octopus

Cleaning Mussels

1. Wash the mussels carefully under cold running water.

2. Remove any soil from the outside by hand and remove the "beard," or byssal threads, which come off easily after wiggling them back and forth a bit.

3. As you clean, discard any open mussels. They are no longer alive and therefore unusable.

How to Open an Oyster

1. Clean the outside of the oyster under cold running water and rub the shell with a brush. Do not place the oysters in water, unless it is seawater.

2. Hold the oyster in a kitchen towel with the backside sticking out. The towel prevents the oyster from moving while you open it. Stick the tip of the oyster knife in the small opening on the back and insert the knife by moving it back and forth.

3. Now crack the oyster with a twist. Use the oyster knife to detach the muscle that clings to the top shell and open the oyster carefully, so you don't lose the liquid inside. Remove any remaining shell pieces with a small brush dipped in saltwater.

How to Open Razor Shells

1. Thoroughly wash the razor shells in cold water.

2. To open the shell, place a small knife at the top edge.

3. Press the shells lightly apart. Carefully cut along the underside of the muscle with the knife and loosen.

4. Discard any that have cracked shells.

4

Cracking a Cooked Lobster

1. First twist the claws toward the inside to separate them from the body.

2. Then separate the tail from the body.

3. Turn the lobster and hold its back. Then, break away its head toward the top.

4. Use a small spoon to remove the tomalley. You can eat it just as it is or use it in lobster sauce, soup, or lobster butter. Crack the head further, and remove and discard the stomach.

5. Push with both hands on the shell to break it.

6. Break the shell by pulling both hands apart. The meat will remain intact.

7. Break the joints of the claws by hand.

8. The joints contain meat. To crack them open and remove the meat, just tap the shell a few times with a knife handle.

9. Cut along the side of the joints with kitchen scissors to get the meat.

10. Open it with your thumb and pull out the meat. Clean off the white protein parts by hand, but do not rinse them off.

11. Tap the pincers on the cutting board to loosen the meat inside. Push the smaller part of the pincer downward and once upward.

12. Carefully remove the pincer so that both tendons come out.

13. Crack the underside of the pincer with the back of the knife. Repeat this step for the top side.

14. Tap from the side, so that the front part comes loose.

15. Use the lobster shells for soups, sauces, or stock. The lobster is now completely cracked open.

10

11

12

13

14

15

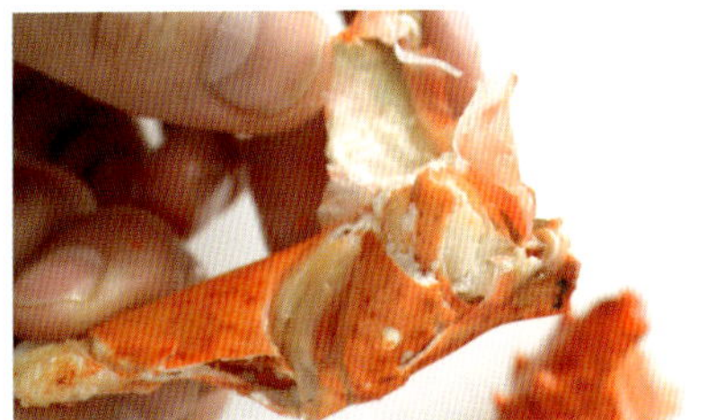

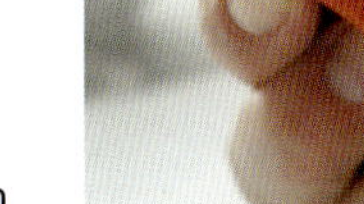

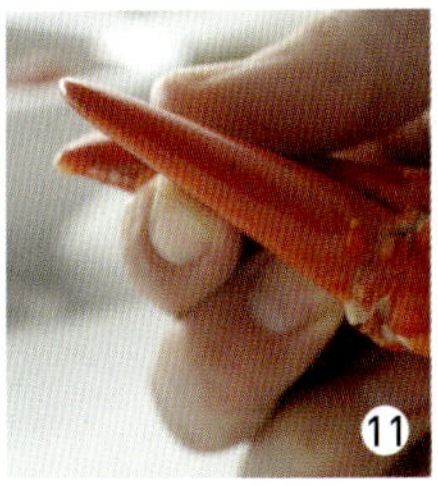

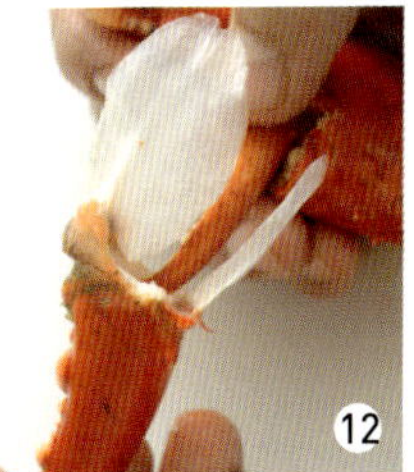

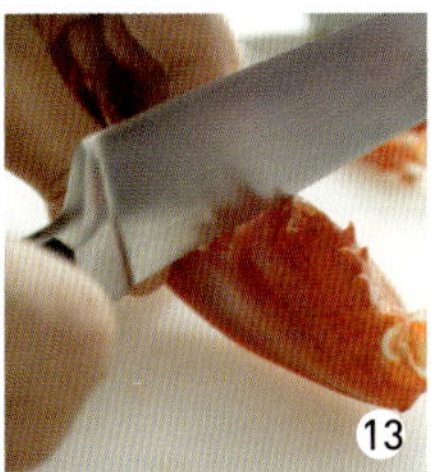

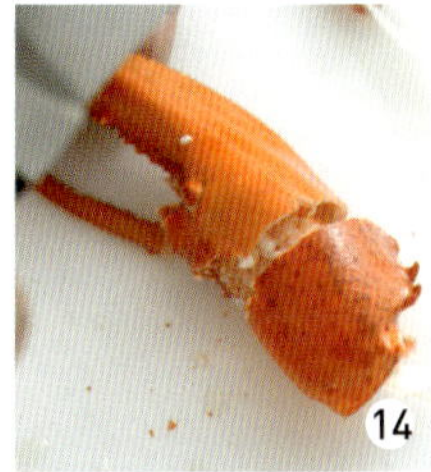

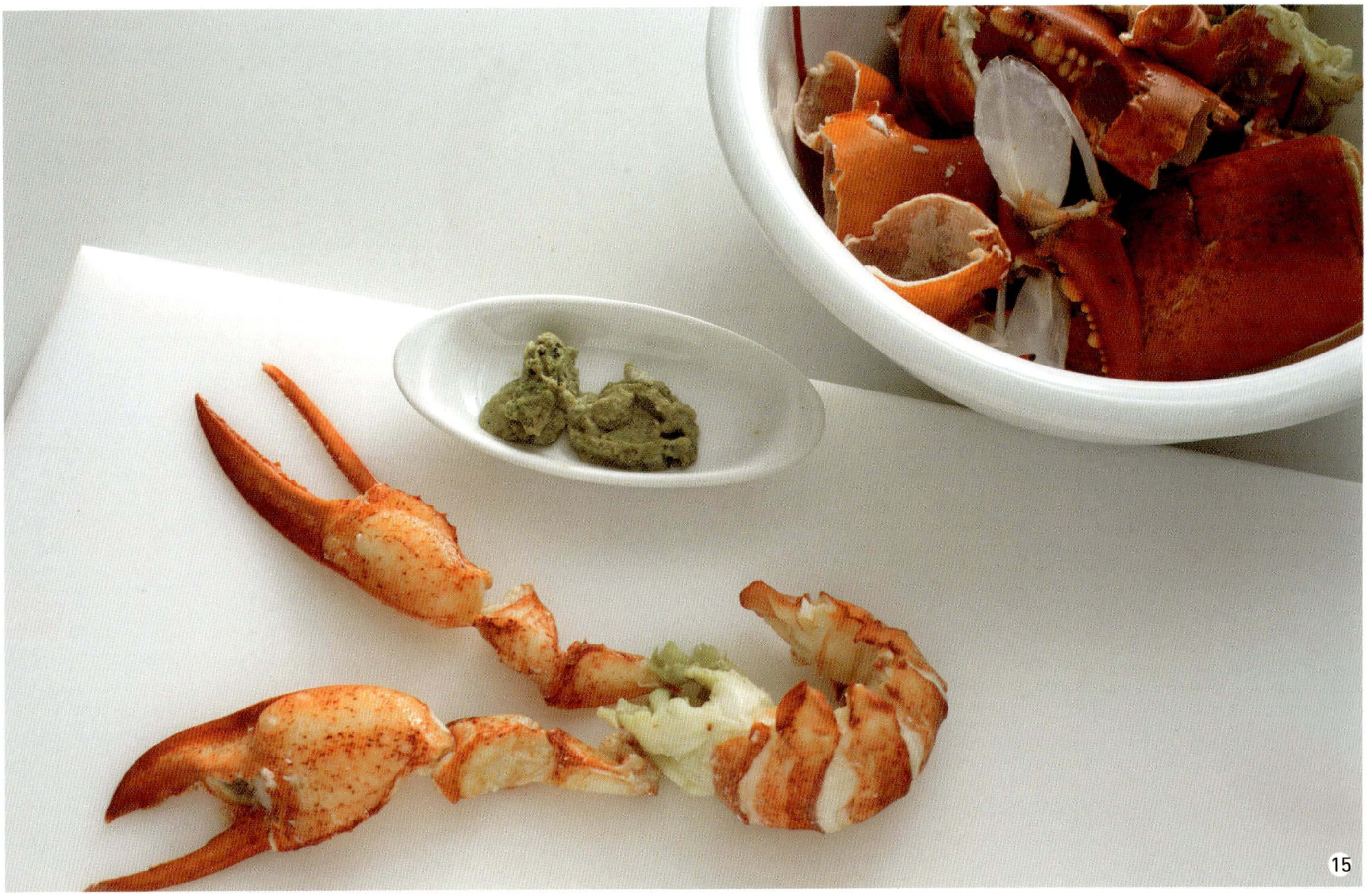

Peeling Shrimp

1. Gently twist the head off the body. The heads and shells can be used to prepare soups, stock, and sauces.

2. Simply remove the shell. Leave the last piece attached at the tail if you want to fry the shrimp whole. If you are using the shrimp to prepare a sauce or ragout, then remove the shell entirely.

3. Make a shallow cut along the length of the back with a knife.

4. Get the tip of the knife under the vein.

5. Remove the vein in one piece. The fresher the shrimp, the easier the veins are to remove.

6. You can determine the freshness of shrimp by their color pattern. Their color bleaches after some time and the shell is only gray.

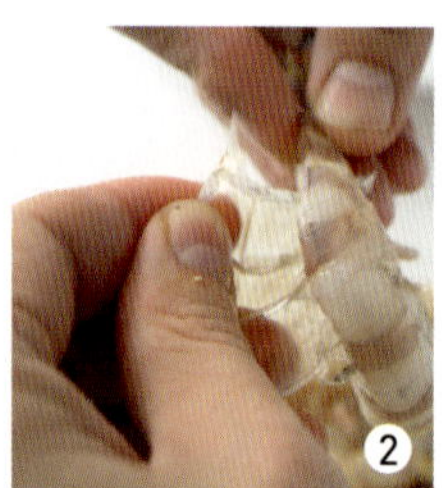

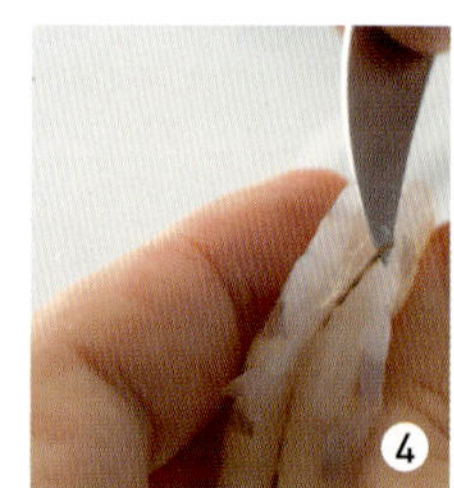

6

Defrosting Crustaceans and Shellfish

1. It is best to defrost peeled shrimp in the refrigerator. Drain the water from defrosting, place the shrimp on paper towels to drain, and then cook as desired. Frozen crustaceans can be defrosted gently and quickly by placing them in a watertight bag in cold water. Do not place them directly in water, because their flavor will leach out.

2. The frozen shrimp on the right is covered with a layer of ice to prevent freezer burn. The frozen shrimp on the left has freezer burn. Freezer burn will make the shrimp lose flavor and become tough.

3. A dark discoloration on the head means that the shrimp is not very fresh.

4. It is best to defrost unpeeled shrimp slowly over the course of 2 hours by placing them side by side on a baking tray in the refrigerator.

5. For faster defrosting, put unpeeled shrimp directly into cold water. Their shell protects the protein-rich meat from leaching.

1

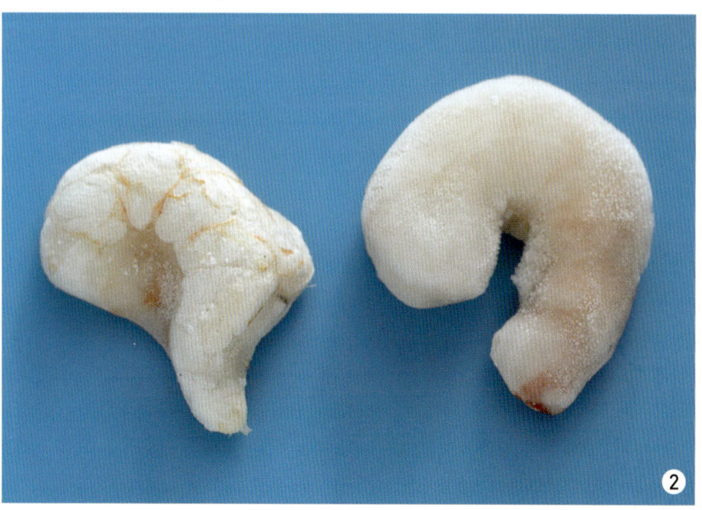

2

3

5

 1 small pineapple

 1 lb 2 oz (500 g) shrimp, cooked

 1⅓ cups (300 ml) Cocktail Sauce (see p. 53)

 4 slices of orange

 4 sprigs celery leaves

Shrimp Cocktail with Cocktail Sauce

1. Pare the pineapple with a knife.

2. Quarter the pineapple lengthwise and cut out the core and brown "eyes" (see p. 654).

3. Cut the pineapple in ¼-inch (5-mm) cubes, about the size of the shrimp.

4. Place the shrimp and the pineapple in a bowl, add the cocktail sauce, and mix. Serve the cocktail in small bowls and garnish with a slice of orange and celery leaves.

■ **Wash the knife and cutting board carefully. The flavors of vegetables, onions, or garlic can be passed on to the fruit.**

Add cooked pieces of asparagus (white and green), sautéed mushrooms, or slices of ripe peach for another delicious version of the shrimp cocktail. It is nice to decorate the cocktail dishes first with finely cut salad greens. Serve with a glass of champagne.

3

4

 1 lb 2 oz (500 g) shrimp, peeled

 1 egg

 1 tbsp soy sauce

 2 tbsp sesame seeds

 1 tbsp black sesame seeds

 1 tsp Sichuan pepper

 ½ bunch watercress

 4 tbsp soy vinaigrette with coriander (see p. 63)

1

2

Sautéed Sesame-Coated Shrimp

1. Devein the peeled shrimp (see p. 484). Separate the yolk from the egg white, combine the egg white with the soy sauce in a bowl and beat.

2. Marinate the shrimp for about 10 minutes in the egg white-soy mixture.

3. Mix the sesame seeds with Sichuan pepper in a bowl and toss the shrimp in this mixture.

4. Heat the oil in a nonstick skillet and sauté the shrimp for about 2 minutes on both sides. Then wash the watercress leaves, drain, and arrange them on the serving plates. Add the shrimp to the plates and sprinkle the soy vinaigrette over them.

■ **Shrimp in a crust of spices taste delicious on arugula, tomato, or marinated asparagus salad.**

3

4

8 garlic cloves

½ bunch fresh parsley

2 dried jalapeño peppers

2 lb 4 oz (1 kg) raw shrimp

⅔ cup (150 ml) extra virgin olive oil

½ tsp coarse sea salt

A few drops of lemon juice

Garlic Shrimp

1. Peel the garlic and cut into thin slices. Wash the parsley, then chop it. Lightly crush the jalapeño peppers. Peel the shrimp.

2. Heat the oil in a skillet over medium heat, add the jalapeño peppers, and the garlic, and brown slightly.

3. After about 1 minute, add the shrimp and sauté for an additional 2 minutes. Add the parsley. Season with salt and a few drops of lemon juice to taste.

Serve with fresh white bread or rice.

■ Mix into the garlic shrimp some chopped spaghetti and a few cubes of tomato. Add a few spoons of cooking water, so the oil binds well with the pasta.

2

3

4 ears of corn

4 lobsters

2 tbsp coarse sea salt

1 pinch of cayenne pepper

½ cup (100 g) butter

1 tsp fine sea salt

Boiled Lobster with Corn and Melted Butter

1. Remove the leaves and silk from the ears of corn, and cut off the stalks. Bring water to a boil in a pot large enough for 4 ears of corn. Do not add salt. It could make the corn tough.

2. Place the corn in the boiling water and simmer for 8 minutes.

3. With a knife, remove the rubber bands from the lobsters' pincers. Use a second pot with 5¼ quarts (5 liters) water and bring to a boil. Season with sea salt and cayenne pepper.

4. Quickly put the lobsters headfirst into the boiling water and return the water to a boil. Then turn off the heat and let the lobsters simmer for 10 minutes.

5. Melt the butter. Place the lobsters directly on the serving plates. Add one corn cob to each plate, sprinkle with the melted butter, and sprinkle some fine sea salt on it. Serve with lobster pliers to crack open the lobster.

■ The price of Canadian lobster is more reasonable. It offers plenty of meat with an ideal weight of 1 lb 2 oz (500 g).

2
3
4
5

 3½ oz (100 g) white bread

 10½ oz (300 g) crabmeat

 ½ bunch fresh cilantro

 2 tbsp crème fraîche (or sour cream)

 3 eggs

 1 pinch of salt

 1 pinch of black pepper

 2 tbsp vegetable oil

Crispy Crab Cakes

1. Cut away the bread crusts and finely chop the bread in a food processor. Put the crabmeat in a mixing bowl and flake it with a fork. This makes it easier to mix it with the other ingredients.

2. Wash the cilantro and mince. Add the crème fraîche (or sour cream) to the crabmeat. Separate two eggs and add the two yolks as well as the remaining whole egg, season with salt and pepper, and mix with the cilantro.

3. Then add half of the grated white bread and mix. Set covered in the refrigerator for 15 minutes. The mixture is easier to work with when cold.

4. With a tablespoon, take some mixture and shape into cakes by hand. Dip them into the remaining breadcrumbs.

5. Heat the oil in a nonstick skillet. Fry the cakes on both sides for 2–3 minutes, until golden brown. Turn them over carefully. Arrange them on serving plates and serve with a dip.

■ **Dip recommendation: Pour 7 oz (200 g) ketchup in a mixing bowl, add 1 tsp finely grated ginger, and mix in a few drops of Tabasco sauce. The cakes can also be prepared with chopped shrimp or with leftovers of other cooked crustaceans instead of the crabmeat.**

2
3
4
5

 4 lb 8 oz (2 kg) crayfish

 3 carrots

 3 scallions

 3 shallots

 2 leeks

 4 celery stalks

 1 garlic clove

 1 bunch fresh dill

 5 cloves

 1 tsp black peppercorns

 3 bay leaves

 1 dried jalapeño pepper

 2¼ cups (500 ml) white wine

 2 tbsp coarse sea salt

 5½ oz (150 g) mayonnaise (see p. 50)

Crayfish in Dill Stock

1. First check whether the crayfish are still moving; if not, discard. Peel and trim the carrots, the scallions, and the shallots. Cut the leeks in half and wash. Cut the celery and the other vegetables into ¼-inch (5-mm) slices. Crush the garlic clove in its peel. Wash the dill and chop.

2. Pour 5¼ quarts (5 liters) water in a large pot, add the cloves, peppercorns, bay leaves, jalapeño pepper, white wine, and sea salt, and bring to a boil. Then add the vegetables and the dill, and simmer for 3 minutes.

3. Place half of the crayfish in the simmering stock. Cover with a lid and bring to a boil. After boiling, remove the crayfish using a large skimmer. Boil the remaining crayfish. Break away the tails and arrange the crayfish with a dash of mayonnaise on a plate. Serve with fresh, lightly toasted white bread.

■ **Simply serve the crayfish in a large bowl on a table, where everyone can have a bite. Savor the crayfish during the summer months with chilled white wine and cocktail sauce.**

2

3

 1 shallot

 5 tbsp red wine vinegar

 1 tbsp water

 24 oysters

1

2

3

Oysters on Ice

1. Peel the shallot and finely dice. Pour the red wine vinegar and the water in a bowl, add the shallot, and mix.

2. Crack the oysters with an oyster knife (see p. 480).

3. Open the oysters and serve on a platter with crushed ice. Place the sauce in a small bowl in the center of the platter.

■ **Garnish the ice with seaweed and the oysters will taste like the sea. Serve with buttered rye bread cut into small pieces and arranged on a small plate. Here size 00 Belon oysters are illustrated. This is a very tasty flat oyster variety, which can be found in the smaller size 0. Rock oysters such as Fines de Claires, Portugaise, Sylter Spezial, or American Blue Point, eaten raw, are true delicacies.**

24 oysters 

2 leeks

2 tsp (10 g) butter 

1 pinch of salt
1 pinch of black pepper 

1 pinch of nutmeg, freshly grated 

7/8 cup (200 ml) Hollandaise Sauce (see p. 152) 

2 lb 4 oz (1 kg) coarse sea salt

Baked Oysters

1. Open the oysters (see p. 480), remove them from their shells, and place in a sieve. Clean the oyster shells and place for 3 to 5 minutes to dry in a preheated oven. Wash the leek and slice diagonally into fine strips.

2. Bring the butter to a froth in a pot, add the leeks, season with salt, pepper, and freshly grated nutmeg, and sauté. Add 3/8 cup (100 ml) water and simmer for 2 to 3 minutes, until the leeks are done and the liquid reduced. Place the leeks in the dried oyster shells and place the oysters on top.

3. Prepare the Hollandaise Sauce (see p. 152) and pour over the oysters. Broil for 2–3 minutes under a preheated broiler. Because of the short cooking time, you must pay attention that the oysters do not brown. Place the oysters on a serving plate on top of the coarse sea salt and serve.

■ **Oysters removed from their shells can be fried like fish in a beer batter and served with tartar sauce, or fried wrapped in bacon and served on sauerkraut.**

 2 lb 4 oz (1 kg) octopus

 2 tbsp coarse sea salt

 1 lemon

 1 sprig fresh thyme

 1⅛ cups (250 ml) white wine

 1 tbsp sweet paprika

 ¼ tsp cayenne pepper

 4 tbsp extra virgin olive oil

Octopus with Lemon Dressing

1. Thoroughly wash the octopus. Turn the body inside out, pull away the entrails, and cut them off with a knife.

2. Rinse thoroughly and remove any remaining skin.

3. Pinch the lower part of the head of the octopus to grip the beak and remove it.

4. Bring the water to a boil in a pot with high sides and put in the octopus with the salt, 1 lemon slice, and the thyme sprig.

5. Let it simmer for about 40 minutes. Cut a piece of the octopus to see whether it is done. Put the juice of ½ the lemon in a mixing bowl. Add the paprika and the cayenne pepper. Mix with the olive oil and 1 tbsp of the cooking liquid of the octopus. Remove the octopus, drain, and slice in pieces. Arrange on plates and sprinkle the spiced lemon dressing over it.

■ In Spain, cooked octopus is often served on cooked potato slices. It is also delicious when served with fresh garlic sauce or on bean salad (see p. 88). The cooking time depends largely on the size of the octopus. This is why it should be tasted to judge whether it is tender.

2
3
4
5

3 shallots

2¼ oz (60 g) celery stalks

1 leek

1 garlic clove

⅛ cup (30 g) butter

2 bay leaves

1 sprig fresh of thyme

1 pinch of salt
1 pinch of black pepper

4 lb 8 oz (2 kg) mussels
(1 lb 2 oz/500 g per person)

⅔ cup (150 ml) white wine

½ bunch fresh parsley

Mussels Steamed in White Wine

1. Peel the shallots and cut into fine strips. Cut the celery and leek into fine strips. Crush the garlic clove in its peel. Melt the butter in a pot. First add the garlic and the shallots, then the bay leaves, the thyme, the celery, and the leek, and sauté briefly. Season with salt and pepper.

2. Add the washed and cleaned mussels (see p. 480), mix with the vegetables, add the white wine, cover the pot with a lid, and let it simmer for 3–5 minutes, until the mussels open. Discard any that have not opened. Wash the parsley, then mince and sprinkle over the mussels. Mix well and serve.

■ Use an empty mussel shell to eat the others without silverware.

2

 2 tomatoes

 2 shallots

 5 basil leaves

 1 bunch fresh parsley

 1 pinch of salt
1 pinch of black pepper

 3 tbsp red wine vinegar

 ½ cup (125 ml) olive oil

 4 lb 8 oz (2 kg) mussels, cooked (see p. 504)

1

Mussels in Herb Marinade

1. Peel the tomatoes, quarter, seed, and dice (see p.346). Peel and chop the shallots finely. Mince the basil leaves. Wash and clean the parsley and mince. Combine and mix in a small bowl.

2. Season with salt and pepper and pour the red wine vinegar over it. Add the olive oil and mix.

3. Remove the meat from the cooked mussels. Mix the mussels into the marinade, cover with plastic wrap, and refrigerate for ½ hour. Arrange the mussels on plates and serve with toasted slices of white bread.

■ **This dish is very delicious made with cockles, New Zealand mussels (also called green mussels), clams, or cooked sea snails. It is especially important not to serve them directly from the refrigerator, but at room temperature.**

2

3

 3 slices white bread

 ½ bunch fresh parsley

 3 sprigs fresh thyme

 2 lb 4 oz (1 kg) razor shells

 2 tbsp soy sauce

 3 tbsp extra virgin olive oil

1

Razor Shells with Herbs and Soy Sauce

1. Cut off the crusts of the white bread and cube the bread. Wash and trim the parsley and the thyme leaves. Put all in the food processor and mix.

2. Wash the razor shells, open with a knife, and place side by side in a baking dish. Sprinkle soy sauce over the razor shells.

3. Spread the herb-bread mixture over the razor shells and sprinkle with olive oil. Bake them for about 10 minutes in the oven preheated to 425°F (220°C/ Gas Mark 7). Serve in the baking dish.

■ The following shellfish can be prepared the same way:

1. Date-shells (elongated and very tasty)
2. New Zealand mussels (very large with a green edge, and tender meat)
3. Clams (delicious with a nutty flavor)

2

3

 8 scallops

 8 bacon slices

 1 tbsp vegetable oil

 1 pinch of salt
1 pinch of black pepper

 8 tbsp coarse sea salt

1

2

Fried Scallops Wrapped in Bacon

1. Remove the meat from the shells and separate the white meat from the orange. Clean the lower shells and remove any remaining parts of the scallop. Dry and set aside until the dish is ready to serve.

2. Place the bacon slices on a work surface. Place the pieces of white scallop meat on one end and roll up in the bacon.

3. Heat the vegetable oil in a skillet. Place the scallops wrapped in bacon in the pan and season with pepper. Do not add salt, because the bacon provides plenty of flavor.

4. Pan-fry the scallops on both sides for about 1 minute, until the bacon is crispy.

5. Place the orange meat in a separate pan with a little oil and quickly fry on both sides. Season lightly with salt and pepper. Spoon the sea salt on small serving plates and arrange the shells firmly on it. Arrange the fried scallops on top of the shells.

■ **This dish is served as an appetizer. However, the scallops can be fried without the bacon and served with asparagus salad or in pumpkin cream soup.**

3

4

5

 2 garlic cloves

 1 bunch fresh parsley

 8 cuttlefish or squids

 1 pinch of salt
1 pinch of black pepper

 1 sprig fresh rosemary

 1 pinch of chile flakes

 4 tbsp extra virgin olive oil

 1¼ cups (300 g) plain yogurt

 1 lemon

Grilled Cuttlefish

1. Peel and dice the garlic. Wash and clean the parsley and mince. Clean the cuttlefish thoroughly. After the innards are removed, dry thoroughly with paper towels. Place on a work surface with the smooth side up and slit crosswise.

2. Place in a baking dish with the cut side on top, season with salt and pepper on the inside, and fill with the parsley and half the garlic. Then turn over.

3. Pluck the rosemary needles, combine with the chile flakes, and spread over the cuttlefish. Season again with salt and pepper and sprinkle 2 tbsp olive oil over it. Then marinate for 15 minutes. You can marinate the cuttlefish the day before preparing this dish.

4. Heat a nonstick grill pan and fry the cuttlefish first on the side with the slits, then turn over. Grill them on each side for about 2 to 3 minutes.

5. Put the yogurt, the remaining garlic, and the remaining olive oil in a mixing bowl. Season with salt and pepper and mix. Cut the lemon in slices and arrange with the cuttlefish on serving plates. Serve with the yogurt dip.

■ **You can use fresh squid for this dish. Cuttlefish and squid taste even more delicious when charbroiled and served with tomato vinaigrette (see p. 63) and fresh white bread.**

2
3
4
5

Poultry

Contents

516 Poultry
516 Cooking Chart
518 How to Cut up Poultry
520 Brown Poultry Sauce
522 Chicken Legs in BBQ Sauce
523 Baked Chicken with Herb Crumbs
524 Chicken Cordon Bleu
526 Traditional Chicken Schnitzels
528 Chicken Schnitzels with Coconut and Curry
530 Turkey with Bread Stuffing
532 Roasted Duck with Apples
534 Roasted Breast of Duck with Orange-Pepper Sauce
536 Stuffed Squab Wrapped in Bacon
538 Sautéed Venetian-Style Poultry Livers
540 Cornish Hens Roasted with Lemon and Garlic
542 Pheasant on Sauerkraut with Mashed Potatoes

Poultry

In earlier times, poultry dealers dressed their wares in front of the customers. The trained eye could gain a lot of insight about the life of poultry by looking at their feet, beaks, or the size of the stomachs. Caged chickens have no claws. Poultry fed mashed foods daily do not develop large, strong stomachs. But supermarkets do not provide reliable signs of quality. Poultry looks mostly the same under plastic wrap. Only occasionally can spots be seen on the skin if the product has been handled too much.

Cooking Chart

Type of Poultry	Weight	Cooking Method	Temperature	Cooking Time
Chicken	2 lb 12 oz (1.2 kg)	Oven	400°F (200°C/Gas Mark 6)	45 minutes
Chicken leg	4 ¼ oz (120 g)	Oven	325°F (160°C/Gas Mark 3)	25 minutes
Duck	3 lb 8 oz (1.6 kg)	Oven	325°F (160°C/Gas Mark 3)	90 minutes
Goose	Approx. 9–11 lb (4–5 kg)	Oven	300–325°F (150–160°C/GM 2–3)	150–180 minutes
Goose breast	10 ½ oz (300 g)	Oven	325°F (160°C/Gas Mark 3)	70 minutes
Goose leg	9 oz (250 g)	Oven	325°F (160°C/Gas Mark 3)	100 minutes
Chicken breast	6–7 oz (180–200 g)	Skillet	Medium heat	10 minutes
Turkey	18 lb (8 kg)	Oven	300°F (150°C/Gas Mark 2)	300 minutes
Duck breast	7–9 oz (200–250 g)	Skillet	Medium heat	10 minutes
Squab	10 ½ oz (300 g)	Oven	410°F (210°C/Gas Mark 6½)	25 minutes
Cornish hens	1 lb (450 g)	Oven	350°F (180°C/Gas Mark 4)	25 minutes
Pheasant	1 lb 12 oz–2 lb 4 oz (800 g–1 kg)	Oven	350°F (180°C/Gas Mark 4)	40 minutes
Quail	4 ½ oz (120 g)	Oven	375°F (190°C/Gas Mark 5)	20 minutes
Chicken for soup	2 lb 12oz (1.2 kg)	Pot	Boil	50 minutes

Cornish hen

Turkey

Squab

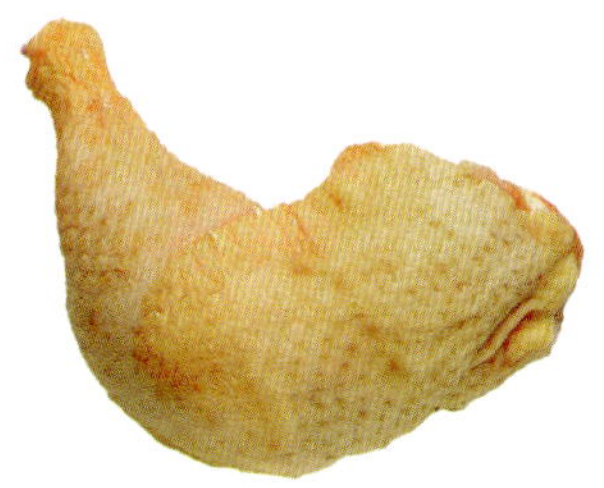

Chicken leg

Duck breast

Chicken wing

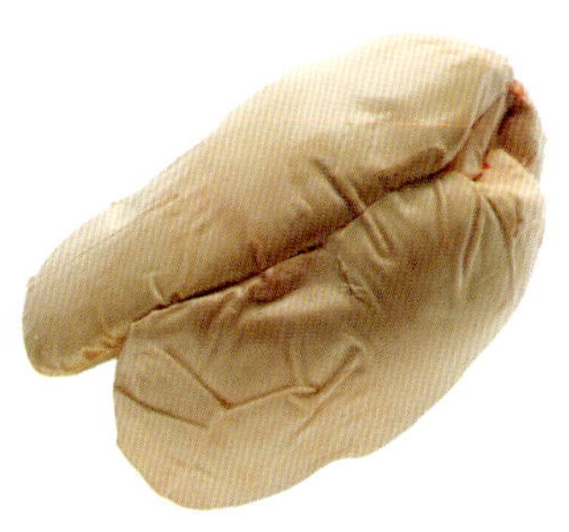

Foie gras

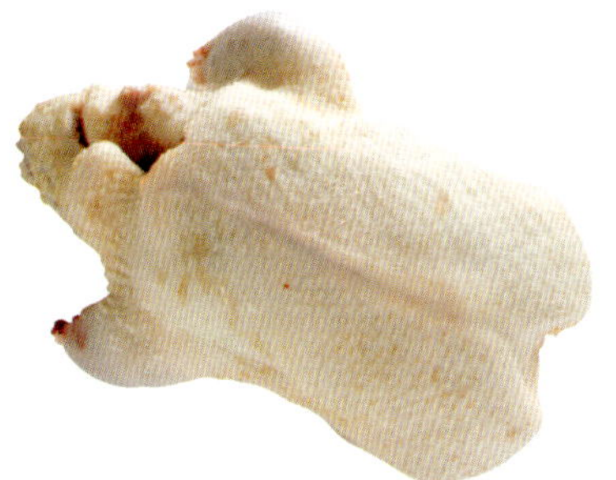

Duck

Chicken

How to Cut up Poultry

1. Remove the foot joints with a knife. Place the poultry on a clean work surface, legs pointing toward the front.

2. Pull the legs away from the body and cut to the bone with a knife.

3. Break the legs off at the joints and turn the poultry over.

4. Remove the thumb-size fillets and cut off the drumsticks.

5. Make an incision around the wing, keeping about 1¼ inches (3 cm) away from the breast, and scrape off the meat to the tip of the wing to expose the bone. Separate the wing with the backside of the knife.

6. Carefully move the skin up to avoid damaging it, and loosen the wishbone with the tip of the knife.

1

2

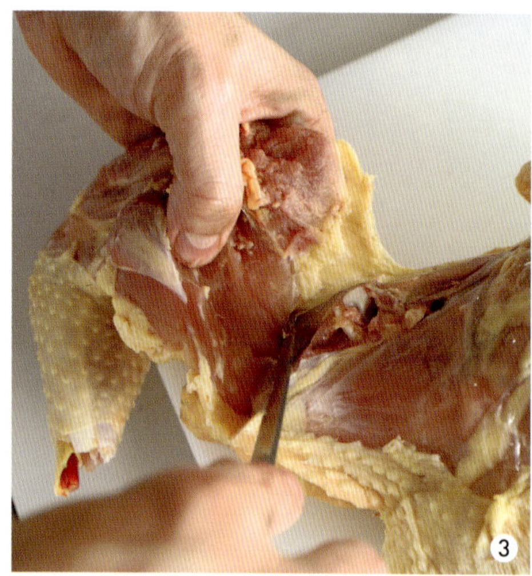

3

4

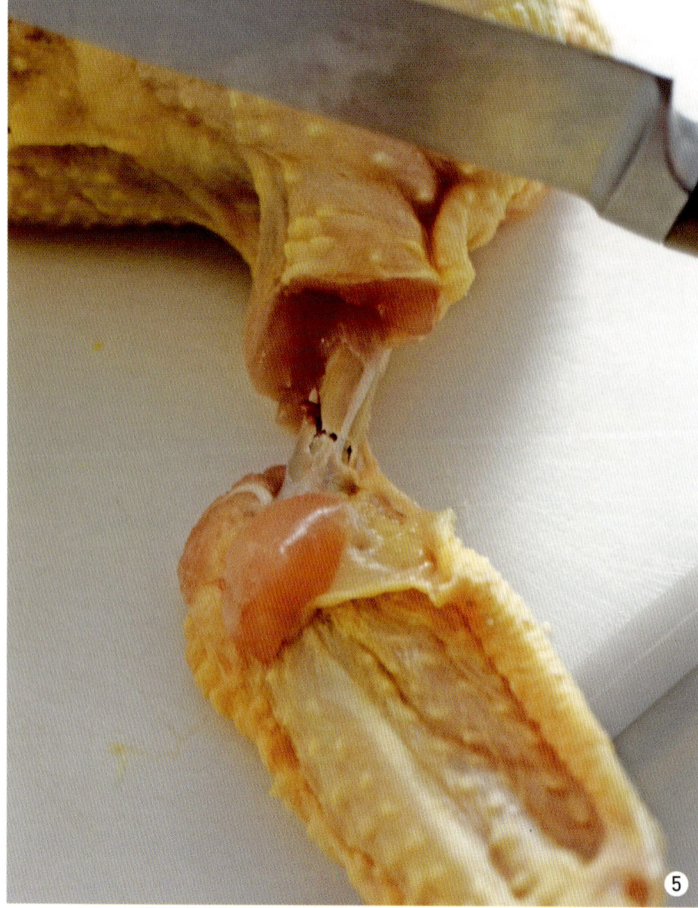

5

7. Carefully remove the wishbone. This will make it easier to cut out the fillet around the breast.

8. Make an incision along the breastbone from where the wishbone was removed, and cut from the abdominal cavity to the neck.

9. Use your hand to turn over the breast fillet, and cut so the drumstick bone remains attached to the fillet.

10. Continue to process the breast fillets, the drumsticks, and the wings. Use the bones for soups or sauces.

■ **You can prepare the liver and kidneys separately and serve them, for example, as an appetizer with mâche.**

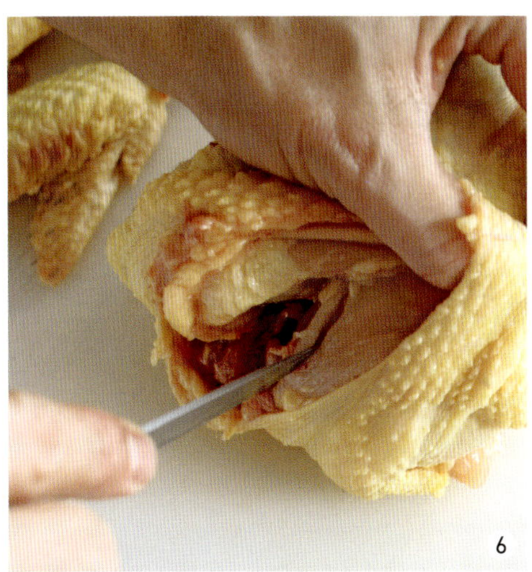

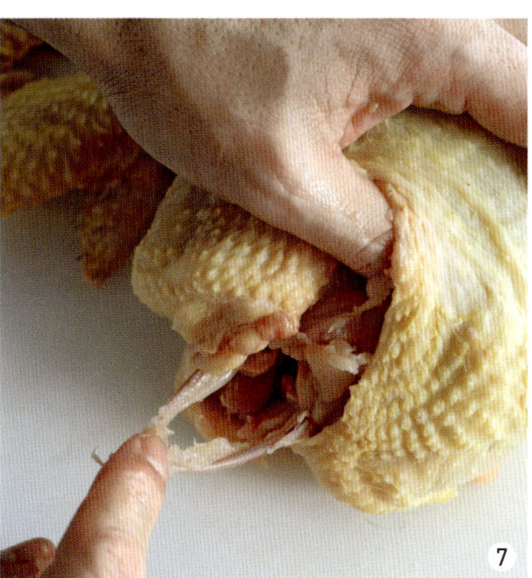

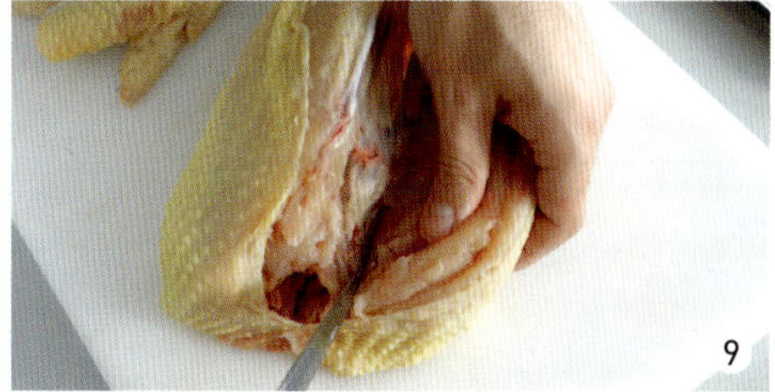

 4 lb 8 oz (2 kg) poultry bones

 3 tbsp vegetable oil

 9 oz (250 g) onions

 3½ oz (100 g) shallots

 5½ oz (150 g) carrots

 5½ oz (150 g) celery stalks

 1 head of garlic

 1 tsp white peppercorns

 5 cloves

 ½ bunch fresh parsley

 2 sprigs fresh rosemary

 3 sprigs fresh thyme

 5 bay leaves

 1 tsp coarse sea salt

 1 tbsp tomato paste

 ⅜ cup (100 ml) white port

 ⅞ cup (200 ml) white wine

 3¼ quarts (3 liters) water

Brown Poultry Sauce

1. Cut the poultry bones into walnut-size pieces with a large meat cleaver or kitchen scissors. Heat the oil in a wide pot and sauté the bones for about 20 minutes, until golden brown. Stir frequently.

2. Peel the onions, the shallots, and the carrots and slice them, as well as the celery stalks, into ¼-inch (5-mm) slices (see p. 344). Combine and sauté them.

3. Cut the head of garlic horizontally in half, combine with the vegetables, and bring to a boil. Sauté for an additional 10 minutes, stirring to prevent the drippings from becoming too dark or burning. Crush the peppercorns and cloves with the flat side of a kitchen knife. Wash the parsley and pluck the leaves. Add the sprigs of rosemary, the thyme, the bay leaves, and the salt to the pan drippings, and sauté at medium heat.

4. Move the sauce to the edge of the pan and put the tomato paste in the open space. Sauté lightly to reduce the acid and to prevent the sauce from becoming too red. Mix well with the sauce and sauté briefly.

5. First add the port and then the white wine to deglaze the pan.

6. Remove any drippings from the bottom of the pot. They will dissolve in the sauce during cooking and provide a roasted flavor.

■ You can use the bones of the wings, neck, or breast. It is important to leave some skin on the bones. It provides flavor for the sauce when sautéed. Properly cooked, the bones contribute body and flavor to the sauce, which can be intensified by adding poultry jus.The brown poultry sauce can be served with any poultry dishes. It is also easy to freeze for future use.

7. Add sufficient cold water to cover the bones by approximately ½ inch (1 cm). Slowly bring to a boil.

8. After the liquid has boiled, skim the froth and fat from the surface and simmer the sauce for about 2 hours. Add the parsley leaves to the sauce about 20 minutes before the end of the cooking time, and continue to simmer.

9. Strain the sauce twice. First, filter the bones through a colander and slightly mash the vegetables. Then strain through a sieve. Bring the sauce to a boil once more. Skim the froth and season with salt and pepper to taste.

 6–8 chicken legs

 1-inch (2.5-cm) piece of fresh ginger

 ⅔ cup (150 ml) barbecue sauce (see p. 56)

 2 tbsp vegetable oil

 1 pinch of salt
1 pinch of black pepper

 ⅜ cup (100 ml) water

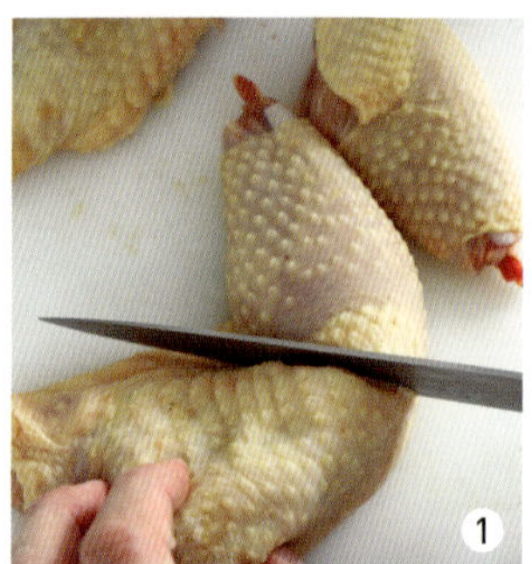

Chicken Legs in BBQ Sauce

1. Cut the chicken legs into two parts at the joint. Make one or two slits in the skin so the meat can better soak up the marinade.

2. Peel and slice the ginger. Place the legs in a baking dish and pour the barbecue sauce and the oil over them. Add the ginger slices. Cover with plastic wrap and let it marinate in the refrigerator for a minimum of 2 hours.

3. Season the legs with salt and pepper on both sides and bake in the oven, preheated to 400°F (200°C/Gas Mark 6), for about 40 minutes. Half way through the baking time, deglaze with water and baste with the marinade. Remove the drumsticks from the oven and serve with salad, toasted bread, or carrots.

■ **It is best to marinate the chicken legs one day before use. This allows the BBQ sauce to properly soak into the meat.**

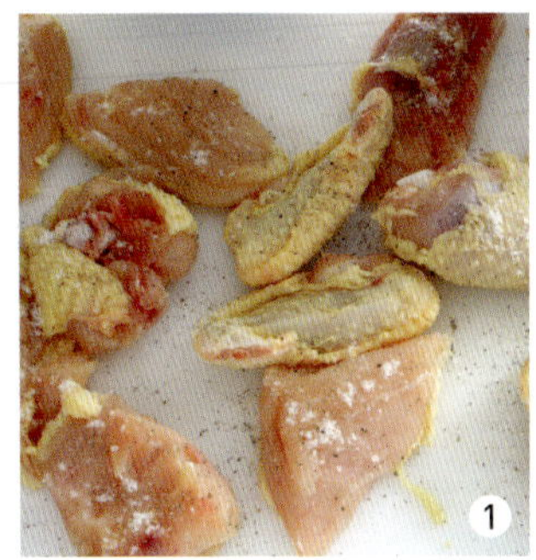

2 sprigs fresh rosemary

2 sprigs fresh thyme

1 whole chicken

1 pinch of salt
1 pinch of black pepper

1 egg

1 tbsp flour

2¾ oz (80 g) white bread slices

3 tbsp olive oil

Baked Chicken with Herb Crumbs

1. Pluck the rosemary needles and thyme leaves from their stems and finely chop them. Cut the chicken into parts (see p. 518). Cut each breast into two pieces. Separate the breast twice. Separate the legs at the joints and cut through each thigh along the bone. Season with salt and pepper.

2. Beat the egg in a mixing bowl. Add the flour, rosemary, thyme, and salt. Mix with a fork until smooth. Cut off the crust from the white bread slices and finely chop in the food processor. Place the chicken pieces in the bowl and turn to coat with the egg mixture. Then add the white breadcrumbs and mix again.

3. Place the chicken pieces on an aluminum baking sheet and sprinkle with some olive oil. Bake in a preheated convection oven at 400°F (200°C/Gas Mark 6) for 40 minutes. You may have to cover the chicken with aluminum foil to prevent the crust from getting too dark. Arrange the chicken in a baking dish and serve with mashed potatoes and carrots.

4 chicken breasts, skinless

1 pinch of salt
1 pinch of black pepper

4 slices cooked ham

2 slices cheese (Gouda or Swiss)

¾ cup (100 g) flour

2 eggs

7 oz (200 g) breadcrumbs

6 tbsp vegetable oil

1 tbsp butter

Chicken Cordon Bleu

1. Cut a pocket lengthwise into each chicken breast. Season the breasts on both sides with salt and pepper, and fill each pocket with a slice of ham and a slice of cheese. Beat the eggs.

2. Fold the chicken breasts over, enveloping the ham and cheese.

3. Seal any open spots and push down a bit on the meat.

4. First dredge the breasts in the flour and remove any excess flour. Then dip them in the beaten eggs, and next in the breadcrumbs.

5. Place the breaded chicken breasts in a heated skillet with oil and butter. Cook on both sides for about 7 minutes over medium heat.

■ **You can also stuff the chicken breasts with prosciutto, Serrano ham, or blue cheeses, such as Gorgonzola or Stilton. The pieces must be breaded well to prevent the melting cheese from running out during cooking. This dish can also be prepared with veal or pork cutlets. They taste delicious with a spinach filling.**

2
3
4
5

 4 chicken breasts, skinless

 1 pinch of salt
1 pinch of pepper

 2 eggs

 1 dash mineral water

 ¾ cup (100 g) flour

 14 oz (400 g) breadcrumbs

 6 tbsp oil

 1 tbsp butter

1

2

3

4

Traditional Chicken Schnitzels

1. Remove any tendons from the chicken breasts. Season on both sides with salt and pepper.

2. Season the eggs with pepper, combine with the mineral water, and beat well with a fork.

3. Then dust the chicken breasts with the flour, removing any excess.

4. Dip in the egg until the breasts are completely covered.

5. Dredge the breasts in fine breadcrumbs. Never push down on the coating. This would prevent it from becoming fluffy.

6. Heat the oil and butter in a skillet.

7. Place the schnitzels in the skillet and sauté in the oil and butter mixture.

8. Toss lightly in the skillet to cover the schnitzels with the fat. This ensures that the meat gets done on the top.

9. After about 5 minutes, turn the schnitzels over and sauté for an additional 5 minutes. Keep tossing the pan so the batter becomes very crisp.

10. Remove the schnitzels from the skillet and drain on paper towels.

Arrange on serving plates and serve with parsley potatoes or cucumber salad.

■ To make the meat even more tender and flavorful, marinate the cut chicken breasts for 2 hours in a mixture of yogurt and hot mustard.

5
6
7
8
9
10

4 chicken breasts, skinless and boneless

1 pinch of salt
1 pinch of pepper

¾ cup (100 g) flour

2 eggs

9 oz (250 g) fine coconut flakes

1 tsp curry powder

½ cup (125 ml) vegetable oil

Chicken Schnitzels with Coconut and Curry

1. Remove the tendons from the chicken breasts. Season with salt and pepper. Lightly dust with flour and remove any excess.

2. Beat the eggs well and dip the floured chicken breasts in the eggs.

3. Place the coconut flakes in a wide dish and combine with the curry.

4. Dip the chicken breasts in the coconut flakes.

5. Put the oil in a skillet and sauté the chicken pieces for about 5 minutes over medium heat.

6. Turn them and sauté for an additional 5 minutes.

7. Remove the schnitzels and drain on a plate covered with paper towels.

Arrange on serving plates and serve with almond rice and spicy hot spinach leaves.

■ You can prepare chicken legs the same way. Bone the legs and lightly pound. Bread them and cook them the same way. The meat from the legs becomes a bit tougher than the breasts and must be sautéed for an additional 3 minutes.

2
3
4
5
6
7

3⅛ cups (720 g) butter

6 eggs

1½ tbsp dried marjoram

1 pinch of salt
1 pinch of black pepper

½ tsp of nutmeg, freshly grated

9 oz (250 g) poultry livers

1 lb 2 oz (500 g) sliced white bread

1⅓ cups (300 ml) heavy cream

1 turkey (approx. 13–15 lb/6–7 kg)

5 carrots

3 onions

3 celery stalks

1⅛ cups (250 ml) sweet cider

3⅓ cups (750 ml) poultry stock or water

2 sprigs fresh thyme

Turkey with Bread Stuffing

1. Beat the butter at room temperature in a large mixing bowl until creamy. Add 1 egg, the dried marjoram, the salt, the black pepper, and the grated nutmeg, and continue to beat this mixture until the egg is completely absorbed. Add the other eggs one by one.

2. Clean the poultry livers, cut into 1¼-inch (3-cm) slices, and combine with the butter mixture.

3. Cut the slices of white bread, including the crust, into ½-inch (1-cm) cubes and put into a mixing bowl. Pour the heavy cream over it and let it soak for about 10 minutes.

4. Carefully combine the butter mixture with the bread cubes with a wooden spoon so that the bread cubes keep their shape.

5. Clean the cavities of the turkey well and remove any remaining giblets. Season the outside and inside generously with salt and pepper. Stuff the turkey, but make sure that the stuffing does not come out at the neck.

6. Truss the turkey with cotton string and place on a roasting pan. Peel the carrots and onions. Wash them and cut them with the celery stalks and into 2-inch (5-cm) pieces.

+ 5 hours of cooking time

■ **You can add cooked chestnuts, steamed apples, dried apricots, or sautéed pieces of pumpkin to the stuffing. Serve with sweet potatoes and cranberry sauce.**

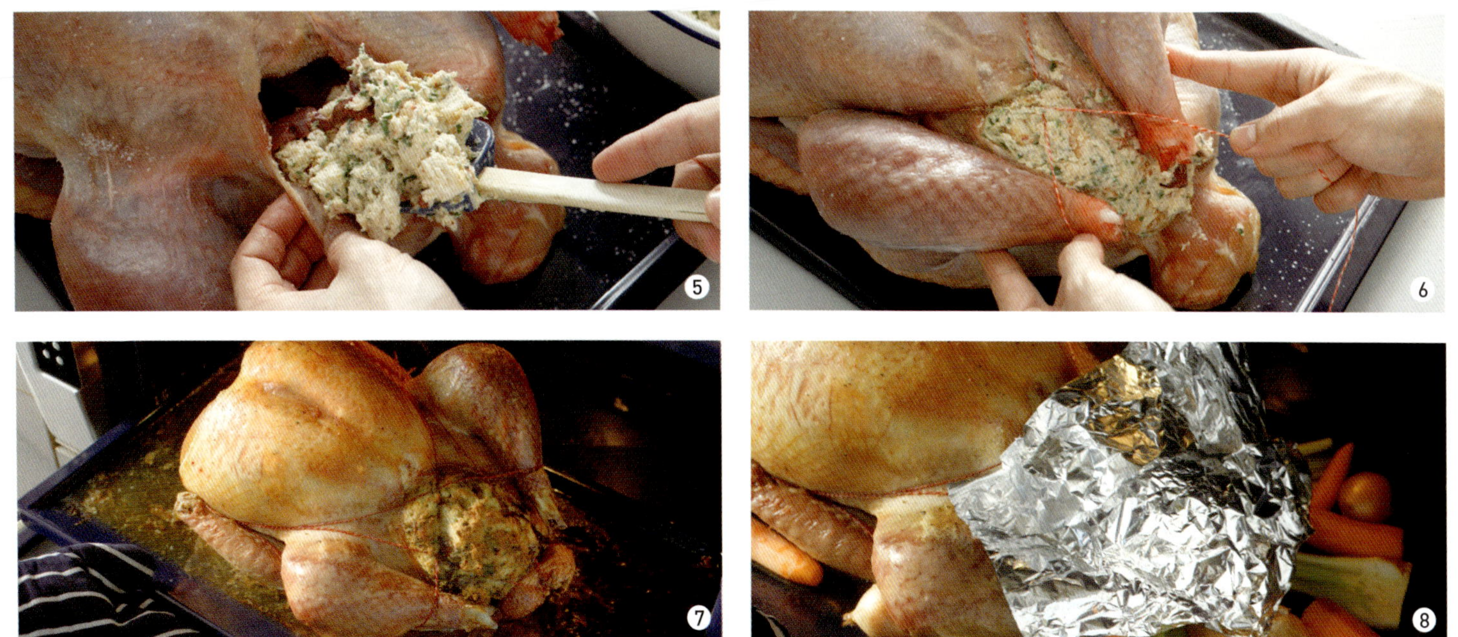

7. Pour the sweet cider over the turkey and put it into the oven preheated to 300°F (150°C/Gas Mark 2). Roast for 4 hours and baste from time to time with the jus. Increase the amount of jus periodically by adding some water or poultry stock (see p. 134).

8. After 4 hours, lay the sprigs of thyme around the turkey and add the vegetables. Cover the stuffing with aluminum foil and pour 2¼ cups (500 ml) stock in the pan. Roast for an hour and turn over the vegetables occasionally. Remove them from the sauce and place them in a skillet. Pour the jus through a sieve. Place the turkey on a cutting board and serve with the jus.

1 whole duck

3 shallots

1 small apple

1 pinch of salt
1 pinch of black pepper

1 garlic clove

½ bouquet of fresh marjoram

1⅛ cups (250 ml) water

Roasted Duck with Apples

1. Purchase the duck ready to cook at the butcher or meat market. Make sure they pack the neck, wings, and giblets separately. Peel and halve the shallots. Quarter the apple and remove the core. Then slice the quarters in half. Clean the inside of the duck and rub dry with paper towels. Season with salt and pepper. Stuff the duck with the whole garlic clove, the apple slices, and a sprig of marjoram.

2. Close the opening with toothpicks and tie with cotton string. Cut off the ends of the toothpicks with the scissors on both sides. This prevents the liquid from oozing out and keeps the flavor in the duck. Pluck any remaining pinfeathers from the skin using small pliers.

3. Season the outside of the duck with salt and pepper and rub in the seasonings well.

4. Place the duck on a suitable baking dish and lay the neck, wings, and giblets around the outside of the duck. Pour in half of the water and cook on the lower shelf of an oven set on convection, if available, and preheated to 350°F (180°C/Gas Mark 4).

■ **Serve the duck with potato cakes, Brussels sprouts, red cabbage, or sauerkraut. Strain the jus using a fine sieve and serve as sauce. This jus is highly concentrated, so sprinkle it lightly over the side dishes.**

5. Baste the duck with the jus. After about 45 minutes, add the remaining water and roast the duck for another 45 minutes. As soon as the roast is done, loosen the cotton string with a knife and remove the toothpicks. Place the duck on a large serving platter and garnish with a few sprigs of marjoram.

 4 duck breasts (7 oz/200 g each)

 2 oranges

 1 pinch of salt
1 pinch of pepper

 1 tbsp vegetable oil

 2 tsp (10 cl) Cointreau

 7/8 cup (200 ml) orange juice

 2 tbsp pickled green peppercorns

Roasted Breast of Duck with Orange-Pepper Sauce

1. Place the duck breasts on a cutting board with the skin side up. Cut off any excess skin. With a sharp knife, cut the skin in a crisscross pattern.

2. Wash the oranges well under hot running water and dry. Finely grate the zest using a grater. Take a knife and carefully cut off any white pith. Then slice the oranges.

3. Season the duck breasts on both sides with salt and pepper. Heat oil in a skillet and place the breasts in the pan skin-side down.

4. Sauté the breasts at medium heat for about 10 minutes. During this time, spoon up the fat from the duck and keep pouring it over the pieces. Continue to cook it on the skin side until the skin is very crisp.

5. Arrange the duck breasts with the skin side up on a serving platter. Let them rest. Drain the fat from the pan, place the orange peel in the pan, and add the Cointreau and orange juice. Put in the peppercorns and orange slices and heat through.

Arrange together with the duck breasts on serving plates.

■ **Carefully remove the tendons from the insides of the duck breasts with a knife. They do not get tender during this short cooking time.**

2
3
4
5

4 squab

4 slices white bread

1 shallot

½ bunch fresh parsley

½ cup (100 g) butter, at room temperature

2 eggs

1 pinch of salt
1 pinch of pepper

1 pinch of nutmeg, freshly grated

8 bacon slices

4 garlic cloves

10 juniper berries

2 tbsp vegetable oil

4 sprigs fresh rosemary

1

Stuffed Squab Wrapped in Bacon

1. Have the butcher prepare the squab so they are ready to cook. Finely cube the hearts and livers. Remove the crust from the white bread and cut the bread into ¼-inch (5-mm) cubes. Peel the shallot and finely dice. Wash the parsley, then mince. Beat the butter in a bowl until creamy. Separate the eggs and add the yolks one by one to the butter. Season with salt and pepper. Add the nutmeg and mix with a wire whisk. Then add the shallot and parsley.

2. Add the liver, the heart, and the white bread cubes, and mix carefully.

3. Rub the insides of the squab with paper towels and remove any skin and blood residue. Season inside and out with salt and pepper and fill with the stuffing.

4. Wrap each of the squab with 2 slices of bacon and tie together with a cotton string. With the flat side of a knife, crush the unpeeled garlic and the juniper berries.

5. Heat the oil in a skillet and place the squab with the rosemary, the juniper berries, and the garlic in the pan. Sauté back-side up first, then on their backs. Set the oven to convection, if available, and preheat to 410°F (210°C/Gas Mark 6½). Roast the squab for about 25 minutes and baste with the jus continuously. Remove the squab; take off the cotton string and halve the squab lengthwise, using a sharp knife. Arrange on plates and serve.

■ Place any excess stuffing in a buttered soufflé dish and bake in the oven for about 15 minutes at 400°F (200°C/Gas Mark 6). The butter makes it easier to turn out later. Pumpkin gratin and salsify, which is also called vegetable oyster, make wonderful side dishes to complement the squab dinner.

2
3
4
5

 2 shallots

 1 lb 5 oz (600 g) poultry livers

 1 sprig fresh oregano

 3 tbsp (40 g) butter

 1 pinch of salt
1 pinch of black pepper

 1½ oz (40 g) pine nuts

 1 oz (30 g) raisins

 4 tbsp (60 ml) balsamic vinegar

 ⅜ cup (100 ml) brown poultry sauce (see p. 520)

Sautéed Venetian-Style Poultry Livers

1. Peel the shallots and finely dice. Clean the poultry livers, removing any tendons and veins. Pluck the oregano leaves and mince. Froth the butter in a skillet and add the livers.

2. Season with salt and pepper and sear.

3. Turn the pieces of liver over carefully. Season with salt and pepper. Season the livers in the pan, otherwise they will become dry and tough.

4. Add the shallots, pine nuts, and raisins and sauté for about 1 minute. Sprinkle the oregano over them.

5. Add the balsamic vinegar and simmer. Add the brown poultry sauce. Reheat quickly and serve immediately.

■ **This dish tastes delicious when served with mashed potatoes, fried cornmeal, or salad topped with Parmesan shavings and vinaigrette.**

2
3
4
5

1 head of garlic

1 lemon

1 bunch fresh parsley

4 Cornish hens (approx. 12 oz/ 350 g each)

1 pinch of salt
1 pinch of pepper

10½ oz (300 g) pearl onions

¼ cup (60 g) butter

Cornish Hens Roasted with Lemon and Garlic

1. Set the head of garlic stem up on the work surface, and press down with the palm of your hand to loosen the garlic cloves. Remove the outer skin, and crush the cloves still in the remaining skin. Rinse the lemon under hot water and cut into ¼-inch (5-mm) slices. Wash the parsley. Dress the Cornish hens, clean them, and dry the insides with paper towels.

2. Season the insides and outsides of the hens well with salt and pepper. Stuff with the crushed garlic cloves and the parsley. Set aside some of the parsley for garnish.

3. Place the stuffed hens in a baking dish. Wash the small onions and remove the skins. Cut off the root ends. Arrange the onions around the Cornish hens. Distribute the butter over the meat.

4. Roast for 25 minutes in the oven preheated to 350°F (180°C/Gas Mark 4). Garnish with the lemon slices. Add ⅜ cup (100 ml) water. Baste with the pan drippings and roast for an additional 15 minutes. Remove from the oven. Tuck the remaining parsley into the hens and serve with the onions and the pan drippings.

■ Pluck the remaining pinfeathers with fishbone pliers, but be careful not to nick the skin. The white meat would dry out at these spots. Cornish hens taste just as delicious when served cold. Serve with any type of potato dish.

2
3
4

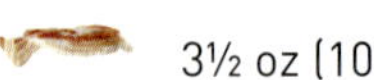 3½ oz (100 g) lard

 1 tsp juniper berries

 ½ bunch fresh thyme

 5 shallots

 1 pheasant (approx. 2 lb 4 oz/1 kg)

 1 pinch of salt
1 pinch of black pepper

 5 bay leaves

 5½ oz (150 g) green grapes

 1 lb 2 oz (500 g) sauerkraut with bacon (see p. 398)

 4 tsp (20 g) butter

 3 tbsp (40 ml) dry vermouth

 2 tbsp (30 ml) vegetable oil

Pheasant on Sauerkraut with Mashed Potatoes

1. Place the lard on a plate. Crush the juniper berries with the flat side of a large kitchen knife and chop. Pluck the thyme leaves from 2 sprigs, combine them with the juniper berries, and sprinkle over the lard slices.

2. Peel the shallots and quarter. Set 3 sprigs of thyme aside. Chop the remaining sprigs. Clean the pheasant thoroughly inside and out. Remove any remaining pinfeathers and possible pellets. Then season the pheasant inside and out with salt and pepper. Stuff with the shallots, the chopped thyme, and two bay leaves. Peel the grapes with a small kitchen knife. Wrap the pheasant with the seasoned lard. It prevents the meat from drying out during roasting. In addition, it provides extra flavor. Place 2 sprigs thyme and the remaining bay leaves on top of the legs.

3. Tie the pheasant with cotton string to keep the lard in place during roasting. Also tie the bay leaves and thyme sprigs.

4. Heat the wine sauerkraut. Melt the butter in a skillet until it froths. Add the peeled grapes and toss in the pan. Pour over the vermouth and add the sauerkraut.

■ **Lard is bacon fat. It is mostly used to bard or wrap meat. One pheasant serves 4, if a soup is served prior to the main pheasant course or the pheasant is served as an appetizer. For all other occasions, you should prepare 2 pheasants. Homemade mashed potatoes make a delicious side dish. Serve with ⅔ cup (150 ml) brown poultry sauce or prepare it from the pheasant's carcass.**

5. Heat the oil in a skillet. Sauté the pheasant on both sides for about 5 minutes and pour the pan drippings over it frequently. Place it in the baking dish in the oven preheated to 350°F (180°C/Gas Mark 4) for about 40 minutes. Baste the pheasant with its own juices occasionally. Remove the cotton string after roasting. Carve the breast and remove the legs and then serve with wine sauerkraut and the lard.

Beef & Veal

Contents

546 Types of Beef and Veal Cuts
546 Cooking Chart
548 How to Cut and Trim Veal Fillet
550 How to Cut and Trim Beef Fillet
552 Degrees of Doneness for Beef
554 Chili con Carne
556 Roast Beef
558 Stewed Beef with Vegetables and Herbs
560 Beef with Onions and Fried Potatoes
562 Beef Tenderloin in Chive Bouillon with Spring Vegetables
564 Beef Tenderloin in Green Peppercorn Cream Sauce
566 Beef Tournedos Rossini with Goose Liver and Truffle Sauce
568 Grilled T-Bone Steak with Onion Rings and Baked Potatoes
570 Beef Stroganoff with Pickles and Button Mushrooms
572 Traditional Hamburgers with Onion Relish
574 Indian Beef Curry with Black Cardamom and Cinnamon
576 Meatloaf with Sauce and Parsley Potatoes
578 Vietnamese Beef Stew with Ginger
580 Veal Roast with Root Vegetables and New Potatoes
582 Braised Veal Shanks with Gremolata (Osso Buco)
586 Veal Tenderloin in Puff Pastry with Herbs
588 Veal Kidneys in Mustard Cream Sauce with Mashed Onion Potatoes
590 Sautéed Veal Patties
592 Veal Cutlets in Almond-Bread Crust
594 Saltimbocca alla Romana with Sage and Prosciutto
596 Wiener Schnitzels

Types of Beef and Veal Cuts

The quality of beef and veal is not easy to detect visually. Lighting at the butcher counter can be deceptive and conceal the true color of meat. You are usually not allowed to touch the product. In general, female calves and cows taste better than their male counterparts. The ox is the exception to this rule. It is desirable for the beef to have a layer of fat. This layer is an important carrier of flavor. There is no way to discern the quality of beef by country of origin or breed. For example, there is a top-quality variety of beef called Charolais that is also sold under the same name in an inferior quality.

Cooking Chart

GM = Gas Mark

Type of Meat	Weight	Cooking Method	Temperature	Cooking Time	Notes
Rump roast	4 lb (1.8 kg)	Oven	325°F (160°C/GM 3)	120 minutes	Cover with lid
Roast beef	4 lb 8 oz (2 kg)	Oven	400°F (200°C/GM 6)	40 minutes	Sear
Beef sirloin	7 oz (200 g)	Skillet	Medium heat	6 minutes (medium)	
Beef tenderloin	7 oz (200 g)	Skillet	Medium heat	5 minutes	
T-bone steak	1 lb 2 oz (500 g)	Grill pan	High heat	12 minutes (medium)	Grease first
Beef olive	approx. 10½ oz (300 g)	Pot with lid	Low heat	90 minutes	Sear first
Beef tournedos	2¼ oz (60 g)	Skillet	Medium heat	4 minutes	
Beef sirloin tips	3½ oz (100 g)	Skillet	High heat	2 minutes	
Beef, boiled	3 lb 8 oz (1.6 kg)	Pot	Low heat	80 minutes	
Hamburger	7 oz (200 g)	Skillet	Medium heat	4 minutes	
Meatloaf	4 lb 8 oz (2 kg)	Oven	375°F (190°C/GM 5)	80 minutes	
Entrecote	9 oz (250 g)	Skillet	Medium heat	8 minutes (medium)	
Veal leg, boned and rolled	3–3 lb 5 oz (1.3–1.5 kg)	Oven	325°F (160°C/GM 3)	90 minutes	
Whole veal leg	4–5 lb 5 oz (1.8–2.4 kg)	Oven	340°F (170°C/GM 3½)	120 minutes	
Veal roast, lean	4 lb 8 oz (2 kg)	Oven	300°F (150°C/GM 2)	100 minutes	
Veal breast, stuffed	5 lb 8 oz (2.5 kg)	Oven	300°F (150°C/GM 2)	100 minutes	
Veal chops	10½ oz (300 g)	Skillet	Medium heat	12 minutes	
Veal loin	7 oz (200 g)	Skillet	Medium heat	10 minutes	
Veal medallions	2¼ oz (60 g)	Skillet	Medium heat	10 minutes	
Veal roast	3 lb 5 oz (1.5 kg)	Oven	350°F (180°C/GM 4)	90 minutes	
Osso bucco or veal shanks	14 oz (400 g)	Pot with lid	Medium heat	120 minutes	10 minutes
Veal cheeks	7 oz (200 g)	Pot with lid	Medium heat	120 minutes	Also possible in the oven
Hamburger patties	3½ oz (100 g)	Skillet	Medium heat	8 minutes	
Veal schnitzel	3¼ oz (90 g)	Skillet	Medium heat	5 minutes	
Calf liver	3½ oz (100 g) slices	Skillet	Medium heat	1 – 2 minutes	
Calf kidneys	In small lobes	Skillet	High heat	1 minutes	
Calf tongue	1 lb 2 oz (500 g)	Pot	Medium heat	60 minutes	Cook in vegetable broth

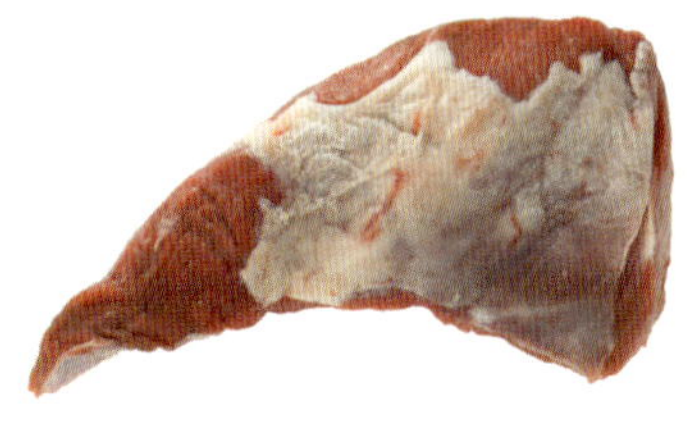

Fillet of beef

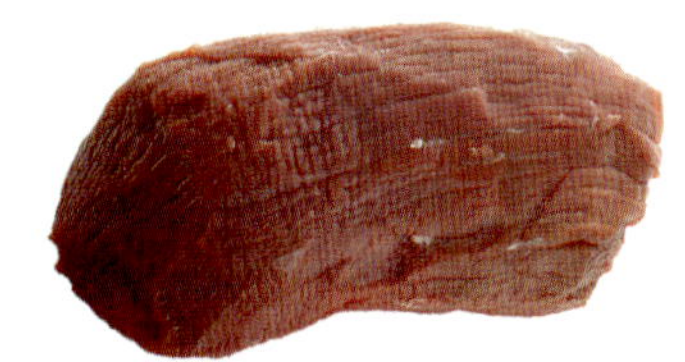

Rump roast

Roast beef

T-bone steak

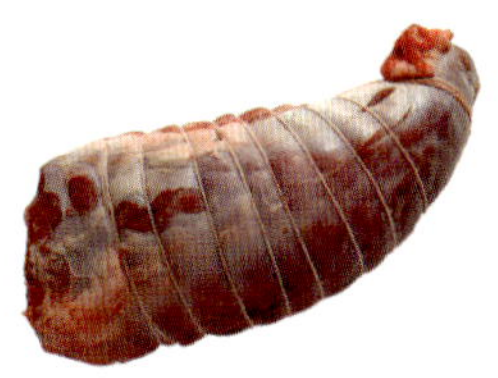

Veal roast

Calf bones

Calf kidneys or rognons

Veal cutlet

Whole tenderloin

Beef tenderloin (tournedos)

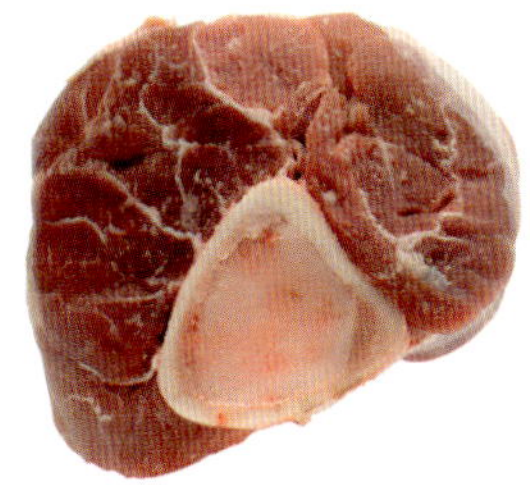

Veal shank

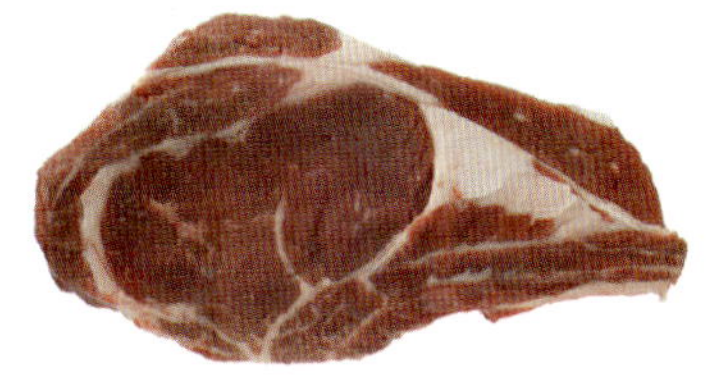

Beef steak

How to Cut and Trim Veal Fillet

1. Carefully remove the outer skin with a medium-size knife and on one side expose the long cord, which is also called the chain.

2. Carefully separate the chain from the fillet.

3. Cut with the knife under the outer sinews to separate them from the meat.

4. Hold the sinew taught and cut off with the knife. Hold the knife on an angle and slice toward the top to cut off as little meat as possible.

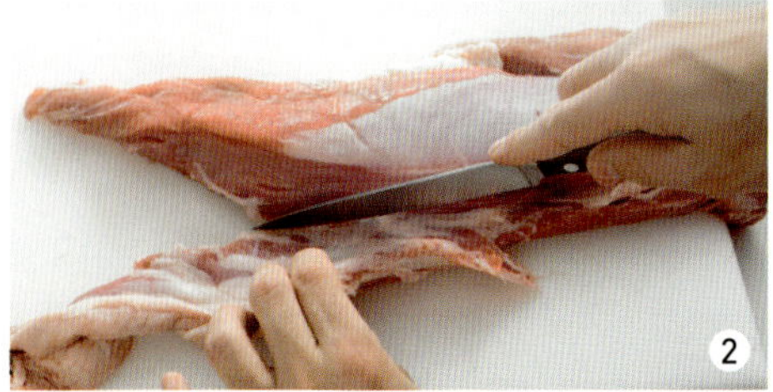

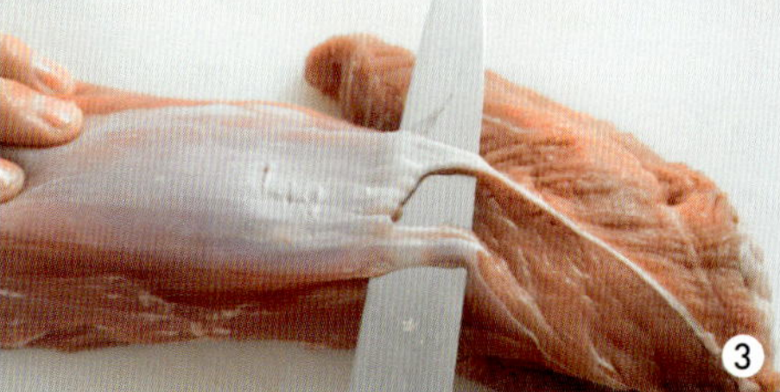

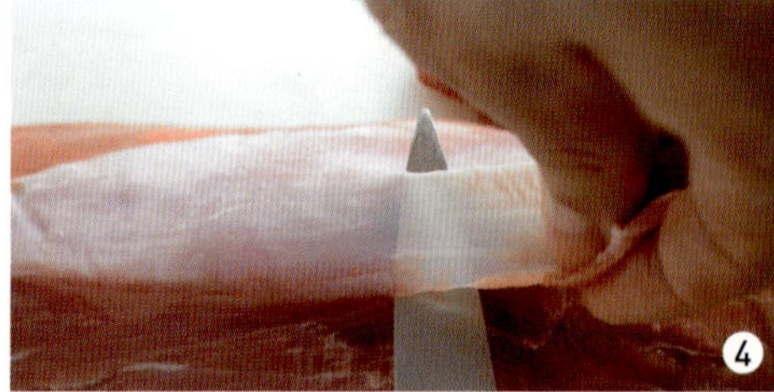

5. Turn the fillet over and remove any remaining small tendons or skin.

6. The fillet is ready to cook as soon as it is free of sinew and skin.

7. Separate the fillet tip and the head part, which is attached to the top of the fillet. Cut the center into medallions. Cut the tip of the fillet and the upper part into small pieces and use for stews.

8. Use the sinew and skin for sauces. Remove the remaining sinew from the chain and use for fillings or stuffing.

8

How to Cut and Trim Beef Fillet

To prepare a whole fillet of beef to cut into portions, first separate the fatty strand on the side (the chain) with a knife, then remove the uppermost white sinew. Turn the fillet over and cut off the outermost white sinew and skin, then trim and use as follows:

1. Use the fillet tips for stews.

2. Cut 1½–1¾ oz (40–50 g) filets mignons and use for light meals or for stews. Sear them briefly on each side.

3. Cut tournedos, each weighing about 2¼–2½ oz (60–70 g), and sear them briefly on each side or poach.

4. Cut fillet steaks of 7 oz (200 g) each from the center-cut, or one Chateaubriand weighing 14 oz–1 lb 5 oz (400–600 g). This is the prime cut of beef.

5. From the fillet head, where the meat is less fibrous, cut fillet steaks each weighing 7–10½ oz (200–300 g).

6. Use the fillet chain for stews and Asian pan dishes.

7. Cut 2½-inch (6-cm) pieces from the lower fillet chain and sauté in a grill pan. These flavorful pieces can also be used in stews.

8. Use the cuts from the head of the fillet for Asian stir fry dishes.

9. Use the end of the fillet head for stews.

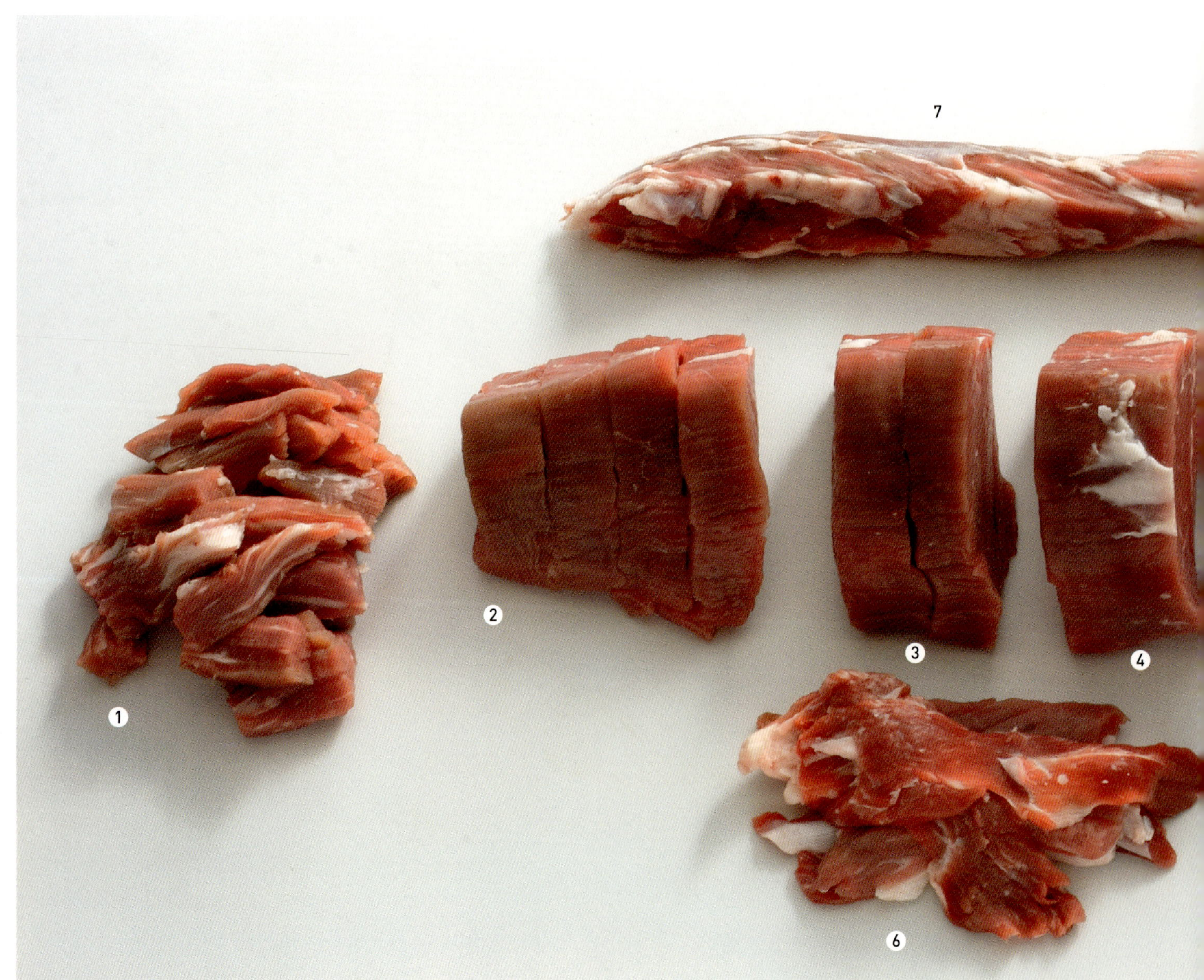

■ Wrap the tenderloin in fatty bacon and tie with a cotton string. After roasting you can either discard the bacon or serve.

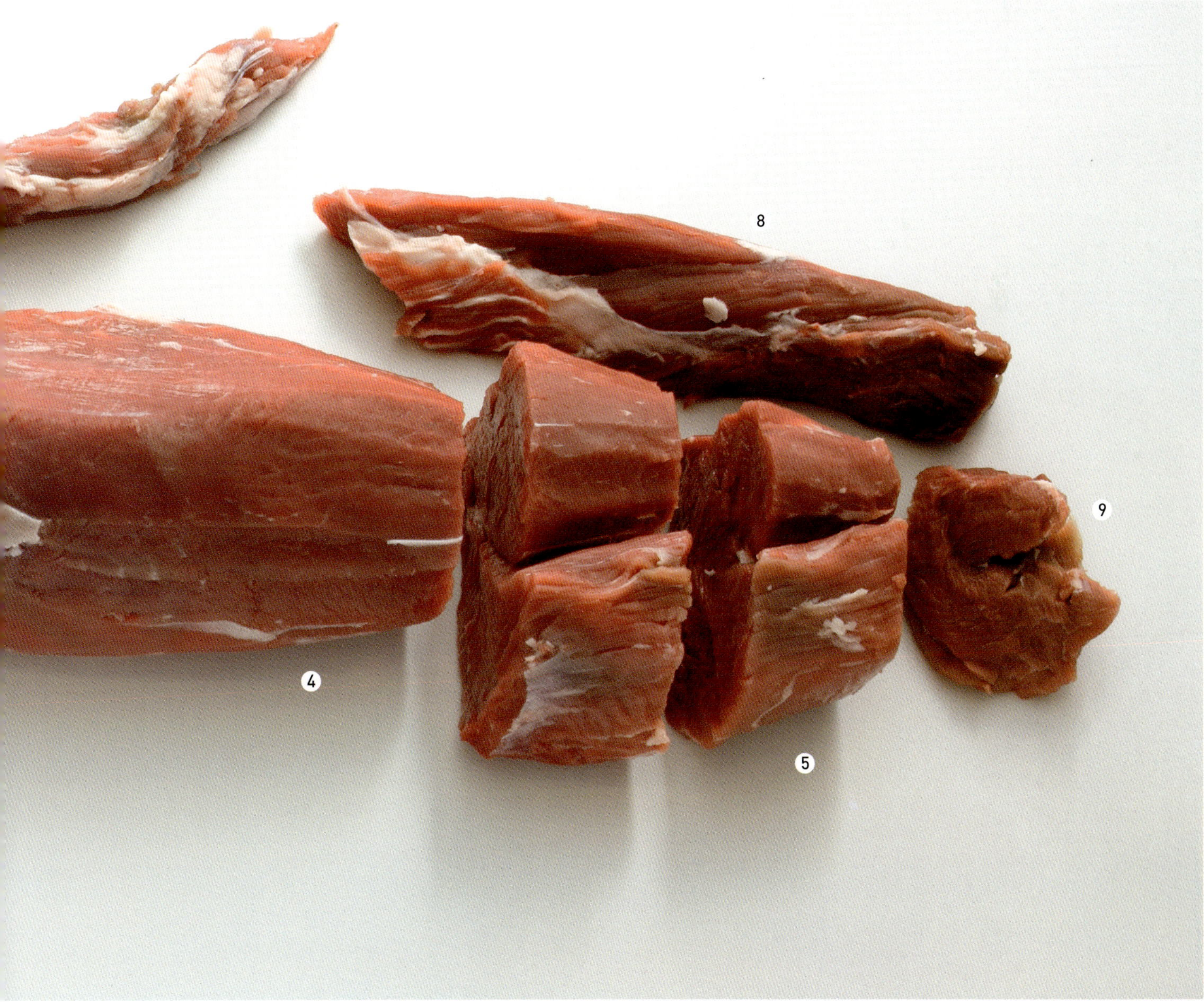

Degrees of Doneness for Beef

Beef Tenderloin

Rare/bleu: The meat is sautéed for 1 minute on each side and is raw on the inside.

Medium rare/saignant/bloody: The meat is sautéed for 3 minutes on each side. It has a pink center with a bloody core.

Medium/medium/pink: This is by far the most popular degree of doneness. The meat is sautéed for 5 minutes on each side. It remains pink on the inside; however, the core is no longer bloody.

Medium well/à point/half-done: The meat is sautéed for 6 minutes on each side. It is slightly pink on the inside. However, there are no bloody juices when cut.

Well done/bien cuit: The meat is sautéed for 8 minutes on each side and is well done on the inside. There are no juices when cut.

6 oz (175 g) green bell pepper

3½ oz (100 g) red bell pepper

3 onions

2 garlic cloves

1 lb 10 oz (750 g) lean beef (shoulder)

14 oz (400 g) cooked pinto beans

3 tbsp brown sugar

3/8 cup (100 ml) white wine vinegar

4 tbsp vegetable oil

5 cloves

2 bay leaves

1 pinch of salt
1 pinch of black pepper

1 tbsp sweet paprika

½ tbsp flour

2 chipotle peppers in adobo (marinade)

1 lb 2 oz (500 g) canned peeled tomatoes

3/8 cup (100 ml) sour cream

2¾ oz (80 g) grated Swiss cheese

1

Chili con Carne

1. Wash and trim the green and red bell peppers. Cut into ¼-inch (5-mm) cubes. Peel the onions and the garlic and finely chop. Cut the beef into ¼-inch (5-mm) cubes. Drain the beans in a strainer. Dissolve in a pot the brown sugar in 3/8 cup (100 ml) water until it caramelizes. Deglaze with the white wine vinegar and simmer to reduce the liquid. Add the vegetable oil and the garlic, and sauté.

2. Crush the cloves with a knife. Add the bay leaves, the onions, and the peppers. Sauté for about 10 minutes.

3. Add the meat cubes. Season with salt and pepper, and sauté slowly for 10 minutes.

4. Dust with paprika and flour—the flour binds the chili. Add the marinated chipotle peppers and sauté for an additional 5 minutes.

5. Put the peeled tomatoes in a bowl and blend with a handheld blender. Then add to the meat, cover the pot with a lid, and let it slowly simmer for about 1 hour. Stir occasionally. After 45 minutes, add the beans and simmer for 15 minutes. Serve, pour sour cream over it, and sprinkle with the grated cheese.

■ Chili con Carne can also be prepared using ground beef, or kidney beans instead of pinto beans. In addition, you can add fresh corn or small pieces of corn on the cob.

2
3
4
5

 2 slices white bread

 3 lb 5 oz (1.5 kg) roast beef

 1 tsp sea salt

 1 pinch of black pepper

 3 tbsp vegetable oil

 1 tbsp hot mustard

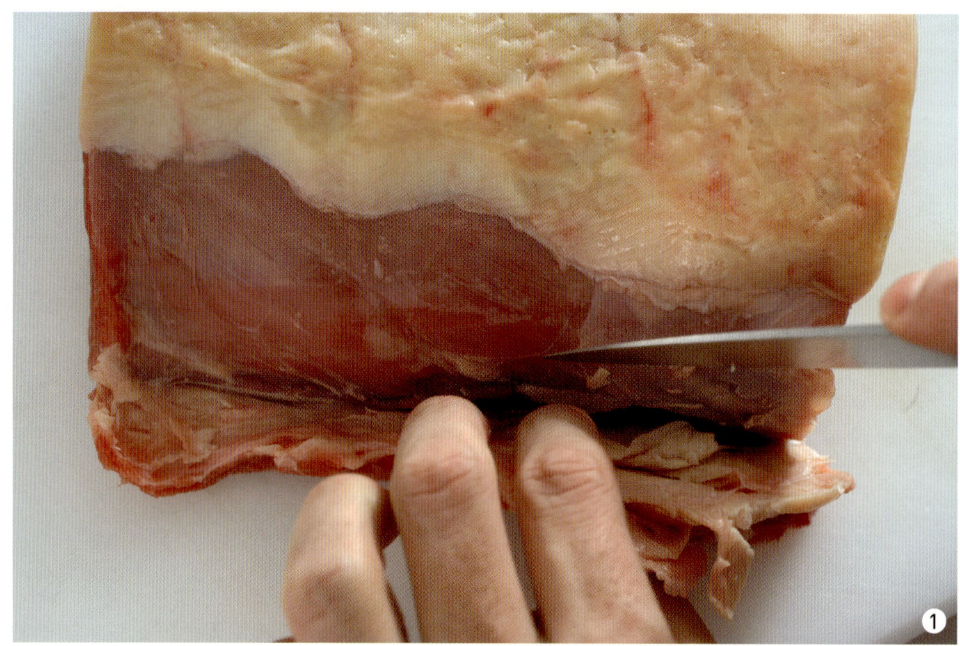

Roast Beef

1. Remove the crust from the white bread and chop up the bread in the food processor. Trim the outer tendons from the meat. Cut off excess fat, leaving about ¼ inch (5 mm) of fat on the meat. Turn the meat over, remove the tendons and skin, and trim nicely.

2. Make small incisions in the fat layer in various locations. This makes it easier to slice the meat after roasting. In addition, these cuts allow the fat to cook better, making the roast beef wonderfully crispy.

3. Season the meat with salt and pepper on all sides and rub in the seasoning.

4. Heat the oil in the skillet; place the meat in it, and sauté for about 2 minutes on each side.

5. Grease the baking sheet with a bit of oil and place the sautéed meat on it. Brush the mustard on the top side and sprinkle breadcrumbs over it. Place the roast beef in the oven preheated to 400°F (210°C/Gas Mark 6½) and set on convection, if available. Roast for about 25 minutes. Remove and place on a serving platter, and let it sit for about 5 minutes before slicing.

■ **Serve potato gratin or baked potatoes with roast beef. Pepper cream sauce and green beans are welcome and delicious additions. Another option is to let the roast beef cool, then thinly slice it and serve with fried potatoes and tartar sauce (see p. 52).**

2
3
4
5

 5 juniper berries

 5 white peppercorns

 2 onions

 5¾ oz (160 g) carrots

 5¾ oz (160 g) leeks

 5¾ oz (160 g) celery stalks

 1 tbsp coarse sea salt

 2 lb 4 oz (1 kg) beef for stew

 2 cloves

 1 bay leaf

 3 sprigs fresh parsley

 ½ bunch fresh chives

Stewed Beef with Vegetables and Herbs

1. With the flat blade of a knife, lightly crush the juniper berries and the peppercorns.

2. Cut the root ends off the onions and halve them, leaving the peel on. Wash the vegetables and pare. Peel the carrots and halve. Cut the leeks and celery stalks in 2 or 3 pieces, depending on their size.

3. In a large pot, bring water and salt to a boil and simmer the beef for about 1 hour.

4. After 1 hour, add the cut vegetables, cloves, and bay leaf, and let it simmer for another hour.

5. Season with salt and pepper to taste.

Cut the vegetables in bite-size pieces and arrange them on a serving platter together with the beef. Sprinkle some parsley leaves and snipped chives over it.

■ **Serve with parsley potatoes, fried potatoes, or creamed spinach. It tastes delicious with tartar sauce.**

2
3
4
5

 7 oz (200 g) onions

 1 tsp sweet paprika

 1 tbsp flour

 4½ cups (1 liter) vegetable oil

 3 shallots

 ⅛ cup (30 g) butter

 ½ tsp dried marjoram

 1 tsp tomato paste

 ⅜ cup (100 ml) beer

 1⅛ cups (250 ml) veal stock

 1 lb 12 oz (800 g) fried potatoes

 4 pickles

 1 bunch fresh chives

 4 roast beef slices (7 oz/200 g each)

 1 pinch of salt
1 pinch of black pepper

Beef with Onions and Fried Potatoes

1. Peel the onions and finely slice. Dust with the flour and the paprika and mix well.

2. Heat the oil in a pot to 325°F (160°C), but save 2 tbsp of oil for later. Fry the onion rings in two batches until golden brown. Remove and drain them on paper towels. Add a dash of salt.

3. Peel the shallots and finely dice. Froth the butter in a skillet and sauté the shallots until golden brown. Then add the dried marjoram and the tomato paste and sauté lightly.

4. Add the beer to the pan drippings and reduce the liquid. Add the veal stock and reduce the liquid to a quarter of its volume. In the meantime, prepare fried potatoes. Cut the pickles in half. Wash the chives and mince.

5. Lightly pound the meat and season with salt and pepper. Heat the 2 tbsp oil in a skillet and sauté the meat for about 2 minutes on each side.

Arrange the fried potatoes and the meat on serving plates. Pour the sauce over it and garnish with the onions and chives. Serve with a pickle.

■ **This dish is especially tender and delicious if you use pieces of tenderloin instead of roast beef.**

2
3
4
5

 1 bunch carrots

 1 head of romanesco (or cauliflower)

 5½ oz (150 g) green beans

 10 asparagus stalks

 2 tbsp coarse sea salt

 3½ oz (100 g) peas

 ½ bunch fresh chives

 2⅔ cups (600 ml) beef stock

 1 lb 12 oz (800 g) beef tenderloin

 1 pinch of salt
1 pinch of black pepper

 ½ cup (120 g) butter, cold

 1 pinch of nutmeg, freshly grated

Beef Tenderloin in Chive Bouillon with Spring Vegetables

1. Peel the carrots and cut into 2-inch (5-cm) pieces. Cut the romanesco into small florets. Remove the stem of the green beans. Peel the asparagus stalks and cut into 2-inch (5-cm) pieces. Bring salted water to a boil in a large pot. Prepare a bowl with cold water and ice cubes to cool down the cooked vegetables quickly and stop the cooking process.

2. First cook the carrots and the green beans, then the romanesco florets and asparagus pieces, and lastly the peas. Refresh with cold water. Wash the chives, trim, and slice.

3. Put the beef stock in a cooking pot and simmer for 5 minutes. Prepare the beef tenderloin and cut into 8 equal portions. Season with salt and pepper and place in the bouillon. Take the pot off the burner and let it sit for 6 minutes. Remove the tenderloins. Place on a plate and cover with aluminum foil to keep warm.

4. Slice the cold butter, add it to the bouillon, and bring to a boil. Use a beater to blend the butter into the mixture thoroughly. Season with salt and pepper and nutmeg to taste, and add the chives.

■ **As side dishes serve fresh white bread, parsley potatoes, or steamed rice.**

5. Place the vegetables in a sieve and drain. Then add those vegetables to the bouillon and reheat. Arrange in deep soup dishes and place the tenderloins on top.

1¾ cups (400 ml) Green Peppercorn Cream Sauce (see p. 148)

4 shallots

2 sprigs fresh tarragon

4 beef tenderloins (7 oz/200 g each)

1 pinch of salt
1 pinch of pepper

3 tbsp vegetable oil

¼ cup (60 g) butter

Beef Tenderloin in Green Peppercorn Cream Sauce

1. First prepare the Green Peppercorn Cream Sauce. Then peel the shallots and finely dice. Wash the tarragon, pick off the leaves, and chop. Season the tenderloins on both sides with salt and pepper.

2. Heat the oil and butter in a pot until foamy, and place the tenderloins in it.

3. Sauté the tenderloins and pour the butter-oil mixture repeatedly over them.

4. Turn over the tenderloins and cook to desired doneness while basting with the butter-oil mixture.

5. Move the tenderloins to the edge of the pot, add the shallot dice, and sauté until golden brown. Then add the tarragon, mix, and distribute the shallot over the tenderloins. Place one tenderloin in the center of each serving plate. Pour the pepper cream sauce around them.

Serve with Potato Gratin (see p. 314).

■ Place the sautéed beef tenderloins on a plate, cover with aluminum foil, and let it sit for about 3 minutes. Add the meat juices to the sauce. The result is an evenly rosy and juicy piece of meat.

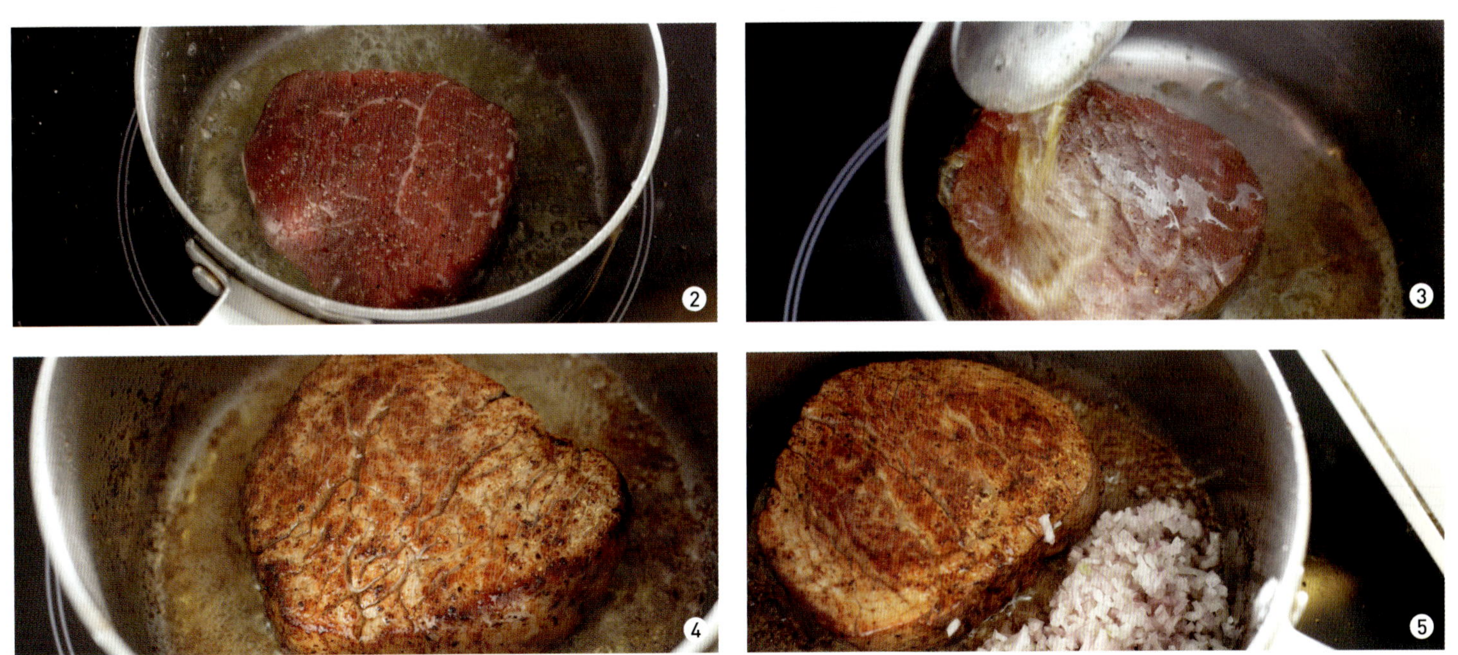
2
3
4
5

 2¼ oz (60 g) black winter truffle

 ¼ cup (50 g) butter, cold

 1 pinch of salt
1 pinch of black pepper

 3 tbsp (40 ml) Madeira

 ⅞ cup (200 ml) gravy (see p. 138)

 10½ oz (300 g) beef tenderloin/ tournedos

 5½ oz (150 g) fresh goose liver

 1 tsp flour

 2 tbsp vegetable oil

 4 slices white bread

Beef Tournedos Rossini with Goose Liver and Truffle Sauce

1. Wash the black truffle, brush, and cut into 1⁄16-inch (1-mm) thin slices. Froth half of the butter in a skillet. Heat the truffle slices in it and season with salt and pepper. Pour the Madeira over them and simmer.

2. Add the gravy, bring to a boil, and set aside.

3. Cut the beef tenderloin into four equal portions. Cut the goose liver into four equal slices. Season the tenderloins and goose liver with salt and pepper. Dust the goose liver lightly with flour.

4. Heat 1 tbsp oil and 2 tsp (10 g) butter in a skillet and sauté the beef medallions on both sides to your preference. For medium doneness, sauté for about 3 minutes on each side.

5. Heat 1 tbsp oil in a nonstick skillet. Sauté the liver slices for about 30 seconds on each side. Combine the cooking fat with the remaining cold butter and add it to the sauce. Cut the crusts off the white bread and lightly toast. Arrange the beef tenderloin on the toast on a serving plate, top it with goose liver, and pour the sauce over it.

■ **Goose liver is easier to sauté and does not disintegrate if you place it in the freezer for 10 minutes prior to cooking. Alternatively, you can use duck liver. However, you should always use fatty liver or foie gras.**

2
3
4
5

 4 potatoes

 2 tsp (10 g) butter

 1 pinch of salt
1 pinch of black pepper

 2 T-bone steaks, 14 oz (400 g) each

 1 tsp coarse sea salt

 Black peppercorns

 3 tbsp vegetable oil

 3 white onions

 1 tsp sweet paprika

 1 tbsp flour

 4½ cups (1 liter) oil

 ⅜ cup (100 ml) BBQ sauce
(see p. 56)

Grilled T-Bone Steak with Onion Rings and Baked Potatoes

1. Wash the potatoes and cook for 10 minutes in salted water. Grease four pieces of aluminum foil with butter. Season the foil with salt and pepper and wrap the precooked potatoes in it. Bake in the oven at 400°F (200°C/Gas Mark 6) for 45 minutes. Season both steaks on both sides with a dash of coarse sea salt and pepper. Rub oil over them. Heat a large ridged grill pan and fry the meat for 1 minute on all sides.

2. Then grill for another 6 minutes.

3. Turn the steaks over and grill for an additional 6 minutes.

4. Peel the onions and cut into ¾-inch (2-cm) slices. Separate the rings, and dust them first with the paprika and then with the flour.

5. In a wide pan, heat the oil to 325°F (160°C) and fry the onion rings for about 3 minutes, until golden brown. Remove and drain them on paper towels, then season them with salt. Place the steaks on a cutting board. Separate the fillet from the entrecote. Then cut into ½-inch (1-cm) thick slices and arrange them together with the baked potatoes and fried onion rings and the BBQ sauce on serving plates. Sprinkle some coarse sea salt and freshly ground pepper over the meat.

■ **Freshly made French fries and spinach leaves or creamed spinach taste delicious with the steak.**

2
3
4
5

 1 lb 5 oz (600 g) beef tenderloin

 3½ oz (100 g) button mushrooms

 2 pickled gherkins

 5¾ oz (160 g) canned red beets

 2 shallots

 ¼ cup (50 g) butter

 1 pinch of salt
1 pinch of black pepper

 1 tbsp vegetable oil

 4 tbsp pickle juice

 1⅛ cups (250 ml) gravy (see p. 138)

 7 oz (200 g) crème fraîche
(or sour cream)

 ½ tsp hot mustard

 1 pinch of sugar

Beef Stroganoff with Pickles and Button Mushrooms

1. Cut the tenderloin into thin 2-inch (5-cm) long strips. Clean the mushrooms and slice. Cut the pickles and the red beets into strips. Set aside. Peel the shallots and finely dice.

2. Melt 3 tbsp (40 g) butter in a skillet and add the beef strips. Season with salt and pepper. Fry briefly until light brown on all sides. Remove and place on a plate. Cover with aluminum foil to keep warm.

3. Pour the oil in the same skillet and brown the shallot dice. Add the mushroom slices, season with salt and pepper, and fry briefly. Then add the pickle juice and reduce the liquid.

4. Pour the gravy into the skillet and bring to a boil. Add any juices from the tenderloin.

5. Add the crème fraîche (or sour cream). Season with freshly ground black pepper.

6. Place the beef strips in the sauce and add the gherkin slices. Mix the mustard into the sauce, but do not heat.

7. Melt the remaining butter in a pan and briefly sauté the red beet strips. Season with salt and sugar, then arrange the beef strips on serving plates and garnish with the beets.

■ **This dish is just as tasty if prepared with top sirloin. You may serve it with added sour cream and steamed rice.**

5

6

7

4 onions

2 tbsp sugar

1 bay leaf

1 pinch of salt
1 pinch of black pepper

⅜ cup (100 ml) fruit vinegar

1 lb 12 oz (800 g) lean ground beef

2 tbsp oil

8 lettuce leaves

2 tomatoes

2 pickles

4 soft sesame-seed hamburger buns

4 tsp mayonnaise

1 tbsp mustard, medium hot

4 tsp ketchup

Traditional Hamburgers with Onion Relish

1. Peel, halve, and thinly slice the onions. Combine them with the sugar, bay leaf, ground black pepper, salt, and fruit vinegar, and place in a skillet. Then add ⅞ cup (200 ml) water and slowly simmer for 25 minutes. The onion relish is ready when the liquid is completely reduced and the mixture is jamlike.

2. From the ground beef, form 4 hamburger patties of equal size. Heat the oil in a nonstick skillet and place the hamburgers in it. Season with salt and pepper, and sauté for about 2 minutes.

3. Turn the patties over. Season with salt and pepper, and sauté for an additional 2 minutes.

4. Wash the lettuce leaves. Slice the tomatoes and pickles. Cut the sesame-seed buns in half and toast them. Put mayonnaise on the bottom half of the buns. Place a lettuce leaf on top and add one patty. Brush the mustard on the patty.

5. Add slices of tomato and top with the onion relish. Place the pickle slices on top. Put ketchup on the top part of the bun and place on the hamburger patty.

■ **Hamburgers are best served with fresh homemade French fries. You can use other spicy sauces, crisp bacon strips, or fresh onion rings. If you like, add 1 slice of cheddar cheese and, voilà, the hamburger is now a cheeseburger.**

3

4

5

 5 tbsp vegetable oil

 3 cinnamon sticks

 8 black cardamom pods

 1 tbsp black mustard seeds

 ½ tsp cumin

 1 tbsp turmeric

 1 lb 2 oz (500 g) onions

 3 garlic cloves

 2 lb 4 oz (1 kg) beef shoulder

 1 tsp salt
1 pinch freshly ground black pepper

 1 tbsp jaggery (or brown sugar)

 1¾ cups (400 ml) canned peeled tomatoes

 3 bay leaves

Indian Beef Curry with Black Cardamom and Cinnamon

1. Heat the vegetable oil in a cooking pot. Add the cinnamon sticks, cardamom pods, mustard seeds, cumin, and turmeric. Lightly toast to intensify the flavor.

2. Peel the onions and the garlic. Cut each onion into eight pieces and mince the garlic. Add the mixture to the pot and sauté lightly. In the meantime, cut the beef into 1¼-inch (3-cm) cubes.

3. Season the beef with salt, coarsely ground pepper, and the sugar. Put this mixture into the pot. Sauté for 5 minutes.

4. Add the peeled tomatoes and the bay leaves. Put a lid over it and gently simmer for about 50 minutes. Occasionally, add some water to make a fine sauce.

Serve with steamed basmati rice.

■ Create an Indian curry paste with the following ingredients: 3 red chili peppers, 5½ oz (150 g) shallots, 5 garlic cloves, ¼ oz (10 g) galangal, ¼ oz (10 g) fresh ginger, ¼ oz (8 g) fresh turmeric root (or, as an alternative use 1 tsp ground turmeric), 2 tbsp coriander seeds, ½ tsp anise seeds, 5 cloves, ½ tsp fennel seeds, and 1 stalk of lemon grass. First, grind the solid spices in a mortar. Add the other ingredients one by one until pastelike. Use this paste with fish, poultry, or vegetables. Store in a glass jar or freeze.

2
3
4

 1 lb 10 oz (750 g) ground beef

 1 large onion

 4 small day-old bread rolls

 2¼ cups (500 ml) milk

 2 eggs

 2 tsp sweet paprika

 1 pinch of salt
1 pinch of black pepper

 1 tsp dried marjoram

 1 tbsp hot mustard

 1 tsp cornstarch

Meatloaf with Sauce and Parsley Potatoes

1. Place the ground beef in a bowl and add the peeled and finely chopped onion.

2. Pour the milk into a dish and add an equal amount of water. Soak the rolls in this mixture for 20 minutes.

3. Squeeze the liquid from the rolls and combine them with the eggs, the paprika, the salt and pepper, the marjoram, and the hot mustard. Add them to the ground beef. Mix well and season to taste.

4. Place the meat mixture in a buttered baking dish and smooth with your moistened hand.

5. Bake for about 1 hour at 375°F (190°C/Gas Mark 5) in a preheated oven. Occasionally, add some water and pour it over the meatloaf. Remove the meatloaf from the baking dish and slice. Bind the sauce with the cornstarch, after mixing it with a little bit of water.

Pour the sauce over the slices of meatloaf. Serve with parsley potatoes.

■ **Add a dash of fresh heavy cream to your sauce. It tastes delicious and it stretches the sauce, just in case you get more company for dinner than expected.**

2
3
4
5

2 heads of romanesco (or cauliflower)

3 shallots

2 tomatoes

1 bunch fresh cilantro

1-inch (2.5-cm) piece of fresh ginger

14 oz (400 g) beef tenderloin

4 tbsp oyster sauce

4 tbsp peanut oil

1 garlic clove

1 pinch of sugar

1 lime

Vietnamese Beef Stew with Ginger

1. Wash the romanesco and divide it into florets; also cut up the stem. Peel the shallots and slice them lengthwise. Quarter the tomatoes, deseed, and cut each quarter twice. Wash the cilantro and chop. Peel the ginger and finely slice. Remove any fat or tendons from the beef tenderloin und cut the meat into ¾-inch (2-cm) wide and 1¼-inch (3-cm) long slices. Place in a bowl, combine with the oyster sauce, and marinate for 20 minutes.

2. Slowly sauté the romanesco florets with half of the oil in a nonstick wok for about 3 minutes. Then pour in the rest of the oil from the side.

3. Peel the garlic clove and mince. Add it to the oil and sear. Then add the marinated beef strips and sear for 1 minute while stirring.

4. Add the shallot strips, ginger, and tomato pieces, and toss. Fry only briefly, so the vegetables stay crispy.

5. Then add the cut cilantro, the sugar, and the juice of the lime. Mix it only once and serve.

■ **You can mix cooked cellophane or glass noodles, or wide rice noodles into the dish. You need about 7 oz (200 g) cooked noodles for this recipe.**

2
3
4
5

3 lb 5 oz (1.5 kg) veal roast from the lower side

1 pinch of salt
1 pinch of white pepper

5 sprigs fresh rosemary

1 tbsp flour

7 oz (200 g) carrots

10½ oz (300 g) young onions

5½ oz (150 g) celeriac

7 cloves

¼ cup (60 g) butter

3 tbsp vegetable oil

2 bay leaves

⅜ cup (100 ml) white wine

1 lb 12 oz (800 g) new potatoes

1

Veal Roast with Root Vegetables and New Potatoes

1. Season the roast with salt and pepper. Leave the tendons and fat on the meat; they make the roast juicier. Cover with the rosemary sprigs and tie with a cotton string. Then dust with flour.

2. Peel the carrots and celeriac and cut them up. Peel and halve the onions. Put them with the cloves in a baking dish. Distribute the butter among them. Season the vegetables lightly with salt and pepper.

3. Heat the oil in a nonstick skillet and sauté the veal roast evenly on all sides until golden brown.

4. Then add it to the vegetables and put it in the oven preheated to 350°F (180°C/Gas Mark 4). Add the bay leaves. Roast for 30 minutes and baste frequently with the pan drippings. Add 3 tbsp (50 ml) white wine every 10 minutes.

5. In the meantime, peel the potatoes and cook in a pot of salted water for about 10 minutes. Drain and add them to the roast. Cook for an additional hour in the oven at 350°F (170°C/Gas Mark 3½). Baste frequently with the pan drippings and turn the roast and the vegetables over occasionally. Remove from the oven. Arrange the vegetables, the potatoes, and the sauce on serving plates. Remove the cotton string and rosemary sprigs from the roast. Slice the roast and arrange it on the plates.

■ **If the meat is too lean, your roast can dry out. Both the neck and shoulder are well suited to this dish. The added vegetables are a wonderful side dish and create a natural sauce that does not need binding.**

2
3
4
5

6 slices of veal shank, 7–10½ oz (200–300 g) each

1 tsp salt
1 pinch of black pepper

2 tbsp flour

9 oz (250 g) carrots

5½ oz (150 g) onions

5 garlic cloves

3½ oz (100 g) celery stalks

3½ oz (100 g) leeks

½ bunch fresh parsley

1 orange

1 lemon

1 tsp fennel seeds

⅓ cup (90 g) butter

3 tbsp olive oil

1 tbsp tomato paste

1⅛ cups (250 ml) white wine

9 oz (250 g) canned peeled tomatoes

2¼ cups (500 ml) veal bouillon

1 bay leaf

2 sprigs fresh thyme

Braised Veal Shanks with Gremolata (Osso Buco)

1. Dry the veal pieces with paper towels. Season with salt and pepper and dust with flour.

2. Peel the carrots and onions. Wash the celery stalks and leeks. Finely dice the vegetables (see Brunoise, p. 344). Peel and press three of the garlic cloves.

3. For the gremolata, mince the parsley leaves, 2 peeled garlic cloves, 2 strips each of orange and lemon peels, a few celery leaves, and the fennel seeds. Mix with ¼ cup (50 g) butter.

4. Heat the oil in a large pot that is wide enough to fit all the veal pieces side by side. Slowly sauté them for 10 minutes on each side.

»

■ **Don't heat the meat too much. It would cause the pieces to curl up.**

4

5. Then place two veal pieces on top of the others and put the remaining butter in the available space. Let it foam, then sauté the garlic and the tomato paste.

6. Put the onions, carrots, leeks, and celeriac into the pot. Sauté lightly and distribute around the veal. Continue to sauté for another 10 minutes and turn the meat over occasionally. Deglaze with the white wine and simmer.

7. Then add the peeled tomatoes, veal bouillon, bay leaf, and thyme sprigs. Cover with a lid and braise the veal slowly for about 2 hours. Turn the pieces over occasionally and make sure they are covered with sauce. If necessary, add some water. Then season with salt and pepper to taste and arrange on serving plates. Spoon the gremolata over the veal. Serve with risotto flecked with saffron threads.

■ The gremolata can also be prepared with fresh marjoram or fennel. The butter takes on all the flavors and is added to the finished veal with the sauce to complete the dish.

6

7

 2 lb 4 oz (1 kg) veal tenderloin

 1 pinch of salt
1 pinch of black pepper

 2 tbsp vegetable oil

 5½ oz (150 g) lean veal

 3½ oz (100 g) cooked ham

 2 eggs

 ⅓ cup (70 ml) heavy cream

 1 tbsp cognac

 3½ oz (100 g) button mushrooms

 3 tbsp (40 g) butter

 1 pinch of nutmeg, freshly grated

 ⅞ cup (200 ml) Madeira

 1 oz (30 g) pistachios

 ½ bunch fresh parsley

 9 oz (250 g) puff pastry dough

Veal Tenderloin in Puff Pastry with Herbs

1. Remove all skin and tendons from the veal tenderloin and cut into four equal portions. Season with salt and pepper. Heat the oil in a skillet and sear the veal tenderloin on both sides. Place on a plate to cool. Cut the veal and cooked ham into ¼-inch (5-mm) cubes and place in the food processor. Add salt, pepper, 1 egg, 3 tbsp (50 ml) heavy cream, and the cognac. Mix for about 1 minute.

2. Wash the mushrooms and chop finely. Melt the butter in a large skillet and sauté the mushrooms. Season with salt and pepper and sprinkle with freshly grated nutmeg. Add the Madeira. Place in a bowl to cool. Finely chop the pistachios in the food processor and place in a bowl. Wash and mince the parsley. As soon as all ingredients are cool, combine the paste with the parsley and mix well.

3. Spread the sautéed veal tenderloin with the mushroom-herb mixture until the pieces are completely covered.

4. Roll out the puff pastry dough ¼-inch (5-mm) thick and separate into 4 equal squares. Place each veal tenderloin in the center of a square. Separate the egg and beat the egg yolk with 1 tbsp heavy cream. Brush this mixture onto the edges of the puff pastry and wrap each piece into a package. Lightly press the dough to seal.

■ Serve with a truffle sauce (see Tournedos Rossini p. 566), an herb or Mushroom Cream Sauce (see p. 149), or with fresh chanterelles.

5. Place the veal pastries with the smooth side on top on a baking sheet covered with parchment paper. Brush the remaining egg mixture on them and make a diamond pattern in the dough with the back of a knife. Bake for about 25 minutes in the oven preheated to 425°F (220°C/Gas Mark 7). Use the convection setting, if available. After half of the baking time, reduce the heat to 400°F (200°C/Gas Mark 6). Then arrange the veal tenderloins on a serving platter.

 1 lb 12 oz (800 g) veal kidneys

 1 shallot

 7 oz (200 g) green beans

 1 tbsp salt

 2 lb 4 oz (1 kg) mashed potatoes (see p. 336)

 2 onions

 4 tbsp vegetable oil

 1 pinch of black pepper

 ½ bunch fresh parsley

 4 tsp (20 g) butter

 3 tbsp (40 ml) white port

 1⅓ cups (300 ml) heavy cream

 1 tbsp coarse mustard

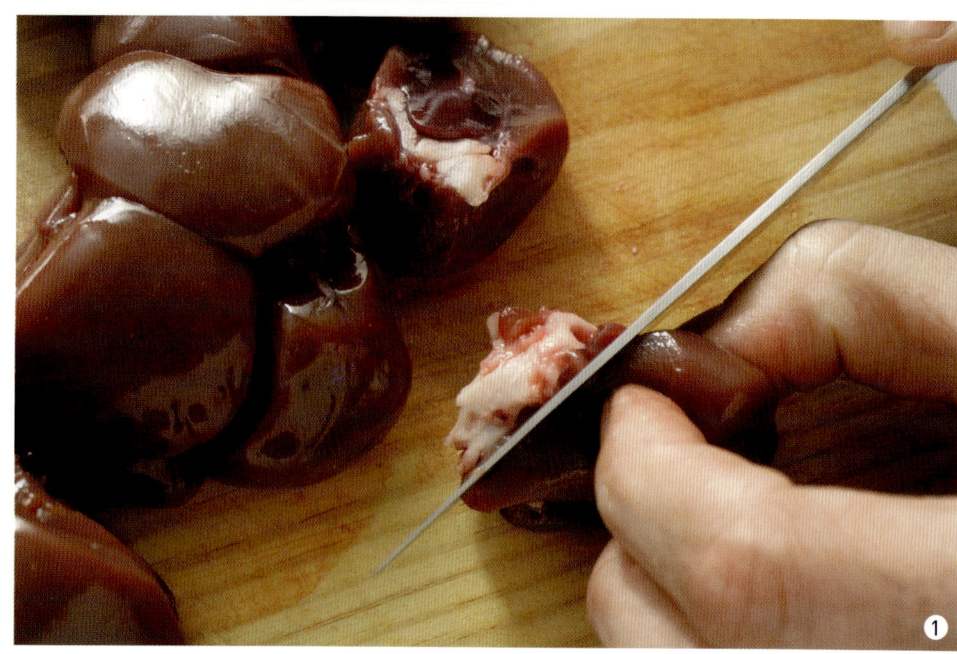

Veal Kidneys in Mustard Cream Sauce with Mashed Onion Potatoes

1. Separate the kidneys into loaves and cut away any fat with the knife. Peel the shallot and finely dice it. Clean the beans, remove any stems, and cut into ¾-inch (2-cm) pieces. Cook in a pot of boiling salted water for about 3 minutes. Then place in water with ice cubes to cool. This helps to preserve the beans' green color.

2. Prepare the mashed potatoes. Peel the onions, halve, cut into strips, and sauté them in 2 tbsp oil until golden brown, then fold into the mashed potatoes. Heat the remaining oil in a nonstick skillet. Add the kidneys, season with salt and pepper, and sear on all sides.

3. Place the kidneys in a sieve and drain. Wash and trim the parsley. Mince.

4. Heat the butter in a skillet until frothy and sauté the shallots. Add the white port and reduce the liquid. Add heavy cream and again reduce the liquid to about half.

5. Add the well-drained kidneys and the coarse mustard. Mix and reheat, then mix in the green beans and the minced parsley. Arrange on serving plates together with the mashed onion potatoes.

■ You may sear the kidneys with vegetables, such as small mushrooms, whole pearl onions, small carrots pieces, or green beans, and add gin and brown gravy.

2
3
4
5

 ½ garlic clove

 3½ oz (100 g) cooked ham

 5 tbsp butter

 2 onions

 1 tsp marjoram

 ½ bunch fresh parsley

 1 lb 2 oz (500 g) ground veal

 4 slices white bread

 ⅔ cup (150 ml) milk

 1 pinch of salt
1 pinch of black pepper

 1 tbsp mustard

 2 eggs

Sautéed Veal Patties

1. Peel the garlic and chop finely. Cut the ham into small cubes.

2. Brown both in 2 tbsp of butter. Add the peeled and cubed onions and sauté until light brown. Remove from the stove and mix in the marjoram. Wash the parsley and mince.

3. Add the veal to the white bread slices soaked in milk and squeeze-dried well.

4. Add the cooled onion-ham mixture. Season with salt and pepper. Add the mustard and the eggs.

5. Mix well, using your hands.

6. Moisten your hands and form 8 equal-size patties.

7. Carefully sauté the patties in 3 tbsp butter for about 5 minutes on each side.

8. Baste the patties continuously with the jus. This keeps them juicy.

Arrange on plates and serve with mustard, potato salad, or fried potatoes.

■ **Instead of cooked ham, you can use finely cubed bacon, which adds additional zest to your patties.**

5
6
7
8

 4 veal cutlets, 5¾ oz (160 g) each

 1 pinch of salt
1 pinch of pepper

 ¾ cup (100 g) flour

 2 eggs

 10½ oz (300 g) breadcrumbs

 3½ oz (100 g) slivered almonds

 5 tbsp vegetable oil

 ⅛ cup (30 g) butter

Veal Cutlets in Almond-Bread Crust

1. Lightly pound the cutlets with the blade of a large kitchen knife.

2. Season with salt and pepper.

3. Coat the cutlets in the flour and remove any excess.

4. Put the eggs into a bowl and beat. Dip the cutlets in the egg, completely coating the meat.

5. Pour the breadcrumbs and the slivered almonds into a wide dish, mix, and bread the cutlets.

6. Pour the oil and the butter into a skillet, and heat until frothy. Place the cutlets in the pan. Carefully sauté and turn over after 3 minutes.

7. Sauté for an additional 3 minutes on the other side, continuously basting with the jus.

8. Remove from the pan and drain on paper towels.

Arrange on plates; serve with parsley potatoes and garnish with lemon slices.

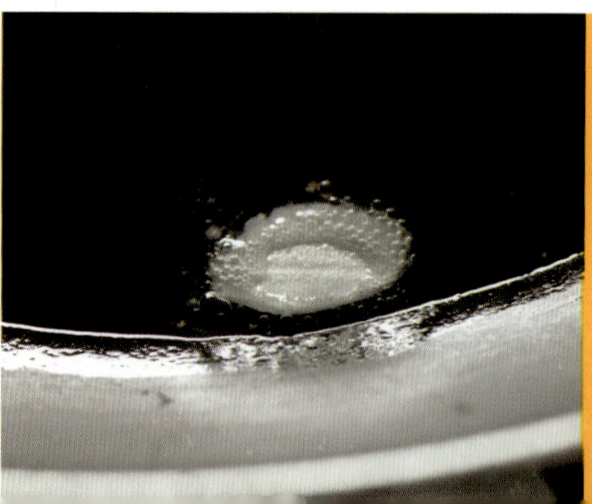

■ **Drop an almond slice into the oil. When it bubbles, the oil is the right temperature.**

3
4
5
6
7
8

8 veal cutlets, sliced thin (2½ oz/70 g each)

1 pinch of salt
1 pinch of pepper

3 sprigs fresh sage

8 slices of prosciutto

1 lb 12 oz (800 g) roasted potatoes, (see p. 326)

1 tbsp olive oil

¼ cup (60 g) butter

⅜ cup (100 ml) marsala wine

⅔ cup (150 ml) veal stock

Saltimbocca alla Romana with Sage and Prosciutto

1. Lightly pound the small cutlets and season with salt and pepper on both sides. Use little salt, because the prosciutto is already salty. Top the cutlets with sage leaves.

2. Place the prosciutto slices on the cutlets and press with your hand. You may use toothpicks to hold them in place, though they prevent the Saltimbocca from frying evenly. Prepare the roasted potatoes.

3. Heat the olive oil and half of the butter in a skillet. Place the cutlets with the prosciutto on the bottom into the skillet and sauté for about 2 minutes over medium heat. Then turn over and sauté for an additional 2 minutes.

4. Pour the Marsala over the Saltimbocca and remove them from the skillet. Add the veal stock to the meat juice and reduce to about half of the volume.

5. Bind the sauce with the remaining butter and put the meat back into the sauce. Then arrange the meat and roasted potatoes on serving plates and garnish with oregano.

■ Use cutlets from the loin or top rounds. You can serve this dish with spinach leaves, Vichy carrots, or green beans. Instead of marsala, you can use Madeira or sweet white wine.

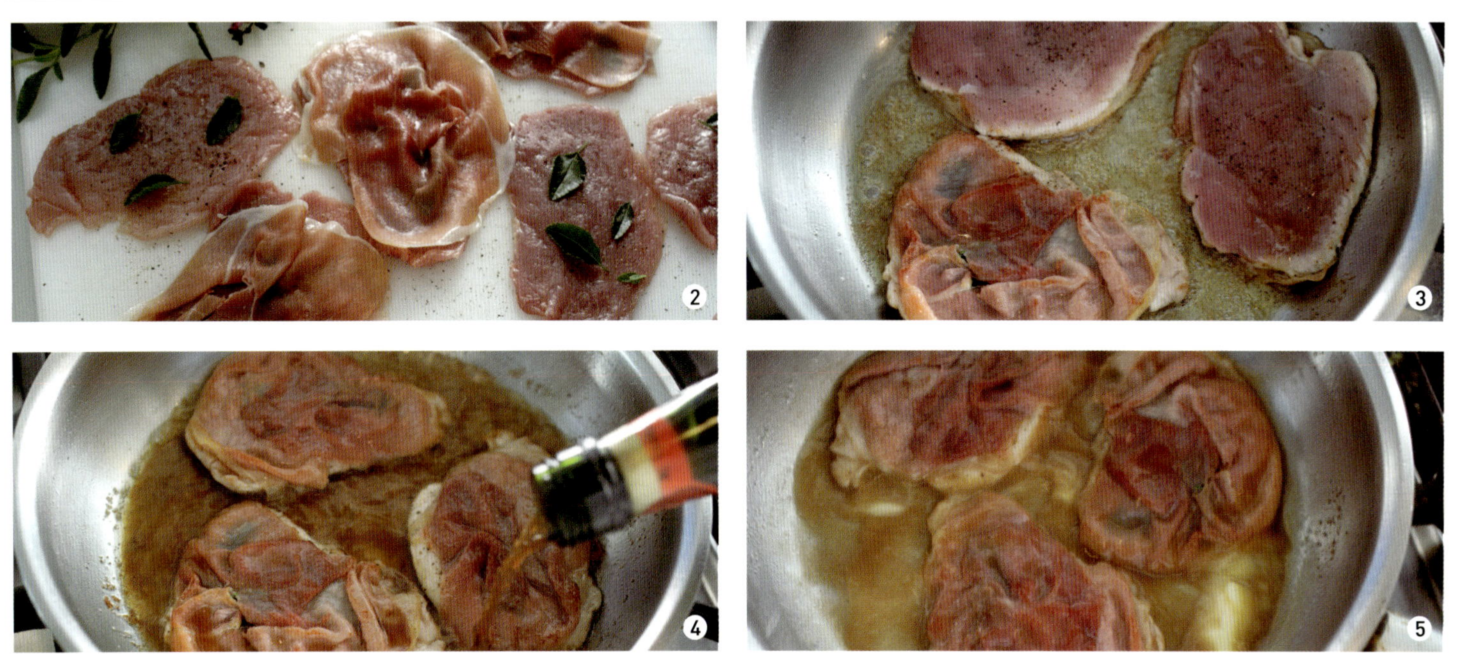
2
3
4
5

 8 slices of top round of veal (2½ oz /70 g each)

 1 pinch of salt
1 pinch of pepper

 2 lb 4 oz (1 kg) potatoes

 ⅓ cup (80 g) butter

 1 bunch parsley

 ⅓ cup (80 ml) vegetable oil

 5½ oz (150 g) pastry flour

 3 eggs

 12 oz (350 g) breadcrumbs

 1 lemon

1

Wiener Schnitzels

1. Pound the veal cutlets on both sides with a meat mallet. Then season with salt and pepper on both sides. Peel the potatoes and halve or quarter them depending on size, and boil in salted water for about 20 minutes. Drain and put 1½ oz (40 g) of the butter on the potatoes. Wash and clean the parsley and set aside.

2. Coat the seasoned schnitzels on both sides with flour and remove excess. Crack the eggs in a bowl and beat with a fork. Add a dash of water. This helps the coating to rise during frying.

3. Then coat the veal cutlets with the beaten egg. Make sure it is covered with the egg on all sides so that the coating sticks.

4. Place the breadcrumbs in a deep dish and put the schnitzels in the crumbs. Coat them on all sides with the crumbs and lightly press the coating on. However, do not press hard; this would prevent the batter from puffing up during frying.

5. Pour the oil and the remaining butter into a large skillet and let it froth. Then add the schnitzels and fry for 2 minutes.

6. Carefully turn the schnitzels over with a fork and fry for an additional 3 minutes. Remove and place on paper towels to drain. Chop the parsley and add it to the cooked potatoes. Arrange the schnitzels and the potatoes on serving plates and garnish with lemon wedges.

■ **After the schnitzel is breaded, place it on a cutting board that has previously been covered with breadcrumbs. This assures that the batter does not soak through, even if the breaded schnitzel has to sit for a few minutes. An anchovy fillet rolled around capers and placed on a slice of lemon is the traditional garnish for Viennese schnitzel.**

2
3
4
5
6

Pork

Contents

600 Pork
600 Cooking Chart
602 Pork Roast with Sauce and Caraway Potatoes
604 Suckling Pig Leg with Honey and Pineapple
606 Pork Goulash with Paprika and Butter Noodles
608 Spareribs Glazed with BBQ Sauce
610 Pork Belly Grilled with an Asian Marinade
612 Ground Pork Meatballs Cooked in Coconut-Curry Sauce
614 Pork Chops Grilled with a Mexican Marinade
616 Pork Neck Steaks Baked in a Pistachio Crust
618 Pork Steaks Baked with Pears and Gorgonzola Cheese
620 Pork Tenderloin with Mango-Peppercorn Sauce and Thai Basil

Pork

Nearly ivory white, odorless, firm meat without moistness is the hallmark of good pork. Pork tastes best when it comes from free-range farms, particularly if the animals were fed acorns and chestnuts.

The meat of intensively factory-farmed pigs ("turbo pigs") can be disappointing: their flesh is watery and they have enormous chops and hams. The characteristic fat has been bred out. Pigs of that kind are not supposed to be as fat as a pig. There are hardly any reliable signs of quality. Nevertheless, when buying pork, we should make sure that it is dry and is not exuding any liquid. Meat that turns gray quickly also comes from intensively farmed pigs in the industrial sector. For best results, the fat should be removed only after the pork has been roasted or stewed: it's an important flavor enhancer. If the pork has been wrapped in paper by your butcher, it will keep for about two days in your refrigerator at a temperature of (35°F) 2°C.

In France, there is a well-known saying: *Tout est bon dans le cochon*, everything on a pig is good. Indeed, expert butchers know how to make full use of this animal. The blood becomes blood sausage and the intestines are made into sausage casings. The breast can be smoked or cured. The belly and the neck are far fatter than tenderloin: that is not a disadvantage. As we have already said; fat is an important flavor enhancer.

Cooking Chart

Product	Weight	Method	Temperature	Time	Notes
Roast pork with crackling (Cut into the crackling with a razor blade)	4 lb (1.8 kg)	Oven	350°F (180°C/ Gas Mark 4)	100 minutes	
Rolled pork roast	3 lb 5 oz (1.5 kg)	Oven	325°F (160°C/GM 3)	110 minutes	
Smoked pork roast, uncooked	3 lb 8 oz (1.6 kg)	Oven	300°F (150°C/GM 2)	70 minutes	
Pork tenderloin medallions	2¼ oz (60 g)	Skillet	Medium heat	8 minutes	
Ground pork	4 lb 8 oz (2 kg)	Oven	325°F (160°C/GM 3)	80 minutes	
Suckling pig leg	5–5lb8oz(2.2–2.5kg)	Oven	325°F (160°C/GM 3)	90 minutes	
Goulash	large cubes	Saucepan with lid	Low heat	70 minutes of stewing	20 minutes of gentle sautéing
Knuckle of pork	2 lb 12 oz (1.2 kg)	Oven	350°F (180°C/GM 4)	80 minutes	
Spareribs	2 lb 4 oz (1 kg)	Oven	325°F (160°C/GM 3)	40 minutes	
Ground pork meatballs	1 lb 2 oz (500 g)	Oven	350°F (180°C/GM 4)	25 minutes	
Pork chops	9 oz (250 g)	Skillet	Medium heat	6 minutes	
Pork neck steaks	10½ oz (300 g)	Skillet	Medium heat	10 minutes	

Pork tenderloin

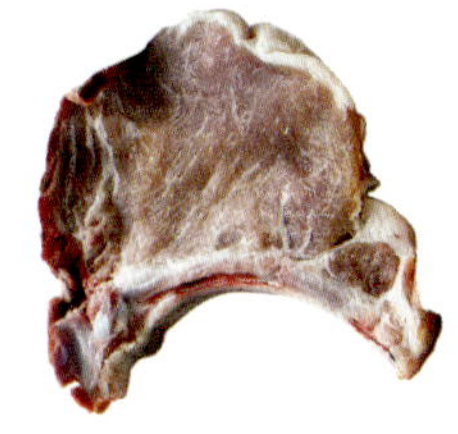

Pork roast

Pork chop

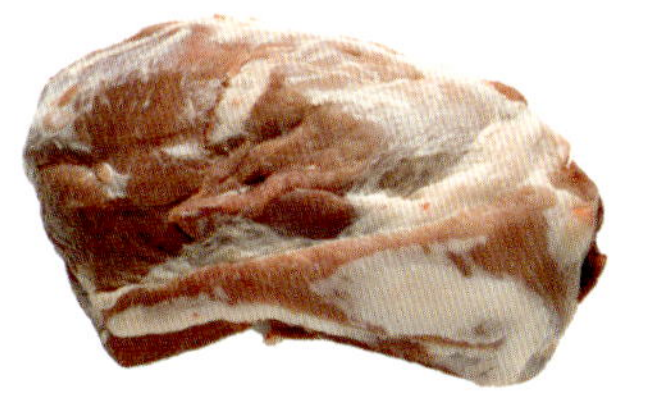

Pork neck

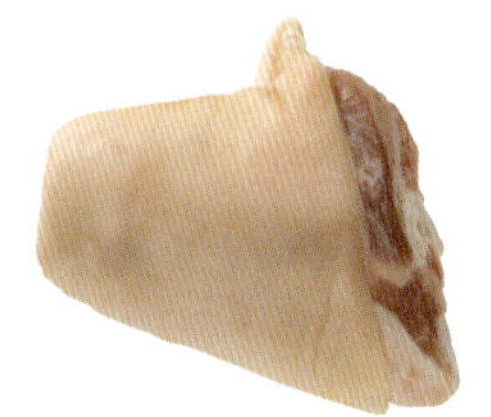

Ham hock

Ground pork

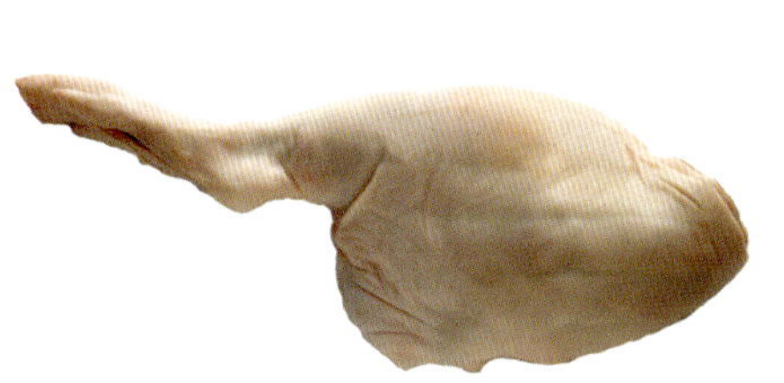

Suckling pig leg

Spareribs

Pork belly for a rolled pork toast

Ribs

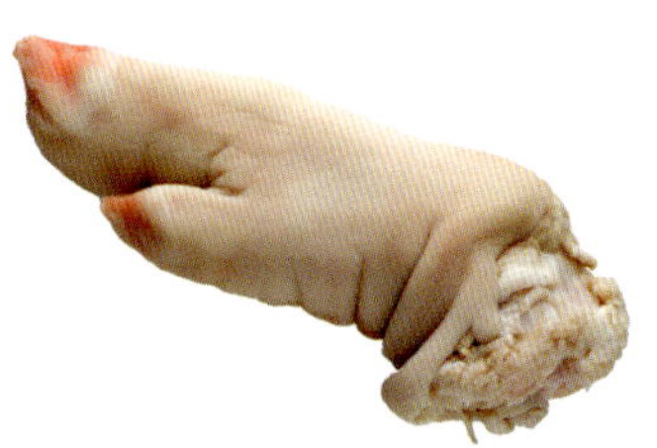

Pig's foot

Pig's ears

1 pork shoulder with rind, weighing 2 lb 4 oz (1 kg)

½ tsp caraway seeds

2 tbsp vegetable oil

2 lb 4 oz (1 kg) Caraway Potatoes (see p. 309)

2 garlic cloves

1 pinch of salt
1 pinch of black pepper

2 carrots

¼ celeriac

4 onions

1⅛ cup (250 ml) water

⅔ cup (150 ml) beer

Pork Roast with Sauce and Caraway Potatoes

1. Put the pork shoulder on a work surface and, with a very sharp knife or razor blade, make approximately ¼-inch (5-mm) deep slits in the rind in a diamond-shape pattern. Rub in the caraway seeds. Drizzle the meat with the vegetable oil, so the spices will adhere to the roast. Prepare the Caraway Potatoes for baking and set them aside.

2. Peel the garlic cloves and dice them finely. Rub the freshly ground black pepper, the garlic, and the salt gently into the scored pork shoulder. Peel the carrots and the celeriac and cut them up into big pieces.

3. Then, rub off the loose outer skins of the onions with your hands and cut off the root bases. There is always residual dirt in these areas. Put the unpeeled onions in a roasting dish with the pork roast. Add ⅞ cup (200 ml) water and put the roast into the oven, preheated to 325°F (160°C/Gas Mark 3), oven for 40 minutes.

4. Baste the roast repeatedly with the pan juices. After 40 minutes, put the Caraway Potatoes into the same oven on the bottom rack. Cook the roast and the potatoes for 40 minutes longer. Pour the beer over the roast and add the root vegetables. Increase the temperature

■ **Roast pork is also delicious with sauerkraut, red cabbage, or Vichy carrots. This recipe can also be prepared with pork neck or pork knuckle.**

to 350°F (180°C/Gas Mark 4) for the last 10 minutes of cooking and refrain from basting the roast during this time, so the skin can crisp. Remove it from the oven, carve it, and serve it with the potatoes and the root vegetables.

 1 tsp salt

 1 onion studded with cloves and a bay leaf

 2 carrots

 3½ oz (100 g) celeriac

 1–2 suckling pig legs

 1 pineapple

 1 tbsp cloves

 3 tbsp acacia honey

 1 pinch of cinnamon

 2 tbsp vegetable oil

Suckling Pig Leg with Honey and Pineapple

1. For best results, use small suckling piglet legs, each weighing 1 lb 12 oz (800 g). Two legs are needed for four people. In a large pot, bring to a boil the water with the salt, the onion studded with cloves and bay leaves, the peeled carrots, and the peeled celeriac. Add the legs and simmer them for 5 minutes. Remove the legs and let them cool on a cutting board, so that you can handle them.

2. Score the skin with a very sharp knife or razor blade at ½-inch (1-cm) intervals. Peel the pineapple (see p. 654), cut it into ½-inch (1-cm) slices, and set them aside. Stick the cloves into the slits in the skin.

3. Put the meat into a roasting dish and drizzle it with the acacia honey. Bake it in the oven, preheated to 325°F (160°C/Gas Mark 3), for 1½ hours. Baste it frequently with water and the pan juices that are being created. In this way, the skin will become crispy over time. Season the pineapple slices lightly with salt, dust them with cinnamon, and rub them with oil. Fry them on both sides for 1 minute in a nonstick pan. Arrange them on plates and put the suckling pig legs on top.

■ **Serve them with mashed potatoes, roasted beets, fried sweet-potato slices, or glazed carrots. The sweet-potato slices can also be added to the suckling pig legs half an hour before the end of cooking to absorb the pan juices.**

2

3

1 pork shoulder, weighing 2 lb 4 oz (1 kg)

1 tsp salt
1 pinch of black pepper

2 tbsp sweet paprika

1 tsp dried marjoram

1 tbsp flour

10½ oz (300 g) onions

3 garlic cloves

⅔ oz (20 g) parsley stems

1½ oz (40 g) pork lard

½ lemon

½ tsp caraway seeds

4 tsp (20 g) butter

1 tbsp tomato paste

2¼ cups (500 ml) poultry or beef stock

1 lb 2 oz (500 g) fresh ribbon noodles (see p. 200)

1 bunch fresh chives

1

Pork Goulash with Paprika and Butter Noodles

1. Cut the pork shoulder into 1½-inch (4-cm) cubes. Leave the sinew and the fat on the meat; it will make the goulash tender and juicy. Put the cubed meat into a bowl, season it with the salt, the pepper, the paprika, and the marjoram, and dust it with the flour.

2. Mix everything well with your hands. Peel and halve the onions, and cut them into strips. Peel 2 garlic cloves and dice them finely. Tie the parsley stems together with cotton string to form a little bouquet.

3. Heat the pork lard in a large pot, and add first the diced garlic and then the onions to it. Sauté them gently until the onions are translucent. Finely chop the remaining garlic clove, 1 piece of lemon zest, and the caraway seeds for the seasoning mix, and combine them with the butter that has been brought to room temperature. Then put the mixture in the refrigerator to chill.

4. Put the meat in the pot and sauté it gently for 10 minutes, being careful not to brown it. Add the tomato paste to a space that has been cleared in the pot, and brown it slightly. Mix it with the meat, cover the pot, and cook it for 10 minutes longer.

■ For a Szegedin goulash, add 1 lb 2 oz (500 g) cooked sauerkraut and mix ⅔ cup (150 g) crème fraîche or sour cream into the goulash. Serve it with cooked parsley potatoes, bread dumplings, or napkin dumplings.

5. Pour in the stock and replace the lid on the pot. Cook slowly for 1 hour. Stir it occasionally and add some water if necessary. After 45 minutes, add the parsley bouquet. Remove it 15 minutes later, add the chilled herb butter, and mix the goulash well. Arrange the goulash on plates, and serve it with freshly cooked ribbon noodles tossed in butter and sprinkled with finely snipped chives.

2 lb 4 oz (1 kg) pork spareribs

13 cups (3 liters) water

1⅛ cups (250 ml) fruit vinegar

¾ cup (150 g) sugar

2 bay leaves

8 black peppercorns

3 shallots

⅔ cup (150 ml) BBQ Sauce
(see p. 56)

1

Spareribs Glazed with BBQ Sauce

1. Have your butcher cut through the spareribs lengthwise. Bring the water to a boil in a large pot. Add the vinegar, sugar, bay leaves, peppercorns, and unpeeled shallots to the pot, and let it simmer for approximately 5 minutes. Add the spareribs and simmer them gently in the broth for approximately 10 minutes. Remove the pot from the heat and let the spareribs cool in the broth overnight, if possible, but for at least 3 hours in the refrigerator. Remove the spareribs from the broth and let them drain.

2. Brush the spareribs generously with BBQ sauce and put them on a baking sheet. Then roast them in the oven, preheated to 325°F (160°C/Gas Mark 3), oven for approximately 40 minutes. During cooking, turn the spareribs and coat them with BBQ Sauce once more. Cook the ribs at low heat to avoid burning the honey.

You can also prepare the spareribs in advance and marinate them in the BBQ Sauce in the refrigerator. Alternatively, the spareribs can be broiled and served with roasted or baked potatoes, or with a salad.

+ 3 hours for chilling

■ The BBQ Sauce can be used as the basis of a marinade for Sichuan-style spareribs. To this recipe, add grated fresh ginger root, finely chopped dried chili peppers, and crushed star anise mixed with onion or dill seeds. Serve them with fried rice or fried noodles and vegetables.

2

 1 thumb-size piece of fresh ginger

 ½ tsp Thai red curry paste

 4 tbsp oyster sauce

 3 tbsp vegetable oil

 1 lb 12 oz (800 g) pork belly

 1 lime

1

2

Pork Belly Grilled with an Asian Marinade

1. Finely grate the fresh ginger into a bowl.

2. Add the curry paste.

3. Pour in the oyster sauce.

4. Add the vegetable oil and stir the mixture well.

5. Slice the pork belly and put it into a suitable container. Pour the marinade over it and mix it well. For best results, marinate the meat for at least 1 hour. Grill the slices on both sides for approximately 5 minutes in a ridged grill pan.

Sprinkle them with juice from the quartered lime and serve with white bread or baked potatoes.

■ **You can also marinate pork chops or pork neck in this mixture and then cook them in a ridged grill pan or on the grill.**

Yellow Curry
3

4

5

1 lb 2 oz (500 g) ground pork

2 tbsp oyster sauce

1 can (14 oz/400 g) coconut milk

1 tsp Thai red curry paste

10½ oz (300 g) canned corn kernels

2 tbsp slivered almonds

Ground Pork Meatballs Cooked in Coconut-Curry Sauce

1. Mix the ground pork with the oyster sauce and shape into small balls. Put them into a flat casserole dish. Pour the coconut milk into a tall container. Scrape the can well.

2. Add the curry paste to the coconut milk.

3. Using a handheld blender, blend the mixture briefly, until the curry paste dissolves.

4. Pour the sauce over the pork meatballs. Drain the corn kernels in a sieve and sprinkle them over the meatballs. Sprinkle them with the slivered almonds and bake them for approximately 25 minutes in an oven preheated to 350°F (180°C/Gas Mark 4). Cover them with aluminum foil, if necessary, so the almond slivers don't burn. Arrange the meatballs in bowls.

■ **Milder yellow curry paste can be used instead of the red curry paste. Baby peas can be added to the sauce as well.**

3

4

 1 small can salsa

 1 pinch of black pepper

 2 sprigs fresh rosemary

 8 pork chops, each weighing 4½ oz (120 g)

 2 tbsp olive oil

 1 pinch of salt

Pork Chops Grilled with a Mexican Marinade

1. Put the salsa in a bowl.

2. Add some freshly ground black pepper and freshly plucked rosemary needles to the sauce.

3. Put the pork chops on a platter and pour the marinade over the meat.

4. Turn the chops and brush the other side with the marinade as well. Sprinkle the chops with a little olive oil.

5. Cover the pork chops with plastic wrap and let them marinate in the refrigerator for at least 1 hour (but ideally, for 3–4 hours). Grill them on both sides for approximately 3 minutes in a ridged grill pan and season them with salt. Serve them with bell peppers, baked potatoes, or a tomato salad.

■ Buy a whole saddle of pork and cut it into 1¼-inch (3-cm) cubes. Thread the cubes of pork onto skewers, alternating them with bell pepper pieces and diced onions, and season them with the marinade. Then grill them slowly over a barbecue or grill them in a ridged grill pan.

2
3
4
5

 1 lb 5 oz (600 g) pork neck

 1 pinch of salt
1 pinch of black pepper

 ½ tsp cinnamon

 ¾ cup (100 g) flour

 2 eggs

 9 oz (250 g) shelled pistachios

 3 tbsp vegetable oil

 1 tbsp butter

1

2

3

Pork Neck Steaks Baked in a Pistachio Crust

1. Cut the pork neck into small steaks and season them well on both sides with salt, black pepper, and ground cinnamon.

2. Dredge the meat in flour and shake off any excess. Dip the steaks in the beaten eggs, so the meat is fully covered.

3. Chop the pistachios with a large knife and put them in a flat container. Put the egg-dipped steaks into the pistachios.

4. Coat the pork steaks well with the chopped pistachios and press down on the coating lightly.

5. Heat the vegetable oil and butter in a skillet until it froths, and add the steaks.

6. Brown the steaks on both sides at medium heat for approximately 5 minutes and let them drain briefly on paper towels. Arrange them on plates and serve them with carrots, cauliflower, and couscous.

■ **Fry small pistachio-coated pork medallions, top with Gorgonzola cheese, and broil them briefly.**

4

5

6

 2 ripe pears

 1 tbsp butter

 1 tbsp sugar

 1 pinch of black pepper

 2 sprigs fresh thyme

 4 pork neck steaks, each weighing approx. 4½ oz (130 g)

 1 pinch of salt

 1 tbsp vegetable oil

 4½ oz (120 g) Gorgonzola cheese

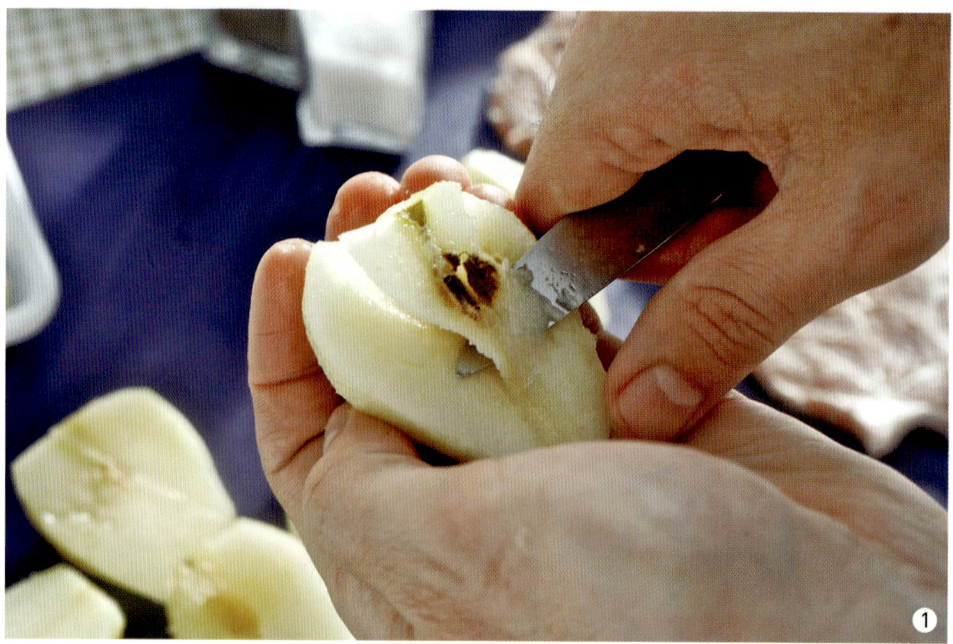

Pork Steaks Baked with Pears and Gorgonzola Cheese

1. Peel the pears, cut them in half, and cut out the cores with a sharp knife. Cut the pears lengthwise into segments.

2. Melt the butter with the sugar in a skillet. Add the pear segments, season them with freshly ground pepper, and add the thyme. Toss everything in the skillet and let the mixture caramelize slightly.

3. Season the pork neck steaks with salt and freshly ground black pepper. Sear the steaks on both sides in vegetable oil in a nonstick skillet and put them into a baking dish or onto a baking sheet.

4. Put pear segments on top of each steak.

5. Lay the Gorgonzola cheese on top, put the dish in an oven preheated to 350°F (180°C/Gas Mark 4) with a broiler, and broil it for 2–3 minutes. Arrange the steaks on plates and pour the pan juices over them. Serve them with potatoes or pasta.

■ **Variation: You can use dried fruit, such as plums, apples, or apricots, cooked in red wine instead of pears.**

2
3
4
5

 1 ripe mango

 2 oranges

 1 white onion

 ¼ cup (60 g) butter

 1 tbsp honey

 6 stems of green peppercorns

 1 pinch of salt

 1 lb 5 oz (600 g) pork tenderloin

 2 tbsp vegetable oil

 1 pinch of black pepper

 2 sprigs fresh Thai basil

Pork Tenderloin with Mango-Peppercorn Sauce and Thai Basil

1. Peel the mango, remove the fruit from the pit with a knife, and chop it into ¼-inch (5-mm) cubes. Use a vegetable peeler to pare a strip of zest from an orange and chop it finely. Squeeze the oranges and set the juice aside. Peel the onion and dice it finely. Melt 1½ oz (40 g) of the butter in a long-handled saucepan. Gently sauté the diced onion until it is translucent, and then add the mango cubes.

2. Add the strips of orange zest and the honey, and sauté gently for 5 minutes.

3. Strip the green peppercorns off two stems and reserve the rest for use as a garnish. Add the peppercorns and the orange juice to the sauce, season it with salt, and let it simmer gently for approximately 10 minutes. Meanwhile, cut the clean, trimmed pork tenderloin into 8 medallions.

4. Let the oil and the remaining butter foam in a nonstick skillet. Season the medallions on both sides with salt and pepper and add them to the skillet. Fry them on both sides for approximately 5 minutes and baste them with the pan juices. Put portions of mango sauce on plates and lay 2 medallions on top of each portion. Garnish each plate with a green peppercorn stem and some Thai basil leaves.

■ **You can replace half of the mango with pineapple when you are preparing the mango sauce. You can also use curry powder, ginger, or chili peppers to season it more intensely.**

2
3
4

Lamb & Wild Game

Contents

624 Lamb and Wild Game
624 Cooking Chart
626 Roast Leg of Lamb with Herbs and Garlic
628 Irish Stew with Young Cabbage and Carrots
630 Pink Roast Rack of Lamb with Rosemary
632 Grilled Marinated Lamb
634 Larded Saddle of Hare with Cranberry Pears
636 Medallions of Venison with Savoy Cabbage, Celery Puree, and Morel Sauce
640 Whole Leg of Venison with Mushroom Cream Sauce
642 Venison Ragout with Diced Vegetables and Mashed Potatoes
646 Stewed Haunch of Rabbit in Paprika Cream Sauce

Lamb and Wild Game

In order to enjoy really good game, you need to know a hunter. But these days you can also purchase high-quality, farm-raised "wild" game.

Hare: Female hares taste better than their male counterparts. The males are tougher and more solid. The lighter the color of the meat is, the younger the animal. A red to a reddish black color is a sign of an old tough hare. Young hare is more tender and is suitable for roasting. Older animals are suitable for marinating and for stews.

Venison: Meat from deer, antelope, caribou, elk, and moose are all classified as venison. Stags have dark, almost-brown meat, whereas the meat of hinds turns out somewhat paler. The color of fallow deer meat is similar to that of mutton. The smaller the animal is, the lighter and more delicate its meat. It is also the case that female animals taste better than their male counterparts.

Lamb: Good lamb is pale pink or almost white with a snowy white, solid layer of fat. This fat layer should be firm to the touch. If you are allowed to touch the meat, warm your hands first, before sliding them over the fat layer. If the lamb is too old, your fingers will subsequently have the typical, pungent smell of mutton. A dull red, almost purple or downright black color is a bad sign. This kind of lamb also comes from older animals and tastes like mutton. You should also be careful with respect to large chops or fillets. A normal lamb weighs between 32 and 35 lb (14 and 15 kg). Anything heavier than 40 lb (18 kg) is considered to be mutton. In the case of lamb as well, female animals are tastier than their male counterparts. Lamb can be stored in the cold section of your refrigerator at 32–36°F (0–2°C) for two days.

Cooking Chart

Product	Weight	Method	Temperature	Time	Notes
Leg of lamb	3 lb 5 oz–4 lb (1.5–1.8 kg)	Oven	320°F (160°C/Gas Mark 3)	100 minutes	
Lamb's liver	10½ oz (300 g)	Skillet	Medium heat	2 minutes	Cut into ½-inch (1 cm) slices
Saddle/rack of lamb	14 oz (400 g)	Oven	320°F (160°C/Gas Mark 3)	20 minutes	
Lamb chop	2¼ oz (60 g)	Grill pan	Medium heat	5 minutes	Rub the chop with oil in advance, so that it doesn't stick to the grill pan
Fillet of lamb	1½ oz (40 g)	Skillet	Medium heat	4 minutes	
Shoulder of lamb	3 lb –3 lb 5 oz (1.3–1.5 kg)	Oven	390°F (200°C/Gas Mark 6)	45 minutes	
Saddle of venison	Whole, 4 lb 8 oz (2 kg)	Oven	350°F (180°C/ Gas Mark 4)	35 minutes	Sear on all sides in advance
Roast venison (female)	2 lb 12 oz–3 lb 5 oz (1.2–1.5 kg)	Oven	320°F (160°C/ Gas Mark 3)	45 minutes	
Knuckle of lamb	9–10½ oz (250–300 g)	Oven	320°F (160°C/Gas Mark 3)	90 minutes	
Roast venison (male)	4 lb 8 oz (2 kg)	Oven	320°F (160°C/Gas Mark 3)	70 minutes	
Venison medallion	2¼ oz (60 g)	Skillet	Medium heat	10 minutes	
Haunch of venison	2 lb 4 oz (1 kg)	Oven	340°F (170°C/Gas Mark 3½)	25 minutes	
Rabbit	3 lb (1.3 kg)	Oven	320°F (160°C/Gas Mark 3)	40 minutes	
Saddle of hare	1 lb (450 g)	Oven	340°F (170°C/Gas Mark 3½)	20 minutes	
Leg of hare	14 oz (400 g)	Saucepan with a lid	Medium heat	70 minutes	Stew
Leg of rabbit	9 oz (250 g)	Skillet with a lid	Medium heat	30 minutes	

Leg of venison

Venison medallions

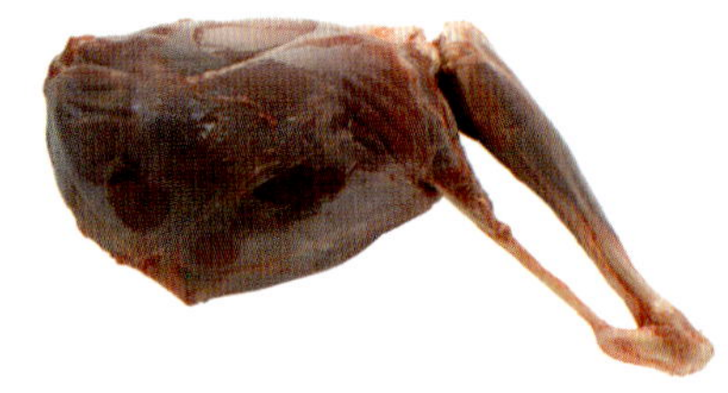

Haunch of venison

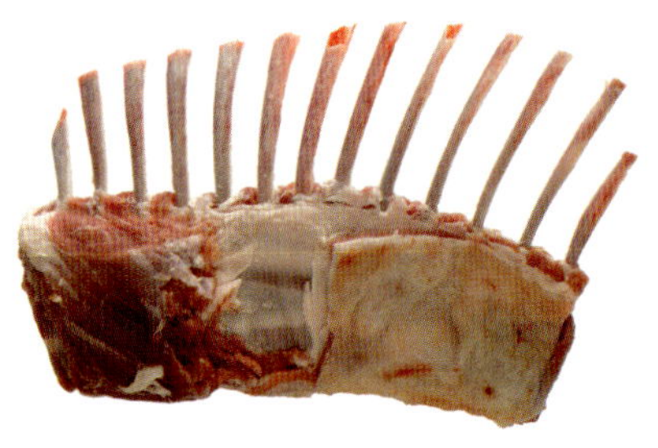

Rack of lamb

Lamb chop

Leg of lamb

Saddle of hare

Rabbit

Loin of venison

½ cup (125 ml) olive oil

2 sprigs fresh thyme

1 sprig fresh rosemary

1 tsp fennel seeds

1 pinch of salt
1 pinch of black pepper

1 leg of lamb, weighing about 4 lb (1.8 kg)

1 head garlic

1

2

Roast Leg of Lamb with Herbs and Garlic

1. For the marinade, pour the olive oil in a bowl, pluck the thyme leaves off the sprigs, and add them to the oil.

2. Pluck the rosemary needles, use a knife to chop them somewhat, and add them with the fennel seeds to the oil. Combine all of the ingredients and season with salt and freshly ground black pepper.

3. Put the leg of lamb into a roasting pan along with some lamb bones, and rub the leg of lamb thoroughly with the herbed oil. Separate the individual garlic cloves from the head and crush them lightly in a bowl with the heel of your hand. Put the garlic on the leg of lamb.

4. Put the leg of lamb in an oven preheated to 400°F (200°C/Gas Mark 6) and roast it for 30 minutes. Turn the roast frequently and baste it with its juices. Reduce the temperature to 350°F (180°C/ Gas Mark 4) and roast it for another hour. While the lamb is roasting, occasionally add some water to the pan drippings to create a sauce.

Arrange the leg of lamb on a platter. Add the unstrained sauce from which only the bones have been removed. Serve the roast leg of lamb with potatoes en papillote or couscous salad.

■ **Finely chop parsley, tarragon, marjoram, and lemon and orange zests, and mix them with butter. Let the mixture foam in a skillet and pour it over the leg of lamb.**

3

4

 1 leg of lamb (3 lb/1.3 kg)

 1 bunch fresh parsley

 1 sprig fresh tarragon

 5 shallots

 5½ oz (150 g) carrots

 3 onions

 1 head young cabbage

 2 garlic cloves

 10½ oz (300 g) potatoes

 2 tbsp vegetable oil

 1 tsp salt
1 pinch of black pepper

 ½ tsp tomato paste

 1 bay leaf

 5⅓ cups (1.2 liters) beef broth

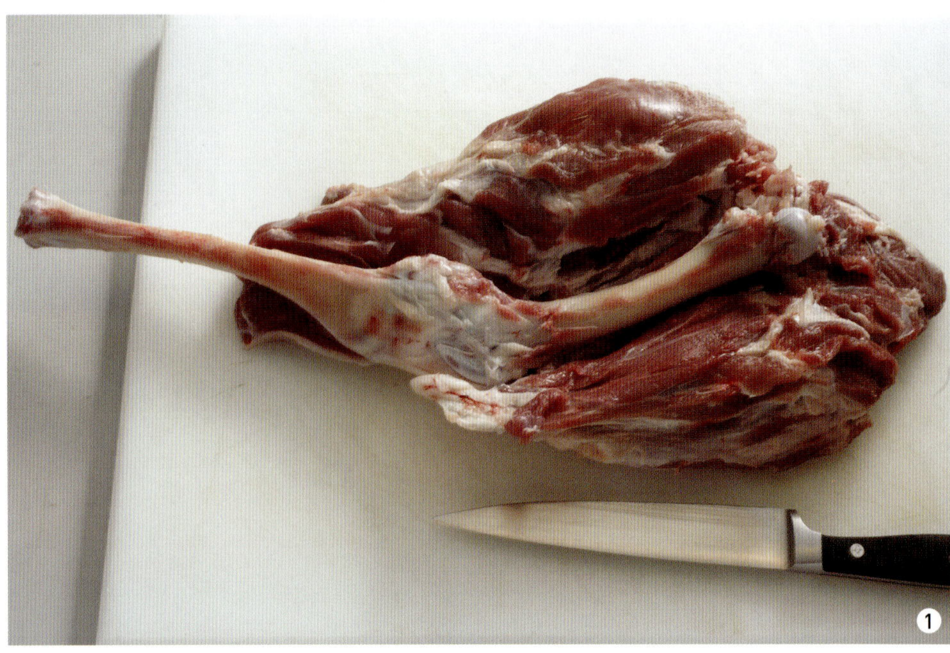

Irish Stew with Young Cabbage and Carrots

1. Cut into the leg of lamb along the bone and remove it carefully from the meat with the tip of your knife. Remove the fat from the skin and the gristle. Cut the meat into 1¼-inch (3-cm) pieces. Wash the parsley and the tarragon, pluck the leaves, and set them aside. They will only be chopped shortly before they are added to the dish in order to preserve their flavor and their essential oils.

2. Peel and halve the shallots. Peel the carrots and cut them diagonally into ½-inch (1-cm) slices. Peel and halve the onions and cut them into strips. Remove the outer leaves from the young cabbage, cut it in half, remove the stalk, and wash the head. Cut it into 1¼-inch (3-cm) cubes. Peel the garlic cloves and dice them finely. Peel the potatoes and cut them into 1¼-inch (3-cm) cubes.

3. Heat the oil in a saucepan, add the garlic first and then the onion strips, and cook them until they are translucent. Season the diced meat with salt and pepper, and add it to the pan. Sauté it gently for 10 minutes. Bring the meat to the edge of the pan, put the tomato paste in the clear space created, and brown it somewhat, briefly, and then mix it with the meat. Add the bay leaf to the mixture.

■ **Lamb shoulder can be used instead of leg of lamb, but it will have to be cooked for 15 minutes longer, because it is more marbled. The quantity of vegetables can be augmented or other vegetables can be used according to your preference. Green beans, celery, and savoy cabbage or parsley root are every bit as delicious in this stew.**

4. Pour the broth over the meat or use water as a substitute. You will need to season the meat more if you use water instead of broth. Bring the stew to a boil and let it simmer for 15 minutes with the lid on.

5. Add the carrots, the shallots, and the potatoes and let the stew simmer for 10 more minutes with the lid on. Add the cabbage, mix all of the ingredients thoroughly, and simmer the stew for 20 minutes longer. Staggering the times at which the ingredients are added lets all of the ingredients cook through without becoming overcooked. Finally, chop the parsley and the tarragon finely, stir them into the pot, and serve the stew on soup plates.

2 saddles of lamb, each weighing 1¼–1½ lb (1–1.2 kg)

1 pinch of salt
1 pinch of black pepper

3 tbsp olive oil

6 garlic cloves, crushed

2 sprigs fresh rosemary

⅛ cup (30 g) butter

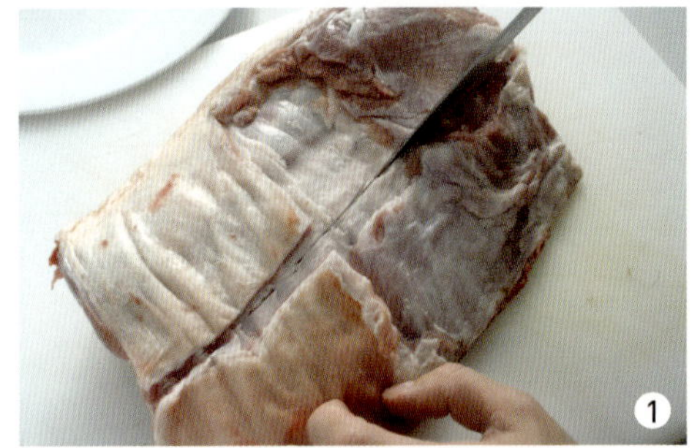

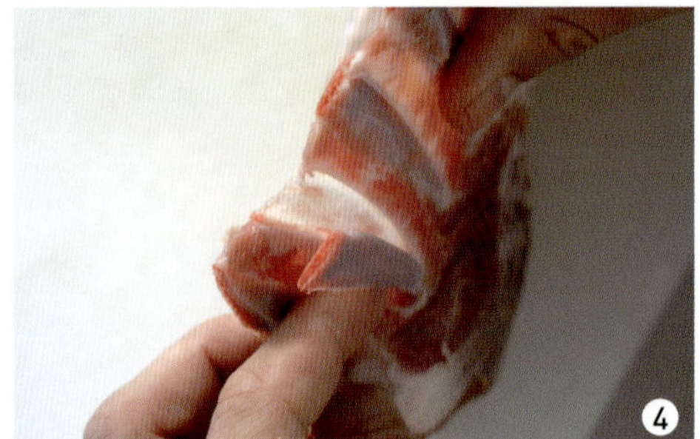

Pink Roast Rack of Lamb with Rosemary

1. Instead of saddle of lamb, you can use prepared racks of lamb, but you will still need to clean the ribs. Put the saddles of lamb on a cutting board and cut into the skin under the loin fillet at a depth of ½ inch (1 cm).

2. Trim the skin and the meat from the ribs.

3. Shave the skin off the bone with the knife, so that it is easier to remove.

4. Carefully loosen the skin from the bone with your fingers, until the bone is exposed and clean.

5. Turn it over and cut this part of the skin off.

6. Cut along the backbone and remove the white sinew carefully. Continue cutting on the back to the ribs.

7. Turn it over again to separate the rack of lamb from the backbone with sharp kitchen shears.

8. Remove any small bits of sinew and bones from the separated rack of lamb and season it with salt and pepper on both sides.

9. Heat the oil in a wide, ovenproof skillet and put the rack of lamb into the skillet with its top side facing downward. Add the garlic and the rosemary sprigs to the rack. Baste the lamb with the pan drippings and turn it over after 5 minutes.

■ **The rack of lamb can also be roasted with a pecan-lemon marinade. Chop the pecans coarsely, cut 2 pieces of lemon zest into fine strips, and mix them with 1 sprig fresh rosemary, 2 tbsp of olive oil, and 1 tsp of coarse mustard. Roast the lamb with this mixture for the last 5 minutes of cooking. Potatoes au gratin and green beans are very suitable accompaniments to the rack of lamb.**

10. After you turn it over, place the rosemary sprigs on the top of the rack of lamb again, so it doesn't burn in the skillet, and add the butter. Roast the rack of lamb in an oven preheated to 350°F (180°C/Gas Mark 4) for approximately 10 minutes, and continue to baste it with the pan drippings. Remove it from the oven, cover it with aluminum foil, and let it rest for 3 minutes. Cut it and serve.

 1 sprig fresh rosemary

 1 sprig fresh thyme

 ½ bunch fresh parsley

 3 garlic cloves

 1 lb 12 oz (800 g) lamb chops

 4 tbsp olive oil

 1 pinch of salt
1 pinch of black pepper

Grilled Marinated Lamb

1. Wash the herbs, remove any withered parts, pluck the leaves, and chop them finely with a sharp kitchen knife.

2. Peel the garlic cloves and use a garlic press to crush them onto the chops.

3. Sprinkle the chopped herbs, olive oil, and freshly ground black pepper on the chops and mix everything together. Marinate the chops for approximately 30 minutes.

4. Season the lamb chops with salt and grill them on both sides in a ridged grill pan or on a backyard barbecue grill, until they are pink inside (approximately 2 minutes per side).

Arrange the chops on plates and serve them with garlic bread or grilled vegetables.

■ **The following herbs and spices can be used to marinate the lamb chops: sage, mint and lemon zest, cinnamon, ground cardamom, and curry powder and honey (for an Asian flavor). Serve these chops with couscous and a yogurt dip.**

3

4

7 oz (200 g) salt pork or bacon

2 saddles of hare, each weighing 1 lb 12 oz (800 g)

4 pears

1 tsp salt
1 pinch of black pepper

¼ cup (60 ml) vegetable oil

10 juniper berries

5 bay leaves

1 sprig fresh rosemary

3 tbsp (40 g) butter

1 tbsp brown sugar

6 tsp cranberry jelly

Larded Saddle of Hare with Cranberry Pears

1. Put the salt pork in the freezer for half an hour or so. This makes it more solid and easier to handle. Remove the skin and the membrane from both saddles of hare. Cut the pork into 2-inch (5-cm) long by ¼-inch (5-mm) thick strips. Hook the pork to the back end of a larding needle.

2. Carefully stick the point of the needle into the meat and guide it through until the pork is evenly distributed in the saddle and protrudes somewhat. Repeat this procedure every ¾ inch (2 cm). Larding makes the meat juicier.

3. Peel the pears, cut them in half, and remove the cores with a melon baller. Leave the stem on the pear to make it more visually attractive.

4. Season the saddle of hare with salt and pepper. Heat the oil in a skillet, sear both fillets on one side, and them turn them over. Crush the juniper berries, then add them with the bay leaves and garnish the dish with a rosemary sprig. Roast the hare slowly in an oven preheated to 340°F (170°C/Gas Mark 3½) for approximately 20 minutes and baste it frequently with its juices.

■ **For best results, use small, red Bartlett pears. Serve the saddle of hare accompanied by small potato cakes, finger noodles, or a porcini cream sauce** **(see p. 149).**

5. Meanwhile, melt the butter in a skillet and sprinkle in half of the sugar. Lay the pear halves in the skillet with their cut surface facing down, Sprinkle them with the remaining sugar and sauté them slowly, until they are golden yellow. Turn the pear halves over and fill them with the cranberry jelly. Remove the hare fillets carefully from the saddles with a knife and cut them diagonally into ¾-inch (2-cm) thick slices. Pour the pan juices over the meat, transfer it to a platter, and serve it with the pears.

 1 head savoy cabbage

 2 tbsp salt

 2 shallots

 1 lb 10 oz (750 g) celery

 ½ bunch fresh parsley

 ½ cup (100 g) butter

 1 pinch of black pepper

 1 pinch of nutmeg, freshly grated

 1 tbsp fruit vinegar

 4½ cups (750 ml) game or poultry stock

 9 oz (250 g) morels

 1 venison backstrap, weighing approximately 1 lb 10 oz (750 g)

 1 sprig fresh rosemary

 2 tbsp oil

 8 juniper berries

 3 tbsp (50 ml) Madeira wine

 1⅓ cups (300 ml) brown gravy (see p. 138)

 1⅛ cups (250 ml) cream

 2 tbsp whipped cream

Medallions of Venison with Savoy Cabbage, Celery Puree, and Morel Sauce

1. Remove the outer leaves from the cabbage, cut it into quarters, and remove the stalk. Wash the quarters and cut them into fine strips, diagonally. Cook the cabbage in boiling salted water for 10 seconds, remove it, and let it cool in cold water. Drain. Peel the shallots and dice them finely. Peel the celery, cut it into 1¼-inch (3 cm) cubes, and cook it in a saucepan with boiling, salted water for approximately 2 minutes. Remove the celery and chill it under cold running water. Wash the parsley, pluck the leaves, and chop them finely.

2. Let 4 tsp (20 g) of the butter foam in a long-handled saucepan and gently sauté half of the diced shallots. Add the cooked cabbage and season it with salt, pepper, and nutmeg. Pour in half of the poultry stock and let it simmer gently for 15 minutes, until the cabbage is soft. Meanwhile, heat another 4 tsp (20 g) butter in another long-handled saucepan and gently sauté the rest of the diced shallots. Add the celery, season the mixture with nutmeg, and add the fruit vinegar. Pour in the remaining poultry stock and gently steam the celery with the lid on, until it is soft.

»

■ **Serve Brussels sprouts, glazed apples, morel sauce with cream, red cabbage, spaetzle, finger noodles, various mushrooms, or potato cakes with chives as an accompaniment to these medallions.**

3

3. Clean the morels, remove their stems, and wash them briefly in lukewarm water. Remove them immediately and put them on paper towels to drain. If mushrooms are left in water for too long, they absorb liquid and release it into the skillet again when they are sautéed.

4. Cut the saddle of venison into 8 evenly sized medallions and pound them lightly with the heel of your hand. Season them with salt and pepper and sprinkle them with the plucked rosemary needles.

5. Let the oil foam with 4 tsp (20 g) of the butter in a skillet and add the venison medallions. Crush the juniper berries and add them to the meat. Sauté the medallions gently on both sides for approximately 5 minutes and baste them repeatedly with the pan juices.

6. Meanwhile, let the remaining butter foam in a skillet, add the well-drained morels, season them with salt and nutmeg, and sauté them quickly. Add the Madeira wine and boil it down.

7. Add the brown gravy, preferably a game sauce that has been prepared from the bones. Simmer the mushrooms for 5 minutes longer.

8. Pour 3/8 cup (100 ml) cream into the cooked savoy cabbage and stir it well. Let it cook briefly and top it off with the whipped cream and the chopped parsley. Pour the remaining cream on the steamed celery and let it simmer as well for 5 minutes longer, then use a handheld blender to puree it. Put a mound of pureed celery and a mound of cabbage on a plate, add two medallions, top them with the morel sauce, and serve.

■ **These medallions go nicely with other side dishes and sauces as well. Mushrooms, such as chanterelles, porcini, or shiitakes, can also be used for the sauce. The sauce can be enhanced with cream and orange liqueur. Other side dishes, such as green beans with bacon, glazed apples, salsify, or golden pumpkin cakes, are perfect accompaniments to this dish.**

5
6
7
8

 1¾ oz (50 g) salt

 2 sprigs fresh rosemary

 2 sprigs fresh thyme

 2 bay leaves

 1 lemon

 1 tsp juniper berries

 10 cloves

 1 tsp black peppercorns

 1 leg of venison, weighing 2 lb 4 oz (1 kg)

 ½ bunch fresh parsley

 5 shallots

 5 bacon slices

 9 oz (250 g) small porcini mushrooms

 3 tbsp vegetable oil

 3 tbsp (40 g) butter

 1 pinch of nutmeg, freshly grated

 3 tbsp (40 ml) red port wine

 ⅞ cup (200 ml) brown gravy (see p. 138)

 ⅞ cup (200 ml) cream

 3½ oz (100 g) crème fraîche (or sour cream)

 3 tbsp cranberry jelly

Whole Leg of Venison with Mushroom Cream Sauce

1. To season the leg of venison, prepare seasoning salt in the blender, using salt, plucked rosemary needles and thyme leaves, bay leaves, the juice of ½ lemon, juniper berries, cloves, and black peppercorns. Blend everything to a fine seasoning salt. Store in a preserving jar.

2. Have your butcher remove the shank so that you have only the meat to roast. Rub the roast on all sides with the seasoning mix and let it rest briefly, so that the flavors seep in. Wash the parsley, pluck the leaves, and chop them finely. Peel the shallots, dice two of them finely, and cut the rest in quarters lengthwise. Cut the bacon into ¾-inch (2-cm) strips.

3. Clean the porcini mushrooms, remove any impurities, and cut them into ¼-inch (5-mm) slices.

4. Heat the oil in a skillet and sear the leg of venison on all sides. Then, roast it in the oven, preheated to 350°F (170°C/Gas Mark 3½), for 10 minutes.

5. Arrange the quartered onions and the bacon strips around the leg of venison and roast it at 325°F (160°C/Gas Mark 3) for 20 minutes longer. Baste it frequently with the pan juices.

6. Let the butter foam in a nonstick skillet. Gently sauté the porcini mushroom slices and season them with salt and nutmeg.

■ **This dish is delicious when served with handmade spaetzle, crisp potato cakes, or finger noodles. Cranberry preserves (homemade if possible), wild mushrooms, and a celeriac puree provide the finishing touches for this feast of wild game.**

Add the finely diced shallots and continue to sauté them gently until they are translucent. Add the red port wine and let the mixture cook down.

7. Add the brown gravy and let the mixture cook down to one third of its original volume.

8. Add the cream and crème fraîche (or sour cream) to the sauce and bring it to a boil once again. Season it with the cranberry jelly to taste and remove it from the heat.

9. It's important to use small porcini mushrooms and not to let them disintegrate. They must be firm in the sauce.

Stir the juice from the leg of venison into the porcini mushroom sauce. Pour the sauce onto a platter, and place the leg of venison on top.

1 leg of venison, weighing 3 lb 5 oz (1.5 kg)

2 onions

2 carrots

1 celeriac

5 bay leaves

2 sprigs fresh thyme

2 sprigs fresh rosemary

5 black peppercorns

8 juniper berries

2 cloves

5 allspice berries

4½ cups (1 liter) robust red wine

7 oz (200 g) button mushrooms

1 apple

5½ oz (150 g) bacon

½ cup (120 ml) vegetable oil

2 tbsp balsamic vinegar

1 tsp salt
1 pinch of black pepper

1 tbsp flour

»

1

Venison Ragout with Diced Vegetables and Mashed Potatoes

1. Remove the leg of venison from the bone and cut into 1¼-inch (3-cm) strips first and then into ¼-inch (3-cm) cubes. Peel the onions, carrots, and celeriac, and cut into ¼-inch (2-cm) cubes. Reserve half of the celeriac for garnishing.

2. Put the venison in a large bowl and smother it with the vegetables. Add the bay leaves, thyme sprigs, rosemary sprigs, crushed peppercorns, juniper berries, cloves, and allspice berries. Pour in the red wine and cover the meat.

3. For best results, marinate the venison in the refrigerator for 24 hours. Mix the ingredients carefully every now and again.

4. After the meat has been marinated, put it into a large sieve and let it drain. Put the marinade in a saucepan and slowly bring it to a boil. Remove the foam, which will float to the top, so that it cannot be boiled down in the sauce. Use this marinade later as additional liquid for the

+ 24 hours marinating

■ Be sure to take time to marinate the meat. Prepare venison, wild boar, or hare ragouts in this manner. Real wild game ragouts are still thickened with ⅜ cup (100 ml) of blood at the end. This gives it a unique flavor, which is not to everyone's taste.

stew. Separate the pieces of meat from the vegetables and let them to drain on paper towels. Store the vegetables separately.

5. Clean and quarter the button mushrooms. Set aside two-thirds of the mushrooms for the garnish. Core the apple and cut it into ¾-inch (2-cm) pieces. Cut the bacon into ¼-inch (5-mm) strips first and then into ½-inch (1 cm) pieces. Heat 3 tbsp (40 ml) of the oil in a wide saucepan and lightly sauté one-third of the bacon strips, one-third of the button mushrooms, and all of the apple pieces. Sprinkle the mixture with the balsamic vinegar.

6. Add the drained vegetables from the marinade and sauté the mixture gently until the vegetables are softened. Place them in a bowl.

7. Season the venison with salt and pepper and dust it with flour. Put 4 tbsp (60 ml) oil into the wide saucepan and spread out the pieces of meat in the pan to brown them. You may need to brown them in two batches; it will begin to steam if it is too crowded.

»

 1 tbsp tomato paste

 ⅜ cup (100 ml) cognac

 ⅜ cup (100 ml) red port wine

 3⅓ cups (750 ml) game or poultry stock

 1 lb 12 oz (800 g) mashed potatoes (see p. 336)

 3 slices white bread

 ⅓ cup (80 g) butter

8. Move the meat to the edge of the pan and brown the tomato paste slightly in the free space. Mix it with the meat and fry it for another 5 minutes.

9. Add the vegetables to the meat, mix everything well, and cook the mixture for another 5 minutes, until residue builds up on the bottom of the pan. Deglaze these drippings with cognac, and let the sauce cook down. If there is a fresh buildup of drippings, deglaze the pan with port wine, and let the sauce cook down again.

10. Pour in the boiled marinade, cover the pan, and let the mixture simmer for approximately 45 minutes. Add the game or poultry stock and let it simmer for 20 minutes longer. In the meantime, prepare the mashed potatoes. Cut the crust off the slices of white bread and chop the slices finely in a food processor Melt the butter in a small saucepan and fry the breadcrumbs until they are golden. Remove the venison ragout from the heat. Remove the pieces of meat from the ragout and put them into another pan, Make sure that no vegetables or herbs adhere to the meat. This process is called *pressing out*. Bring the sauce to a boil again and pass it through a fine sieve over the meat. Squeeze the vegetables well. Cut the remaining half of the celeriac into strips measuring 1½ inches (4 cm) in length and ½ inch (1 cm) in width. Cook these strips in boiling salted water for 2 minutes and then chill them. Heat the remaining oil in a nonstick skillet, sear the remaining button mushrooms, and add the remaining bacon strips to the skillet. Season lightly with salt and pepper and add the pieces of celeriac, tossing continuously. Arrange the mashed potatoes on plates and sprinkle them with the toasted breadcrumbs. Arrange the venison ragout on the side, spoon the button mushroom, bacon, and celeriac pieces on top of it and serve.

■ **Serve the ragout with cranberry sauce or mushrooms. Cook Brussels sprouts in salted water and sauté them with onions and diced ham to make another delicious accompaniment for this dish.**

9

10

4 rabbit haunches

1 pinch of salt
1 pinch of black pepper

3 tsp sweet paprika

2 small onions

⅛ cup (30 g) butter

2¼ cups (500 ml) poultry or vegetable stock

1¾ cups (400 ml) cream

Stewed Haunch of Rabbit in Paprika Cream Sauce

1. Season the rabbit haunches with salt, black pepper, and paprika.

2. Peel the onions and dice them finely. Sauté them gently in the butter in a wide saucepan until they are translucent, and add the rabbit haunches. Brown slightly on both sides.

3. Add the poultry stock and stew it with the lid on for approximately 30 minutes.

4. Turn the haunches occasionally. You may have to add water if the stew evaporates quickly. The bottom of the pan should be covered with a ½-inch (1-cm) layer of liquid.

5. Add the cream and let the rabbit haunches simmer gently in the sauce. You may need to add more salt and pepper to season the stew.

Serve the rabbit stew with bread dumplings or ribbon noodles.

■ **A whole jointed rabbit can be prepared in the same manner. If you omit the ground paprika and add 9 oz (250 g) sliced mushrooms, such as button mushrooms, or other wild fungi, after you brown the rabbit, you'll get a wonderful mushroom sauce that should be served with steamed rice.**

2
3
4
5

Fruit & Desserts

Contents

650 Fruit Varieties
652 Peeling and Pitting Mangoes
652 Halving and Pitting Apricots
653 Scraping Out Vanilla Beans, Vanilla Sugar
653 Peeling Kiwis
654 Cutting Honeydew Melons
654 Cutting Pineapple
655 Segmenting Oranges
655 Hollowing Out Apples
656 Simple Fruit Salad
657 Exotic Fruit Salad
658 Bavarian Cream
660 Vanilla Ice Cream Parfait
662 Little Fruit Tarts
664 Pineapple Fritters
665 Apple Fritters
666 Egg Rolls with Cherry Filling
668 Tapioca-Coconut Pudding
670 Sweet Gnocchi with Almond Crumbs
672 Pavlova with Berries and Vanilla Cream
674 Panna Cotta with Coffee
676 White Chocolate Mousse with Maple Syrup
678 Dark Chocolate Mousse
680 Sweet Sushi with Strawberries and Toasted Quinoa
682 Strawberry Yogurt Mousse
683 Banana Mousse
684 Hot Zabaglione
684 Pistachio Zabaglione
684 Campari Zabaglione
686 Baked Peaches with Lavender
688 Tiramisu
690 Vanilla Soufflé
692 Walnut Soufflé
694 Vanilla Sauce
694 Chocolate Sauce
694 Caramel Sauce
695 Strawberry Sauce
695 Apricot Sauce
695 Kiwi Sauce
696 Wine Chaudeau
698 Cold Wine Cream

Fruit Varieties

Beautiful fruit isn't always good fruit. For the most part, shriveled organic items have more flavor than shiny fruit from the supermarket. Always be sure to buy fresh fruit that's in season, from local growers if possible.

Red currants

Raspberries

Strawberry

Starking apple

Fuji apple

Golden Delicious apple

Galia melon

Cantaloupe melon

Watermelon

Sugar pear

Nashi pear

Conference pear

Green plum

Apricot

Kiwifruit

Blood orange

Pink grapefruit

Mandarin orange

Formosa papaya

Pomegranate

Mango

Peeling and Pitting Mangoes

1. Remove the mango skin with a small knife or a vegetable peeler.

2. Cut off the flesh of the mango along both sides of the pit.

3. Loosen the flesh that adheres to the pit.

4. Both mango halves and the small pieces of fruit are now ready for use.

Halving and Pitting Apricots

1. Cut the apricots in half lengthwise.

2. Twist the halves with your hands in opposite directions so that one half comes loose from the pit.

3. Remove the pit from the other half with a knife.

4. Work with the apricot halves quickly. Otherwise, the cut surface will become brown.

Peaches and nectarines can be pitted in the same way.

Scraping Out Vanilla Beans, Vanilla Sugar

1. Hold the vanilla bean by one end and use the knife to cut it in half lengthwise.

2. Scrape the seeds out of the whole vanilla bean with the tip of the knife.

3. Dark vanilla beans lend desserts and sauces an aromatic flavor.

4. Store the scraped-out vanilla beans with granulated sugar in a preserving jar. If the pod has hardened, put it into the food processor with the sugar, and blend them until you have a fine mixture.

5. Homemade vanilla sugar can be used for desserts, cakes, and sauces.

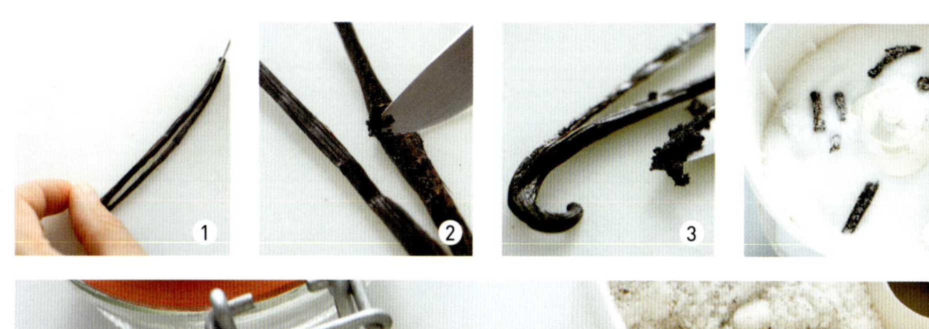

Peeling Kiwis

1. Cut ¼ inch (5 mm) off the bottom and trim the top to the same extent around the core, but do not sever it completely.

2. Then, simply fold the top back and the little stalk will also be removed. Twist the top slightly to accomplish this.

3. Stand the kiwi upright and pare the skin off from the top to the bottom.

4. Cut and use the kiwi as you like.

Cutting Honeydew Melons

1. Cut the melon in half lengthwise.

2. Remove the core with a small spoon.

3. You can make little boats by dividing the melon halves several times. Then cut it away from the rind, leaving a little tag so that the flesh doesn't slip when it is being eaten.

4. Little melon balls can also be scooped out with a melon baller.

5. The scooped-out melon half can be used as a decorative bowl.

1

2

3

4

5

Cutting Pineapple

1. Cut a 1¼-inch (3-cm) thick round off the top and the bottom.

2. Cut the skin off from top to bottom at a thickness of approximately ½ inch (1 cm).

3. Remove the remaining eyes with a V-shape cut.

4. Cut the flesh into ½-inch (1-cm) thick slices and scoop out the woody center with a melon baller.

1

2

3

4

Segmenting Oranges

1. Cut a 1¼-inch (1-cm) round off the top and off the bottom.

2. Remove the outer peel and the white pith from top to bottom.

3. Hold the peeled orange in your hand, slice it into segments to the middle of the fruit, and remove them.

1

2

3

Hollowing Out Apples

1. Cut the top off the apple at a thickness of half an inch (1.5 cm).

2. Remove the core with a melon baller.

3. Then scoop out the flesh of the apple so that it can be cooked later with a filling.

1

2

3

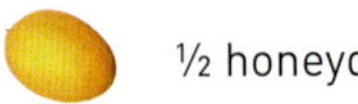 ½ honeydew melon

 2 bananas

 2 apples

 3 oranges

 9 oz (250 g) red grapes

 1 lime

 3 tbsp honey

 10 mint leaves

Simple Fruit Salad

1. Peel and halve the melon, remove the seeds with a spoon, and cut the flesh into ½- x ¾-inch (1.5- x 2-cm) pieces. Peel the bananas and cut them into ½-inch (1-cm) slices. Peel the apples, remove the cores, and dice the flesh into ½-inch (1.5-cm) pieces. Segment the oranges (see p. 655).

2. Halve the grapes and remove the seeds with the tip of the knife, if necessary.

3. Squeeze the lime through a strainer over the fruit salad, so that none of the pulp is included. The acid will prevent the fruit from discoloring. Finally, add the honey and the chopped mint leaves, mix the ingredients, and chill the fruit salad before serving it.

- ½ honeydew melon 
- 1 mango  
- 3 oranges  
- 3 kiwis 
- 2 limes 
- ⅓ cup (60 g) vanilla sugar 
- 4 passion fruits 
- 6 strawberries 
- 1 pinch of lime zest 
- 1 vanilla bean
- 2 tbsp grated coconut  

Exotic Fruit Salad

1. Cut the melon in half, remove the seeds with a spoon, and scoop out balls with a melon baller. Peel the mango and cut it in half, remove the pit, and dice the flesh. Peel and segment the oranges (see p. 655). Peel the kiwis, cut them in half, and slice them.

2. Squeeze the limes by hand and add them to the salad. The volatile oils of the zest will add an even more exotic taste to the fruit salad. Wash them with hot water in advance.

3. Add the sugar. Cut the passion fruits in half, scoop out the insides with a spoon, and add them to the salad. Let the salad marinate for ½ hour. Remove the lime zest from the salad. Finally, slice the strawberries thinly lengthwise and use them to garnish the fruit salad. Garnish to taste with lime zest, vanilla, and grated coconut. Arrange the fruit salad in one of the hollowed-out melon halves.

5 eggs

⅔ cup (130 g) sugar

2¼ cups (500 ml) milk

1 vanilla bean

8 gelatin sheets

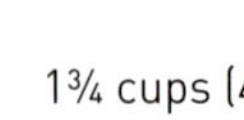
1¾ cups (400 ml) heavy cream

Bavarian Cream

1. Separate the eggs and whisk the egg yolks with the sugar, until the mixture is almost white. Prepare a double boiler on the stove, being careful the bowl does not touch the water.

2. In the meantime, boil the milk with the vanilla bean and the vanilla seeds, and using the wire whisk, stir it gradually into the egg/sugar mixture.

3. Heat the mixture slowly in the water bath, stirring it continuously with a wooden spoon so that the egg doesn't coagulate at the rim of the bowl.

4. Heat the milk, stirring it until the egg thickens the mixture. It's the right consistency when a line drawn with your finger on the back of a wooden spoon holds its shape.

5. Soak the gelatin sheets in cold water for 10 minutes, squeeze them, and then mix them with the reserved cream. Whip this mixture over a bowl containing ice water until it's cold and thick.

+ 3 hours to chill

■ **To make a coffee cream, boil 4 cups of strong espresso and stir it into the mixture before folding in the cream. Increase the number of gelatin sheets to 9.**

6. Carefully fold just a little whipped cream into the egg mixture to temper the mixture and avoid cooking the eggs.

7. Fold in the rest of the cream and turn the whisk with your wrist in a stirring motion. Pour the cream into dishes or glasses, cover them and let them chill in the refrigerator. Serve the cream with fruit sauce or fresh fruit.

 ¾ cup (150 g) sugar

 ½ cup (125 ml) water

 3 eggs

 1 vanilla bean

 2 tsp (10 ml) amaretto

 2¼ cups (500 ml) cream

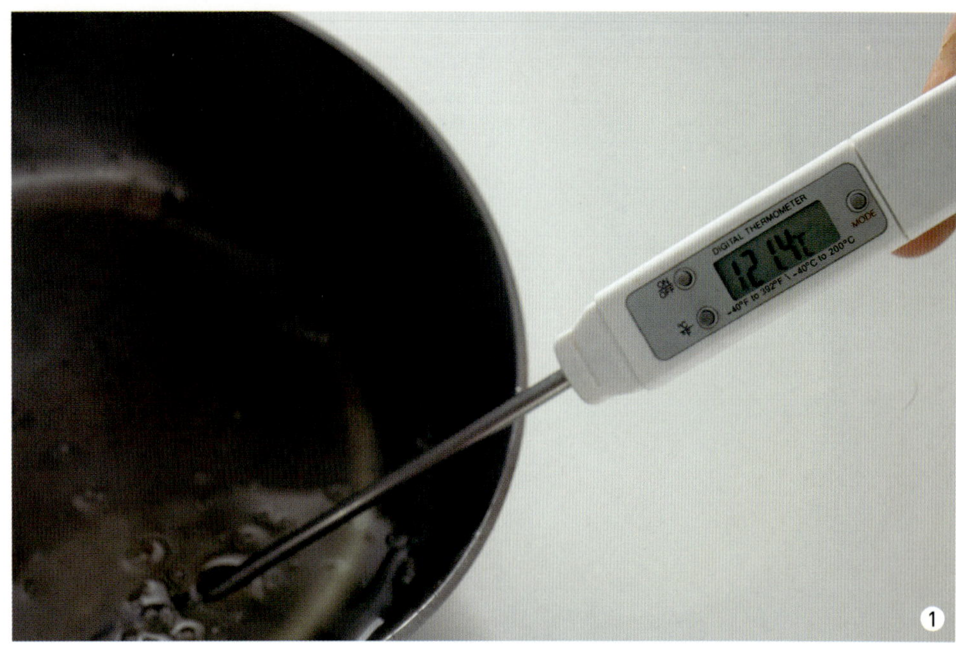

Vanilla Ice Cream Parfait

1. Add the sugar to the water and heat to 250°F (121°C). Use a candy thermometer. Do not stir.

2. Separate the eggs and put the egg yolks into a metal bowl. Mix the cooked sugar little by little with the egg whites. Beat it continuously with a wire whisk, so the egg doesn't coagulate.

3. Mix in the scraped out vanilla seeds and the amaretto, whip the mixture with the whisk until it is creamy, and stir it over a chilled water bath until it is cold again.

4. Beat the chilled cream until stiff peaks form. Stir one-third of the cream into the egg mixture with a wire whisk. Fold in the rest of the cream carefully to keep the parfait fluffy.

5. Put the mixture in a mold and put it in the freezer compartment for at least 6 hours. Hold the mold under running hot water briefly and turn out the parfait. Use a hot knife to cut ½-inch (1-cm) slices and serve them immediately. Wrap the rest of the parfait in clear plastic wrap for future use.

Variations on the parfait can be made by adding any of the following ingredients:

1. 7 oz (200 g) strawberry puree
2. 5½ oz (150 g) passion fruit puree, 3 tbsp (50 ml) coconut liqueur
3. 1¾ oz (50 g) roasted almonds, 4½ oz (120 g) coarsely chopped amarena cherries, 4 tsp (20 ml) cherry liqueur
4. 7 oz (200 g) apricot puree, 4 tsp (20 ml) amaretto

+ 6 hours to freeze

■ You can also surprise your guests with an ice cream soufflé by making a collar from parchment paper, putting it into a miniature soufflé dish, and pouring in some parfait mixture. Freeze and then remove the paper. The parfait creates the effect of a soufflé, but it is made of ice cream.

2
3
4
5

 1⅛ cups (250 ml) milk

 ⅜ cup (80 g) sugar

 3 eggs

 ⅔ oz (20 g) cornstarch

 ⅛ cup (30 g) butter

 1 vanilla bean

 9 oz (250 g) puff pastry

 7 oz (200 g) mixed berries

 3 tbsp (50 ml) water

 ⅛ cup (30 g) sugar

 3 tbsp (50 ml) white wine

 1½ gelatin sheets

 ¼ oz (10 g) confectioners' sugar

 1 orange

Little Fruit Tarts

1. Take 4 tbsp of the milk and mix it with the sugar, the yolk of 1 egg, and the cornstarch. Cut the butter into small pieces and refrigerate it. Cut the vanilla bean in half lengthwise and scrape it out with the back of a knife. Bring the rest of the milk, the seeds, and the scraped bean to a boil. Pour it through a sieve and put it back on the stove. Pour the prepared mixture of egg yolk, sugar, and cornstarch slowly into the milk and let the cream thicken.

2. Stir the cream and the chilled butter over ice water, cover it, and let it chill.

3. Cut the puff pastry into triangles and strips and assemble them as shown in the photograph. Brush them completely with the yolks of the remaining eggs and prick the tart bottoms with a fork.

4. Bake the little tarts at 350°F (180°C/Gas Mark 4) in the oven for 12–15 minutes, and then let them cool. Fill them with the vanilla cream to just below the rim.

5. Top the vanilla cream with fresh fruit. Meanwhile, bring the water, sugar, and white wine to a boil, dissolve the softened gelatin in this mixture, and let it cool. Coat the berries with the glaze so that they stay fresh and the little tarts are shiny. Dust them with confectioners' sugar and decorate them with a twist of orange zest before serving.

■ The little tarts can be topped with any kind of berries you like. A large slice of puff pastry with vanilla cream and fresh strawberries is also a delicious alternative to a cake.

2
3
4
5

1 pineapple

2 eggs

1 pinch of salt

6⅔ cups (1.5 liters) vegetable oil

1 cup (120 g) flour

⅓ cup (60 g) sugar

½ cup (125 ml) milk

3 tbsp (40 ml) dark rum

1 oz (30 g) coconut flakes

1

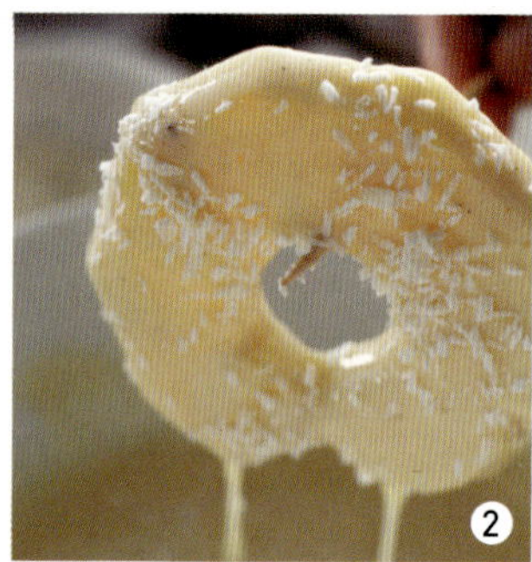
2

3

Pineapple Fritters

1. Peel the pineapple and remove the core. Then cut the fruit into ¼-inch (5-mm) thick slices and set them aside. Separate the eggs and beat the egg whites with the salt until stiff peaks form. Cover the container and put it into the refrigerator for future use. Put the vegetable oil in a saucepan and heat it to 350°F (180°C). Meanwhile, mix the flour, the sugar, the egg yolk, the milk, and the rum until smooth, and fold in the egg whites.

2. Dip the pineapple slices in the batter and sprinkle them with coconut flakes.

3. Fry the pineapple fritters at 325°F (160°C) until golden brown. Drain them well on paper towels, sprinkle them with the remaining coconut flakes, and serve.

3 eggs 

2⅓ cups (300 g) flour 

⅔ oz (20 g) baking powder 

⅓ cup (60 g) sugar 

1½ cups (350 ml) milk 

4 apples 

½ lemon 

1 pinch of salt 

6 cups (1.5 liter) vegetable oil 

1 tbsp vanilla sugar 

Apple Fritters

1. Separate the eggs and mix the egg yolk with flour, baking powder, sugar, and milk, until smooth. Gradually, stir in ⅔ cup (160 ml) of the vegetable oil. Peel the apples and remove the core with a baller. Cut the apples into ¼-inch (5-mm) thick slices and rub them with the cut lemon to prevent them from browning.

2. Beat the egg whites with a pinch of salt until stiff peaks form and fold them into the batter carefully. Put the remaining vegetable oil in a saucepan and heat it to 350°F (160°C). You can check that the correct temperature has been reached by holding a wooden skewer in it—the oil will bubble up.

3. Dip the apples in the batter and immediately slide them into the hot oil. Fry the apple fritters until they are golden brown. Let them drain well on paper towels, dust them with vanilla sugar, and serve them with vanilla sauce (see p. 694).

■ **You can create delicious apple chips by deep-frying apple skins in oil.**

 8 ladyfingers

 10½ oz (300 g) juicy cherries

 2 tbsp sugar

 ½ tsp cinnamon

 4 tsp cherry liqueur

 1 package egg roll wrappers (measuring 4½ x 4½ inches/12 x 12 cm)

 1 egg white

 2 quarts (2 liters) vegetable oil for deep frying

 ¼ oz (10 g) confectioners' sugar

Egg Rolls with Cherry Filling

1. Use your fingers to crush the ladyfingers coarsely in a bowl.

2. Wash the cherries, cut them in half, and remove the pits. Add the cherries to the ladyfingers.

3. Season with the two tbsp of sugar and the ground cinnamon.

4. Drizzle with cherry liqueur and mix well.

5. Lay the wrappers out on the work surface. Put two tbsp of the cherry filling in the center of each wrapper. Paint the sides with egg white.

6. Fold two opposite corners into the center and paint the edges with egg white.

7. Fold in the third corner and paint the lower section with egg white again.

8. Fold the lower section onto the filling and press it down lightly. Paint the upper section with egg white and roll the wrap up completely.

9. Put the oil in a large saucepan and heat it to 325°F (160°C). Deep-fry the egg rolls in the pan for approximately 5 minutes, until they are golden.

10. Remove the egg rolls and drain them on paper towels.

Arrange them on plates with napkins and sprinkle them with confectioners' sugar.

■ These egg rolls can also be filled with other fruit, such as plums, morello cherries, mangoes, bananas, or grapes. When they are prepared this way, they look like miniature strudels. Fillings with yogurt or vanilla cream are also an option, although you will need to use some soaked broken ladyfingers to make the filling thicker.

5
6
7
8
9
10

 2⅞ cups (650 ml) coconut milk

 4½ oz (120 g) coarsely ground tapioca

 ¼ cup (60 g) brown cane sugar

 1 vanilla bean

 1 pinch of salt

 ⅜ cup (100 ml) orange juice

 3 star anise pods

 1 tbsp sugar

 ¼ oz (10 g) cornstarch

 4 tsp (20 ml) orange liqueur

 2 oranges

Tapioca-Coconut Pudding

1. Put the coconut milk in a saucepan and bring it to a boil, let the tapioca dribble in slowly, and stir it in with a wire whisk.

2. Add the brown sugar and let the pudding simmer gently for five minutes. Scrape out the vanilla bean and add the vanilla seeds and the salt.

3. The pudding is ready once it is firm. Pour it into glasses or bowls, cover them with plastic wrap directly on the pudding (so it doesn't form a skin) and let the pudding cool.

4. Bring the orange juice, the star anise, and the sugar to a boil.

5. Mix the cornstarch with the orange liqueur and thicken the orange juice with this mixture.

6. Segment two oranges and add the slices to the thickened sauce. Remove the sauce from the heat and let it cool down. Pour it over the tapioca pudding and serve.

■ **The coconut milk must not be thickened. If the pudding sticks to the bottom of the pan, stop stirring it and pour it out immediately. Green tea ice cream or stewed papaya is a perfect accompaniment to this pudding.**

3
4
5
6

½ cup (100 g) butter

3½ oz (100 g) ground almonds

3 tbsp sugar

3 tbsp breadcrumbs

1 tsp ground cinnamon

1 lb 2 oz (500 g) cooked potato gnocchi

¼ oz (10 g) confectioners' sugar

1

2

3

Sweet Gnocchi with Almond Crumbs

1. Melt the butter in a nonstick skillet and add the ground almonds and the sugar.

2. Add the breadcrumbs to the pan.

3. Sprinkle the cinnamon on the mixture.

4. Gently toast the crumbs in the butter for approximately five minutes, stirring frequently.

5. Add the cooked gnocchi to the skillet and turn them in the breadcrumbs.

6. Cook the gnocchi in the crumbs for another 2 minutes, until they are completely coated by the crumbs.

Arrange the gnocchi on plates and sprinkle them with confectioners' sugar.

■ **Finger noodles or other gnocchi that are mixed with pumpkin, poppy seeds, or various nuts can also be prepared in this manner. Be sure the almond breadcrumbs are well browned and sweetened, and that the gnocchi have a neutral taste. Ground poppy seeds with sugar and butter are also particularly delicious with these gnocchi.**

4

5

6

 4 eggs

 2⅓ cups (260 g) confectioners' sugar

 7 oz (200 g) raspberries

 7 oz (200 g) strawberries

 1⅛ cups (250 ml) heavy cream

 1 vanilla bean

Pavlova with Berries and Vanilla Cream

1. Separate the eggs, add the chilled egg white to the bowl, and beat it with a whisk until semistiff peaks form. Gradually add the confectioners' sugar and beat the mixture with a whisk, until stiff.

2. Use a scraper to put the beaten egg whites into a piping bag.

3. Pipe the egg white mixture in spirals onto a baking sheet covered with parchment paper. Bake it in the oven for approximately 35 minutes at 250°F (120°C/Gas Mark ½). Reduce the temperature to 125°F (60°C) and let the meringues dry for 4 hours.

4. Trim the berries, wash them, and put them into a bowl.

5. Cut the baked meringue spirals with a sharp, serrated knife. Whip the cream with seeds scraped out of the vanilla bean and put the mixture on the lower halves of the meringue spirals. Put the berries on top of the cream, set the lids on top at an angle, and serve.

+ 4 hours for drying

■ **Try making a miniature version of these meringue cases. They won't take as long to dry and can be served as an afternoon snack. They can also be prepared in advance and filled only just before they are served. You can also use fruit sherbet as a filling instead of fresh fruit.**

2
3
4
5

½ vanilla bean

2¼ cups (500 ml) cream

½ cup (100 g) sugar

1 tbsp coffee beans

3 gelatin sheets

Panna Cotta with Coffee

1. Cut the vanilla bean lengthwise, scrape out the seeds with the back of a knife, and add them to the cream. Bring the cream with the scraped vanilla bean, the sugar, and the coffee beans to a boil. Let the gelatin sheets soften in cold water for approximately 10 minutes.

2. Set the boiled cream mixture aside. Add the softened, squeezed, and drained gelatin and dissolve it.

3. Pour the cream through a sieve into a measuring cup.

4. Pour it into glasses and let it chill in the refrigerator for at least 3 hours, so the panna cotta can set. Put the glasses into hot water briefly and turn out the panna cotta onto serving plates.

210

■ **Sprinkle the panna cotta with crushed almond cookies or Amarettini and garnish it with amarena cherries. For a lighter panna cotta, use milk as a substitute for half of the cream.**

3

4

1 envelope gelatin powder

3⅛ cup (700 ml) milk

3½ oz (100 g) white chocolate

3 tbsp (50 ml) maple syrup

White Chocolate Mousse with Maple Syrup

1. Put the gelatin powder into 4 tbsp of cold water, stir it, and let it soak for 10 minutes.

2. Heat the milk. Reserve 2 tbsp. Break the chocolate into pieces and dissolve it in the milk.

3. Mix the gelatin with the reserved hot milk, and then add it to the chocolate-milk mixture and stir it until it dissolves completely.

4. Pour the chocolate mousse into a siphon with the aid of a funnel.

5. Add the maple syrup. Close the siphon when it contains 3⅓ cups (750 ml) of the mixture, and shake it well. Let it cool in the refrigerator for approximately one hour.

To serve, mount two cartridges and squirt the fluffy mousse into small bowls.

■ **The mousse can be prepared in advance. At the last minute, you can serve it fresh in glasses and it will taste particularly frothy. Dark chocolate, nougat, or even fruit purees can be added to the milk. However, fruit purees should not be cooked further, and the amount of gelatin must be increased by half because of the acid in the fruit. Otherwise, the puree would be too runny.**

2
3
4
5

5½ oz (150 g) bittersweet chocolate

2 eggs

3 tbsp sugar

1 tbsp reduced-fat cocoa powder

4 tsp (20 ml) cognac

3 tbsp (50 ml) espresso

1 pinch of salt

⅞ cup (200 ml) cream

4 tbsp chocolate shavings

Dark Chocolate Mousse

1. Put the bittersweet chocolate in a heatproof bowl and set the bowl over a saucepan of barely simmering water to let it melt slowly.

2. Separate the eggs, store the egg whites in the refrigerator, and whisk the egg yolk with the sugar until it foams. Stir the cocoa, cognac, and espresso into the egg mixture.

3. Add the warm melted chocolate.

4. Stir in the chocolate until everything is mixed well.

5. Beat the egg whites with a pinch of salt until stiff peaks form, and fold them into the chocolate mix with the wire whisk. Fold in the whipped cream, and let the mousse chill in the refrigerator for at least 2 hours. To serve, scoop out a portion with a spoon and decorate it with some chocolate shavings.

■ **Put a ripe banana with two pieces of finely chopped, candied ginger, the juice of ½ orange, and ½ vanilla bean in a saucepan and bring them to a boil. Add the mixture as an intermediate layer in the chocolate mousse and let it chill. Chocolate and bananas are an excellent combination and will turn the mousse into a wonderful dessert.**

2
3
4
5

9 oz (250 g) strawberries

14 oz (400 g) sushi rice

3½ oz (100 g) quinoa

2 tbsp mango jelly

4 tsp (20 g) butter

2 tbsp brown sugar

1

2

Sweet Sushi with Strawberries and Toasted Quinoa

1. Wash and hull the strawberries, and cut them into slices. Cook the sushi rice (see p. 235) and the quinoa (see p. 275).

2. Using two tablespoons, make small oblong mounds out of the sushi rice and put a dab of mango jelly on each one.

3. Decorate each sushi shape with 2 strawberry slices.

4. Heat the butter and the brown sugar in a skillet.

5. Add the boiled quinoa to the butter and toast it.

Put some toasted quinoa seeds on top of each piece of strawberry sushi and serve them. Serve maple syrup or honey as a dipping sauce.

■ This sweet sushi can be served with various thinly sliced fruit. Mangoes, papayas, oranges, melons, plums, or cherries are particularly suitable for this.

3

4

5

1 tbsp lemon juice

½ cup (130 g) low-fat Greek-style yogurt

4½ oz (130 g) crème fraîche (or sour cream)

⅞ cup (90 g) confectioners' sugar

5½ oz (150 g) strawberry puree

4 gelatin sheets

½ cup (125 ml) heavy cream

2 eggs

⅛ cup (30 g) sugar

3 strawberries

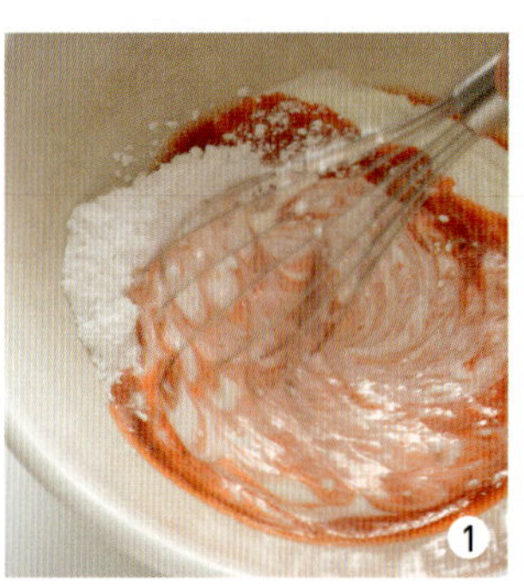

Strawberry Yogurt Mousse

1. Squeeze half the lemon and combine the juice with the yogurt, crème fraîche (or sour cream), confectioners' sugar, and two thirds of the strawberry puree. Soften the gelatin sheets in cold water for 10 minutes, squeeze the moisture out of them, and let them dissolve in a small saucepan. Then mix the gelatin with the yogurt.

2. Whip the cream until stiff peaks form, and fold it into the mixture with a wire whisk.

3. Separate the eggs, beat the egg whites and the sugar until stiff peaks form, and fold them into the mixture slowly. Pour the mixture into glasses and put them in the refrigerator to chill for an hour. Add a little strawberry puree on top before serving it, and decorate it with strawberry slices.

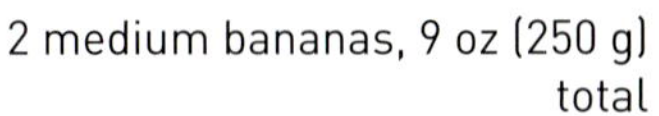

2 medium bananas, 9 oz (250 g) total

2 lemons

3 tbsp banana liqueur

2 tbsp butter

2½ gelatin sheets

½ cup (125 ml) heavy cream

2 eggs

⅓ cup (65 g) sugar

2 tsp vanilla sugar

4 tbsp chocolate sauce (see p. 694)

Banana Mousse

1. Cut the bananas into thin slices. Squeeze the lemons and drizzle the juice onto the banana slices to prevent browning. Bring the bananas, the banana liqueur, and the butter to a brief boil in a saucepan, puree the mixture with a handheld blender, and strain it through a sieve. Let the gelatin sheets soften in cold water for approximately 10 minutes, squeeze the moisture out of them, let them dissolve in a small saucepan, and stir the liquid into the banana puree. Then set the mixture aside to cool.

2. Whip the cream until semistiff peaks form, and fold it carefully into the cooled banana puree.

3. Separate the eggs. Beat the egg whites until they are light and fluffy, and then add the sugar and the vanilla sugar carefully to the egg white foam. Continue beating the egg whites until stiff peaks form, fold them into the mousse, and pour the mousse into individual glasses. Put the glasses in the refrigerator to chill for at least 2 hours. Garnish the mousse with some unpeeled banana slices and drizzle chocolate sauce on top.

■ **You will need approximately 3 bananas to yield 9 oz (250 g) of peeled bananas. You must weigh the bananas for the mousse to be a success.**

160

6 eggs

½ cup (100 g) sugar

⅞ cup (200 ml) sparkling wine

3 tbsp (50 ml) dessert wine

½ lemon

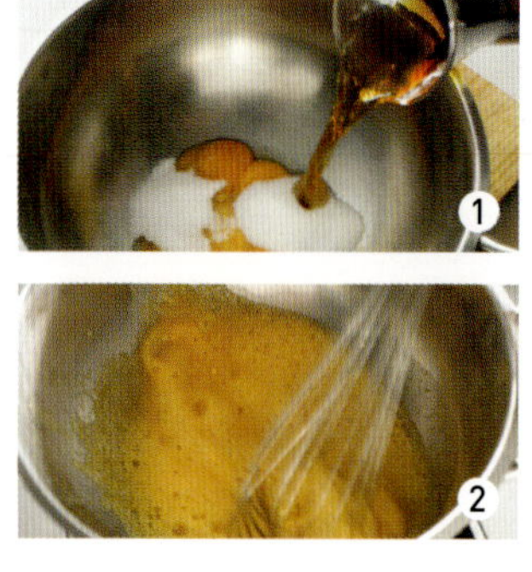

1. Hot Zabaglione

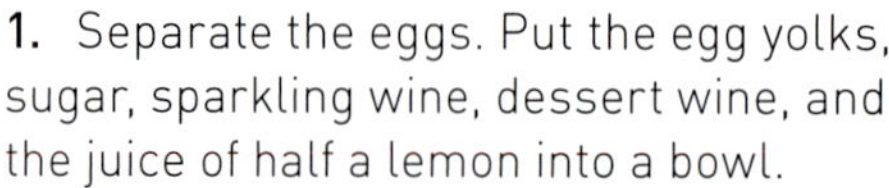

1. Separate the eggs. Put the egg yolks, sugar, sparkling wine, dessert wine, and the juice of half a lemon into a bowl.

2. Beat the mixture over a water bath. As you work, be careful to whisk evenly, scraping the edges of the bowl, or lumps will form.

3. The mixture will become lighter in color and more viscous, and it will increase in volume.

4. The zabaglione is ready when it is creamy and shiny.

Pour it into glasses and serve immediately.

2. Pistachio Zabaglione

Separate **4 eggs**. Beat the egg yolks with **⅓ cup (60 g) sugar** and **⅜ cup (100 ml) sparkling wine** in a water bath as with the basic zabaglione. Heat **1 sheet of softened gelatin**, dissolve it, and add it to the zabaglione. Stir this mixture over a bowl of ice water until it is cold. Grind **2¼ oz (60 g) shelled pistachio nuts** very finely in a blender until they are almost like a paste, and add them to the zabaglione. Then, whip **⅜ cup (100 ml) cream** until semistiff peaks form, and fold it in.

Pour the zabaglione into glasses and serve it with fresh raspberries, raspberry sorbet, vanilla ice cream, or poached peaches.

3. Campari Zabaglione

Separate **4 eggs**. Beat the egg yolks with **⅓ cup (60 g) sugar** and **⅓ cup (80 ml) Campari** in a water bath as with the basic zabaglione. Finely grate some **orange zest** and add it to the zabaglione. Cut an **orange in half** and squeeze it. Heat **1 sheet of gelatin** in the orange juice, dissolve it, and add it to the zabaglione. Stir this mixture over a bowl of ice water until it is cold. Then, whip **⅔ cup (150 ml) cream** until semistiff peaks form, and fold it in.

Pour the zabaglione into glasses and serve it with stewed fruit or pistachio ice cream.

1
2
3

 ½ cup (120 g) butter

 ¼ cup (60 g) brown sugar

 3 eggs

 1¾ oz (50 g) slivered almonds

 3½ oz (100 g) white breadcrumbs

 4 peaches

 8 sprigs fresh lavender

 1 vanilla bean

 4 tsp honey

 8 tsp peach liqueur

Baked Peaches with Lavender

1. Beat the butter and the brown sugar, at room temperature, until they are fluffy. Separate the eggs and stir the egg yolks in gradually.

2. Dry roast the slivered almonds in a skillet until they are golden, and then let them cool. Add the almonds and the breadcrumbs to the butter-egg mixture and mix well.

3. Score the peach skins lightly with a knife, and put the fruit into boiling water for approximately 10–15 seconds. Then remove them with a skimmer and place them in ice water to cool.

4. Remove the skins from the peaches and cut them in half. Remove the pits and put the peach halves, with the cut side facing upward, in a dish where lavender sprigs have already been placed.

5. Fill the peaches with the almond mixture. Cut the vanilla bean in half lengthwise and divide it into 1¼-inch (3-cm) lengths. Drizzle the peaches with honey and peach liqueur and bake them in the oven at 425°F (220°C/Gas Mark 7) for approximately 20 minutes. Arrange them on plates, decorate them with the vanilla beans, and serve them with vanilla ice cream or lavender honey, as you prefer.

■ Baked apples with raisin filling: 3 tbsp (40 g) fluffy whipped butter, 2¼ oz (60 g) lightly toasted, coarsely chopped almonds, 1½ oz (40 g) raisins (softened in 2 tbsp tea), 1¾ oz (50 g) crustless white bread cubes, 1¾ oz (50 g) diced almond paste, 8 small, red apples with stems, 1 tbsp butter to grease the baking dish, 1 tbsp sugar, 1 tbsp honey, 5 cloves, and 2 cinnamon sticks. Prepare these ingredients in the same way as the peaches and cook them for the same length of time.

2
3
4
5

 4 eggs

 ⅜ cup (80 g) sugar

 ½ vanilla bean

 3 tbsp (40 ml) cognac

 4 tsp (20 ml) Grand Marnier

 1 lb 2 oz (500 g) mascarpone cheese

 5½ oz (150 g) ladyfingers

 ⅞ cup (200 ml) espresso

 ¼ cup (30 g) cocoa powder

Tiramisu

1. Separate the eggs, and beat the egg yolks with the sugar and the seeds scraped out of the vanilla beans until the mixture is fluffy.

2. Add the cognac and the Grand Marnier and stir them in.

3. Add the mascarpone cheese and whisk it into the mixture.

4. Dip the ladyfingers in the espresso for a maximum of 3 seconds, so that they are not completely saturated.

5. Put the ingredients in alternating layers in a bowl. Start with a layer of ladyfingers, then add a layer of the mascarpone cream, and repeat the process. Top off the dessert with a mascarpone layer and set it in the refrigerator for at least 1 hour. Sprinkle it with the unsweetened cocoa and serve.

+ 1 hour to cool

■ **Kitchen doctor: If the cream becomes lumpy, you can add some hot milk and stir it in, until the mixture is smooth again.**

2
3
4
5

5 eggs

2¾ oz (80 g) ladyfingers

3 tbsp (40 ml) Grand Marnier

¼ cup (50 g) butter

1 vanilla bean

1 oz (30 g) cornstarch

⅞ cup (200 ml) milk

½ cup (100 g) sugar

1 pinch of salt

Vanilla Soufflé

1. Separate the eggs, cover 1 egg white, and set it aside to chill in the refrigerator for future use. Cut the ladyfingers into ¼-inch (5-mm) cubes and marinate them in the Grand Marnier. Let ⅛ cup (30 g) of the butter soften at room temperature so it may be used to grease ramekin molds. Cut the vanilla bean in half lengthwise and scrape out the seeds with the back of a knife. Beat the separated egg whites until stiff peaks form, cover them, and set them aside to chill in the refrigerator. Mix the cornstarch with 3 tbsp (40 ml) of the cold milk. Put the remaining milk in a saucepan, add the rest of the butter, ⅓ cup (70 g) sugar, the vanilla seeds, the scraped bean, and the salt, and bring the mixture to a boil.

2. Use a brush to coat the ramekin molds evenly with the softened butter. Put some sugar into the molds and twist them at a slight angle to dust the entire mold. Follow the same procedure with the other ramekin.

3. When the milk has come to a boil, add the cold milk and the cornstarch, and stir the mixture continuously with the wire whisk for 2 minutes on the stove. The dissolved cornstarch will thicken the milk. Cover the mixture with plastic wrap and let it cool. Preheat a convection oven, if available, to 350°F (180°C/Gas Mark 4). Line a baking pan with parchment paper, pour in water until it has reached a depth of 2 fingers, and put it into the oven until the water starts to boil. The parchment paper will ensure that no bubbles, which could impair the soufflé's rising, will be created during baking.

■ **Cover the soufflé with plastic wrap while it is cooling to prevent a skin from forming.**

4. Stir the egg yolks into the cooled mixture. The mixture must be cool to prevent the egg from coagulating. Put the mixture through a sieve to remove any lumps.

5. Fold the stiffly beaten egg whites carefully into the egg yolk mixture with a rubber scraper. Stir it gently, so that none of the trapped air will escape. Divide the ladyfinger cubes among the ramekin molds.

6. Spoon the soufflé mixture on top of the ladyfinger cubes. Place the ramekin molds in the water bath in the baking dish and bake the soufflés at 350°F (180°C/ Gas Mark 4) for 20 minutes. The soufflés are ready as soon as they are golden yellow and reach a height of ¾–1¼ inches (2–3 cm) above the rims of the ramekin molds. Never open the oven while the soufflés are baking, otherwise they will not puff up sufficiently. Serve the soufflés as quickly as possible, so they don't fall. The basic rule is: Guests wait for a soufflé, but soufflés don't wait for guests.

 ¼ cup (50 g) butter

 ⅛ cup (20 g) flour

 1 vanilla bean

 2¾ oz (80 g) shelled walnuts

 ⅔ oz (20 g) chocolate

 3 eggs

 ⅜ cup (80 g) sugar

 ⅞ cup (200 ml) milk

 ⅔ oz (20 g) confectioners' sugar

Walnut Soufflé

1. Let ⅛ cup (30 g) of the butter soften at room temperature and mix it with the flour in a small container until a homogeneous mass is created. This is also called beurre manié and is used as a thickener. Cut the vanilla bean in half lengthwise and scrape out the seeds with the back of a knife. Coarsely chop the walnuts and the chocolate. Separate the eggs. Beat the separated egg whites until they form soft peaks, cover them, and set them aside in the refrigerator to chill. Grease the ramekin molds with the remaining butter and dust them with sugar (see the Vanilla Soufflé recipe, pp. 690–91).

2. Bring the milk to a boil with the chopped walnuts, the scraped bean, and the vanilla seeds. After boiling, remove the beans from the milk and stir in the prepared beurre manié.

3. Simmer the mixture for 3 minutes, stirring continuously, until it becomes considerably thicker. Then cover it with plastic wrap and let it cool. Meanwhile, preheat the oven to 400°F (200°C/Gas Mark 6) and prepare a water bath for the ramekin molds. To do this, line a baking pan with parchment paper and pour in water until it has reached a depth of 2 fingers. Put it in the oven until the water starts to boil. When the mixture has cooled to room temperature, stir in the egg yolks. Remove the beaten egg whites from the refrigerator and fold them in carefully with a dough scraper. Fill the ramekin molds two thirds full with the mixture and bake them in the water bath, at 400°F (200°C/Gas Mark 6) for 20 minutes, until the soufflés rise to a height of ¾ inch (2 cm) above the ramekin rims. Sprinkle them with confectioners' sugar and serve immediately.

■ You can use this basic recipe to whip up different kinds of soufflés in no time. Just substitute other ingredients for the walnuts. For best results, use hazelnuts, chestnut puree, roasted almonds, or grated coconut. However, if you are using coconut and chocolate, white chocolate should be used because dark chocolate would be overpowering.

2

3

Vanilla Sauce

Cut **1 vanilla bean** in half lengthwise and scrape out the seeds with the back of a knife. Add the seed and the bean to **1⅛ cups (250 ml) milk** in a saucepan and bring it to a boil. Meanwhile, separate **6 eggs**, combine the egg yolks with **¼ cup (50 g) sugar**, and beat them until they are fluffy. Bring water to a boil in a long-handled saucepan. As soon as the milk boils, pour it through a sieve so that none of the residue from the vanilla bean is included in the sauce. Add the hot milk gradually to the egg-sugar mixture, stirring continuously. Heat the mixture over the prepared water bath and stir it until it has thickened enough to coat the back of a spoon. Finally, stir it over a bowl of ice water until it is cold.

Kitchen doctor: If the sauce becomes too hot, it will coagulate. If this happens, pour it through a fine sieve. Stir 1 tbsp of cornstarch into 2 tbsp of milk, and whisk them into the hot vanilla sauce. Return the sauce to a boil and it will be creamy once again.

Chocolate Sauce

Bring **½ cup (125 ml) milk**, **⅜ cup (100 ml) cream**, and **half a scraped vanilla bean** to a boil slowly. Chop **3½ oz (100 g) bittersweet chocolate** and **1¾ oz (50 g) milk chocolate** into small pieces with a knife and add them to the milk. Stir the mixture slowly with a whisk and dissolve the chocolate. Then, remove it from the heat, take out the vanilla bean and stir in **2 tsp (10 ml) cognac**, **⅛ cup (20 g) sugar**, and **3 tbsp (40 ml) vegetable oil**. Pour the sauce through a fine sieve and serve it at room temperature, if possible.

■ **Variation: Use hazelnut oil in place of the vegetable oil.**

Caramel Sauce

Cook **¼ cup (50 g) sugar** and **⅜ cup (100 ml) water** in a small long-handled saucepan at low heat. Let it simmer until the sugar is golden brown and evenly caramelized. Then, add **3 tbsp (50 ml) water** to prevent the sugar from browning further. Simmer it again gently, until the water has evaporated (approximately 5 minutes). Then, pour in **1⅛ cups (250 ml) milk**. Cut **1 vanilla bean** in half lengthwise and scrape out the seeds with the back of a knife. Add the bean and the seeds to the milk and bring the mixture to a boil in a saucepan. Meanwhile, separate **6 eggs**, combine the egg yolks with **⅛ cup (30 g) sugar** and beat them until they are fluffy. Prepare a water bath by putting water in a long-handled saucepan and bring it to a boil. As soon as the milk boils, pour it through a sieve, so that no lumps are included in the sauce. Add the hot milk gradually to the egg-sugar mixture, stirring continuously. Heat the mixture over the prepared water bath and stir it until it has thickened enough to coat the back of a spoon. Finally, stir it over a bowl of ice water until it is cold.

Strawberry Sauce

Wash **9 oz (250 g) strawberries**, hull them, and remove any rotten spots, if necessary. Sprinkle **½ cup (50 g) confectioners' sugar** on the strawberries, pour **⅓ cup (80 ml) mineral water** over them, and puree everything with a handheld blender to make a thin sauce. Finally, pour it through a fine sieve and serve.

Apricot Sauce

Put **5 apricots** into boiling water for 10 seconds and plunge them into cold water immediately to chill them. Remove the skin with a small knife, cut the fruit in half, and remove the pits. Put the apricot halves, the juice of **half a lemon**, **½ cup (50 g) confectioners' sugar**, and **⅓ cup (80 ml) mineral water** in a bowl, and mix everything with a handheld blender. Then pour the mixture through a fine sieve and press the fruit pulp through with a spoon or a scraper.

Kiwi Sauce

Peel **4 kiwis**, put them in a bowl with **½ cup (50 g) confectioners' sugar** and **⅓ cup (80 ml) mineral water**, and mix them with a handheld blender. Pour the mixture through a fine sieve.

■ **Kiwis cannot be used with any dairy products, because they contain a curdling enzyme (just like pineapples do).**

8 eggs

1 cup (200 g) sugar

A large pinch of ground cinnamon

3½ cups (800 ml) red wine

Wine Chaudeau

1. Separate the eggs and put the egg yolks in a round stainless steel bowl. Add the sugar and the ground cinnamon to the egg yolks.

2. Pour in the red wine and mix it in with a wire whisk. Put ¾ inch (2 cm) water into a long-handled saucepan and bring it to a boil.

3. Set the stainless steel bowl on the saucepan with the boiling water, so that it is heated by the steam.

4. Beat the mixture vigorously, so that its volume is increased threefold and it is rich and creamy as it runs off the whisk. Remove the custard from the heat and pour it into glasses. Serve it hot with some cinnamon sprinkled on top.

■ **Hot red wine chaudeau is very delicious when it is served with baked pears, peaches, or apples. If you substitute prosecco or marsala for the red wine, you will produce a mouthwatering zabaglione.**

2
3
4

 4 eggs

 ½ cup (100 g) sugar

 1 pinch of cinnamon

 1¾ cups (400 ml) red wine

 2 gelatin sheets

 10½ oz (300 g) whipping cream

 8 ladyfingers

Cold Wine Cream

1. Whip up a wine chaudeau from the egg yolks, sugar, ground cinnamon, and ⅞ cup (200 ml) of the red wine (see p. 696). Soften the gelatin sheets in cold water for approximately 10 minutes, then squeeze them and dissolve them in the wine chaudeau. Pour the mixture into a bowl and let it cool.

2. Meanwhile, let the remainder of the red wine reduce to a volume of 4 tbsp. Whip the cream until soft peaks form.

3. Add the cream and almost all the red wine reduction to the cold wine chaudeau.

4. Fold the cream and the reduction carefully into the cold wine chaudeau. The red wine reduction will impart the necessary color to the wine chaudeau and will also intensify its flavor. Break the ladyfingers into pieces with your fingers and put them in glasses. Add the wine cream and let it cool for a good hour. To finish, mix the remaining red wine reduction with sugar to taste and drizzle it over the wine cream.

+ 1 hour to cool

■ **White wine can also be used for this cold wine cream. If you make a white wine cream, use white wine to make the wine reduction as well. Small, fresh, seeded white grapes can also be added to the cookies. Red grapes go better with the red wine cream.**

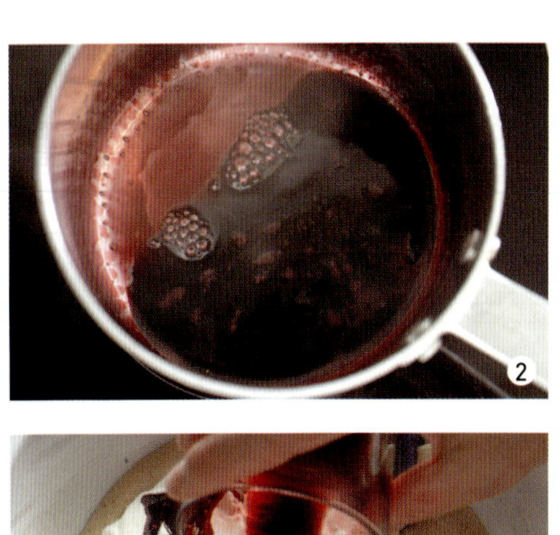
2 
3

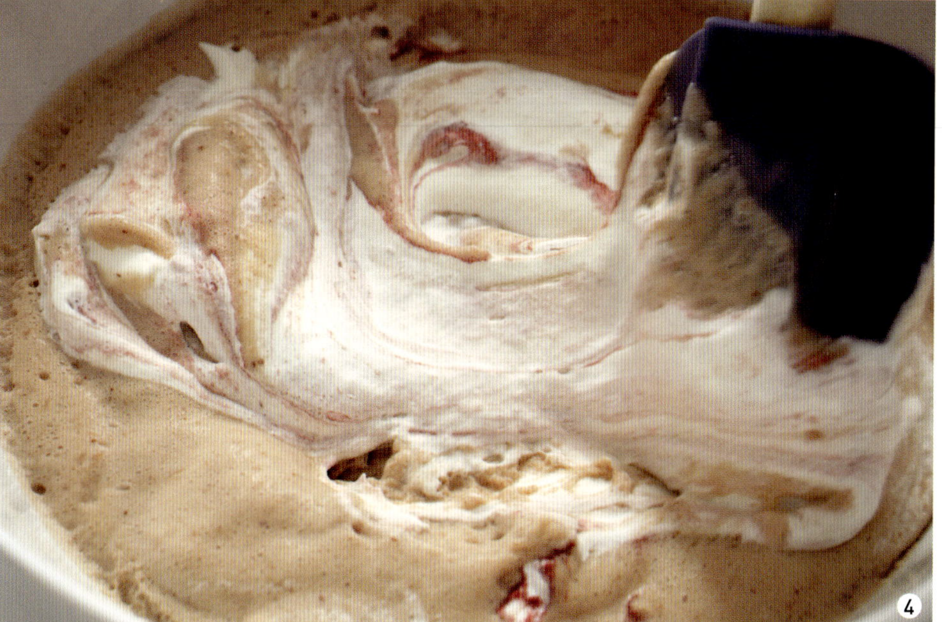
4

Cakes & Bread

Contents

702 Sweet Pie Dough
704 Jam-Filled Cookies
706 Sponge Cake
708 Strawberry Swiss Roll
710 Chocolate Brownies
711 Walnut Caramel Brownies
712 Yeast Dough
713 Candied Fruit Snail Rolls
714 Butter Pecan Cookies
716 German Cheesecake
718 Red Currant and Blueberry Meringue Cake
720 Homemade Bread with Sea Salt
722 Sunday Rolls with Poppy Seeds
724 Pizza Dough
725 Vegetable Pizza
726 Rosemary Focaccia with Porcini Mushrooms and Apricots
728 Mini Baguettes with Olives and Onion
730 Mexican Corn Bread with Green Chili Peppers

 3¼ cups (400 g) flour

 ⅞ cup (200 g) unsalted butter, cut into small pieces and chilled

 ½ cup (100 g) granulated sugar

 1 pinch of salt

 2 eggs

Sweet Pie Dough

1. Place the flour, the chilled butter pieces, the sugar, and the salt together on a work surface.

2. Using both hands, quickly rub the butter into the flour. If it is worked too long, the butter will get warm and the dough will crumble later.

3. Next add 1 egg and 1 egg yolk and work them in. Store the remaining egg white in the refrigerator for later use.

4. Briskly and thoroughly knead the dough until it is smooth. (If it's elastic, you've overdeveloped the gluten and it will be tough.)

Wrap it in clear plastic wrap and refrigerate it for at least 1 hour. Then continue working with it as desired.

Makes about 1 lb 10 oz (750 g).

■ Substitute finely chopped almonds for a quarter of the flour. Then prepare the dough as described, form into cookies, and bake until golden brown.

3

4

1 lb 2 oz (500 g) Sweet Pie Dough (see p. 702)

2 tbsp flour, for dusting

3½ oz (100 g) any fruit jam (e.g. raspberry, red currant, or apricot)

1 tbsp confectioners' sugar

Jam-Filled Cookies

1. Roll out the dough on a flour-dusted surface to a thickness of slightly less than ⅛ inch (2 mm). Continuously flip the dough as you roll, sprinkling more flour each time, so it doesn't stick to the countertop.

2. Cut out desired shapes from the dough. Work quickly. If the dough gets too warm, return it to the refrigerator.

3. Put the cookies on a baking sheet lined with parchment paper, and bake in an oven preheated to 400°F (200°C/Gas Mark 4). Keep an eye on the cookies while baking. Because they are rolled out so thinly, they can quickly get too brown. Baking time is usually around 8–10 minutes.

4. Remove the cookies from the baking sheet using the parchment paper and let them cool. Spread jam on half of the cookies.

5. Lay the other halves over them.

Sprinkle with confectioners' sugar and arrange on a plate.

■ **If there are no cookie cutters handy, use the rim of a glass.**

2
3
4 

5

8 eggs

⅔ cup (120 g) granulated sugar

1 pinch of salt

½ cup (60 g) pastry flour

⅓ cup (40 g) cornstarch

Sponge Cake

1. Separate the eggs and add the egg yolks to a mixing bowl. Set aside 4 of the egg whites. Store the remaining egg white in the refrigerator for later use. Add ⅓ cup (60 g) of the sugar to the egg yolks.

2. Beat the egg yolks and sugar for about 5 minutes, until the mixture is pale yellow.

3. Slowly beat the 4 egg whites and salt in another bowl. Stir in the remaining sugar a little at a time and beat with a mixer on a medium speed until stiff peaks form, then on the highest speed for 30 seconds. Add the beaten egg whites to the egg yolks and carefully fold them in using a rubber spatula.

4. Sift the flour and cornstarch using a fine sieve. This keeps any flour lumps from making it into the sponge cake.

5. Then carefully mix them in using a rubber spatula, without hitting the sides of the bowl. This would "shock" the sponge cake batter slightly, keeping it from rising properly. It must have a lot of air for the cake to be spongy.

6. Line an 11- x 16-inch (30- x 40-cm) sheet pan with parchment paper, put in the batter, and smooth it over. In an oven preheated to 375°F (190°C/Gas Mark 5), bake the sponge cake for about 10 minutes, until it is golden yellow. Remove it from the oven and let it cool slightly before working with it further.

■ To make a chocolate sponge cake, fold in ¼ cup (20 g) of preferably low-fat cocoa powder. Then bake as directed. Chocolate sponge cake tastes great rolled with cherries and cherry jam.

3
4
5
6

1 sponge cake (see p. 706)

1 tbsp granulated sugar

7 oz (200 g) strawberries

7 oz (200 g) strawberry jam

Strawberry Swiss Roll

1. Flip the baked sponge cake onto a piece of parchment paper sprinkled with sugar. Carefully pull off the top layer of parchment paper.

2. Carefully roll up the sponge cake with the paper and let it cool. If it is cooled rolled up, it won't break later when it is rolled again. In the meantime, clean the strawberries and cut them into thin slices.

3. Unroll the sponge cake and spread the strawberry jam over it. Evenly distribute the sliced strawberries over the jam.

4. Next roll up the filled sponge cake using both hands, applying a light pressure to keep any hollow spaces out of the roll. Let the finished roll rest another 15 minutes and then cut it into slices about 1 inch thick. Arrange on a platter and serve with fresh whipped cream, as desired.

■ Rubbing the top sheet of parchment paper with moist paper towels will make it easier to pull it off the top the sponge cake after it is flipped out of the pan.

2
3
4

1⅛ cups (250 g) unsalted butter

2¼ cups (450 g) granulated sugar

¼ cup (50 g) vanilla sugar

4 eggs

2 cups (180 g) unsweetened cocoa

2 cups (250 g) flour

1 tsp baking powder

1 pinch of salt

1½ cups (150 g) ground almonds

Chocolate Brownies

1. Slowly melt the butter in a wide pot. Mix in the granulated sugar and vanilla sugar. Remove from the heat, and stir in the eggs one at a time.

2. Stir the unsweetened cocoa into the butter-sugar mixture using a whisk, then add the sifted flour, baking powder, salt, and the ground almonds, mixing everything evenly.

3. Put the batter in a nonstick pan and smooth the surface. In an oven preheated to 350°F (180°C/Gas Mark 4), bake the brownies for about 35 minutes. Remove the pan from the oven and let it cool. Take the brownies out of the pan and cut them into 1½-inch (4-cm) squares. If possible, serve the brownies warm with a scoop of vanilla ice cream.

■ **For more chocolate flavor, coarsely chop some bittersweet chocolate and stir it into the brownie batter, then bake.**

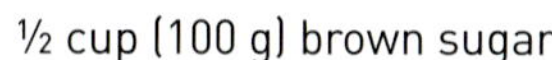
½ cup (100 g) brown sugar 

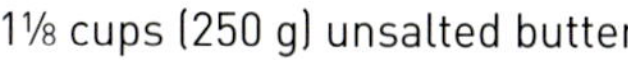
1⅛ cups (250 g) unsalted butter 

2 cups (400 g) granulated sugar 

⅛ cup (30 g) vanilla sugar 

10 oz (280 g) walnuts 

4 eggs

1¾ cups (180 g) unsweetened cocoa powder 

1¾ cups (220 g) flour 

1 tsp baking powder 

1 pinch of salt 

Walnut Caramel Brownies

1. In a wide pot over a medium heat, let the brown sugar caramelize. Then pour in ⅓ cup (100 ml) of cold water to dissolve the caramelized sugar. Add the butter, letting it melt, and remove the pot from the heat. Mix in both sugars. Coarsely chop 7 oz (200 g) of the walnuts and set them aside.

2. Stir in the eggs a little at a time first, then the unsweetened cocoa. With a sifter, sift the flour, baking powder, and salt into the mixture. Evenly mix in the coarsely chopped walnuts.

3. Put the batter in a nonstick pan and smooth the surface. Distribute the remaining walnuts over the surface. In an oven preheated to 350°F (180°C/Gas Mark 4), bake the brownies for about 35 minutes. Remove the pan from the oven and let the brownies cool. Take the brownies out of the pan and cut them into 1½-inch (4-cm) squares. If possible, serve the brownies warm with a scoop of vanilla ice cream and caramel sauce.

■ **Brownies also taste good with a variety of other nuts, such as macadamias, pecans, or Brazil nuts, mixed in—increase the portion of nuts by half again.**

60 

 1½ cups (350 ml) milk

 ½ cup (100 g) unsalted butter

 4 cups (500 g) flour

 2 tbsp active dry yeast

 1 pinch of salt

 ⅛ cup (80 g) granulated sugar

 2 eggs

Yeast Dough

1. Warm the milk and butter until the butter begins to melt. Sift the flour into a bowl and make a depression in the middle. Crumble the yeast into the depression, and then sprinkle the salt and half of the sugar over the yeast. Pour in a quarter of the warm milk and, using a wooden spoon, stir the contents in the depression to make a bread starter. Keep adding in flour from the sides a little at a time. The starter in the middle should have the consistency of pancake batter because this will best let the yeast expand. Cover with a towel and let it rise in a warm place for about 15 minutes.

2. Crack both eggs and add them. Mix in the remaining sugar and warm milk a little at a time, along with the rest of the flour.

3. Punch the dough until it no longer sticks to the bowl and its surface is smooth. This means the flour is worked in well and the dough will rise evenly. Cover the dough with a towel again, and let it rise for 30 minutes. After this rise, the dough can be worked further, for example for a fruit streusel cake.

■ The finished dough can be covered and stored in the refrigerator. This retards the rising of the dough, allowing it to be prepared the night before any further use. However, the dough must be brought back to room temperature and kneaded again before baking.

⅓ cup (50 g) flour, for dusting 

1 portion of yeast dough (see opposite page) 

7 oz (200 g) candied fruit 

⅔ cup (100 g) raisins 

⅓ cup (30 g) dried unsweetened coconut 

⅛ cup (30 g) unsalted butter 

¼ cup (50 g) granulated sugar 

⅞ cup (200 ml) cream 

1 egg 

Candied Fruit Snail Rolls

1. Using a rolling pin, roll out the dough on a flour-coated surface to a thickness of slightly less than ½ inch (1 cm). Cut the candied fruit into roughly ⅛-inch (2-mm) pieces, mix them with the raisins and coconut, then distribute over the dough. Next roll up the dough.

2. Grease a baking dish with the butter and coat with the sugar. Cut the dough roll into 1¼-inch (3-cm) thick slices, and place them side by side in the dish. Cover them with a towel and let rise for 30 minutes.

3. Using a whisk, whip the cream and the egg in a bowl. Pour the mixture over the snail rolls after they have risen. In an oven preheated to 350°F (180°C/ Gas Mark 4), bake for about 35 minutes, until golden brown. Remove, let cool, and serve. Serve with vanilla sauce and whipped cream as desired.

■ **If the dough tears during rolling, simply pull a little dough over the torn area and press it together again using your fingers.**

 ½ cup (100 g) unsalted butter

 1 cup (100 g) confectioners' sugar

 ⅜ cup (80 g) granulated sugar

 ½ tsp salt

 5½ oz (150 g) pecans

 1⅜ cups (175 g) pastry flour

 1 tsp baking powder

 1 egg

 ½ cup (60 g) flour, for dusting

Butter Pecan Cookies

1. Rub the butter into the confectioners' sugar, sugar, and salt with your hands, quickly so the butter doesn't get too warm. Finely grind half the pecans, then coarsely chop the rest.

2. Sift the flour and baking powder over the butter and work in as with Sweet Pie Dough (see p. 702). Mix the nuts into the dough.

3. Next add the egg, and knead everything into a uniform dough. Proceed briskly so the dough doesn't get too soft and sticky.

4. Roll the dough into a 2-inch (5-cm) roll, cover it in clear plastic wrap, and put it in the refrigerator to chill for 1 hour. This makes the dough much easier to work with.

5. Lay a piece of parchment paper on a baking sheet. Cut the dough into ¾-inch (2-cm) slices and spread them out on the baking sheet, leaving a little space between them. In an oven preheated to 350°F (180°C/Gas Mark 4), bake them for about 20 minutes, until golden yellow. Remove the cookies from the oven and let cool. For best results, store them in a sealable container. The cookies taste good with cold milk, fresh coffee, or hot chocolate.

■ **For chocolate chip cookies, work 7 oz (200 g) of coarsely chopped dark or white chocolate and the nuts into the dough. Then bake as directed.**

2
3
4
5

 1 lb 12 oz (800 g) low-fat yogurt

 7/8 cup (200 ml) milk

 3/8 cup (100 ml) cream

 5 eggs

 1 lemon

 1/4 cup (50 g) unsalted butter

 3/8 cup (80 g) vanilla sugar

 3/4 cup (90 g) cornstarch

 1 pinch of salt

 2/3 cup (120 g) granulated sugar

 9 oz (250 g) Sweet Pie Dough (see p. 702)

German Cheesecake

1. Put the yogurt in a bowl and mix it with the milk and cream until smooth. Separate the eggs and put the egg whites in a covered bowl in the refrigerator. Rinse the lemon with hot water, and finely grate the zest. Cut the lemon in half and squeeze the juice into a bowl. Melt the butter in a pot on the stove or in a microwave.

2. Add the egg yolk, melted butter, half the vanilla sugar, lemon juice, lemon zest, and cornstarch to the yogurt mixture, and stir everything with a whisk until smooth.

3. Beat the cold egg whites with the salt and sugar until creamy peaks form, and then fold them into the yogurt mixture.

4. Roll out the dough to a thickness of slightly less than 1/4 inch (5 mm), and place it in a nonstick springform pan. Cut any excess crust from around the edges with a knife. Fill the crust with the cheesecake batter and smooth the surface. Put the pan in an oven preheated to 425°F (220°C/Gas Mark 7). After about 5 minutes remove the cake from the oven. Insert a knife into the skin that develops on top of the cake and make a cut all along the crust. Put the pan back into the oven and bake another 15 minutes. Then take it out again, let the cake sink a little after having risen, and turn the oven down to 325°F (160°C/Gas Mark 3). Then let the cake bake for another 35 minutes.

5. Remove the cake from the oven, let it cool, and take it out of the springform pan. Put in on a cake platter and cut the pieces. Serve it warm with the remaining vanilla sugar sprinkled on top.

■ German cheesecake tastes especially good slightly warm, but it's harder to cut that way—so be careful. Add 1¾ oz (50 g) of rum-soaked raisins to the yogurt batter if desired.

2
3
4
5

 3 eggs

 1¼ cups (250 g) granulated sugar

 1 tbsp vanilla sugar

 ⅜ cup (100 ml) milk

 ½ cup (120 g) unsalted butter

 2¼ cups (280 g) flour

 2 tsp baking powder

 1 pinch of salt

 1 tsp cornstarch

 7 oz (200 g) red currants

 7 oz (200 g) blueberries

Red Currant and Blueberry Meringue Cake

1. Separate the eggs. Beat the egg yolks with ¾ cup (150 g) of the granulated sugar and the vanilla sugar in a mixing bowl, until peaks form. Put the egg whites in a bowl in the refrigerator. Bring the milk and ½ cup (100 g) butter to a boil, pour it into the sugar-egg mixture, and stir well.

2. Sift 2 cups (250 g) flour and the baking powder into the bowl and mix everything into a batter.

3. Grease an 11-inch (28-cm) springform pan with butter and coat with the remaining flour. Then fill with the batter and, in an oven preheated to 350°F (180°C/Gas Mark 4), bake for about 18 minutes. Remove the cake from the oven and let it cool a bit.

4. Using a mixer, beat the egg whites, a pinch of salt, and the remaining sugar until creamy. Add the cornstarch and beat on the highest setting for 1 minute, until stiff peaks form. Remove any damaged berries, hold back 1 tbsp of each fruit, and mix the remainder carefully into the egg whites. This makes a fruity meringue.

5. Spread the meringue over the baked bottom.

6. Sprinkle the remaining berries over the meringue. Set the oven to 425°F (220°C/Gas Mark 7). Place the cake on the middle rack and bake it again for about 15 minutes. Remove the pan from the oven and let it cool. Finally, cut it into pieces.

■ After the cake bottom has cooled, spread 1¼-inch (3-cm) thick layers of vanilla and chocolate ice cream over it. Cover with the meringue and bake for 5 minutes at 480°F (250°C/Gas Mark 10). Remove it from the oven and serve immediately. This makes an especially delicious and festive dessert.

2
3
4
5
6

 2 cups (250 g) rye flour

 4 cups (500 g) all-purpose flour

 2⅞ cups (650 ml) lukewarm water

 1 tsp sea salt

 1 tbsp active dry yeast

 1 tsp granulated sugar

 4 tsp (20 g) unsalted butter

 1 tbsp oil

 ⅓ cup (50 g) flour, for dusting

1

Homemade Bread with Sea Salt

1. Sift 1⅛ cups (150 g) of rye flour and 1⅛ cups (150 g) of all-purpose flour into a bowl. Stir in 2¼ cups (500 ml) of lukewarm water and the sea salt, then let the dough sit for 1 hour.

2. Stir the yeast and the sugar in ⅜ cup (100 ml) of lukewarm water, then let it proof for 15 minutes.

3. Add the yeast mixture, the room-temperature butter, and the oil to the dough, and mix everything together.

4. Add the remaining all-purpose and rye flours a little at a time, and mix everything into a smooth dough. In a stand mixer fitted with a dough hook, knead the dough for 5 minutes.

5. Cover it with a towel and let it rise for at least 1 hour.

6. Place the dough on a floured surface, shape into a long loaf, and lay it on a baking sheet. Sprinkle more flour over it, cover it with a towel, and let it rise for 15 minutes.

7. Using a knife, slash the top of the loaf several times. Bake it in an oven preheated to 410°F (210°C/Gas Mark 6½) for about 50 minutes. Remove the bread from the oven and let it cool. Slice the bread and spread butter on it.

+ 2¾ hours rising time

■ **For a beautiful crust, pour an espresso cupful of water on the hot oven floor, and then quickly close the oven again.**

2
3
4
5
6
7

4 cups (500 g) whole-wheat flour

2 tbsp active dry yeast

1 tsp granulated sugar

½ tsp salt

⅓ cup (80 g) unsalted butter

1⅓ cups (300 ml) lukewarm water

3½ oz (100 g) poppy seeds

Sunday Rolls with Poppy Seeds

1. Sift the flour into a bowl and make a depression in the middle. Crumble the yeast into it, add the sugar and salt, then with the butter and ⅜ cup (100 ml) of lukewarm water, stir it to form a bread starter (see p. 712). Cover with a towel, and let it rise for 15 minutes. Stir the remaining water into the dough and then, in a stand mixer fitted with a dough hook, knead the dough for 5 minutes. Cover with a towel again, and let it rise in a warm place for 30 minutes.

2. Roll out the dough on a floured surface and cut it into 1¾-oz (50-g) pieces.

3. Knead each piece once, from the outside inward.

4. Form each into a round roll, tucking the top of the dough under the bottom to form a taut "skin."

5. Brush a little water over the tops and roll them in the poppy seeds.

6. Put the rolls on a baking sheet lined with parchment paper, and cut crosses into the tops with scissors. Then cover the rolls with a towel and let them rise for another 20 minutes. Next, put them on the middle rack in an oven preheated to 425°F (220°C/Gas Mark 7). Pour an espresso cupful of water into the oven. The steam makes the rolls crisp. Bake the Sunday rolls for about 20 minutes or until golden. Then remove them from the oven and serve warm.

Makes 18 rolls.

+ 65 minutes rising time

■ Round off the Sunday roll tops with different ingredients as desired—for example, with chopped pistachios, sunflower seeds, sesame seeds, green pumpkin seeds, chopped hazelnuts, or walnuts.

2
3
4
5
6

4 cups (500 g) pastry flour

2 tsp active dry yeast

1 tsp salt

1 egg

2 tbsp olive oil

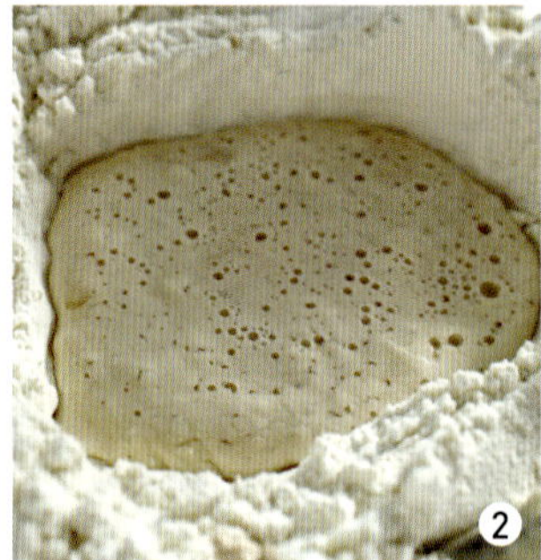

Pizza Dough

1. Pile the flour on a work surface and make a depression in the middle. Put the crumbled yeast in it, then pour in 1⅛ cup (250 ml) of lukewarm water and add 1 tsp salt. Using a fork, stir to form a bread starter, and then let it rise for 15 minutes.

2. The starter has risen properly when bubbles form on the surface and it has doubled in size.

3. Next add the egg and 2 tablespoons of olive oil to the bread starter.

4. Stir to combine with a fork.

5. Use your hands to work the dough. Add lukewarm water a little at a time.

6. Add enough water so that all the flour is taken up and the dough can be kneaded.

7. Work the dough with the backs of your hands and then knead thoroughly. The pizza dough becomes elastic this way and will roll out better later.

8. Cover the dough with a towel and let it rise for 30 minutes.

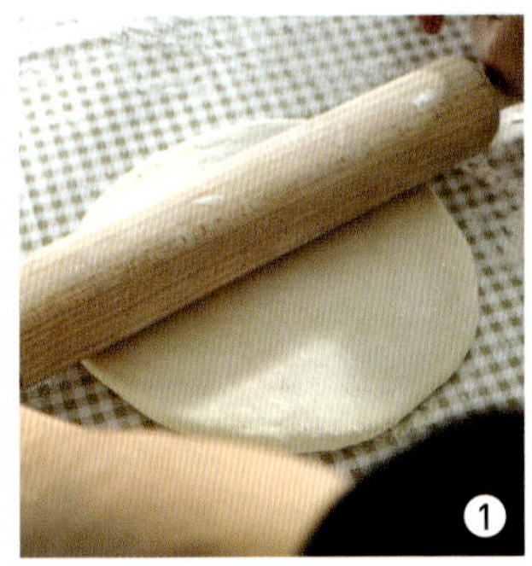

1 lb 12 oz (800 g) pizza dough 

7 oz (200 g) spinach leaves 

1 tsp salt 

$1\frac{3}{4}$ cups (400 ml) tomato sauce (see p. 144) 

3 tomatoes 

1 red onion 

2 balls of mozzarella 

4 tbsp cold-pressed olive oil 

1 tsp dried oregano

Vegetable Pizza

1. Cut the pizza dough into quarters and roll each out. Put the rolled-out pizza dough on a baking sheet lined with parchment paper. Briefly let the spinach leaves wilt in boiling water, shake them out in a sieve, and cool them off under cold running water. Thoroughly squeeze out the spinach and coarsely chop it.

2. On the pizza crusts, spread the tomato sauce first, and then distribute the spinach leaves. Remove the stems from the tomatoes and cut them into $\frac{1}{8}$-in (3-mm) slices. Peel the red onion and cut it into thin rings. Cut the mozzarella balls into $\frac{1}{8}$-in (3-mm) slices.

3. Lay these ingredients flat on the pizzas. Meanwhile, preheat the oven to 450°F (230°C/Gas Mark 8). Drizzle each layered pizza with olive oil and sprinkle it with oregano. Bake for about 12 minutes in the oven. Remove them from the oven, divide them among plates, and serve. The entire pizza dough can also be spread over the baking sheet if the oven is too small for multiple pizzas. Cut this sheet pizza into rectangles and serve.

■ **Pizza can be topped to your taste: with ham, anchovies, banana peppers, olives, antipasto vegetables, Bolognese sauce, different cheeses, and more. Sprinkle grated cheese directly over the tomato sauce before putting on the remaining ingredients.**

 4 cups (500 g) pastry flour

 1⅛ cups (250 ml) lukewarm water

 1 pinch of salt

 1 tbsp active dry yeast

 1½ oz (40 g) dried porcini mushrooms

 1 egg

 3 tbsp (50 ml) extra virgin olive oil

 7 oz (200 g) dried apricots

 2 tbsp apple cider vinegar

 1 tbsp vegetable oil

 1 sprig fresh rosemary

 10 bay leaves

 1 tsp coarse, purified sea salt

 3 tbsp honey

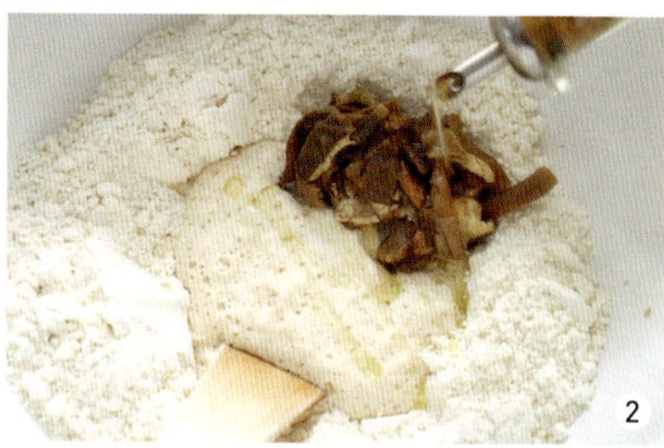

Rosemary Focaccia with Porcini Mushrooms and Apricots

1. Sift the flour into a large bowl and make a depression in the middle. Add 3 tbsp (50 ml) of lukewarm water and salt, crumble the yeast into it, and stir to form a bread starter. Mix the yeast with the water and as much flour as needed to make a fluid batter. Cover it with a towel and let it rise for 15 minutes. In the meantime, cover the porcini mushrooms with cold water and soak them.

2. Add the egg, the soaked, drained, and coarsely chopped porcini mushrooms, and the olive oil to the bread starter. Next work in the remaining water a little at a time and beat the dough until it is elastic and forms bubbles.

3. Then shape the dough into a ball, sprinkle with flour, cover it with a towel, and let it stand for 30 minutes. In the meantime, add the dried apricots to a bowl and pour the vinegar over them. Cover and let them marinate.

4. Meanwhile, the dough should have risen and tripled in size.

5. Thoroughly stir the dough with a wooden spoon, then cover it with a towel and let it rise again for 20 minutes.

6. The dough is ready when it doubles in size.

+ 80 minutes rising time

■ **This focaccia can be baked with fresh tomatoes, oregano, black olives, and feta cheese on top, or as is.**

7. Put the dough on a baking sheet greased with vegetable oil, and spread it out to the edges with both hands.

8. Remove the rosemary needles from their stems and sprinkle them over the dough. Press the marinated apricots and bay leaves lightly into the dough and sprinkle with the coarse sea salt. Lastly, drizzle with the honey.

9. Let the finished dough rise for another 15 minutes. In an oven preheated to 350°F (180°C/Gas Mark 4), bake the dough for about 35 minutes. Remove and let it cool on the baking sheet. Finally, cut into pieces and serve.

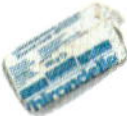 2 tbsp active dry yeast

 1 tbsp (20 g) honey

 3⅛ cups (700 ml) lukewarm water

 3 medium onions

 3 tbsp olive oil

 4½ oz (120 g) sourdough starter (see box)

 2 lb 10 oz (1.2 kg) all-purpose flour

 ¼ cup (40 g) cornmeal

 1¾ oz (50 g) pitted black olives

 1 tsp salt

Mini Baguettes with Olives and Onion

1. Dissolve the yeast and honey in lukewarm water and let stand for 10 minutes. Peel the onions, cut them in half, and slice them. Brown them slowly in a pan with olive oil and then let them cool a little.

2. Put the sourdough, the sifted flour, the cornmeal, the coarsely chopped olives, the onions, and the salt in a bowl.

3. Pour in the yeast-honey mix and work the dough with a wooden spoon until bubbles form. Using a stand mixer fitted with a dough hook, knead the dough for about 5 minutes.

4. Cover the dough with a towel, and let it rise for 30 minutes in a warm place.

5. Taking the dough from the bowl, put it on a flour-coated surface, and knead it vigorously. Then divide it into 2½-oz (70-g) pieces, roll them into balls, and sprinkle them with flour.

6. Next roll the balls of dough with both hands into little wands with tapered ends and then put them on a baking sheet lined with parchment paper. Brush them with water, and let rise for another 30 minutes.

+ 65 minutes rising time

■ **A sourdough starter can easily be made by doing the following: take ⅓ cup (60 g) whole-wheat flour and mix it with 4 tbsp (60 ml) water. Cover the dough with clear plastic wrap and let it ferment at room temperature for 24 hours.**

7. Sprinkle the mini baguettes with flour and, using a knife, lightly cut diagonal lines into them. Put them in an oven preheated to 450°F (230°C/Gas Mark 8), pour a little water on the oven floor, and immediately close the door. While the steam rises, the bread rises again and becomes crisp. Bake the mini baguettes for about 25 minutes. Remove and let them cool on a rack. Serve them with a hearty spread, or dip them in herbed yogurt.

 1¼ cups (200 g) cornmeal

 1 tsp salt

 ⅞ cup (200 ml) boiling water

 2 tbsp active dry yeast

 1 pinch of granulated sugar

 ⅞ cup (200 ml) lukewarm water

 2 tbsp olive oil

 ⅛ cup (30 g) unsalted butter

 2 cups (250 g) flour

 2¾ oz (80 g) medium-hot green chili peppers

Mexican Corn Bread with Green Chili Peppers

1. Stir the cornmeal, salt, and the boiling water together and let it sit for 10 minutes to soften the cornmeal.

2. Pour the lukewarm water over the yeast and add the sugar. Crush the yeast with a wooden spoon until it has completely dissolved.

3. Add the yeast mix, the oil, 1 tbsp (15 g) of the butter, the flour, and the ½-inch (1-cm) diced green chili peppers to the cornmeal preparation.

4. Next, mix everything with a wooden spoon and beat the dough vigorously until bubbles form.

5. Grease a loaf pan with the remaining butter and coat with a little cornmeal. Fill the pan with the dough, cover, and let it rise in a warm place for 30 minutes. Bake for about 45 minutes in an oven set to 375°F (190°C/Gas Mark 5). Let it cool for 20 minutes and remove it from the pan. The corn bread tastes best served warm with fresh butter.

+ 40 minutes rising time

■ **Green jalapeños, black olives, or diced, hot salami can also be mixed in.**

2
3
4
5

Cheese

Contents

734 Where Does Cheese Come From?
736 Cheese Categories
738 The Cheeseboard
742 Cheese Fondue

Where Does Cheese Come From?

Cheese is one of the oldest foods made by human beings. Researchers would have us believe that it already existed in Neolithic times, at the end of the fifth and the beginning of the fourth century BC. The Code of the Babylonian King Hammurabi mentions cheese, bread, and beer as early as 1750 BC. The Romans discovered tasty varieties of cheese in Gaul (France), which were in great demand in Rome, "if they survived the trip." The more detailed the historical chronicles were for an era, the more extensively the historians also wrote stories on cheese.

Actual cheese production is simple: warm unpasteurised milk curdles on its own. If you let the whey, which mainly consists of water, drain off, you will be left with cheese, even if it is only a very sour cream cheese. The milk will curdle more dependably if you add rennet—a natural substance, which is found not only in the stomachs of calves, sheep, and other mammals, but also in many plants. It was known to shepherds and nomads who often stored their milk in pouches made from the stomachs of goats or sheep, whose natural rennet accelerated cheese production. Cheese was not just produced for reasons of taste: large quantities of milk could be be preserved quickly as cheese.

Of course, cheese was always made from the milk that was available at the time. We still see cheese made from the milk of cows, sheep, and goats on our menus today. The milk of water buffalo is traditionally used to make Italian mozzarella, even though a lot of mozzarella is made from cow's milk today.

A Finnish cheese called *Ilves* is traditionally made from reindeer milk. In Jordan, herdsmen use the milk of sheep, goats, cows, and camels for their *labaneh* (yogurt cheese).

Cheese is still produced today using the same basic principles: letting the milk curdle first, removing the whey, and then salting, washing, and finally aging the cheese.

Proper storage and aging of the cheese are important. Only fresh cheese needs practically no time to mature. Depending on the type, cheese can be stored for many years. Such is the case of Parmesan, which is dried and grated over various dishes, and which requires ample time to mature.

Cheese Categories

Fresh cheese: For this kind of cheese, rennet is usually simply stirred into the milk and allowed to stand. Fresh cheese has a high moisture content and is not pressed, but salt is rubbed onto or into it. It is mild and has a milky taste.

Pressed cheese that is not reheated: Also known as "semifirm cheese." This category includes Pecorino Romano, Edam, Gouda, Reblochon, Cheddar, and Cantal, among others.

The curds are skimmed off, crushed, and put into molds. The whey is pressed out. The "raw cheese" is then removed from the mold and put into a salt bath. While it is ripening, it is regularly salted, turned, and brushed. The brushing process imparts an even color to the rind.

Pressed cheese that is reheated: This category includes Gruyère, Emmental, Parmesan, Comté, and Beaufort. They are traditionally made with "evening milk" (milk which is taken from the cow in the evening) that is left to rest overnight and then mixed with morning milk on the following day. Rennet is added to the cheese at 91°F (33°C) and then the mixture is heated up to 127°F (53°C; this process is also called cooking). The season is also important. Cheese made with "summer milk," when cows are eating grass and wild herbs in mountain pastures, is more flavorful than "winter milk" cheese, which comes from animals that are fed with hay.

Cheese with edible mold: Camembert, Brillat-Savarin, and Brie de Meaux are examples of this category. They are neither pressed nor cooked, but salted after thickening, and sprayed with *Penicillium candidum*. This allows the fine, furlike growth of mold to sprout on these cheese varieties.

Cheese with a washed rind: Cheeses such as Époisses, Maroilles, Livarot, Münster, Remoudou, Langres, and Limburger have a strong smell, but they range from surprisingly mild to hearty in taste. This type of cheese is washed regularly with a weak saline solution and turned over.

Cheese with a natural rind: These include Chabichou de Poitou, Saint-Maure de Touraine, and Crottin de Chavignol, and other sheep and goat cheese from the Loire Valley, Spain, or Italy. First of all, the milk is heated to 86°F (30°C), then the curd is cut and ladled into containers.

Blue cheese: Examples are Stilton, Gorgonzola, Fourme d'Ambert, and Roquefort.

Most varieties of blue cheese are produced from cow's milk. The most prominent representative of this category is among the exceptions: sheep's milk is used to make Roquefort, France's first cheese to receive an AOC (controlled denomination of origin). To begin with, rennet for blue cheese is added to milk at temperatures of around 86°F (30°C). Later on, the curds are poured into a mold that is lined with cloth. Even after the cheese leaves the mold, it remains in the cloth initially and is turned regularly to let the whey drain. The wheel is salted and injected with *Penicillium roqueforti* or *Penicillium gorgonzola*.

Processed cheese: The Swiss sapsago variety falls into this category, for instance.

It is created by melting down pressed cheese. Butter, cream, milk, and often flavoring agents are added.

Raw milk cheese: This is made from unpasteurized milk and in this process the taste is better preserved. For example, a raw milk cheese can taste different in the summertime than it does in winter, because cows also eat different food, depending on the season. Due to long maturing times and a lot of manual work, such as washing the cheese with marc (brandy distilled from grape skins and seeds), delicacies like this are also substantially more expensive than cheese made from pasteurized milk. If you are lucky, you'll find them on the cheese trolleys of better restaurants or in specialty cheese stores.

The United States completely prohibits the import of raw milk cheese. One reason for prohibitions of this kind is hygiene regulations. By means of pasteurization, whereby milk is rapidly heated up to 194°F (90°C), harmful germs such as malignant listeriosis bacteria, which also lurk in sausage, raw ground meat, or smoked fish, are effectively killed. Getting sick from cheese can be serious, and the legal requirements for raw milk cheese are strict: animals must not have any diseases that are transferable by means of milk, and the germ content must not exceed a specific limit. Last but not least, even in small, artisanal, working cheese dairies, all procedures must be hygienic. Dim, mold-covered cellars have been replaced by stainless steel, and computers monitor the temperature and air humidity.

Storing cheese properly: Cheese is always palatable and appetizing if it is served under a glass dome, and this sight is also sure to please your guests. However, strictly speaking, a cheese dome is nothing other than expensive fly protection. It originates from times when cheese was stored in cool cellars. Cheese would still be well cared for today under a cheese dome, provided the cellar is not overheated. Most cheese varieties will do well at temperatures of 46–50°F (8–10°C) and with 80–90 percent air humidity. Modern cheese makers have sophisticated aging cellars where the air humidity and temperature are strictly monitored.

At home, you can confidently store cheese in the vegetable compartment of your refrigerator, provided you remember to take it out at the right time before eating it. Cold cheese doesn't develop its full flavor and, for discerning palates, it is as interesting as cold coffee.

Seals of quality: DOC, DO, and AOC? Like good wine, good cheese also has its designations of origin. This guarantees that the cheese was produced using traditional methods.

It is very important to make sure that your cheese actually did receive the seal of quality. A name such as Camembert or Gorgonzola alone has not stood for traditional production for a long time. Many cheese names are not legally protected. The supposedly original cheese can be produced quite legally in any country.

Distinctions

AOC (Appellation d'Origine Contrôlée): Guaranteed Origin Appelation, France.
Label Rouge: Red label, France.
DOC (Denominazione di Origine Controllata): Guaranteed Origin Appelation, Italy.
DO (Denominación de Origen): Guaranteed Origin Appelation, Spain.

British Cheese Awards: No regulation of the origin or source of the cheese, but a kind of "taste Olympics" for cheese dairies and producers in the "fresh cheese," "soft cheese," and "blue cheese" sectors, etc. The very best cheeses are awarded the title of "Supreme Champion."

PDO and PGI: These are distinctions awarded on the European level, on the model of the French AOC. The Protected Designation of Origin (PDO) and the Protected Geographical Indication (PGI) indicate that the product must be produced, processed, and manufactured in a specific geographical area in accordance with a recognized, stipulated process.

The Cheeseboard

You start with the mildest cheese and end with the most pungent one. That is the one cardinal rule for cheeseboards. Many good restaurants offer an assortment of cheeses made from the milk of sheep, goats, and cows at various stages of ripeness and of different colors and shapes. Blue cheese, rolled in ashes, for example, golden yellow and pale white cheeses, maybe a good ripe Époisses, which is "spooned" onto the plate (possibly accompanied by grapes, walnuts, and figs), and the most varied types of bread.

Alternatively, you can train your taste in cheese by tasting only one variety, such as Comté, at various stages of ripeness.

Of course, you should note that raw milk cheese will not taste the same throughout the whole year.

What Can You Drink with Cheese?

"Only red wine goes with cheese" is the common wisdom. It is often a stopgap solution born from the fact that some red wine is left over from the main course and so is then served with the cheese. Of course, red wine often goes well with cheese, but unfortunately the wine gets the short end of the stick in many partnerships. Great wines are overwhelmed by the taste of strong cheeses and tasty lightweight wines do not go well with spicy cheese flavors. In general, wine and cheese do not complement each other but are often competitors. In many cases, white wines are an interesting, tasty alternative.

The typical beverages of a region are often very good partners for local cheese varieties. Both have tolerated each other for centuries, sometimes very happily and sometimes only out of necessity. Why not try drinking cider with a cheese from Normandy, beer with a German or Belgian cheese, and red or white wine with Italian and French cheese?

In addition, there are other classic combinations where you can't go wrong. For blue cheese, something "sweet" is always a good choice. A good Port with Stilton or a Sauternes with Roquefort is always delectable.

Some cheeses

Allgäuer Emmentaler (Allgäu Emmental)

Germany · cow's milk
Maturing time: 3–4 months
Use: As a snack, for breakfast, as a cheese course, or as a topping for gratins, sauces, and salads
Fat content: Approximately 45 %
Weight: 88–198 lb (40–90 kg)
Shape: Wheel shaped
Goes well with: Beer

Appenzeller (1)

Switzerland · cow's milk
Maturing time: 3–4 months
Special feature: A herbal brine, which is a liquid made with salt, pepper, white wine, and various spices, is rubbed onto it.
Use: As a cheese course or snack
Fat content: 45 %
Weight: 13 lb 4 oz–17 lb 10 oz (6–8 kg)
Shape: Wheel shaped

Ardi Gasna

France · sheep's milk
Special feature: Also sold under the names Ossau, Iraty, Brebis, Pyrénées.
Use: As a snack or as a dessert with cherry jam
Fat content: Approximately 50 %
Weight: 6 lb 10 oz–11 lb (3–5 kg)
Shape: Wheel shaped
Goes well with: An Irouléguy wine

2

3

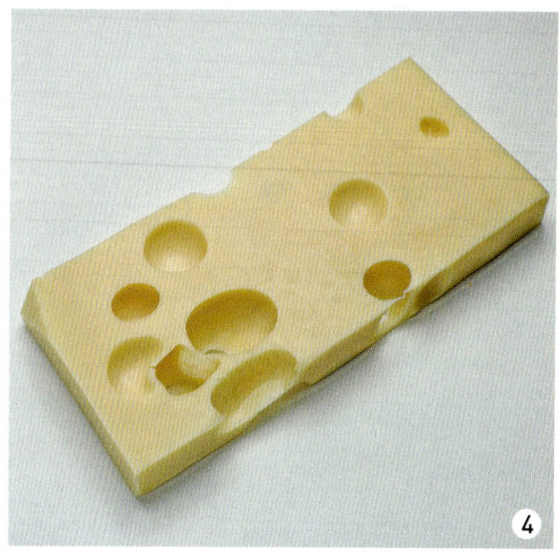
4

Banon

France · various kinds of milk
Special feature: Cow's milk Banon is wrapped in chestnut leaves and bound with raffia. If Banon is rolled in summer savory, it is called "pebre d'ai."
Use: As a cheese course. It is put into a carefully sealed container with Schnapps, cloves, bay leaves, pepper, salt, and thyme, and eaten at Christmas or New Year.
Fat content: Approximately 50 %
Weight: 3½ oz (100 g)
Shape: A disk wrapped in chestnut leaves
Goes well with: A red wine from Provence

Brie

France · cow's milk
Maturing time: At least 1 month
Use: As a cheese course, for Brie croquettes
Fat content: 45 % and higher
Weight: 2 lb 10 oz (1.2 kg) for Brie de Coulommiers, 4 lb 8 oz–6 lb 8 oz (2–3 kg) for Brie de Meaux, 3 lb 5 oz (1.5 kg) or more for Brie de Melun
Shape: Wheel shaped
Goes well with: A Pommard or a Pomerol

Cabrales

Spain · cow's, sheep's, and goat's milk blue cheese
Maturing time: 3 months in limestone caves
Use: As a cheese course
Fat content: Variable
Weight: 5 lb 8 oz–6 lb 8 oz (2.5–3 kg)
Shape: Cylindrical
Goes well with: A robust red wine

Camembert (2)

France · cow's milk
Maturing time: 12 days
Special feature: Experts always perform the softness test by pressing the cheese between their thumb and hand, on the outside—never on the middle—of the cheese. Camembert cheese actually ripens from the outside in. Always store Camembert cheese in a cool place, but not in the refrigerator.
Use: As a cheese course and for Camembert cheese croquettes
Fat content: 45 % and higher
Weight: 9 oz (250 g)
Shape: Disk shaped

Cheddar (3)

England · cow's milk
Maturing time: 6–24 months
Special feature: The name cheddar is not protected, so it can be produced all over the world.
Use: For breakfast and salads, as a topping for gratins, or as a cheese course
Fat content: 45–50 %
Weight: 55–77 lb (25–35 kg)
Shape: Cylindrical

Edam

Holland · cow's milk
Maturing time: 2–3 months for the young version and 12–18 months for ripened Edam cheese
Use: Melted for breakfast, as a cheese course, or a snack
Fat content: 30–48 %
Weight: 3 lb 5 oz (1.5 kg)
Shape: A wax-covered sphere
Goes well with: Beer or a robust red wine

Emmental (4)

Switzerland · cow's milk
Maturing time: 8–10 months
Use: As a cheese course, a snack, for melting, as a topping for gratins, and for salads
Fat content: 45 % and higher
Weight: 176–287 lb (80–130 kg)
Shape: Wheel shaped with a rounded edge
Goes well with: A rather fruity Swiss white wine

Époisses

France · cow's milk
Maturing time: 2–3 months, or 30–40 days if it is washed in Marc de Bourgogne (brandy distilled from crushed grape skins and seeds)
Special feature: The optimal stage of ripeness is attained when the reddish brown rind almost collapses in the center.
Use: As a cheese course
Fat content: 50 %
Weight: 9–10½ oz (250–300 g)
Shape: Disk shaped
Goes well with: A robust red Burgundy wine

Feta

Greece · originally sheep's milk
Maturing time: at least 1 month in brine
Special feature: If you don't like the taste of salt, you can immerse it in water for a couple of minutes.
Use: Traditionally for a Greek salad, as a snack, or as a topping for gratins
Fat content: 40–50 %
Weight: Variable
Shape: Variable, from cubes to blocks

5

6

7

Gorgonzola (5)

Italy · cow's milk
Maturing time: 2–4 months
Use: As a cheese course and for salads and pasta
Fat content: 48 %
Weight: 13 lb 3½ oz–26 lb 7 oz (6–12 kg)
Shape: Drum shaped

Gouda (6)

Holland · cow's milk
Maturing time: 2–3 months for the young cheese, 6 months for the middle-aged variant, and 12 months, at least, for the mature one
Use: For breakfast, as an intermediate course, or a cheese course
Fat content: 40–48 %
Weight: 6 lb 8 oz–22 lb (3–10 kg)
Shape: Wheel shaped with rounded edges
Goes well with: Beer

Gruyère (7)

Switzerland · cow's milk
Maturing time: 4–8 months
Special feature: It is only produced from June to September. 106 gallons (400 liters) of milk produce 77 lb (35 kg) of cheese.
Use: As a cheese course or for fondue
Fat content: 45–46 %
Weight: 44–99 lb (20–45 kg)
Shape: Wheel shaped

Idiazabal

Spain · sheep's milk
Maturing time: 1–2 months
Special feature: It is smoked over a hawthorn and beechwood fire.
Use: As a cheese course, snack, or for grating
Fat content: 45–55 %
Weight: 2 lb 4 oz–4 lb 8 oz (1–2 kg)
Shape: Cylindrical
Goes well with: A Rioja wine

Jarlsberg

Norway · cow's milk
Use: As a cheese course or as a topping for gratins
Fat content: Approximately 45 %
Weight: 22 lb (10 kg)
Shape: Wheel shaped

Limburger

Germany · cow's milk
Maturing time: 2–3 months
Use: As a cheese course or snack
Fat content: 40 % and higher
Weight: 7 oz–1 lb 10 oz (200–750 g)
Shape: Bar shaped

Manchego

Spain · sheep's milk
Maturing time: 9–12 months for the "viejo" (aged) version and 2–3 months for the "curado" (cured) version
Use: As a cheese course or snack, or use the aged version for grating
Fat content: 57 %
Weight: 4 lb 8 oz–7 lb 11 oz (2–3.5 kg)
Shape: Cylindrical

Mascarpone (8)

Italy · cow's milk
Special feature: Mascarpone is produced by skimming off cream from the milk used for Parmesan production and adding lactic acid bacteria to it.
Use: For desserts or for baking
Fat content: 70 % and higher
Weight: Variable
Shape: Variable

Mozzarella

Italy · cow's milk, buffalo milk
Maturing time: 1–3 days
Special feature: Authentic mozzarella is elastic, not hard like the white pizza chunks that you often find in stores.
Use: As a topping for gratins and pizza, or in salads
Fat content: 45 % when made from cow's milk, 50 % from buffalo milk
Weight: Variable
Shape: Variable

Münster

France · cow's milk
Maturing time: 3 months
Special feature: It is washed every 2 days with lightly salted water or Marc de Bourgogne (brandy distilled from crushed grape skins and seeds).
Use: As a cheese course or snack
Fat content: 45 % and higher
Weight: 4½ oz–13 lb 4 oz (120 g–6 kg)
Shape: Round
Goes well with: Gewürztraminer wine

8

9

10

Parmesan (9)

Italy · cow's milk
Maturing time: At least 1 year for the "vecchio" (aged) version , at least 3 years for the "stravecchio" (extra-aged) version
Use: As a cheese course and for grating
Fat content: 32 %
Weight: 53–88 lb (24–40 kg)
Shape: Cylindrical with a rounded edge

Pecorino

Italy · sheep's milk
Pecorino Romano
Maturing time: 8–12 months

Pecorino Sardo
Maturing time: 20–60 days of storage for the young, sweet kind, known as "dolce," or 12 months and more for the well-ripened "maturo" (aged) kind
Use: For pasta dishes or as a topping for gratins

Pecorino Toscano
Maturing time: 6 months for the "crosta nero" (the kind with the black rind)
Use: As a cheese course, for salads and for grating
Fat content: 36–40 %
Weight: Variable
Shape: Cylindrical

Ricotta

Italy · cow's milk, occasionally sheep's milk, or goat's milk as well
Maturing time: 1–5 days
Use: For desserts, ravioli, and lasagna
Fat content: 20–30 %
Weight: Variable
Shape: Variable

Roquefort (10)

France · sheep's milk
Maturing time: 3 months and longer
Special feature: It ripens in the damp caves of Cambalou. Traditionally, loaves of rye bread are laid out and allowed to mold. The bloom is then dried and added to the cheese.
Use: As a cheese course, for salads, and for pasta dishes
Fat content: 52 % and higher
Weight: 5 lb 8 oz–6 lb 6 oz (2.5–2.9 kg)
Shape: Cylindrical
Goes well with: Sweet wines, such as Sauternes

Saint-Marcellin

France · cow's milk
Maturing time: 4–6 weeks
Use: As a cheese course
Fat content: 40–50 %
Weight: 2¾ oz (80 g)
Shape: Disk-shaped

Saint-Nectaire

France · cow's milk
Special feature: An individually crafted farmer cheese that is identified by an oval, green label. By contrast, the label of the dairy Saint-Nectaire, which is produced in cooperatives and cheese factories, is square.
Use: As a cheese course or snack
Fat content: 45 %
Weight: 3 lb 5 oz (1.5 kg)
Shape: Wheel shaped

Serra da Estrela

Portugal · sheep's milk
Maturing time: 1–4 months
Special feature: It is a "vegetarian cheese." Its rennet comes from the blossoms and leaves of one of the thistles growing in Portugal.
Use: As a cheese course or snack
Fat content: 45–50 %

Stilton

England · cow's milk
Maturing time: 6–12 months
Special feature: Stilton should not be confused with white Stilton. The latter has no blue mold at all and has a neutral taste.
Use: As a cheese course
Fat content: 48–55 %
Weight: 4 lb 8 oz–17 lb 10 oz (2–8 kg)
Shape: Drum shaped
Goes well with: Port wine

Tête de Moine

Switzerland · cow's milk
Maturing time: 2–3 months
Use: As a cheese course or snack
Fat content: 50 %
Weight: 1 lb 9 oz–4 lb 8 oz (700 g–2 kg)
Shape: Drum shaped

7 oz (200 g) Gruyère cheese

7 oz (200 g) Appenzeller cheese

12 oz (350 g) Swiss cheese

1⅛ cups (250 ml) white wine

1 garlic clove

1 pinch of nutmeg, freshly grated

1 dash of black pepper

⅔ oz (20 g) cornstarch

Cheese Fondue

1. Cut the rind off the Gruyère, the Appenzeller, and the Swiss cheeses, and grate them coarsely.

2. Put the white wine, the peeled garlic clove, and the nutmeg into a saucepan and bring the mixture to a boil.

3. Add all of the grated cheeses and season it with freshly ground black pepper.

4. Stir the mixture constantly with a wire whisk, until the cheese combines with the liquid and melts.

5. Stir the cornstarch into 3 tbsp of water until no lumps remain and pour this mixture slowly into the hot cheese fondue, stirring it constantly.

6. Let it come to a boil again until the cornstarch thickens the cheese fondue. Pour the mixture into a cheese fondue pot and serve it with a generous amount of white bread, small unpeeled boiled potatoes, pickled vegetables, and fresh black pepper.

■ At the end, mix 3 tbsp (40 ml) of kirsch (cherry brandy) into the cheese fondue or serve the kirsch in chilled glasses as an accompaniment to the fondue. The cheese fondue will have a more intense flavor if the grated cheese rind is also included. The rind will dissolve when cooking and will add a spicy, pungent character to the dish.

2
3
4
5
6

Wine

Contents

746 The Most Famous Wine-Growing Regions
748 Grape Varieties
749 Wine Production
750 Champagne
752 Sweet Wines
754 What Is on the Label?
756 Enjoying Wine
758 Buying and Storing Wine
758 Glossary

The Most Famous Wine-Growing Regions

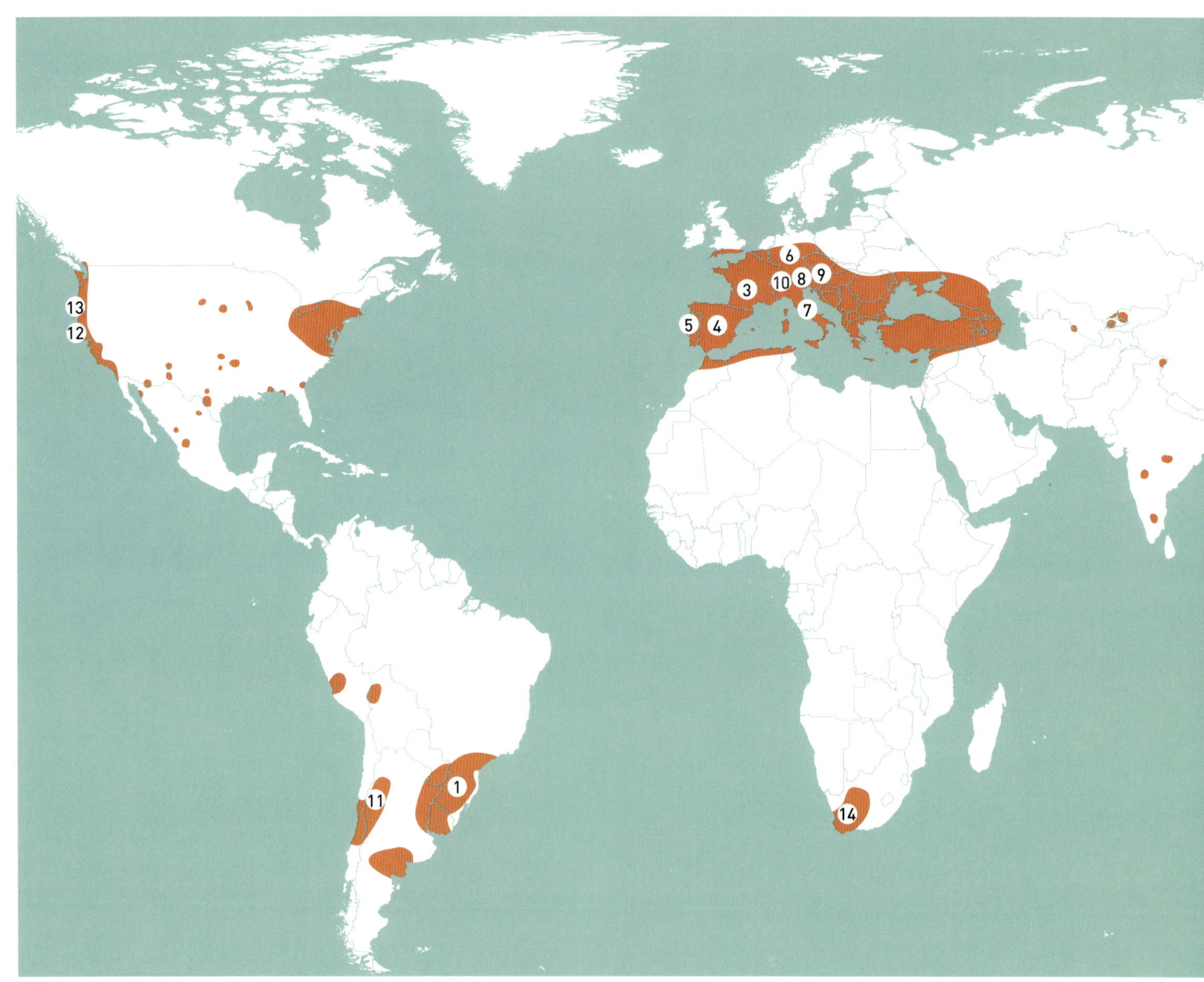

Argentina (1): This emerging wine-growing country is particularly famous for its cultivation of the Malbec grape. Spanish conquerors introduced vines into the southern hemisphere in the middle of the sixteenth century. Today, the region of Mendoza, with a good 900 vintners on more than 57,000 sq miles (148,000 sq kilometers) is responsible for over 80 percent of the wine production in the country.

Australia (2): Riesling (Rhine Riesling), Shiraz, Cabernet, and Chardonnay are cultivated there. Among others, the wines of the area around Adelaide and the Barossa Valley are famous.

France, Beaujolais (3): This region is famous for light wines. Nowadays, approximately one-third of the production of the Beaujolais vineyards is dedicated to meeting the demand for Beaujolais Nouveau. Of the 89,000 acres (36,000 hectares) that are planted with Gamay grapes, 56,000 (22,500) are in the Beaujolais region. Approximately 38 million Beaujolais Nouveau bottles are produced per year.

France, Bordeaux (3): Arguably the most famous wine-growing region in the world. The northerly Bordeaux region produces Médoc, Pomerol, Saint-Émilion; wonderful sweet wines come from the Sauternes region in the south. Since 1855, the Châteaux du Médoc (castles of the Médoc) have been classified from first to fifth of the grands crus. This classification was changed only once, in 1973.

France, Champagne (3): The most famous wine in the world may be produced only in the area around Reims and Épernay. Only Champagne from good years becomes vintage Champagne. Most commercial brands do not bear a date. Some of them are a blend of more than 40 raw wines from various locations and vintages.

France, Burgundy (3): The region from which Chablis and Beaujolais originate. A very confusing region for the uninitiated; even somebody who focuses on big names will be spoiled with so many choices. The 124 acres (50 hectares) of the famous Clos de Vougeot are shared among 80 vintners, and no wine is like any other.

France, Alsace (3): Alsace is one of the leading white wine regions. Depending on the vintner, the wines range from extremely dry to very sweet.

Spain, Jerez de la Frontera (4): The home of sherry, a vintageless wine made with Palomino grapes and ripened by use of the solera system. The old ripened sherry is stored in the lower rows of barrels in the wine cellar, whereas younger wines are stored in the barrels above them. Sherry from the bottom row of barrels is tasted and sold. As soon as a third of the barrel is removed, it is refilled from somewhat younger barrels whose contents, in turn, are blended with still younger ones.

Spain, Ribera del Duero (4): Intense, powerful, prestigious red wines from the environs of Valladolid, cultivated along the Duero River. Main grape variety: Tinta del País; one of the most renowned producers is the Bodega Vega Sicilia.

Spain, Rioja (4): The first wine-growing region of Spain whose wines were awarded the DO (*Denominación de Origen*) seal (in 1926). The grape varieties Tempranillo, Graciano, and Garnacha produce remarkable red wines, and white Riojas are made from Viura, Malvasia, and Garnacha Blanca grapes.

Portugal, Douro (5): The port wine region—it's not actually a wine, but is made from a blend of eau-de-vie (a type of brandy) and wine. Old vintage Port is rare.

Germany, Moselle (6): Excellent Rieslings, wonderful *Trockenbeerenauslesen* ("dry berry selections"), and ice wines in good years. The home of many top German vintners. Unfortunately, there are also still many particularly popular bulk wines here.

Germany, Rheingau (6): Premium Rieslings from the environs of Mainz and Wiesbaden. Good, dry quality wines are sometimes called "first growth" here.

Italy, Piedmont (7): The home of Barbaresco and Barolo, in northern Italy near Turin. Top class among Italian red wines. Nebbiolo grapes are grown there.

Italy, Tuscany (7): The best-known wine from Tuscany is Chianti—alongside some good classic reserve Chiantis, there are certainly many bulk wines. The viticultural star of the region is Brunello di Montalcino, one of Italy's greatest red wines. Grape varieties: Trebbiano and Sangiovese.

Austria, Wachau (8): Grüner Veltliner and Riesling thrive splendidly on the 3,500 acres (1,400 hectares) of the Wachau area of the Danube Valley between Melk and Krems. The steep terraces, which are full of vines, are every bit as impressive as the local wines.

Hungary, Tokaj (9): This region has one of the greatest sweet wines in the world. "Noble rotten" grapes of the Furmint variety, which are affected by the *Botrytis cinerea* fungus, are picked to make true Tokaj wine.

Switzerland, Wallis (10): Wallis is the representative of all the great Swiss wines, which are so seldom available in other countries. More than 22,700 vintners share 12,911 acres (5,225 hectares) of grape vines. The grape variety Fendant is grown on 30 percent of that area.

Chile (11): It is only since the middle of the nineteenth century that wine has been grown systematically in Chile. Cabernet Sauvignon and Merlot produce good red wines. In accordance with prevailing taste, a lot of Chardonnay grapes have also been grown since then. The Maipo region is your safest bet for Chilean wines.

US, Napa Valley (12): Representative of all good California wines. Mostly Cabernet Sauvignon and Chardonnay are grown, but Zinfandel, a Californian specialty, is also worth sampling. Red Zinfandel is an impressive wine that can be compared with a good Barolo.

US, Oregon (13): This region is a "late bloomer." It is only since the 1960s that viticulture has been pursued here systematically and on a large scale. There are now more than 300 wineries. The most important varieties are Pinot Noir, Pinot Gris, Chardonnay, Merlot, and Riesling.

South Africa (14): Chardonnay, Cabernet Sauvignon, and Shiraz are the stars of the South African repertoire. Good wines come from the Stellenbosch and Paarl regions, in particular.

Grape Varieties

Cabernet Sauvignon (1): One of the best red wine grapes in the world and the most important component of many Bordeaux wines (of which the other grape varieties are Merlot, Cabernet Franc, and Petit Verdot). Their wines are mostly dark red, rich in acidity, full of tannin, and ready for laying down.

Chardonnay (2): A variety that is especially renowned in the Burgundy region (Chablis, Puligny-Montrachet, and Mersault), as well as in the Champagne region. It produces rich, fine wines with balanced acidity that are ready for laying down. Also grown in California, South Africa, Italy, and Australia.

Gewürztraminer: A white wine grape that is widespread in Germany and in Alsace. They often yield highly flavored and "spicy" wines, which are even a good accompaniment to Asian cuisine. In the Jura region, this grape variety is known as Savagnin and it is used to make "vin jaune" (yellow wine).

Muscatel (3): White wine grapes that are not only planted in Germany and in Alsace, but also in southern countries. Fresh and acidic, these are used mainly for wines that are supposed to be consumed young.

Nebbiolo: The grape from which Barolo and Barbaresco, the most renowned red wines of Piedmont, are made. It guarantees full-bodied, robust red wines, and is also grown in California and other regions.

Pinot Noir (4): Represents a small percentage of grapes in Champagne and causes quite a stir in Burgundy for Clos de Vougeot or Chambertin. It produces dark red, fruity wines. Pinot Noir is also used for Champagne (and blended with Chardonnay).

Riesling (5): The grape used for some of the best white wines of the world, it is particularly widespread throughout Germany and in Alsace. Versatile vines: both dry and sweet wines are produced from Riesling grapes.

Sangiovese: An excellent Italian red wine grape that produces most Chianti wines.

Sauvignon Blanc: A grape variety that is used for Sancerre and Pouilly Fumé, and also provides acidity and freshness in sweet Sauternes wines. It is also the most important white Bordeaux wine grape. Depending on the wine-growing region, Sauvignon wines can range from very light to quite heavy.

Syrah (6): A red wine grape particularly widespread in South Africa and Australia, which has a distinctive, dark red color. It produces potent wines with a high alcohol content.

Merlot: This red wine grape variety, popular all over the world, comes originally from the Bordeaux region.

Tempranillo: A Spanish red wine grape variety. The name is a diminutive form of the Spanish word for "early," as Tempranillo grapes ripen earlier than other varietals.

Wine Production

After the grape harvest [1] and selection by hand in the vineyard [2], red wine grapes are initially cleaned, i.e. stems and combs are removed. The remaining mixture of fruit pulp, seeds, and skins ends up in a fermenting container.

White grapes, however, are crushed before fermentation. For them, only the must is fermented and never the skins. If the must doesn't have a sufficiently high sugar content, must or sugar is occasionally added. This is called chaptalization, and increases the alcohol content by 1 to 1.5 percentage points.

The "mixture" remains in the fermenting vat with a good supply of air at a temperature of approximately 86°C (30°C). The yeast cultures develop, the sugar is converted into alcohol and releases carbon dioxide. This is alcoholic fermentation, which lasts for approximately five to eight days. The wine obtains its color and its tannin from the solid part of the mixture, which is called the *chapeau* (cap) by vintners, because it rises to the top, due to the pressure from the carbon dioxide. The cap must be mixed with the must every day [3]. Wines that are to be laid down must be particularly rich in tannins and, therefore, they require a longer period of mash fermentation, of approximately two to three weeks.

Nowadays, fermentation usually occurs in stainless steel tanks. They are more hygienic than wooden or concrete containers and do not alter the taste of the wine. Besides, you can monitor developments inside the tanks, and thus also the fermentation process.

Red wines are pumped around the tanks several times a day in order to extract the color and tannins from the skins more effectively.

Then the fermentation vat is tapped [4]. The so-called "free run," i.e. the pure juice, is separated from the "marc," the pomace with the solids. The latter is used for "press wine" [5] when it is pressed to extract more juice.

The free run and the press wine are put into separate fermentation vats at a temperature of 64–68°F (18–20°C). This is where malolactic fermentation occurs. This process converts the malic acid in the wine into lactic acid. The wine loses some acidity and becomes less tart. This is where the winemaking process itself ends and the aging process begins.

Carbon dioxide and cloudy matter are removed from the wine. A quite old technique is clarification with egg white, which makes the wine clear and removes excessive coloring. Numerous red wines are aged in oak barrels [6]. The new wood adds a touch of vanilla to the wine.

Then the cellar master [7] goes to work. It is his job to discover the suitable blend of grapes and the proper ratio of free run wine and press wine.

Champagne

Champagne: Whenever we hear the word "Champagne," we associate this region less with Chagall and Joan of Arc than we do with Dom Pérignon, the monk who discovered Champagne in 1688.

Unlike wine, Champagne is purposefully oriented and attuned to a clientele. Raw wines from various locations and up to ten varied vintages are married by the cellar master to create the desired taste, and are sweetened with a greater or smaller dose of sugar (dissolved in wine). That sounds like "adulteration," but it is real alchemy. Brut Champagne (very dry Champagne) always tastes the same, no matter where or when it is drunk. The classification above Brut is called "Champagne millésimé"—a vintage Champagne that is only produced in particularly good years.

Its well-known competitors are Winzersekt, sparkling wine, Cava, Crémant, or Spumante, and come from Germany, the United States, Spain, France, and Italy. Bottles of those wines are less expensive than "authentic Champagne," but they are not second rate by any means. It is no wonder, because many vintners produce their sparkling wines in exactly the same way as the more expensive competition. Although Champagne may only be produced in the Champagne region, the production process is practiced all over the world.

Many commercially available sparkling wines do not undergo a second round of fermentation in the bottle, as Champagne does, but are fermented in huge pressurized tanks, in accordance with the Charmat method. This does not necessarily detract from the quality—in the opinion of oenologists, the quality of the raw wine is more important than the fermentation process. Californian sparkling wines, in particular, are regularly awarded prizes.

The grape varieties:
Pinot Meunier: A red grape variety. It produces fruity wines with little acidity and is often used during the blending process to make the Champagne more mellow or to blend the two other grape varieties better. It is planted on approximately 48 percent of the cultivated area.

Pinot Noir: A red grape variety. It makes Champagne more potent and is planted on approximately 28 percent of the cultivated area. A wine made from the two Pinots, or only one of them, may be called "blanc de noirs" (white wine from red grapes).

Chardonnay: A white grape variety, cultivated on 24 percent of the appellation. It adds freshness, delicacy, and lightness to Champagne and makes it more sparkling. Champagne made from 100 percent Chardonnay grapes is called "blanc de blancs" (white wine from white grapes).

"Terroirs" and "crus": Grand cru sites (which are classified with the highest valuation of 100 percent) are located in the Côte des Blancs and Montagne de Reims growing areas.

Rosé: There are two approved methods for the production of rosé Champagne. Either a rosé wine is subjected to the classic *méthode champenoise* (Champagne method), or white Champagne is blended with a small amount of red wine (10–15 percent). The calculation "red + white = rosé" is allowed by French law exclusively in the region of Champagne.

Mysterious abbreviations: Two tiny letters beside the name of the producer provide information about the true origin of their Champagne:

CM: *Coopérative de manipulation*—Champagne from a cooperative
MA: *Marque auxiliaire* (subsidiary brand), *Marque d'acheteur* (buyer's brand)—A Champagne bottler's subsidiary brand. It can be bottled specially for consumption in restaurants and it's rarely good if it's a supermarket brand.
NM: *Négociant manipulant*—Champagne from a Champagne company
RC: *Récoltant coopérateur*—Champagne from a vintner who is a member of a cooperative
RM: *Récoltant manipulant*—Champagne from a grower
SR: *Société de récoltants*—Product of an association of growers

Tips for enjoying Champagne

- Pay attention to how the wine merchant stores the Champagne. Champagne does not like harsh neon light, high temperatures, or fluctuating temperatures. It is best if stored at approximately 55°F (13°C) in the dark.

- Young Champagnes and most *blancs de blancs* are served very cold (at approximately 45°F/7°C); vintage and robust Champagnes may be somewhat warmer (approximately 48–50°F/9–10°C).

- It is only on advertising posters from the *Belle Époque* that Champagne is drunk out of goblets. To enjoy Champagne at its best, you need flutes or tulip-shape glasses.

- Don't hesitate to store some bottles of good vintages. Champagne does not "die" and thus does not turn into vinegar when stored properly, but it does lose some of its sparkle over time, becomes mellower and more full-bodied, and sometimes takes on a hint of Madeira wine.

Sweet Wines

It was a bad year for Marquis Romain-Bertrand de Lur-Saluces. In 1847, he gave the employees at his vineyard instructions that the grape harvest should not begin until his return from a hunting trip to Russia. The nobleman's trip lasted longer than anticipated and the grapes had fallen prey to a fungus by the time he returned home. However, this did not deter him from harvesting them. A blessing in disguise; the outcome was an excellent sweet wine with an incomparable taste: Château d'Yquem. So goes the legend. Curiously enough, almost the same anecdote is told about the neighboring Château Suduiraut. The only differences are the gender of the main character and the century. Actually, a document dated October 4, 1866, discovered in the regional archives of the Département of the Gironde, proved that the delayed grape harvest already was a longstanding tradition in the region.

Botrytis cinerea is the name of the fungus that still affects grapes in the environs of Sauternes and in Germany's best wine locations. Vintners also call it "noble rot," which is almost a contradiction in itself from a linguistic point of view. At exactly the moment when the fungus seems to be destroying the grape, it's improving it. Spores penetrate the skin of the berries and promote the evaporation of water in the fruit pulp. The grapes dry out and the concentation of sugar and fruit substances is increased. In addition, the glycerin content increases, the wine seems "oilier" and smoother, its flavor is similar to honey, and when it is swirled in the glass, it leaves streaks. The rare vintages have been praised in the highest terms by wine critics, who have used terms such as "drinkable light" and "liquid gold."

Noble sweet wines of this kind are a nice accompaniment to *foie gras*. That is a classic combination, but not compulsory. These wines can taste first class if they are served with chicken salad, sweetbreads in a cream sauce, duck à l'orange, or with blue cheese, such as Roquefort. A classic culinary masterpiece is Turbot in Sauternes.

Incidentally, the wines with the honey bouquet are among the most expensive wines in the world. The wines of Egon Müllers Scharzhof in Wiltingen regularly break records for prices at auctions, fetching US$3,330 (2,350 euros) for a bottle of *Trockenbeerenauslese* (a wine made with late harvest grapes affected by *Botrytis cinerea*)—a record for a "young" wine. The 17 acres (7 hectares) at the best locations of the Scharzhofberg vineyard, which have been family owned since 1797, are well known to Asian and American wine connoisseurs. Currently, 50,000 bottles leave this prestigious winery every year, and the *Trockenbeerenauslesen* and ice wines are absolute collectors' items. Yquem still competes with them due to the carefully tended legend. "The summers of the past burn in the bottles of Yquem" wrote François Mauriac, Nobel Prize Laureate for Literature. Even Lenin considered growing these grape vines on Russian soil. However, grapes and the right climate alone are not enough. To make really good use of the effect of the noble rot, each individual grape must be picked at its ideal stage of ripeness.

The grape pickers go through the vines at least five times and select the grapes one by one for each consecutive harvest. The harvest will take about 45 days, as long as it is not stopped by the first drops of rain. The juice alone is so valuable that the wooden collection baskets are sealed with wax.

ALAGA
VIRGEN
SIRVASE FRIO
Pedro Ximen
Su inconfundible
sabor a uva de
Málaga se realza
al beberlo frío.
¡Disfrútelo!
V.L.C.P.R.D.
Añada 2002
López Hermanos, S.A.
Canadá 10 - Málaga
Alc. 17% Vol.
R.E. 410-MA
75 cl. e

What Is on the Label?

Spain

DO (Denominación de Origen): Guaranteed origin appellation. The Spanish equivalent of the DOC and the AOC.
Vino de la tierra: Country wine.

France

AOC (Appellation d'Origine Contrôlée): Guaranteed origin appellation.
VDQS (Vin Délimité de Qualité Supérieure): A superior-quality wine with an indication of its origin.
Vin de pays: Country wine.
Vin de table: Table wine. At its worst, it's blended with wines from other EU countries.
1st to 5th grade cru classé (classified growth): For Médoc or Sauterne wines. This classification originated in 1855 and was modified only once, in 1973, when Mouton-Rothschild moved up into the top category.

Of course, discerning wine lovers will select wine which is bottled by the producer and can be recognized by the notation "Mis(e) en bouteille(s) au château" (bottled at the castle) or "Mis(e) en bouteille(s) à la propriété" (bottled at the estate). The name and address of the bottler are also required, as well as the quantity and specification of the country of origin for export.

Inscriptions such as "bottled in the region"or "Mis(e) en bouteille(s) dans la région" usually mean that the bottle contains a blend of wines from several vintners.

Italy

DOCG (Denominazione di Origine Controllata e Garantita): Controlled and guaranteed origin appellation. For top wines, such as Barolo, Barbaresco, and Brunello di Montalschino.
DOC (Denominazione di Origine Controllata): Controlled origin appellation.
Vini da tavola: Table wines.

Germany

Label:

- Production area for choice wines (e.g. Pfalz, Rheingau, or Nahe)
- Name of the winery
- Vintage
- Bottled by the producer—means that the wine was bottled right at the winery. Other possible bottlers include distributors and importers.
- Information about the vineyard
- Grape variety (e.g. Riesling, Grey Burgundy, and Late Burgundy)
- Information about the quality level of the wine (e.g. Quality wine with distinction)
- Alcohol content of the wine as a percentage of the volume
- Volume contained in the bottle in liters
- Official control number—contains information about the inspection center
- Year of inspection and the producer
- Country of origin: in the case of wines for export

Classification:

Tafelwein: Table wine. Simple, not particularly high-quality wine, which must be enhanced with added sugar before fermentation. If the wine is not called German table wine, then it could be a blend of wines from various countries.

Landwein: Country wine. May not contain more than ¾ oz/quart (18 g/l) of residual sugar, so it is often drier than table wine. From a purely theoretical point of view, it is somewhat better than table wine, but far from being a great vintage.

Qualitätswein bestimmter Anbaugebiete (Q.b.A): Quality wine from specific growing areas. This wine must originate completely from the stipulated region, be produced from approved grape varieties, and have a specific must weight that can vary from region to region. That is why it does not offer any guarantee of quality.

Qualitätswein mit Prädikat (Q.m.P.): Quality wine with distinction. From a purely theoretical perspective, this is Germany's top category of wine. As with the previous category, added sugar (chaptalization) is prohibited and official inspection is required. In addition to this, there are five subcategories, which, again, are based on the must weight. As in the case of the Q.b.A, the same rules do not apply in the Pfalz region as do in the Mosel region:

Designations such as "Grand Vin" (great wine) or "Reserve" (Grandfather's Reserve) have no legal basis and often emanate from the vintner's imagination alone. In addition, imprints with medals and awards do not always vouch for quality. Make sure that the year of the award matches the vintage you are buying.

United States

Front label

- Producer (it's not always the vintner who grew the grapes)
- Grape variety
- AVA (American Viticultural Area)
- Vineyard
- Vintage
- Alcohol content (from 7 to 13.9 %)
- Proportion of sulfites
- Filtered/unfiltered
- Volume contained in the bottle (sometimes on the back label)

Back label

- Description of the wine
- Mandatory government warning

Australia

- Winery, brand, or trade name
- Grape variety or style of wine (such as a dry, red wine). The simple word "wine" is also sufficient.
- Region of origin (optional)
- Vintage (optional)
- Bottle size
- Alcohol content
- Standard drinks content (in numbers: for example, "A bottle contains 7.4 standard drinks")
- A list of allergenic substances (such as sulfites)
- Name and address
- Country of origin

Enjoying Wine

Glasses: Elaborately polished or colored glasses are not recommended. Although they sometimes look decorative, they hide the color of the wine. On the other hand, you absolutely do not need a different glass for each wine. The professionals from the French INAO (Institut National des Appellations d'Origine), who oversee the testing of wine bottled by producers, use just two: one red wine glass and one white wine glass.

As a general rule, do not drink wine out of supposedly solid glasses made of molded glass. Avoid quaint designer shapes (square wine glasses have even driven connoisseurs to desperation). When you are traveling, the glasses that are customarily used in the region are usually best suited to the local wines and are sometimes even based on centuries of experience.

White wine glasses are smaller and tulip shape, and curve inward. Their shape keeps the flavor better in the glass. Red wine glasses are round bodied, because oxygen is good for red wine. The glass can easily be bigger, because red wine, which is drunk warmer, does not increase in temperature as quickly.

Temperature: The ineradicable rule that wine is to be enjoyed at room temperature originates from the time before the invention of central heating. Today, wine is served at the following temperatures:

Around 46–48°F (8–9°C) for Champagne, sparkling wines, and light whites
50–52°F (10–11°C) for heavier whites, such as Rieslings
53–55°F (12–13°C) for great white wines, such as noble Chardonnays
57–59°F (14–15°C) for light Beaujolais-style reds
61–63°F (16–17°C) for young reds
64–66°F (18–19°C) for heavy, full-bodied red wines, such as Barolo and the great Bordeaux wines. In case of doubt, serve the wine preferably a degree too cold. It will eventually warm up on its own.

Corkscrews: There are many varied types of corkscrew. Many of them promise to remove corks without any effort, or attempt to impress us with particularly nice shapes. Basically, all you need is a solid, traditional corkscrew. It will remove the cork reliably without sticking through it, which often causes pieces of cork to fall into the wine.

Decanting: It's not only in restaurants that wines are sometimes decanted (poured into a carafe). In this way, the wine receives a strong dose of oxygen, and older bottles are relieved of sediment (deposits). Many young wines are improved by the addition of oxygen, but you have to be careful with old wines. Many a seasoned old wine has been transformed into a cloudy, lightly alcoholic liquid when decanted hours before drinking. Sommeliers recommend that rare wines should be decanted only shortly before being consumed. However, as with any other rule, there are exceptions. Some old wines are markedly inproved by being decanted hours before consumption.

Wine tasting: If you want to taste several wines one after the other, some basic rules should be followed, no matter whether you are at home or in a restaurant:

· Serve young, light wines first, then follow them with older ones. Otherwise, the young ones will be overwhelmed by the rich taste of the older ones.

· Drink dry wines before sweet ones. Otherwise, the residual sugar will numb your tongue.

· Drink better wines after the less complex ones. In that way, the flavor will increase.

A tasting sip—At first glance, is the color right? Does the wine seem hazy, dusty, or cloudy? Or, on the contrary, is it clear and luminous? Professionals can recognize grape varieties and tell the age of the wine from its color. To better appreciate whether the red has a slight, rather purple shimmer (a sign of a young wine), or its color is reminiscent of mahogany (usually a sign of maturity), you should drink by daylight, because artificial light can distort the color. Also, you should hold the glass by its stem, not as you hold a brandy snifter.

Then, let the wine swirl in the glass. If there are hardly any streaks of wine on the edge of the glass, it's light. If you can see several narrow streaks, it is a heavy wine with a high alcoholic content.

Then the nose test: What does the wine smell like ? Earth, underbrush, wild cherries? Particularly important: watch out for the smell of musty cork. A pervasive smell of cork is always a cause for alarm. It's often due to flawed corks that let too much oxygen in and inflict their taste on the wine through oxidation. How can we recognize the notorious cork smell? Go ahead and take the time to smell a cork: You will find the exact same perfume and taste in the wine also. In short, corked wine is flawed. You can send it back in a restaurant. A weak, characterless bouquet is not a good sign.

Apart from that, it's true that perfume and taste are somewhat subjective. Of course, professionals can recognize immediately whether wine tastes like wild cherries or underbrush, or whether it is nervous, acidic, or rich in tannins.

Finally, the actual tasting sip: Is the wine at the right temperature? What does it taste like? Here, as well, the taste of cork is once again a sign of a flawed wine. Does the wine have a long finish? That means, does the taste stay in your mouth for a long time after you have swallowed it? That is an excellent characteristic.

And do you like it? Obviously, you have the right not to like a wine, even if it was expensive or comes from a famous *château*. From the perspective of other wine drinkers, this doesn't mean that you have no taste. You have your own taste.

Buying Wine

Anyone who wants to buy wine on site from the vintner should be aware that the bottles could be damaged on the way home when they are being transported in the trunk of a car due to severe fluctuations in temperature. External aromas can even penetrate into the bottle via the cork—bags of onions or leaking canisters of gasoline are not ideal companions for a good vintage. After the trip, the wine must first get some more rest. Whites should be laid down for approximately four weeks, whereas reds should be left for approximately eight weeks.

Buying wine

Wine from the Internet

You can find almost any wine on the Internet if you really look, whether from a mail-order hobby business in a garage or a professionally organized range, including everything from inexpensive to rare wines.

Liquor stores

Even if you frequent it every day to buy frozen food or carrots, your supermarket is not a good place for getting the most out of your wine. Months of standing upright under neon lights, at temperatures of around 72°F (22°C), is torture, which only the cheapest, everyday wines can withstand. Look for wines in a reputable store and the selection there will be fitting. Even great Bordeaux wines and Champagnes can be purchased there occasionally at a halfway decent price. The only thing that is left to chance is the advice you receive.

Specialty retailers

A knowledgable wine merchant is the best person to approach when you are buying wine. Many merchants select their wines personally, know the vintners, and can make well-founded recommendations. Most of them store wine correctly and carefully. However, this service means that wines from a specialty retailer are sometimes a little more expensive.

Glossary

Alcohol: Wines have between 8.5 and 15 % alcohol by volume.

AOC (Appellation d'Origine Contrôlée): Controlled Denomination of Origin. The distinction awarded to first-class French wines.

Assemblage: Blending (mixing) of various grape varieties (such as for Bordeaux wine) or blending of the same wine from several vats.

Astringent: A wine with a high tannin content.

Barrique: An oak barrel with a capacity of 59½ gallons (225 liters).

Botrytis cinerea: Rotten grapes do not always lead to lower quality wine. *Botrytis cinerea* is the name of a fungus that affects grapes in the area around Sauternes and in Germany's best wine locations. The spores of the fungus penetrate the skin of the grapes and promote the evaporation of water in the flesh of the fruit. The grapes dry out and the concentation of sugar and fruit substances is thus increased. The glycerine content rises, the wine seems "oilier" and smoother. Its flavor and fragrance are honeylike. Noble sweet wines of this kind go very well with foie gras or blue cheese.

Bottle fermentation: The second fermentation for Champagnes and other sparkling wines that are produced in a traditional manner. As the name implies, this process happens in the bottle.

Brut: French for very dry.

Cava: Spanish sparkling wine.

Cave: Wine cellar.

Champagne method: Fermentation of Champagne in the bottle. In addition to Champagne, wines that are produced in the same way bear the inscription "Méthode classique" or "Méthode traditionelle."

Chaptalisation: Enriching the must with sugar.

Crémant: Sparkling wine.

Cru: French for a good grape-growing area.

Cuvée: A blend of raw wines from different varieties of grape or different vintages.

Decanting: Pouring the wine into a carafe.

Development: Ripening of the wine, mostly in steel tanks or wooden barrels.

DO: Spanish and Italian for controlled denomination of origin.

DOCG: The highest distinction for Italian wines, which is currently applied to only 16 wines (Barolo, Barbaresco, Chianti, etc...).

Dry: Wine with less than ¼ oz (9 g) of residual sugar per quart (liter).

Egg white: Is used to clarify red wine by binding with yeast and agents that cause cloudiness.

Finish: The flavor impression left by wine after it is swallowed.

Fortification: Adding alcohol or brandy to wine. This is done in the production of liqueur wines, such as port.

Grand Cru: A designation for the best locations and wines in French wine-growing areas.

Gran Reserva: Spanish red wines which have aged for at least six years. A Gran Reserva wine spends two years in a wooden barrel.

Ice wine: The grapes are picked at a temperature of 18°F (-8°C) or colder, and pressed in a frozen state. It is at least of as high a quality as a noble sweet wine.

Location: Place and vineyard where the wine was grown.

Liqueur wine: Dessert wine with at least 15 % alcohol per volume (e.g. Sherry, Port, Banyuls, and Madeira).

Magnum: A bottle with a capacity of 1⅔ quarts (1.5 liters).

Mature: A wine that has reached the right age to be served.

Must weight: A unit of measurement of the sugar content (and thus, the potential alcohol content of the wine) on the Öchsle scale.

Noble rot: See *Botrytis cinerea*.

Noble sweet wine: A sweet wine made from wines with noble rot (*Botrytis cinerea*) with 110–128° Öchsle.

Nose: The aroma and bouquet of the wine.

Öchsle: Unit of measurement of the must weight. It explains roughly how much heavier 1 quart (1 liter) of must is than 1 quart (1 liter) of distilled water.

Oxidation: Occurs when the wine is exposed to oxygen for an extended period of time. This is beneficial to some wines, but can lead to negative effects, such as a dull color and a musty aroma in other wines.

Phylloxera: The scientific name for vine pest, an insect that feeds parasitically on grapevines.

Sediment: Suspended particles, which are not a sign of a flawed wine.

Semidry: White wines with a residual sugar content of ¼–⅔ oz (10–18 g) per quart (liter).

Sommelier: A wine waiter or cellar master who is in charge of procuring and storing wines for a restaurant and helps the restaurant patron to select a wine that is a good pairing for the menu selection.

Sulfur: Is added to the wine to preserve it and protect it against oxidation.

Tannin: It is mostly present in red wine due to the fermentation of the grape skins and their aging in oak barrels.

Tartar: Acidic deposits in white wines. It's intrinsically harmless and not an indication of poor quality.

Tastevin: A silver tasting cup that is purely decorative nowadays.

Trockenbeerenauslese: A German noble sweet wine with at least 150° Öchsle.

Vinification: Winemaking.

Vintage: The year a wine was made.

MATUSA

Glossary

Bain-marie (Double boiler): This is primarily a hot water bath where food is kept warm. However, it serves other purposes, such as melting chocolate for cakes, custards, and desserts. In addition, when you are making a classic chocolate mousse, the egg white is beaten over a warm water bath to make the mousse particularly airy and firm. The water bath is indispensable when you are preparing warm, whipped sauces such as a hollandaise or a béarnaise sauce, because it guarantees that the preparation will be problem-free. Egg yolks are heated slowly and thus reach the proper volume so as to bind well with the melted butter at a later stage.

Baking: The item is cooked in an ovenproof dish or on a baking sheet in a preheated oven. The food is cooked by means of hot air, either in a conventional or a convection oven. The temperature that is used most frequently is 350°F (180°C/Gas Mark 4) and ideal for cakes, baked goods, cookies, roasting, fish, and poultry. You need 400–425°F (200–220°C/ Gas Mark 6–7) to bake flaky pastry and soufflés, and for browning casseroles. Lower temperatures from 300–325°F (150°–160°C/Gas Mark 2–3) are best for gentle cooking of fish dishes as well as slow roasting (poultry or veal). As a rule of thumb: the lower the temperature, the longer the cooking time.

Barding: Leaner pieces of meat, especially saddle of venison, pheasant, or rack of rabbit, are wrapped in slices of bacon and tied with cotton string. In that way, the pieces of meat remain nice and juicy, do not dry out, and also acquire a good flavor.

Basting: The food is moistened repeatedly by drizzling the juices that collect in the dish or on the baking sheet over it. You can also use wine, broth, or even plain water for this purpose. The food will remain nice and juicy and will not dry out if you baste it constantly. This natural sauce is particularly flavorsome, because it contains all of the essential flavors of the food.

Beating: Soups, sauces, and desserts are best whipped with an electric handheld blender. In that way, they are not only blended, but they are also fluffy and foamy.

Beurre manié: Equal parts of flour and soft butter are kneaded together, and the resulting flakes are whisked into a hot liquid. This quick thickener, which has a delicate buttery taste, is easy to handle, because no lumps form during the cooking process due to the butter-flour combination.

Binding: Sauces and soups can be bound with egg yolk; after the egg yolk has been stirred in, the liquid must not be boiled.

Blanching: Vegetables such as spinach, savoy cabbage, leeks, and carrots are briefly cooked in an ample amount of boiling water. It is important to plunge them into ice water afterward. In this way, the vegetables remain crisp and retain their original color. Depending on the recipe, after the blanching process, the vegetables are reheated in hot broth or butter and then they are served.

Blini: Russian, yeast-leavened, buckwheat pancakes cooked in special small pans. For better binding, the buckwheat flour is mixed with whole-wheat flour. Traditionally, they are served with caviar, but they also taste particularly delicious when served as an accompaniment to braised meat and game.

Boiling: Cooking food in an ample amount of liquid. During the entire cooking time, the temperature should be approximately 212°F (100°C).

Bouquet garni: A small bunch of various fresh cooking herbs tied together. The bouquet garni is removed before the dish is served.

Braising: The food is cooked with some fat and a little liquid in an open pot. This cooking method is particularly suitable for beef, vegetable, and fish dishes.

Broiling: Food is cooked on a rack without the addition of fat. The food acquires a wonderful, smoky flavor. Grilling is to be particularly recommended for people who are calorie-conscious in their eating habits. Meat, fish, poultry, and also vegetables can be cooked without added fat.

Canapé: Small, bite-sized slices of bread with various toppings such as smoked salmon, *foie gras*, caviar, smoked duck breast, ham, etc...

Carcasses: The bones and skeleton of poultry or fish that are used in the preparation of sauces and stocks.

Carving: Cutting meat or fish pieces into individual slices. Carving is best done on a board with a juice-well and with a special carving set of cutlery.

Celestine: Finely sliced pancake strips as a garnish for clear broths.

Chiffonade: Finely chopped strips of lettuce that are served with shrimp cocktail.

Chinois: A conical sieve for straining sauces and soups.

Clarifying: Removing all cloudy substances from soups, stocks, or jellies by means of lightly beaten egg white. Egg white starts to coagulate at 160°F (70°C), and the coagulating egg white traps the impurities so that they can be skimmed off effortlessly. The broth also acquires a more intense flavor. Venison or game broths are suitable for clarifying, but so are vegetable and fish soups (which are clarified only with egg white and vegetables and without meat, of course).

Coating: Sprinkling buttered soufflé and baking molds with granulated sugar so that the contents slip easily out of the molds when they are turned upside down.

Cocotte: An ovenproof oval dish made of porcelain or stoneware.

Concassée: Blanched, peeled tomatoes, quartered, seeded, and finely chopped.

Consommé: This is also called clear soup and must be clarified. Double consommé is clarified with double the quantity of clarifying ingredients. By using a raft (see opposite), the broth acquires an intense flavor.

Cooling: It is important to do this to soups, stews, or other dishes that are supposed to be stored. Put them in a cool place (on the balcony in winter) and let them cool to room temperature, then cover them and store them in the refrigerator. You can put soup that is still warm into the refrigerator, but the amount should be no more than two portions, and the refrigerator should be set at the maximum cooling temperature for a short time.

Crêpes: Thin pancakes prepared from a batter and fried in oil. The pancakes are cooked in a skillet until they are light brown. They can be served sweet with jam or chocolate cream, or also savory, stuffed with a vegetable filling.

Crumbing: Slices of meat or fish are dredged in flour, dipped in beaten egg, finally coated in breadcrumbs before being fried in hot fat. The food becomes particularly crisp on the outside and remains moist on the inside, when this method is used.

Deep-frying: This cooking method involves submerging the food in hot fat to make it crisp on the outside: for example, peeled, raw potatoes cut into small pieces, shrimp and vegetables in tempura batter, baked semolina dumplings for soups, as well as sweet items such as doughnuts, apple fritters, etc... After the food is cooked and crisp, it is removed from the fat with a skimmer and left to drain on paper towels. Care must be taken, because hot fat often splatters out of the pan. It's a good idea to use an electric deep-fryer with a mechanism for accurately setting the temperature, not only to guard against splattering fat, but also due to the unpleasant odor of deep-frying.

Dutch oven: This large ovenproof stockpot is a necessary purchase for anyone who likes stewed dishes, such as oxtail and game ragout. The flavor of the cooked food can develop fully due to the large surface area of the stockpot. There are pots that are just wonderfully suitable for slow roasting of dishes, such as leg of lamb or rolled pork roast.

Duxelles: A stuffing made with finely chopped mushrooms, sautéed with diced onions and herbs. It's traditionally used for Beef Wellington (baked in pastry).

Farce: Finely chopped meat or fish, from which self-contained dishes, such as pike, sausages, or venison dumplings, are made. It also serves as a base for terrines or savory pies, such as terrine of venison or wild boar pie.

Fillet: For meat in the butcher's shop, this refers to the loin. For lamb, rabbit, venison, hare, etc., it designates the saddle and the small "proper" fillets. For poultry, it refers to the boned breasts, and for fish, the portions of flesh that have been removed from the bones, without the head, carcass, or scales.

Filleting: Meat, poultry, wild game, and fish meat are removed from the bones with a sharp knife.

Flambéing: Burning off a liquid with a high percentage of alcohol (such as brandy or Grand Marnier) by igniting it. The most famous dish of this kind is fillet of beef strips in a brandy cream sauce.

Fleurons: Small baked puff pastry decorations in various shapes such as flowers, boats, and lobsters. They are served with fish dishes with sauce or with fricassee of chicken.

Flouring: Coating slices of fish or meat with flour before frying them. The food acquires a tasty crust but remains nice and juicy.

Gazpacho: A cold, Spanish vegetable soup made with tomatoes, cucumber, garlic, red and green bell peppers, and fresh herbs. It tastes particularly good on hot summer days.

Glazing: Adding a shiny surface to, or pouring a glaze onto, vegetables, meat, fish, or desserts. For this purpose, we use either a suitable stock, the food's own pan drippings, a light, cooked caramel, jelly, hot jam, or frosting.

Gnocchi: Little Italian dumplings that are made from potato dough, semolina, ricotta, or bread mixture, and then cooked briefly in salted water.

Gratinéing: Dishes are broiled at 425°F (220°C/ Gas Mark 7) or even higher temperatures, until a brown crust is obtained. Grated cheese, breadcrumbs, or a mixture of both are suitable for topping gratinéed dishes.

Grilling: Fatty joints of meat, such as T-bone steaks or pork chops, can be fried well in a nonstick, coated grill pan without fat.

Jus: The juices released by roasting poultry or meat, and in particular prepared brown sauces made from various types of meat juice.

Kaltschale: A German cold soup made with pureed fruit, such as raspberries, melons, or strawberries, which are finely pureed with lemon juice and white wine, if desired, and seasoned with fresh herbs. It's important to serve it chilled.

Larding needle: An instrument used to insert slender strips of bacon fat or salt pork into particularly lean pieces of meat, such as saddles of venison or hare. The fat prevents the meat from drying out and imparts additional flavor to the lean cut.

Marinade: Mixtures of vinegar, lemon juice, alcohol, yogurt, buttermilk, etc... Marinades can also be enriched by the addition of spices or herbs. They can be used to dress salads or to marinate tender meat. Indeed, meat marinades give sauces the right kick, because the various flavors of herbs, vegetables, and spices are accumulated there.

Marinating: Both meat and fish can be marinated in a sauce. Meat becomes more tender through this process and more flavorful because of the flavors of the marinade. Raw salmon can be marinated with salt, sugar, herbs, and spices. Not only does it become spicier, but it will also keep longer.

Mie de pain: Dry breadcrumbs made from crustless white bread. They are used for stuffings, coating fish, and as a crust for roast lamb, etc.

Minestrone: A classic Italian vegetable soup. The vegetables used vary in each region and according to the season. Beans and noodles are an absolute "must."

Mirepoix: Finely diced vegetables, sometimes with bacon and herbs, toasted in butter, and used as a seasoning for sauces.

Napping: Coating vegetables, meat, or fish with sauces.

Oversalting: If a soup or a sauce is too salty, just diluting it with water will help to alleviate the problem

Pie: Pastry with filling. There are many different types of sweet and savory variations. The typical shape of a pie is a flat bottom with a sloping 2-inch (5-cm) high border. When the pie is covered with a pastry lid, a small opening is cut in the center so that steam can escape and the filling doesn't puff up excessively.

Poaching: Cooking particularly delicate food, such as fish, veal sweetbreads, eggs, or oysters, in hot liquid, below the boiling point.

Profiteroles: Little choux pastry puffs, also called cream puffs, that can have both sweet and spicy fillings.

Raft: Mixture used to clarify stock made from fibrous, lean, and muscular meat—deer veal, for instance. The meat is mixed with root vegetables and herbs, and ground coarsely with a meat grinder. It is then mixed with some beaten egg whites and ice cubes and added to stock. The stock is slowly heated while being stirred constantly. The ingredients should be ice cold for clarifying and the broth must also be cooled down before heating with the raft.

Reduction: A liquid is cooked down until thick. Sauces acquire a particularly aromatic flavor as well as a nice luster if they are reduced several times.

Refreshing: Vegetables, in particular, are briefly plunged into cold water after cooking, so that they retain their color, minerals, and vitamins. The cooked food is then drained in a colander.

Roasting: Roasting is cooking in hot fats and oils that can be heated to high temperatures such as sunflower oil, clarified butter, or goose fat. Due to its high fat content, pork roast can be cooked in the oven and basted frequently with some water only. The rind must always be on top. Due to the high heat, the fat coalesces, acquires a nice color and becomes a solid, very tasty crust.

Roux: A light or dark sauce thickened with flour. Butter is heated, flour is stirred into it, liquid is added gradually, and the sauce is cooked for at least 15 minutes with constant stirring. For a dark roux, the flour is cooked until it has a nice golden color before the liquid is added. As this process reduces the thickening capacity of the flour, the quantity of flour must be increased. Dark roux are used for kidney and liver dishes, and bean and lentil stews.

Royale: Better known as custard royale. Eggs and milk are mixed together, seasoned, and poured into buttered molds and poached in a water bath at 158–176°F (70–80°C).

Salamander: An electrical appliance that is used for broiling and browning dishes. It is comparable to a broiler.

Sautéing: The quick frying of thin slices of meat, fish, or vegetable pieces, while tossing them in a long-handled skillet (known as a *sauteuse* in French).

Simmering: Food is cooked gently at a low heat, whereby it remains juicy and its full flavor is allowed to develop. This method of cooking is used for the production of soups and sauces.

Soufflé: Particularly delicate mixtures that puff up when baked, and can be sweet or savory. A menu whose crowning glory is a chocolate soufflé is certainly always a particularly memorable one.

Soup bones: These are important for the preparation of broths, in order to obtain an intense flavor. Smooth beef bones from the joints and shins are ideal. The marrow bones are the most flavorful. Buying meat from a well-known, trusted butcher or from a guaranteed, organic breeder is the only way we can guard against infections that can be traced back to diseases such as BSE (bovine spongiform encephalopathy).

Steaming: The food is cooked gently in a strainer above simmering water or broth, without the food coming into contact with the liquid. The flavors are particularly well retained using this method. Vegetables remain crisp and flavorful. Fish can also be prepared without any added fat. Preparing food this way is particularly suitable for dieters, small children, and people who have to adhere to a low-fat diet for health reasons, but steaming is also ideal for anyone who enjoys authentic, unadulterated food.

Stewing: This refers to a cooking process that combines searing and simmering. First of all, the food is browned on all sides in hot fat. This process seals the meat and it acquires a slight crust. Browned particles, which are important for the subsequent color and flavor of the food, are created. Then, a liquid of choice is added to the dish and it is covered and placed in a preheated oven to stew. Hearty meat dishes, such as oxtail, goulash, beef for roasting, or lamb ragout are suitable for stewing.

Stock: A basic broth for soups and sauces that is created by simmering veal, beef, game, poultry, or fish. It's important to ensure that stock simmers slowly and that the foam, which forms constantly during this process, is removed with a skimmer. Remove the layer of fat when the stock cools down and the stock will become particularly light and clear.

Suprême: A term for the best part of a butchered animal that is always prepared in the most elegant way. It's also called the best cut.

Sweating: The food is fried with some fat over gentle heat in a skillet, without allowing it to brown.

Tartlets: Miniature tarts made of shortcrust or puff pastry that can have a sweet or savory filling.

Tenderizing: Meat or fish is hammered between two sheets of plastic wrap with a meat mallet or the bottom of a small pot, until it is thin. For example, meat for carpaccio, roulades, or fish for fish rolls is tenderized.

Timbales: Small savory custards or *terrines* that are placed in small baking molds and either baked in the oven or poached in a water bath.

Tiramisu: A very popular dessert from Italy made with ladyfingers dipped in strong coffee, mascarpone, egg yolks, and dusted with cocoa powder.

Tomatizing: Vegetables or bones are mixed with tomato paste, after browning, and then roasted together over medium heat. They can be used to make sauces or soups particularly flavorful.

Trimming: Removing sinew and fat from slaughtered animals of all kinds. The trimmings are used in stocks, broths, and sauces. It's important to have a sharp knife, which you hold flush with the meat so that not too much meat is cut off in the process.

Trussing: Pieces of meat, such as roulades, and poultry are tied with cotton string and thus kept in shape.

Turning: Cutting vegetables and potatoes into desired shapes using a special knife (a small knife with a half-moon-shape blade).

Velouté soups: Pureed and thickened soups are rounded off with an egg-cream mixture. The soup should not be allowed to cook after the thickening agent has been stirred in, or the egg yolk will coagulate.

Vinaigrette: A salad dressing made with oil and vinegar that can be seasoned as desired. Even a meat or fish carpaccio is delicious with an artfully seasoned vinaigrette.

Whole foods: Balanced, varied nutrition, based on healthy, high-quality food, such as whole grain products, naturally raised meat, fish, poultry, and fresh vegetables.

Zesting: A zesting tool is used to remove the peel of unwaxed oranges or lemons in thin strips. There are many commercially available "zesters" with one or more perforations.

Index

A

Aioli ... 53
Allgäuer Emmentaler ... 738
almond oil ... 42
almonds ... 592, 670, 710
aluminum foil ... 14
Appenzeller ... 738
apple vinegar ... 44, 45
apples ... 650
  Apple Chips ... 665
  Apple Crêpes with Crisp Bacon and Maple Syrup ... 126
  Apple Fritters ... 665
  Baked Apples with Raisin Filling ... 686
  hollowing out ... 655
apricots ... 651, 726
  Apricot Sauce ... 695
  halving and pitting ... 652
Arborio rice ... 246, 248
Ardi Gasna ... 738
argan oil ... 42, 43
aromatic rices ... 232
  cooking ... 234
artichokes ... 342
  preparing and cooking ... 345, 356–7
  Tomato and Artichoke Risotto ... 248
arugula ... 67
  Potato Gnocchi with Cherry Tomatoes and Arugula ... 318
asparagus ... 343, 345, 488
  Boiled Asparagus ... 396
  Cream of Asparagus Soup with Mint ... 173
  Green and White Asparagus Salad with Poached Egg ... 72
  Stir-Fried Asparagus ... 396
avocados ... 278
azuki beans ... 269
  cooking ... 268

B

bacon
  Apple Crêpes with Crisp Bacon and Maple Syrup ... 126
  Cheese Spaetzle with Bacon Strips ... 212
  Fried Scallops Wrapped in Bacon ... 510
  Potato and Cucumber Salad with Bacon Strips ... 86
baking powder ... 14, 15
balsamic vinegar ... 44, 45
  Balsamic Vinegar Sauce ... 151
bamboo mat ... 14, 15
bananas
  Banana Crêpes ... 126
  Banana Mousse ... 683
Banon ... 739
basic ingredients ... 12–13
basil
  Basil Croutons ... 164
  Herb-Mustard Vinaigrette ... 63
  preparing ... 54
  Yogurt Sauce with Herbs ... 55
basmati rice ... 232
  Biryani Rice with Lamb ... 254
  cooking ... 234
  Indian Curry Rice with Raisins and Cardamom ... 260
  Sweet Potato Balls with Crisp Basmati Rice Coating ... 334
Batavia lettuce ... 69
bâtonnets ... 344
batter
  Crêpe Batter ... 124
  Salmon in Batter ... 464
  Thyme Batter ... 364
Bavarian Cream ... 658
BBQ Sauce ... 56, 522, 608
bean sprouts ... 67
Béarnaise Sauce ... 154
Béchamel Sauce ... 156
beef ... 544–79
  Beef Carpaccio with Parmesan Cheese and Lemon Juice ... 98
  Beef Mango Salad with Cherry Tomatoes and Mint ... 78
  Beef with Onions and Fried Potatoes ... 560
  Beef Stroganoff with Pickles and Button Mushrooms ... 570
  Beef Tenderloin in Chive Bouillon with Spring Vegetables ... 562
  Beef Tenderloin in Green Peppercorn Cream Sauce ... 564
  Beef Tournedos Rossini with Goose Liver and Truffle Sauce ... 566
  Bolognese ... 158
  buying ... 10, 546
  Chili con Carne ... 554
  cooking chart ... 546
  cuts ... 546, 547
  degrees of doneness ... 552
  fillet, cutting and trimming ... 550–1
  Fried Noodles with Spicy Beef ... 216
  Fried Quail Eggs Canapés with Beef Tartare ... 120
  Gravy/Jus ... 138
  Grilled T-Bone Steak ... 568
  Hamburgers with Onion Relish ... 572
  Hungarian Paprikash with Corn ... 252
  Indian Beef Curry with Black Cardamom and Cinnamon ... 574
  Meatloaf with Sauce and Parsley Potatoes ... 576
  Roast Beef ... 556
  Stewed Beef with Vegetables and Herbs ... 558
  Vietnamese Beef Stew with Ginger ... 578
beet ... 380
bell peppers ... 342, 345
  seeding ... 359
  Vegetable Goulash ... 374
beurre noisette ... 30, 34
black beans ... 269
blender ... 16
blue cheese ... 736
Bolognese Sauce ... 158
  Penne Bolognese ... 202
borlotti beans ... 268
Bouillabaisse ... 178–81
bread
  Bread Stuffing ... 530
  crusty ... 720
  Focaccia ... 726
  Homemade bread with Sea Salt ... 720
  Mexican Corn Bread with Green Chili Peppers ... 730
  Mini Baguettes with Olives and Onion ... 728
  Sourdough Starter ... 728
  Sunday Rolls with Poppy Seeds ... 722
  Yeast Dough ... 712
Brie ... 739
broccoli ... 343, 345
  Broccoli with Asparagus and Seitan ... 418
  Rice Noodles with Broccoli and Green Chili Peppers ... 218
Brown Poultry Sauce ... 520
brown rice ... 232, 233
  Brown Rice Risotto with Kabocha Squash and Lime ... 250
  cooking ... 236, 238, 268
brunoise ... 344
buffalo milk butter ... 32
bulgur ... 269
  Bulgur Mint Salad with Yogurt and Tomatoes ... 276
  cooking ... 268, 271
butter ... 30–7
  beurre noisette ... 30, 34
  clarified butter ... 34
  Herb Butter ... 36
  melted butter ... 34
  salted ... 30
  serving ... 32
  storage ... 30, 32
  Tomato Basil Butter ... 36
  Whipped Butter ... 30
  Whipped Butter Sauce ... 137
Butter Dumplings ... 168
Butter Pecan Cookies ... 714
buttercrunch lettuce ... 66
button mushrooms ... 343, 345, 360, 376, 394, 488, 570

C

cabbage ... 343, 345, 636
Cabrales ... 739
Caesar Dressing ... 59
calf kidneys ... 546
  Veal Kidneys in Mustard Cream Sauce with Mashed Onion Potatoes ... 588
calf liver ... 546
calories ... 21
Camembert ... 739
Campari Zabaglione ... 684
Candied Fruit Snail Rolls ... 713
cannaroni lisci ... 184
cannelloni ... 210
Cantaloupe Melon ... 650
capellini ... 185

Caramel Sauce 694
Caraway Potatoes 309, 602
carp 422, 423
  Carp Fried in Breadcrumbs 434
carrots 342, 353
  Glazed Carrots 390
  preparing and cooking 345, 353
  Vichy Carrots 392
casserole dish 14, 15
catfish 422, 423
  Catfish in Paprika Sauce 429
  Catfish in Root Vegetable Stock 428
cauliflower 345
  Ayurvedic Cauliflower with Tomatoes and Cumin 388
  Corn Fusilli Pasta with Cauliflower and Anchovies 412
  Fluffy Cauliflower Puree 386
cavatappi 185
celeriac 84
celery 354, 636
cellentani 185
Champagne 750
chanterelles 343, 345, 378
Cheddar 739
cheese 732–43
  categories of 736-7
  Cheese Croutons 174
  Cheese Fondue 742
  Cheese Soufflé 114
  Cheese Spaetzle with Bacon Strips 212
  Noodle Casserole with Cheese 194
  Scrambled Eggs with Cheese 105
  storage 736
  types of 738–41
  wine and cheese 738–41
Cheesecake 716
cherries 666
chervil
  Chervil Cream Soup 172
  Green Chervil Cress Sauce 55
  preparing 54
  Yogurt Sauce with Herbs 55
chicken 516, 517
  Baked Chicken with Herb Crumbs 523
  buying 10
  Chicken Cordon Bleu 524
  Chicken and Ham Tortellini 208
  Chicken Legs in BBQ Sauce 522
  Chicken Schnitzels 526
  Chicken Schnitzels with Coconut and Curry 528
  Chicken Soup with Butter Dumplings and Nutmeg 168
  Chicken Stock 134
  Cornish Hens Roasted with Lemon and Garlic 540
  Fresh Chicken Liver Pâté 80
  Shanghai-Style Fried Egg Noodles with Chicken 224
chickpeas 269
  cooking 268
  Indian Chickpea Curry with Cinnamon Yogurt, and Mint 290
chili beans 286
chilis
  Chili con Carne 554
  Chili Pepper Vinegar 46, 47
  cutting 196
  Mexican Chili with Chipotle Peppers 286
  stuffing 359
Chinese cabbage 414
chives 67
  Chive Sauce 137
  Herb-Mustard Vinaigrette 63
  preparing 54
  Swedish Potatoes with Chives 338
  Yogurt Sauce with Herbs 55
chocolate
  Chocolate Brownies 710
  Chocolate Chip Cookies 714
  Chocolate Sauce 694
  Chocolate Sponge Cake 706
  Dark Chocolate Mousse 678
  White Chocolate Mousse with Maple Syrup 676
Choron Sauce 155
cilantro
  Garlic Cilantro Vinegar 46, 47
  Millet Patties with Cilantro and Orange Zest 280
  Soy Vinaigrette with Cilantro 63
clams 479, 506, 508
cockles 506
Cocktail Sauce 53, 488
coconut milk 612
  Curry Sauces 146
  Tapioca-Coconut Pudding 668
cod 428
Coffee Cream 658
colander 14, 15
cold pressed oils 40
Cookies 704, 714
corn
  Boiled Lobster with Corn and Melted Butter 494
  Corn Bread 730
  Corn Fusilli Pasta with Cauliflower and Anchovies 412
  Hungarian Paprikash with Corn 252
cornmeal 269
  cooking 268, 296
  Broiled Cornmeal with Tomatoes and Gorgonzola Cheese 298
couscous 269, 276, 280
  cooking 268, 270
  Couscous Salad on Guacamole and Tomatoes 278
Crab Cakes, Crispy 496
crayfish 478, 479
  Crayfish in Dill Stock 498
crêpes 124-9
  Apple Crêpes 126
  Crêpe Batter 124
  Mirabelle Crêpes 128
crustaceans & shellfish 476–513
  cooking chart 478
  defrosting 486
  types of 478, 479
cucumbers 343, 345
  peeling and seeding 353
  Potato and Cucumber Salad with Bacon Strips 86
Curry Paste 574
Curry Sauces 146
cutters 16, 17
cutting board 16
cuttlefish 478, 479
  Grilled Cuttlefish 512

D

dandelion leaves 66
desserts 656–99
Deviled Eggs 118
diced vegetables 344
Dill Mustard Sauce 53
duck 516, 517
  Cassoulet 284
  Pinto Bean Ragout with Roast Duck Breast 288
  Roasted Breast of Duck with Orange-Pepper Sauce 534
  Roasted Duck with Apples 532
duck eggs 102

E

Edam 739
eel 423
egg noodles
  cooking 190
  Fried Noodles with Spicy Beef 216
  Shanghai-Style Fried Egg Noodles with Chicken 224
eggplants 342
  preparing and cooking 345, 358
  Stuffed Eggplant with Goat Cheese and Oregano Filling 366
eggs 100–29
  Béarnaise Sauce 154
  Boiled Egg 102, 122
  crêpes 124–9
  Deviled Eggs 118
  duck eggs 102
  Eggs Florentine 111
  Fried Eggs 108–9, 111
  Hollandaise Sauce 152
  Italian Frittata 116
  Mayonnaise 50
  Omelets 112
  Pickled Eggs 103
  Poached Egg 110
  quail eggs 102, 120
  Scrambled Eggs 104–7
  Soufflés 114, 690, 692
  Spanish Tortilla 117
  Thousand-Year Egg 103
  Wine Chaudeau 696
Emmental 738, 739
endive 67
Époisses 739
extra virgin oil 40

F

farfalle ... 184
fava beans ... 343, 345
  Fava Beans with Garlic and Onions ... 372
  Mixed Bean Salad with Parsley ... 88
fennel ... 342, 345
  preparing ... 355
fennel seeds ... 288
Feta ... 739
fish
  buying ... 10
  cleaning and scaling ... 424
  cooking chart ... 422, 442
  filleting ... 425
  freshness ... 10, 442, 445
  freshwater fish ... 420–39
  saltwater fish ... 440–75
  storage ... 445
Fish Stock ... 136
fish-bone tongs ... 14, 15
fleur de sel ... 28, 29
flounder ... 442
  Flounder Steamed in Swiss Chard ... 452
food pyramid ... 18–19
food-energy density ... 20
forbidden rice ... 232, 233
Foyot Sauce ... 155
French Dressing ... 58
French Fries ... 38, 304, 324
French Omelet ... 112
frisée ... 66
Frittata ... 116
fruit ... 648–99
  buying ... 10
  types of ... 650–1
Fruit Salads ... 656-7
Fruit Tarts ... 662

G

galia melon ... 650
game
  cooking chart ... 624
  types of ... 624, 625
garam masala ... 320, 332
garlic ... 343
  Garlic Cilantro Vinegar ... 46, 47
  Garlic Shrimp ... 492
  preparing ... 166
garlic press ... 16, 17
Gazpacho ... 162
gefilte fish ... 434
gelatin ... 14, 15
gemelli ... 184
ghee ... 34
ginger, preparing ... 70, 71
glass noodles ... 184, 578
  Fried Glass Noodles in Strawberry Gazpacho ... 228
gnocchi ... 306, 316
  Baked Gnocchi in Tandoori Yogurt Sauce ... 320
  Potato Gnocchi with Cherry Tomatoes and Arugula ... 318
  Sweet Gnocchi with Almond Crumbs ... 670
goose ... 516
goose fat ... 328
goose liver ... 566
Gorgonzola ... 740
  Broiled Cornmeal with Tomatoes and Gorgonzola Cheese ... 298
  Pork Steaks Baked with Pears and Gorgonzola Cheese ... 618
  Tagliatelle in Walnut Gorgonzola Sauce ... 222
Gouda ... 740
grains and legumes ... 266–99
  cooking chart ... 268
grapefruit ... 651
grapeseed oil ... 42, 43
grater ... 14, 15
gratin dish ... 14, 15
Gravy ... 138
grayling ... 423
green beans ... 343, 345
Green Curry Sauce ... 146
Green Peppercorn Cream Sauce ... 148
green plums ... 651
Gremolata ... 582
grill pan ... 14
Gruyère ... 194, 740
gurnard ... 443

H

hake ... 442, 443
  Hake Poached in Spiced Milk ... 474
hake roe ... 443
halibut ... 462
ham
  Ham Aspic ... 74
  Strammer Max ... 109
Hamburgers with Onion Relish ... 572
hare ... 624, 625
  Larded Saddle of Hare with Cranberry Pears ... 634
Hash Browns ... 326
hazelnut oil ... 42, 43
healthy eating ... 18–19
herbs
  Boiled Rice with Herbs ... 240
  Herb Butter ... 36
  Herb-Mustard Vinaigrette ... 63
  preparing ... 54
  Scrambled Eggs with Herbs ... 105
  storage ... 66
Hollandaise Sauce ... 152
horseradish
  Horseradish Crust ... 430
  Horseradish Sauce ... 157
  Lingonberry Horseradish Sauce ... 55
  preparing ... 70, 71

I

Ice Cream Soufflé ... 660
iceberg lettuce ... 66, 68
Idiazabal ... 740
Indian Beef Curry with Black Cardamom and Cinnamon ... 574
Indian Chickpea Curry with Cinnamon Yogurt, and Mint ... 290
Indian Curry Rice with Raisins and Cardamom ... 260
Indian Saffron Potatoes in Coconut Milk ... 332
Irish Stew with Young Cabbage and Carrots ... 628
Italian Frittata ... 116
Italian Vegetable Soup ... 166

J

Jam-Filled Cookies ... 704
Jarlsberg ... 740
John Dory ... 443
julienne ... 344
Jus ... 138

K

kabocha squash
  Brown Rice Risotto with Kabocha Squash and Lime ... 250
  Squash Soup with Cheese Croutons ... 174
kitchen brush ... 16, 17
kitchen shears ... 16, 17
kiwifruit ... 651
  Kiwi Sauce ... 695
  peeling ... 653

L

ladle ... 14, 15
lamb ... 622–33
  Biryani Rice with Lamb ... 254
  cooking chart ... 624
  cuts ... 624, 625
  Grilled Marinated Lamb ... 632
  Irish Stew with Young Cabbage and Carrots ... 628
  Pink Roast Rack of Lamb with Rosemary ... 630
  Roast Leg of Lamb with Herbs and Garlic ... 626
  Tomato Bean Stew with Spicy Lamb Sausage ... 284
lard ... 542
larding ... 634
lasagna ... 184
  Baked Cannelloni with Grilled Vegetables and Mozzarella ... 210
  Lasagna ... 204
leeks ... 342
  Fried Rice Curry with Leeks ... 256
  Potato and Leek Gratin ... 314
  preparing and cooking ... 345, 350
  Quiche Lorraine with Leeks ... 394
  Vichyssoise ... 170
Lemon Rosemary Vinegar ... 46, 47
lentils ... 269
  brown/red ... 269, 273
  cooking ... 268, 272–3
  green ... 268, 269, 272
  Sour Vegetable and Lentil Stew ... 294
  Vegetable Lentil Stew with Italian Sausage ... 292

lettuce ... 66
  rinsing and preparing ... 68–9
Limburger ... 740
Lingonberry Horseradish Sauce ... 55
loaf pan ... 14, 15
lobster ... 478, 479
  Boiled Lobster with Corn and Melted Butter ... 494
  cooking and cracking ... 478, 482–3
  Lobster Bisque ... 176
  Lobster Cocktail with Mushrooms ... 82
lollo biondo ... 66
lollo rosso ... 66
long grain/medium grain/short grain rice ... 232, 233
  cooking ... 236, 239, 268
  Fried Rice ... 258
  Fried Rice Curry with Leeks ... 256
  Hungarian Paprikash with Corn ... 252
  Mexican Brown Rice ... 262
  Rice Pudding with Cinnamon ... 264
  Rice Salad with Curry Mayonnaise and Fruit ... 92
  Spanish Paella ... 244

M

Macaire Potatoes ... 330
mafaldine ... 185
Manchego ... 740
mandarin oranges ... 651
mangoes ... 651
  Beef Mango Salad with Cherry Tomatoes and Mint ... 78
  peeling and pitting ... 652
maple syrup ... 126, 676
Mascarpone ... 740
matchstick potatoes ... 305
Mayonnaise ... 50
measuring cup ... 16, 17
meat fork ... 14, 15
melon baller ... 16
melons ... 650
  cutting ... 654
Meringue ... 672, 718
Mexican Chili with Chipotle Peppers ... 286
Mexican Corn Bread with Green Chili Peppers ... 730
millet ... 269
  cooking ... 268, 274
  Millet Patties with Cilantro and Orange Zest ... 280
mint
  Beef Mango Salad with Cherry Tomatoes and Mint ... 78
  Cream of Asparagus Soup with Mint ... 173
Mirabelle Crêpes ... 128
mirepoix ... 344
miso ... 404
  Miso Soup with Spinach and Tofu ... 406
mixing bowl ... 16, 17
monkfish ... 442, 443
  Monkfish Medallions on a Ragout of Tomatoes with Capers ... 472
morels ... 343, 345, 378, 638
mozzarella ... 740
  Tomatoes au Gratin with Rosemary and Mozzarella Cheese ... 368
Münster ... 740
mushrooms ... 343, 360–1
  Cream of Mushroom Soup ... 173
  French Omelet with Creamed Mushrooms ... 112
  Fried Red Pine Mushrooms on Whole-Wheat Bread ... 376
  Lobster Cocktail with Mushrooms ... 82
  Mushroom Cream Sauce ... 148
  Mushroom Ragout with Nutmeg and Parsley ... 378
  Mushroom Risotto ... 248
  Scrambled Eggs with Mushrooms ... 105
  see also morels; oyster mushrooms; porcini; shitake mushrooms
mussels ... 478, 479, 508
  cleaning and cooking ... 478, 480
  Mussels in Herb Marinade ... 506
  Mussels Steamed in White Wine ... 504
  Spaghetti with Mussels ... 198
Mustard Sauce ... 122, 141, 157
mutton ... 624

N

New Zealand spinach ... 67
Nigiri Sushi ... 242
nonstick pan ... 14, 16, 17
noodles ... 184, 185
  cooking ... 190–1
  Noodle Casserole with Cheese ... 194
  see also egg noodles; glass noodles; rice noodles
nutmeg grater ... 16

O

oak leaf lettuce ... 66
octopus ... 478, 479
  Octopus with Lemon Dressing ... 502
oils ... 38–43
  infused oils ... 42
  olive oil ... 40
  storage ... 40
olive oil ... 40
olive pomace oil ... 40
onions
  dicing and slicing ... 348–9
  Onion Rings ... 568
oranges ... 651
  Roasted Breast of Duck with Orange-Pepper Sauce ... 534
  segmenting ... 655
organic food ... 10
Osso Buco ... 582
oyster mushrooms ... 361, 376, 394
oysters ... 478, 479
  Baked Oysters ... 501
  opening ... 480
  Oysters on Ice ... 500

P

Panna Cotta with Coffee ... 674
papaya ... 651
paper towels ... 16, 17
paprika
  Boiled Rice with Paprika ... 240
  Catfish in Paprika Sauce ... 429
  Hungarian Paprikash with Corn ... 252
  Paprika Cream Sauce ... 150
  parchment paper ... 16, 17
paring knife ... 14
Parisian potatoes ... 305
Parmesan ... 734, 741
  Parmesan Risotto ... 246
parsley ... 67
  Herb-Mustard Vinaigrette ... 63
  parsley bouquet ... 16, 17
  Parsley Potatoes ... 122
  preparing ... 54
  Yogurt Sauce with Herbs ... 55
party food ... 24–5
pasta ... 182–229
  cooking ... 189
  types of ... 184–5
Pasta Dough ... 186
  Spaetzle Dough ... 192
  Spinach Pasta Dough ... 188
pastry cutters ... 16
Pavlova with Berries and Vanilla Cream ... 672
peaches ... 488
  Baked Peaches with Lavender ... 686
peanut oil ... 38
peapods ... 345
  Peapods Stewed with Lettuce and Ham Strips ... 370
pears ... 651
  Larded Saddle of Hare with Cranberry Pears ... 634
  Pork Steaks Baked with Pears and Gorgonzola Cheese ... 618
peas ... 343, 345
  Peapods Stewed with Lettuce and Ham Strips ... 370
Pecan-Lemon Marinade ... 630
Pecorino ... 741
penne ... 185
  Pasta Salad with Tuna and Boiled Egg ... 94
  Penne Bolognese ... 202
pesto
  Genovese Pesto ... 60
  Tomato Mousse with Pesto ... 76
  Tomato Pesto with Black Olives ... 60
pheasant ... 516
  Pheasant on Sauerkraut with Mashed Potatoes ... 542
picnics ... 22–3
pike ... 422, 423
pike-perch ... 422, 423
pineapple ... 620
  cutting ... 654
  Fritters ... 664
  Suckling Pig Leg with Honey and Pineapple ... 604
pinto beans ... 269
  Chili con Carne ... 554
  cooking ... 283
  Mixed Bean Salad with Parsley ... 88
  Pinto Bean Ragout with Roast Duck Breast ... 288

piping bags....16, 17
pistachio oil....42
Pistachio Zabaglione....684
pizza
  Pizza Dough....724
  Vegetable Pizza....725
plaice....442
plant proteins....402–19
plastic wrap....14, 15
pomegranates....651
Pont Neuf Potatoes....305
porcini....343, 345, 378, 640, 726
porgy....442, 443
  Porgy Baked in Salt Crust....460
  Sautéed Porgy Fillets in White Wine with Button Mushrooms....462
pork....598–621
  cooking chart....600
  cuts....600, 601
  Ground Pork Meatballs Cooked in Coconut-Curry Sauce....612
  Pork Chops Grilled with a Mexican Marinade....614
  Pork Tenderloin with Mango-Peppercorn Sauce and Thai Basil....620
  Pork Goulash with Paprika and Butter Noodles....606
  Pork Neck Steaks Baked in a Pistachio Crust....616
  Pork Roast with Sauce and Caraway Potatoes....602–3
  Pork Steaks Baked with Pears and Gorgonzola Cheese....618
pork belly....600, 601
  Pork Belly Grilled with an Asian Marinade....610
potatoes....300–39
  Caraway Potatoes....309, 602
  cooked in their skins....307
  cooking chart....302
  Deep-Fried Potatoes....310
  French Fries....38, 304, 324
  Gnocchi....306, 316, 318, 320, 670
  Golden Potato Cake....326
  Hash Browns....326
  Indian Saffron Potatoes in Coconut Milk....332
  Macaire Potatoes....330
  Mashed Potatoes....336
  Parsley Potatoes....122
  Potato and Cucumber Salad with Bacon Strips....86
  potato cuts....304–5
  Potato Finger Noodles with Sage and Salami....322
  Potato and Leek Gratin....314
  Potato Pancakes with Cured Salmon....432
  Potato Soup with Marjoram....170
  Potato Wedges....305
  Potatoes à la Lyonnaise....304
  Potatoes au Gratin....314
  Potatoes en Papillote with Fresh Herb Yogurt....312
  Roasted Potatoes....326
  Sautéed Potatoes....328
  storage....302
  Swedish Potatoes with Chives....338
  types of....302, 303
  Vichyssoise....170
poultry....514–43
  cooking chart....516
  cutting up....518–19
  types of....516, 517
Poultry Cream Sauce....140
Poultry Livers, Sautéed Venetian-Style....538
pumpkin
  preparing....352
  Pumpkin au Gratin with Fontina and Paprika....384
  see also kabocha squash
pumpkin seed oil....42, 43
pumpkin seeds....352
purslane....67

Q

quail....516
quail eggs....102, 120
  Fried Quail Egg Canapés with Beef Tartare....120
Quiche Lorraine with Leeks....394
quinoa....269, 280
  cooking....268, 275
  Sweet Sushi with Strawberries and Toasted Quinoa....680

R

rabbit....624, 625
  Stewed Haunch of Rabbit in Paprika Cream Sauce....646
radicchio....67
raspberries....650
raspberry vinegar....44, 45
Ratatouille....400
razor shells....478
  opening....481
  Razor Shells with Herbs and Soy Sauce....508
red currants....650
  Red Currant and Blueberry Meringue Cake....718
Red Curry Sauce....146
  Rice Noodles in Red Curry Sauce with Cilantro....226
red kidney beans....269, 554
red wine vinegar....44, 45
redfish....443
Remoulade....52
riccioli....184
rice....230–65
  boiled rice....234–5, 238–40
  steamed rice....236
  types of....232–3
  see also basmati rice; long grain/medium grain/short grain rice; risottos; sushi rice
rice noodles....184, 185
  cooking....191
  Rice Noodles with Broccoli and Green Chili Peppers....218
  Rice Noodles in Red Curry Sauce with Cilantro....226
rice vinegar....44, 45
ricer....14
ricotta....741
  Deep-Fried Beet-Ricotta Pockets....380
  Ricotta Ravioli with Sage Butter....206
rigatoni....184
risottos
  Brown Risotto with Kabocha Squash and Lime....250
  Mushroom Risotto....248
  Parmesan Risotto....246
  risotto rice....232, 233
  Saffron Risotto....246
  Tomato and Artichoke Risotto....248
roasting dish....14, 15
rock salt....28, 29
romaine lettuce....66
Roquefort....741
rosemary
  Lemon Rosemary Vinegar....46, 47
  Rosemary Focaccia with Porcini Mushrooms and Apricots....726
  Tomatoes au Gratin with Rosemary and Mozzarella Cheese....368
Rouille Sauce....52
Russian-Style Eggs....118

S

saffron
  Indian Saffron Potatoes in Coconut Milk....332
  Saffron Risotto....246
Saint-Marcellin....741
Saint-Nectaire....741
salad bowl....14, 15
salad leaves....66–7
salmon....422, 423, 442
  Potato Pancakes with Cured Salmon....432
  Salmon in Batter....464
  Salmon Steaks with Horseradish Butter and Cooked Cucumbers with Dill....430
  Slow-Roasted Salmon....436
salts....28–9
sardines....442, 443
  Fried Sardines....466
  Italian-Style Sardines....466
saucepans....16, 17
sauces....48–63, 137–59, 694–5
Sauerkraut with Bacon....398
  Pheasant on Sauerkraut with Mashed Potatoes....542
  Szegedin Goulash....606
scallops....478, 479
  Fried Scallops Wrapped in Bacon....510
Scrambled Eggs....104–7
sea bass....443
  gutting and preparing....444
  Sea Bass Baked in Puff Pastry....448
sea salt....28, 29
sea snails....506
seaweed....67
  Seaweed Salad with Spinach Leaves and Sesame Dressing....90

seitan 404
Broccoli with Asparagus and Seitan 418
Vegetarian Goulash with Potatoes and Paprika 416
Serra da Estrela 741
sesame seed oil 42
sesame seeds
Sautéed Sesame-Coated Shrimp 490
Sesame-Coated Tuna Fish Sticks 470
Shanghai-Style Fried Egg Noodles with Chicken 224
Shellfish Cream Sauce 143
Shellfish Stock 142
sherry vinegar 44, 45
shitake mushrooms 361
shopping for food 10
shrimp 478, 479
defrosting 486
Garlic Shrimp 492
peeling 484
Sautéed Sesame-Coated Shrimp 490
Shrimp Cocktail with Cocktail Sauce 488
Shrimp Wontons in Vegetable Broth 214
skillet 14, 15
skimmer 16, 17
smoked salt 28, 29
soda siphon 16
sole 443
preparing and cooking 442, 447
Sole in Sage Butter 456
Stuffed Sole Garnished with Potato Scales 458
soufflé dish 16, 17
greasing 114
Soufflé Potatoes 304
soufflés
Cheese Soufflé 114
Ice Cream Soufflé 660
Vanilla Soufflé 690
Walnut Soufflé 692
soup vegetables 344
soups 160–81
Sourdough Starter 728
Soy Vinaigrette with Cilantro 63
Spaetzle Dough 192
Cheese Spaetzle with Bacon Strips 212
spaghetti 184, 185
Spaghetti with Aglio Olio 196
Spaghetti with Mussels 198
Spanish Paella 244
Spanish Tortilla 117
spareribs 600, 601
Spareribs Glazed with BBQ Sauce 608
Sichuan-style Spareribs 608
spatula 16, 17
spinach 342
Boiled Rice with Spinach 240
Creamed Spinach 362
Eggs Florentine 111
Miso Soup with Spinach and Tofu 406
preparing and cooking 345, 351, 362
Seaweed Salad with Spinach Leaves and Sesame Dressing 90
Spinach Pasta Dough 188
Sponge Cake 706
springform pan 16, 17
squab 516, 517
Stuffed Squab Wrapped in Bacon 536
squid 479, 512
Black Tagliatelle with Squid 220
steamer pot 14, 15
Stilton 741
stocks 14, 15, 132–6
Bouillabaisse Stock Base 178
Chicken Stock 134
Fish Stock 136
Shellfish Stock 142
skimming 134
Vegetable Stock 132
Strammer Max 109
straw potatoes 305
strawberries 650
Fried Glass Noodles in Strawberry Gazpacho 228
Strawberry Sauce 695
Strawberry Swiss Roll 708
Strawberry Yogurt Mousse 682
Sweet Sushi with Strawberries and Toasted Quinoa 680
string beans 354
suckling pig leg 600, 601
with Honey and Pineapple 604
sunflower seed oil 42, 43
sushi rice
cooking 235
Nigiri Sushi 242
Sweet Sushi with Strawberries and Toasted Quinoa 680
Swedish Potatoes with Chives 338
Sweet Pie Dough 702
sweet potatoes 302, 303, 308
Sweet Potato Balls with Crisp Basmati Rice Coating 334
Swiss chard 345, 351
Flounder Steamed in Swiss Chard 452

T

tagliatelle 184, 185
Black Tagliatelle with Squid 220
Tagliatelle in Walnut Gorgonzola Sauce 222
tagliolini 184, 185
Tagliolini with Truffles 200
Tapioca-Coconut Pudding 668
tarragon
Herb-Mustard Vinaigrette 63
preparing 54
Tarragon Cream Sauce 141
Yogurt Sauce with Herbs 55
tarragon vinegar 44, 45
Tartar Sauce 52
tempeh 404
Fried Tempeh with Dips 408
terrine mold 14
Tête de Moine 741
Thousand Island Dressing 59
Thousand-Year Egg 103
tilapia 422, 423
Poached Tilapia in Red Wine Butter Sauce 438
Tiramisu 688
tofu 405
Miso Soup with Spinach and Tofu 406
Tofu in Hot Curry Sauce with Thai Basil and Baby Corn 410
tomatoes 342, 345
Boiled Rice with Tomatoes 240
peeling and coring 346–7
Potato Gnocchi with Cherry Tomatoes and Arugula 318
Scrambled Eggs with Tomato 105
seeding 347
Tomato and Artichoke Risotto 248
Tomato Basil Butter 36
Tomato Bean Stew with Spicy Lamb Sausage 284
Tomato Mousse with Pesto 76
Tomato Pesto with Black Olives 60
Tomato Sauce 144
Tomato Soup with Basil Croutons 164
Tomato Vinaigrette 63
Tomatoes au Gratin with Rosemary and Mozzarella Cheese 368
tools and equipment 14–17
toothpicks 16, 17
tortellini 184
Chicken and Ham Tortellini 208
trout 422, 423
Trout Amandine 426
Trout Meunière 426
truffle oil 200
truffle slicer 16, 17
Truffle Vinegar 46, 47
truffles
French Creamy Scrambled Eggs with Truffles 106
Tagliolini with Truffles 200
Truffle Sauce 566
trulli 184
tuna 442, 443
Pasta Salad with Tuna and Boiled Egg 94
Sesame-Coated Tuna Fish Sticks 470
Tuna Steak 468
turbot 443, 462
preparing and cooking 442, 446
Turbot Fillet Fried on the Bone 454
turkey 516, 517
Turkey with Bread Stuffing 530
Turmeric, Boiled Rice with 240
twine 16, 17

V

Vanilla Cardamom Vinegar 46, 47
vanilla beans 653
Vanilla Ice Cream Parfait 660
Vanilla Sauce 694
Vanilla Soufflé 690
vanilla sugar 653
veal
Braised Veal Shanks with Gremolata (Osso Buco) 582
cooking chart 546
cuts 547
fillet, cutting and trimming 548–9
Jus 138

Saltimbocca alla Romana with Sage and Prosciutto 594
Sautéed Veal Patties 590
Veal Cutlets in Almond-Bread Crust 592
Veal Kidneys in Mustard Cream Sauce with Mashed Onion Potatoes 588
Veal Roast with Root Vegetables and New Potatoes 580
Veal Tenderloin in Puff Pastry with Herbs 586
Wiener Schnitzels 596
vegetable bouquet 14, 15
Vegetable Goulash 374, 416
Vegetable Soup, Italian 166
Vegetable Stock 132
vegetables 340–401
buying 10
cooking chart 345
types of 342–3
vegetable cuts 344
venison 624, 625
Medallions of Venison with Savoy Cabbage, Celery Puree, and Morel Sauce 636
Venison Ragout with Diced Vegetables and Mashed Potatoes 642
Whole Leg of Venison with Mushroom Cream Sauce 640
vermicelli 184
Vichy Carrots 392
Vichyssoise 170
Vietnamese Beef Stew with Ginger 578
Vinaigrette 62–3
vinegars 44–7
infused vinegars 44–7
storage 44
virgin olive oil 40

W

Waldorf Salad 84
walnut oil 42, 43
walnuts
peeling 84
Tagliatelle in Walnut Gorgonzola Sauce 222
Walnut Caramel Brownies 711
Walnut Soufflé 692
watercress 67
Green Chervil Cress Sauce 55
watermelon 650
whisk 16
white beans
cooking 268, 282
Mixed Bean Salad with Parsley 88
Tomato Bean Stew with Spicy Lamb Sausage 284
white rice 232, 233
White Wine Sauce 137
white wine vinegar 44, 45
Wiener Schnitzels 596
wild rice 232, 233
wine 744–59
buying 758
Champagne 750
cheese and wine 738–41
Cold Wine Cream 698
enjoying 756
glossary 758
grape varieties 748
production 749
sweet wines 752
Wine Chaudeau 696
wine labels 754–5
wine-growing regions 746–7
wok 16, 17

Y

Yam Chips 96
yeast 14, 15
Yeast Dough 712
Yellow Curry Sauce 146
yogurt
Baked Gnocchi in Tandoori Yogurt Sauce 320
Bulgur Mint Salad with Yogurt and Tomatoes 276
Indian Chickpea Curry with Cinnamon Yogurt, and Mint 290
Strawberry Yogurt Mousse 682
Yogurt Sauce with Herbs 55
Zucchini in a Thyme Batter with Yogurt Sauce 364
yuba 404
Yuba Pockets Filled with Chinese Cabbage and Sweet Soy Sauce 414

Z

Zabaglione 684
zucchini 342, 345
stuffing 352
Zucchini in a Thyme Batter with Yogurt Sauce 364